Manias, Panics, and Crashes

Fifth Edition

Manias, Panics, and Crashes

A History of Financial Crises

Fifth Edition

Charles P. Kindleberger

and

Robert Z. Aliber

John Wiley & Sons, Inc.

Published by John Wiley & Sons, Inc., Hoboken, New Jersey
Published simultaneously in Canada

For general information about our other products and services, please contact our Customer Care Department within the United States at 800-762-2974, outside the United States at 317-572-3993 or fax 317-572-4002.

Wiley also publishes its books in a variety of electronic formats. Some content that appears in print may not be available in electronic books. For more information about Wiley products, visit our website at www.wiley.com.

Library of Congress Cataloging-in-Publication Data:

Kindleberger, Charles Poor, 1910–2003
Manias, panics, and crashes: a history of financial crises / Charles P. Kindleberger.—5th ed.
p. cm.
ISBN 978-0-471-46714-4 (pbk.)
1. Financial crises. 2. Business cycles. 3. Depressions. I. Title.

HB3722.K56 2005
338.5′42—dc22

2005001066

20 19 18 17 16 15 14

Contents

Foreword

Charlie Kindleberger (CPK from now on) was a delightful colleague: perceptive, responsive, curious about everything, full of character, and, above all, lively. Those same qualities are everywhere evident in *Manias, Panics, and Crashes*.

I think that CPK began to work on the book in the spirit of writing a natural history, rather as Darwin must have done at the stage of the *Beagle*—collecting, examining and classifying interesting specimens. Manias, panics, and crashes had the advantage over rodents, birds, and beetles that they were accompanied by the rhetoric of contemporaries, sometimes with insight, sometimes just blather. It was CPK's style as an economic historian to hunt for interesting things to learn, not to pursue a systematic agenda.

Of course, he was an economist by training and experience, and he soon found patterns and regularities, and causes and effects. What caught his eye especially were the irrationalities that seemed so often to enmesh those directly or indirectly enmeshed in the events themselves. By itself that would have been merely entertaining. The story got interesting for CPK with the interaction of behavior and institutions. The occurrence of manias, panics, and crashes, and their ultimate scope, also depended very much on the monetary and capital-market institutions of the time.

CPK could not have known at the start just how hardy a perennial financial crisis would turn out to be. The quarter-century *after* the publication of the first edition featured a whole new level of turbulence in national banking systems, exchange-rate volatility and asset-price bubbles. There was always new material to be digested in successive editions. This history cannot have been merely the result of increasing human irrationality, though CPK would have been charmed by what a German friend of ours called 'Das Gesetz der Verschlechtigung aller Dinge' (the Law of the Deterioration of Everything). Increasing wealth, faster and cheaper communication, and the evolution of national and international financial systems also played an indispensable role, as sketched in Chapter 13, added to this edition by Robert Aliber. CPK's effort at economic history found a subject that does not appear to be going out of style.

The shape of a 'new financial architecture' and the possible utility of a lender of last resort—national and/or international—along with the guidelines that ought to govern it were also among CPK's preoccupations. Those who are engaged in reforming (or at least changing) the system would do well to ponder the lessons that emerge from this book.

One of those lessons is very general, and is most applicable in contexts where irrationality may trump sober calculation. CPK was a skeptic by nature, just the opposite of doctrinaire. He mistrusted iron-clad intellectual systems, whether their proponents were free marketeers or social engineers. In fact, he considered clinging to rigid beliefs in the face of disconcerting evidence to be one of the more dangerous forms of irrationality, especially when it is practiced by those in charge. The international economy would be a safer place if CPK's tolerant skepticism were more common among the powers that be. I am thinking, in particular, about current discussions of the so-called 'Washington consensus,' and the pros and cons of both freely floating exchange rates and unfettered capital markets.

Any reader of this book will come away with the distinct notion that large quantities of liquid capital sloshing around the world should raise the possibility that they will overflow the container. One issue omitted in the book—because it is well outside its scope—is the other side of the ledger: What are the social benefits of free capital flow in its various forms, the analogue of gains from trade? CPK, whose specialties as an economist included international trade, international finance and economic development, would have been sensitive to the need for some pragmatic balancing of risks and benefits. One can only hope that the continued, up-to-date availability of this book will help to spread his open-minded habit of thought.

It seems to me that the Aliber version preserves this basic Kindleberger orientation but imposes a little more order on CPK's occasionally wayward path through his specimen cabinets. More manias, panics, and crashes may plague us, but readers of this book will at least have been inoculated.

ROBERT M. SOLOW

1
Financial Crisis: A Hardy Perennial

The years since the early 1970s are unprecedented in terms of the volatility in the prices of commodities, currencies, real estate and stocks, and the frequency and severity of financial crises. In the second half of the 1980s, Japan experienced a massive bubble in its real estate and in its stock markets. During the same period the prices of real estate and of stocks in Finland, Norway, and Sweden increased even more rapidly than in Japan. In the early 1990s, there was a surge in real estate prices and stock prices in Thailand, Malaysia, Indonesia, and most of the nearby Asian countries; in 1993, stock prices increased by about 100 percent in each of these countries. In the second half of the 1990s, the United States experienced a bubble in the stock market; there was a mania in the prices of the stocks of firms in the new industries like information technology and the dot.coms.

Bubbles always implode; by definition a bubble involves a non-sustainable pattern of price changes or cash flows. The implosion of the asset price bubble in Japan led to the massive failure of a large number of banks and other types of financial firms and more than a decade of sluggish economic growth. The implosion of the asset price bubble in Thailand triggered the contagion effect and led to sharp declines in stock prices throughout the region. The exception to this pattern is that the implosion of the bubble in U.S. stock prices in 2000 led to declines in stock prices for the next several years but the ensuing recession in 2001 was brief and shallow.

The changes in the foreign exchange values of national currencies during this period were often extremely large. At the beginning of the 1970s, the dominant market view was that the foreign exchange value of the U.S. dollar might decline by 10 to 12 percent to compensate for the higher inflation rate in the United States than in Germany and in Japan in the previous few years. In 1971 the United States abandoned the U.S. gold parity of $35 an ounce that had been established in 1934; in the next several years there were two modest increases in the U.S. gold parity although the U.S. Treasury would no longer buy and sell gold. The effort to retain a modified version of the Bretton Woods system of pegged exchange rates that was formalized in the Smithsonian Agreement of 1972 failed and there was a move to floating exchange rates early in 1973; in the 1970s the U.S. dollar lost more than half of its value relative to the German mark and the Japanese yen. The U.S. dollar appreciated significantly in the first half of the 1980s, although not to the levels of the early 1970s. A massive foreign exchange crisis involved the Mexican peso, the Brazilian cruzeiro, the Argentinean peso, and the currencies of many of the other developing countries in the early 1980s. The Finnish markka, the Swedish krona, the British pound, the Italian lira, and the Spanish peseta were devalued in the last six months of 1992; most of these currencies depreciated by 30 percent relative to the German mark. The Mexican peso lost more than half of its value in terms of the U.S. dollar during the presidential transition in Mexico at the end of 1994 and the beginning of 1995. Most of the Asian currencies—the Thai baht, the Malaysian ringgit, the Indonesian rupiah, and the South Korean won—depreciated sharply in the foreign exchange market during the Asian Financial Crisis in the summer and autumn of 1997.

The changes in the market exchange rates for these individual currencies were almost always much larger than those that would have been inferred from the differences between national inflation rates in particular countries. The scope of 'overshooting' and 'undershooting' of national currencies was both more extensive and much larger than in any previous period.

Some of the changes in commodity prices in the period were spectacular. The U.S. dollar price of gold increased from $40 an ounce at the beginning of the 1970s to nearly $1,000 an ounce at the end of that decade; at the end of the 1980s the price was $450, and at the end of the 1990s it was $283. The price of oil was $2.50 a barrel at the beginning of the 1970s and $40 a barrel at the end of that decade; in the mid-1980s the oil price was $12 a barrel and then at the end of the 1980s the price was back at $40 after the Iraqi invasion of Kuwait.

The number of bank failures during the 1980s and the 1990s was much, much larger than in any earlier decades. Several of these failures were isolated national events: Franklin National Bank in New York City and Herstatt AG in Cologne, Germany, made large bets on the changes in currency values in the early 1970s and both banks lost the bets and were forced to close because of the large losses. Crédit Lyonnais, once the largest bank in France and a government-owned firm, made an exceptionally large number of loans associated with the effort to rapidly increase its size and its bad loans eventually cost the French taxpayers more than $30 billion. Three thousand U.S. savings and loan associations and other thrift institutions failed in the 1980s, with losses to the American taxpayers of more than $100 billion. The collapse of the U.S. junk bond market in the early 1990s led to losses of more than $100 billion.

Most of the bank failures in the 1980s and the 1990s were systemic and involved all or most of the banks and financial institutions in a country. When the bubbles in Japanese real estate and stocks imploded, the losses incurred by the Japanese banks were many times their capital and virtually all the Japanese banks became wards of their governments. Similarly when the Mexican currency and the currencies of the other developing countries depreciated sharply in the early 1980s, most of the banks in this group of countries failed because of the combination of their large loan losses and the currency revaluation losses of their domestic borrowers. Virtually all of the banks in Finland, Norway, and Sweden went bankrupt when the bubbles in their real estate and stock markets imploded at the beginning of the 1990s. (Many of the government-owned banks in these various countries incurred comparably large loan losses and would have failed if they were not already in the public sector.) Virtually all of the Mexican banks failed at the end of 1994 when the peso depreciated sharply. Most of the banks in Thailand and Malaysia and South Korea and several of the other Asian countries went bankrupt after the mid-1997 Asian Financial Crisis (the banks in Hong Kong and Singapore were an exception).

These financial crises and bank failures resulted from the implosion of the asset price bubbles or from the sharp depreciations of national currencies in the foreign exchange market; in some cases the foreign exchange crises triggered bank crises and in others the bank crises led to foreign exchange crises. The cost of these bank crises was extremely high in terms of several metrics—the losses incurred by the banks in each country as a ratio of the country's GDP or as a share of government spending, and the slowdowns in the rates of economic growth. The losses incurred by the banks headquartered in Tokyo and Osaka—eventually a burden on the country's taxpayers—were more than 25 percent of Japan's GDP. The losses incurred by the Argentinean banks were

50 percent of its GDP—a lot of money in yen and pesos and U.S. dollars, and a much larger share of GDP than the losses incurred by U.S. banks in the Great Depression of the 1930s.

These bank failures occurred in three different waves: the first at the beginning of the 1980s, the second at the beginning of the 1990s and the third in the second half of the 1990s. The bank failures, the large changes in exchange rates and the asset price bubbles were systematically related and resulted from rapid changes in the economic environment. The 1970s was a decade of accelerating inflation, the largest sustained increase in the U.S. consumer price level in peacetime. The market price of gold surged initially because some investors relied on the cliché that 'gold is a good inflation hedge' as the basis for their price forecasts; however the increase in the gold price was many times larger than the contemporary increase in the U.S. price level. Toward the end of the 1970s investors were buying gold because the price of gold was increasing—and the price was increasing because investors were buying gold. The Hunt brothers from Texas tried to corner the silver market and the price of this precious metal in the 1970s increased even more rapidly than the price of gold.

The prevailing view in the late 1970s was that U.S. and world inflation rates would accelerate. Some analysts predicted that the gold price would increase to $2,500 an ounce; the forecasters in the oil industry and in the banks that were large lenders to firms in the oil industry predicted that the oil price would reach $80 to $90 a barrel by 1990. One of the clichés at the time was that the price of an ounce of gold was more or less the same as the price of twenty barrels of oil.

The range of movement in bond prices and stock prices in the 1970s was much greater than in the several previous decades. In the 1970s the real rates of return on both U.S. dollar bonds and U.S. stocks were negative. In contrast in the 1990s the real rates of return on bonds and on stocks averaged more than 15 percent a year.

The foreign indebtedness of Mexico, Brazil, Argentina, and other developing countries as a group increased from $125 billion in 1972 to $800 billion in 1982. The major international banks headquartered in New York and Chicago and Los Angeles and London and Tokyo increased their loans to governments and government-owned firms in these countries at an average annual rate of 30 percent a year for ten years. The cliché at the time was that governments didn't go bankrupt. During this period the borrowers had a stellar record for paying the interest on their loans on a timely basis—but then they obtained all the cash needed to pay the interest on these loans from the lenders in the form of new loans.

In the autumn of 1979 the Federal Reserve adopted a sharply contractive monetary policy; interest rates on U.S. dollar securities surged. The price of gold peaked in January 1980 as inflationary anticipations were reversed. A severe world recession followed.

In 1982 the Mexican peso, the Brazilian cruzeiro, the Argentinean peso, and the currencies of the other developing countries depreciated sharply, share prices in these countries tumbled, and most of the banks in these countries failed as a result of the large loan losses.

The sharp increase in real estate prices and stock prices in Japan in the 1980s was associated with a boom in the economy; *Japan as Number One: Lessons for America*[1] was a bestseller in the country. The banks headquartered in Tokyo and Osaka increased their deposits and their loans and their capital much more rapidly than banks headquartered in the United States and in Germany and in the other European countries; usually seven or eight of the ten largest banks in the world were Japanese. Then at the beginning of the 1990s real estate prices and stock prices in Japan imploded. Within a few years many of the leading Japanese banks and financial institutions were broke, kaput, bankrupt, and insolvent, and remained in business only because of an implicit understanding that the Japanese government would protect the depositors from financial losses if the banks were closed. A striking story of a mania and a crash—but a crash without a panic, apparently because of the belief that government would socialize the loan losses.

Three of the Nordic countries—Norway, Sweden, and Finland—replicated the Japanese asset price bubble at the same time. A boom in real estate prices and stock prices in the second half of the 1980s associated with financial liberalization was followed by a collapse in real estate prices and stock prices and the failure of the banks.

Mexico had been one of the great economic success stories of the early 1990s as it prepared to enter the North American Free Trade Agreement. The Bank of Mexico had adopted a tough contractive monetary policy that reduced the inflation rate from 140 percent to less than 10 percent in a four-year period; during the same period several hundred government-owned firms were privatized and business regulations were liberalized. Foreign capital flowed to Mexico because the real rates of return on government securities were high and because the prospective profit rates on industrial investments were also high. The universal expectation was that Mexico would become the low-wage, low-cost base for producing automobiles and washing machines and many other manufactured goods for the U.S. and Canadian markets. Because the large inflow of foreign savings led to a real appreciation of the peso, Mexico developed a trade deficit that reached 7 percent of its GDP. Mexico's external debt was 60 percent of its GDP and the country obtained the money to pay the interest on its increasing foreign indebtedness from the inflow of new investments. Then several political incidents, partly associated with the presidential election and transition in 1994, led to a sharp decline in the inflow of foreign funds, the Mexican government was unable to continue to support the peso in the foreign exchange market, and the currency lost more than half of its value in several months. Once again the depreciation of the peso resulted in large loan losses, and the Mexican banks — which had been privatized in the previous several years—failed.

In the mid-1990s real estate prices and stock prices surged in Bangkok, Kuala Lumpur, and Indonesia; these were the 'dragon economies' that seemed likely to emulate the economic successes of the 'Asian tigers' of the previous generation—Taiwan, South Korea, Hong Kong, and Singapore. Japanese firms and European and U.S. firms began to invest in these countries as low-wage, low-cost sources of supply, much as U.S. firms had invested in Mexico as a source of supply for the North American market. European and Japanese banks rapidly increased their loans in these countries. The domestic lenders in Thailand then experienced large loan losses on their domestic credits in the autumn and winter of 1996 because they had not been sufficiently discriminating in their evaluations of the willingness of Thai borrowers to pay the interest on their indebtedness. Foreign lenders sharply reduced their purchases of Thai securities, and then the Bank of Thailand, much like the Bank of Mexico thirty months earlier, did not have the foreign exchange reserves to support its currency in the foreign exchange market. The sharp decline in the foreign exchange value of the Thai baht in early July 1997 led to capital outflows from the other Asian countries and the foreign exchange values of their currencies (except for the Hong Kong dollar and the Chinese yuen, which remained rigidly pegged to the U.S. dollar) declined by 30 percent or more. The Indonesian rupiah lost 80 percent of its value in the foreign exchange market. Most of the banks in the area—except for those in Hong Kong and Singapore—would have been bankrupt in any reasonable 'mark-to-market' test. The crises spread from Asia to Russia, there was a debacle in the ruble, and the country's banking system collapsed in the summer of 1998. Investors then became more cautious and they sold risky securities and bought safer U.S. government securities, with the result that the changes in the relationship between the interest rates on these two groups of securities caused the collapse of Long-Term Capital Management, then the largest U.S. hedge fund.

The immense scope of the financial crashes in the last thirty years reflects in part that there are many more countries in the international financial economy and in part that data collection is more comprehensive. Despite the lack of perfect comparability across different time periods, the conclusion is unmistakable that financial failure has been more extensive and pervasive in the last thirty years than in any previous period.

The 1990s bubble in NASDAQ stocks

Stocks in the United States are traded on either the over-the-counter market or on one of the organized stock exchanges, principally the New York Stock Exchange or the American Stock Exchange or one of the regional exchanges in Boston, Chicago, and Los Angeles/San Francisco. The typical pattern was that shares of young firms would initially be traded on the over-the-counter market and then most of these firms would incur the costs associated with obtaining a listing on the New York Stock Exchange because they believed that such a listing would broaden the market for their stocks and lead to higher prices. Some very successful new firms associated with the information technology revolution of the 1990s—Microsoft, Cisco, Dell, Intel—were exceptions to this pattern; they chose not to obtain a listing on the New York Stock Exchange because they believed that trading stocks electronically in the over-the-counter market was superior to trading stocks by the open-outcry method used on the New York Stock Exchange.

In 1990 the market value of stocks traded on the NASDAQ was 11 percent of that of the New York Stock Exchange; the comparable figures for 1995 and 2000 were 19 percent and 42 percent. The annual average percentage rate of increase in the market value of NASDAQ stocks was 30 percent during the first half of the decade and 46 percent during the next four years. A few of the newer firms traded on the NASDAQ would eventually become as successful and as profitable as Microsoft and Intel and so high prices for their stocks might be warranted. The likelihood that all of the firms whose stocks were traded on the NASDAQ would be as successful as Microsoft was extremely small, since it implied that the profit share of U.S. GDP would be two to three times higher than it ever had been previously.

The bubble in U.S. stock prices in the second half of the 1990s was associated with a remarkable U.S. economic boom; the unemployment rate declined sharply, the inflation rate declined, and the rates of economic growth and productivity both accelerated. The U.S. government developed its largest-ever fiscal surplus in 2000 after having had its largest-ever fiscal deficit in 1990. The remarkable performance of the real economy contributed to the surge in U.S. stock prices that in turn led to the increase in investment spending and consumption spending and an increase in the rate of U.S. economic growth and the spurt in fiscal revenues.

U.S. stock prices began to decline in the spring of 2000; in the next three years U.S. stocks as a group lost about 40 percent of their value while the prices of NASDAQ stocks declined by 80 percent.

One of the themes of this book is that the bubbles in real estate and stocks in Japan in the second half of the 1980s, the similar bubbles in Bangkok and the financial centers in the nearby Asian countries in the mid-1990s, and the bubble in U.S. stock prices in the second half of the 1990s were systematically related. The implosion of the bubble in Japan led to an increase in the flow of money from Japan; some of this money went to Thailand and Malaysia and Indonesia and some went to the United States. The increase in the inflow of money led to the appreciation of their currencies in the foreign exchange market and to increases in the prices of real estate and of securities available in these countries. When the bubbles in the countries in Southeast Asia imploded, there was another surge in the flow of money to the United States as these countries repaid some of their foreign indebtedness; the U.S. dollar appreciated in the foreign exchange market and the annual U.S. trade deficit increased by $150 billion and reached $500 billion.

The increase in the flow of money to a country from abroad almost always led to increases in the prices of securities traded in that country as the domestic sellers of the securities to the foreigners used a very high proportion of their receipts from these sales to buy other securities from other domestic residents. These domestic residents in turn similarly used a large part of their receipts to buy other domestic securities from other domestic residents. These transactions in securities occurred at ever-increasing prices. It's as if the cash from the sale of securities to foreigners was the proverbial 'hot potato' that was rapidly passed from one group of investors to others, at ever-increasing prices.

Manias and credit

The production of books on financial crises is counter-cyclical. A spate of books on the topic appeared in the 1930s following the U.S. stock market bubble in the late 1920s and the subsequent crash and the Great Depression. Relatively few books on the subject appeared during the several decades immediately after World War II, presumably because the recessions from the 1940s to the 1960s were mild.

The first edition of this book was published in 1978, after U.S. stock prices had declined by 50 percent in 1973 and 1974 following a fifteen-year bull market in stocks; the stock market debacle and the U.S. recession led to the bankruptcies of the Penn-Central railroad, several of the large steel companies, and a large number of Wall Street brokerage firms. New York City was on the verge of default on its outstanding bonds and was saved from insolvency by the State of New York. Not quite a crash, unless you were a senior official or a stockholder in one of the firms that failed or the Mayor of New York City.

This edition appears after thirty tumultuous years in global financial markets, a period without a good historical precedent. There was a mania in real estate and stocks in Japan in the 1980s and a crash in the 1990s; during the same period there was a mania in real estate and stocks in Finland and Norway and Sweden and then a crash. There was a mania in U.S. stocks in the second half of the 1990s—the subsequent 40 percent decline in stock prices probably felt like a crash for those who owned large amounts of Enron, MCIWorldCom, and dot.com stocks. Comparisons can be made between the stock market bubbles in the United States in the 1920s and the 1990s, and between these U.S. bubbles and the one in Japan in the 1980s.

The big ten financial bubbles

1. The Dutch Tulip Bulb Bubble 1636
2. The South Sea Bubble 1720
3. The Mississippi Bubble 1720
4. The late 1920s stock price bubble 1927–1929
5. The surge in bank loans to Mexico and other developing countries in the 1970s
6. The bubble in real estate and stocks in Japan 1985–1989
7. The 1985–1989 bubble in real estate and stocks in Finland, Norway and Sweden
8. The bubble in real estate and stocks in Thailand, Malaysia, Indonesia and several other Asian countries 1992–1997
9. The surge in foreign investment in Mexico 1990–1993
10. The bubble in over-the-counter stocks in the United States 1995–2000

The earliest bubble noted in the box involved tulip bulbs in the Netherlands in the seventeenth century, and especially the rare varieties of bulbs. Two of the bubbles—one in Great Britain and one in France—occurred at more or less the same time, at the end of the Napoleonic

Wars. There were manias and financial crises in the nineteenth century that were mostly associated with the failures of banks, often after an extended investment in infrastructure such as canals and railroads. Foreign exchange crises and banking crises were frequent between 1920 and 1940. The percentage increases in stock prices in the last thirty years have been larger than in earlier periods. Bubbles in real estate and in stocks have often occurred together; some countries have experienced a bubble in real estate but not in stocks, while the United States had a stock price bubble in the second half of the 1990s but not one in real estate.

Manias are dramatic but they have been infrequent; only two have occurred in U.S. stocks in two hundred years. Manias generally have been associated with the expansion phase of the business cycle, in part because the euphoria associated with the mania leads to increases in spending. During the mania the increases in the prices of real estate or stocks or in one or several commodities contribute to increases in consumption and investment spending that in turn lead to accelerations in the rates of economic growth. The seers in the economy forecast perpetual economic growth and some venturesome ones proclaim no more recessions—the traditional business cycles of the market economies have become obsolete. The increase in the rate of economic growth induces investors and lenders to become more optimistic about the future and asset prices increase more rapidly—at least for a while.

Manias—especially macro manias—are associated with economic euphoria; business firms become increasingly up-beat and investment spending surges because credit is plentiful. In the second half of the 1980s Japanese industrial firms could borrow as much as they wanted from their friendly bankers in Tokyo and in Osaka; money seemed 'free' (money always seems free in manias) and the Japanese went on a consumption spree and an investment spree. The Japanese purchased ten thousand items of French art. A racetrack entrepreneur from Osaka paid $90 million for Van Gogh's *Portrait of Dr Guichet,* at that time the highest price ever paid for a painting. The Mitsui Real Estate Company paid $625 million for the Exxon Building in New York even though the initial asking price had been $310 million; Mitsui wanted to get in the *Guinness Book of World Records* for paying the highest price ever for an office building. In the second half of the 1990s in the United States newly-established firms in the information technology industry and bio-tech had access to virtually unlimited funds from the venture capitalists who believed they would profit greatly when the shares in these firms were first sold to the public.

During these euphoric periods an increasing number of investors seek short-term capital gains from the increases in the prices of real estate and of stocks rather than from the investment income based on the productive use of these assets. Individuals make down payments on condo apartments in the preconstruction phase of the developments in the anticipation that they will be able to sell these apartments at handsome profits when the buildings have been completed.

Then an event—perhaps a change in government policy, an unexplained failure of a firm previously thought to have been successful—occurs that leads to a pause in the increase in asset prices. Soon, some of the investors who had financed most of their purchases with borrowed money become distress sellers of the real estate or the stocks because the interest payments on the money borrowed to finance their purchases are larger than the investment income on the assets. The prices of these assets decline below their purchase price and now the buyers are 'under water'—the amount owed on the money borrowed to finance the purchase of these assets is larger than their current market value. Their distress sales lead to sharp declines in the prices of the assets and a crash and panic may follow.

The economic situation in a country after several years of bubble-like behavior resembles that of a young person on a bicycle; the rider needs to maintain the forward momentum or the bike becomes unstable. During the mania, asset prices will decline immediately after they stop increasing—there is no plateau, no 'middle ground.' The decline in the prices of some assets leads to the concern that asset prices will decline further and that the financial system will experience 'distress.' The rush to sell these assets before prices decline further becomes self-fulfilling and so precipitous that it resembles a panic. The prices of commodities—houses, buildings, land, stocks, bonds—crash to levels that are 30 to 40 percent of their prices at the peak. Bankruptcies surge, economic activity slows, and unemployment increases.

The features of these manias are never identical and yet there is a similar pattern. The increase in prices of commodities or real estate or stocks is associated with euphoria; household wealth increases and so does spending. There is a sense of 'We never had it so good.' Then the asset prices peak, and then begin to decline. The implosion of a bubble has been associated with declines in the prices of commodities, stocks and real estate, and often these declines have been associated with a crash or a financial crisis. Some financial crises were preceded by a rapid increase in the indebtedness of one or several groups of borrowers rather than by a rapid increase in the price of an asset or a security.

The thesis of this book is that the cycle of manias and panics results from the pro-cyclical changes in the supply of credit; the credit supply increases relatively rapidly in good times, and then when economic growth slackens, the rate of growth of credit has often declined sharply. A mania involves increases in the prices of real estate or stocks or a currency or a commodity in the present and near-future that are not consistent with the prices of the same real estate or stocks in the distant future. The forecasts that the price of oil would increase to $80 a barrel after the earlier increase from $2.50 a barrel at the beginning of the 1970s to $36 at the end of that decade was manic. During the economic expansions investors become increasingly optimistic and more eager to pursue profit opportunities that will pay off in the distant future while the lenders become less risk-averse. Rational exuberance morphs into irrational exuberance, economic euphoria develops and investment spending and consumption spending increase. There is a pervasive sense that it is 'time to get on the train before it leaves the station' and the exceptionally profitable opportunities disappear. Asset prices increase further. An increasingly large share of the purchases of these assets is undertaken in anticipation of short-term capital gains and an exceptionally large share of these purchases is financed with credit.

The financial crises that are analyzed in this book are major both in size and in effect and most are international because they involve several different countries either at the same time or in a causal sequential way.

The term 'bubble' is a generic term for the increases in asset prices in the mania phase of the cycle. Recently, real estate bubbles and stock price bubbles have occurred at more or less the same time in Japan and in some of the Asian countries. The sharp increases in the prices of gold and silver in the late 1970s have been tagged as a bubble, but the increases in the price of crude petroleum in the same years were not; the distinction is that many of the buyers of gold and silver in that tumultuous and inflationary decade anticipated that the prices of both precious metals would continue to increase and that profits could be made from buying and holding these commodities for relatively short periods. In contrast many of the buyers of petroleum were concerned that the disruptions in oil supplies due to actions of the cartel and the war in the Persian Gulf would lead to shortages and increases in prices.

Chain letters, pyramid schemes, Ponzi finance, manias, and bubbles

Chain letters, bubbles, pyramid schemes, Ponzi finance, and manias are somewhat overlapping terms. The generic term is nonsustainable patterns of financial behavior, in that asset prices today are not consistent with asset prices at distant future dates. The Ponzi schemes generally involve promises to pay an interest rate of 30 or 40 or 50 percent a month; the entrepreneurs that develop these schemes always claim they have discovered a new secret formula so they can earn these high rates of return. They make the promised interest payments for the first few months with the money received from their new customers attracted by the promised high rates of return. But by the fourth or fifth month the money received from these new customers is less than the monies promised the first sets of customers and the entrepreneurs go to Brazil or jail or both.

A chain letter is a particular form of pyramid arrangement; the procedure is that individuals receive a letter asking them to send $1 (or $10 or $100) to the name at the top of the pyramid and to send the same letter to five friends or acquaintances within five days; the promise is that within thirty days you will receive $64 for each $1 'investment.'

Pyramid arrangements often involve sharing of commission incomes from the sale of securities or cosmetics or food supplements by those who actually make the sales to those who have recruited them to become sales personnel.

The bubble involves the purchase of an asset, usually real estate or a security, not because of the rate of return on the investment but in anticipation that the asset or security can be sold to someone else at an even higher price; the term 'the greater fool' has been used to suggest the last buyer was always counting on finding someone else to whom the stock or the condo apartment or the baseball cards could be sold.

The term mania describes the frenzied pattern of purchases, often an increase in prices accompanied by an increase in trading volumes; individuals are eager to buy before the prices increase further. The term bubble suggests that when the prices stop increasing, they are likely—indeed almost certain—to decline.

Chain letters and pyramid schemes rarely have macroeconomic consequences, but rather involve isolated segments of the economy and involve the redistribution of income from the late-comers to those who were in early. Asset price bubbles have often been associated with economic euphoria and increases in both business and household spending because the futures are so much brighter, at least until the bubble pops.

Virtually every mania is associated with a robust economic expansion, but only a few economic expansions are associated with a mania. Still the association between manias and economic expansions is sufficiently frequent and sufficiently uniform to merit renewed study.

Some economists have contested the view that the use of the term bubble is appropriate because it suggests irrational behavior that is highly unlikely or implausible; instead they seek to explain the rapid increase in real estate prices or stock prices in terms that are consistent with changes in the economic fundamentals. Thus the surge in the prices of NASDAQ stocks in the 1990s occurred because investors sought to buy shares in firms that would repeat the spectacular successes of Microsoft, Intel, Cisco, Dell, and Amgen.

The policy implications

The appearance of a mania or a bubble raises the policy issue of whether governments should seek to moderate the surge in asset prices to reduce the likelihood or the severity of the ensuing financial crisis or to ease the economic hardship that occurs when asset prices begin to decline. Virtually every large country has established a central bank as a domestic 'lender of last resort' to reduce the likelihood that a shortage of liquidity would cascade into solvency crisis. The practice leads to the question of the role for an international 'lender of last resort' that would assist countries in stabilizing the foreign exchange value of their currencies and reduce the likelihood that a sharp depreciation of the currencies because of a shortage of liquidity would trigger large numbers of bankruptcies.

During a crisis, many firms that had recently appeared robust tumble into bankruptcy because the failure of some firms often leads to a decline in asset prices and a slowdown in the economy. When asset prices decline sharply, government intervention may be desirable to provide the public good of stability. During financial crises the decline in asset prices may be so large and abrupt that the price changes become self-justifying. When asset prices tumble sharply, the surge in the demand for liquidity may drive many individuals and firms into bankruptcy, and the sale of assets in these distressed circumstances may induce further declines in asset prices. At such times a lender of last resort can provide financial stability or attenuate financial instability. The dilemma is that if investors knew in advance that governmental support would be forthcoming under generous dispensations when asset prices fall sharply, markets might break down somewhat more frequently because investors will be less cautious in their purchases of asset and of securities.

The role of the lender of last resort in coping with a crash or panic is fraught with ambiguity and dilemma. Thomas Joplin commented on the behavior of the Bank of England in the crisis of 1825, 'There are times when rules and precedents cannot be broken; others, when they cannot be adhered to with safety.' Breaking the rule establishes a precedent and a new rule that should be adhered to or broken as occasion demands. In these circumstances intervention is an art rather than a science. The general rules that the state should always intervene or that the state should never intervene are both wrong. This same question of intervention reappeared with whether the U.S. government should have rescued Chrysler in 1979, New York City in 1975, and the Continental Illinois Bank in 1984. Similarly, should the Bank of England have rescued Baring Brothers in 1995 after the rogue trader Nick Leeson in its Singapore branch office had depleted the firm's capital through hidden transactions in option contracts? The question appears whenever a group of borrowers or banks or other financial institutions incurs such massive losses that they are likely to be forced to close, at least under their current owners. The United States acted as the lender of last resort at the time of the Mexican financial crisis at the end of 1994. The International Monetary Fund acted as the lender of last resort during the Russian financial crisis of 1998, primarily after prodding by the U.S. and German governments. Neither the United States nor the International Monetary Fund was willing to act as a lender of last resort during the Argentinean financial crisis at the beginning of 2001. The list of episodes highlights that coping with financial crises remains a major contemporary problem.

The conclusion of *The World in Depression, 1929–1939,* was that the 1930s depression was wide, deep, and prolonged because there was no international lender of last resort.[2] Great Britain was unable to act in that capacity because it was exhausted by World War I, obsessed with pegging the British pound to gold at its pre-1914 parity and groggy from the aborted economic recovery of the 1920s. The United States was unwilling to act as an international lender of last resort; at the time few Americans had thought through what the United States might have done in that role. This book extends the analysis of the responsibilities of an international lender of last resort.

The monetary aspects of manias and panics are important and are examined at length in several chapters. The monetarist view—at least one monetarist view—is that the mania would not occur if the rate of growth of the money supply were stabilized or constant. Many of the manias are associated with the surge in the growth of credit, but some are not; a constant money supply growth rate might reduce the frequency of manias but is unlikely to consign them to the dustbins of history. The rate of increase in U.S. stock prices in the second half of the

1920s was exceptionally high relative to the rate of growth of the money supply, and similarly the rate of increase in the prices of NASDAQ stocks in the second half of the 1990s was exceedingly high relative to the rate of growth of the U.S. money supply. Some monetarists distinguish between 'real' financial crises that are caused by the shrinkage of the monetary base or high-powered money and 'pseudo' crises that do not. The financial crises in which the monetary base changes early or late in the process should be distinguished from those in which the money supply did not increase significantly.

The earliest manias discussed in the first edition of this book were the South Sea and Mississippi bubbles of 1719–1720. The earliest manias analyzed in this edition are the *Kipper- und Wipperzeit,* a monetary crisis from 1619 to 1622 at the outbreak of the Thirty Years War, and the much-discussed 'tulipmania' of 1636–1637. The view that there was a bubble in tulip bulbs in the Dutch Republic followed from widespread recognition at the time that exotic specimens of tulips are difficult to breed, but once bred propagate easily—and hence their prices would decline sharply.[3]

The early historical treatment centered on the European experiences. The most recent crisis noted in this edition is that of Argentina in 2001. The attention to the financial crises in Great Britain in the nineteenth century reflects both the central importance of London in international financial arrangements and the abundant writings by contemporary analysts. In contrast Amsterdam was the dominant financial power for much of the eighteenth century, but these experiences have been slighted because of the difficulties in accessing the Dutch literature.

The chapter-by-chapter story

The background to the analysis, and a model of speculation, credit expansion, financial distress at the peak, and then crisis that ends in a panic and crash is presented in Chapter 2. The model follows the early classical ideas of 'overtrading' followed by 'revulsion' and 'discredit'—musty terms used by earlier generations of economists including Adam Smith, John Stuart Mill, Knut Wicksell, and Irving Fisher. The same concepts were developed by the late Hyman Minsky, who argued that the financial system is unstable, fragile, and prone to crisis. The Minsky model has great explanatory power for earlier crises in the United States and in Western Europe, for the asset price bubbles in Japan in the second half of the 1980s and in Thailand and Malaysia and the other countries in Southeast Asia in the mid-1990s, and for the bubble in U.S. stocks, especially those traded on the NASDAQ, at the end of the 1990s.

The mania phase of the economic expansion is the subject of Chapter 3. The central issue is whether speculation can be destabilizing as well as stabilizing—in other words, whether markets are always rational. The nature of the outside, exogenous shock that triggers the mania is examined in different historical settings including the onset and the end of a war, a series of good harvests and a series of bad harvests, the opening of new markets and of new sources of supply and the development of different innovations—the railroad, electricity, and e-mail. A particular recent form of displacement that shocks the system has been financial liberalization or deregulation in Japan, the Scandinavian countries, some of the Asian countries, Mexico, and Russia. Deregulation has led to monetary expansion, foreign borrowing, and speculative investment.[4]

Investors have speculated in commodity exports, commodity imports, agricultural land at home and abroad, urban building sites, railroads, new banks, discount houses, stocks, bonds (both foreign and domestic), glamour stocks, conglomerates, condominiums, shopping centers and office buildings. Moderate excesses burn themselves out without damage to the economy although individual investors encounter large losses. One question is whether the euphoria of the economic upswing endangers financial stability only if it involves at least two or more objects of speculation, a bad harvest, say, along with a railroad mania or an orgy of land speculation, or a bubble in real estate and in stocks at the same time.

The monetary dimensions of both manias and panics are analyzed in Chapter 4. The occasions when a boom or a panic has been triggered by a monetary event—a recoinage, a discovery of precious metals, a change in the ratio of the prices of gold and silver under bimetallism, an unexpected success of some flotation of a stock or bond, a sharp reduction in interest rates as a result of a massive debt conversion, or a rapid expansion of the monetary base—are noted. A sharp increase in interest rates may also cause trouble through disintermediation, as depositors flee banks and thrift institutions; the long-term securities still owned by these institutions fall in price. Innovations in finance, as in productive processes, can shock the system and lead to overinvestment in some types of financial services.[5]

The difficulty of managing the monetary mechanism to avoid manias and bubbles is stressed in this edition. Money is a public good but monetary arrangements can be exploited by private parties. Banking, moreover, is difficult to regulate. The current generation of monetarists insists that many, perhaps most, of the cyclical difficulties of the past have resulted from mismanagement of the monetary mechanism. Such mistakes were frequent and serious. The argument advanced in Chapter 4, however, is that even when the supply of money was nearly adjusted to the demands of an economy the monetary mechanism did not stay right for very long. When government produces one quantity of the public good, money, the public may proceed to produce many close substitutes for money, just as lawyers find new loopholes in tax laws about as fast as legislation closes up older loopholes. The evolution of money from coins to bank notes, bills of exchange, bank deposits and finance paper illustrates the point. The Currency School might be right about the need for a fixed supply of money, but it is wrong to believe that the money supply could be fixed forever.

The emphasis in Chapter 5 is on the domestic aspects of the crisis stage. One question is whether manias can be halted by official warning—moral suasion or jawboning. The evidence suggests that they cannot, or at least that many crises followed warnings that were intended to head them off. One widely noted remark was that of Alan Greenspan, chairman of the Federal Reserve Board, who stated on December 6, 1996, that he thought that the U.S. stock market was irrationally exuberant. The Dow Jones industrial average was 6,600; subsequently the Dow peaked at 11,700. The NASDAQ had been at 1,300 at the time of the Greenspan remark and peaked at more than 5,000 four years later. A similar warning had been issued in February 1929 by Paul M. Warburg, a private banker who was one of the fathers of the Federal Reserve system, without slowing for long the stock market's upward climb. The nature of the event that ultimately produces a turning point is discussed: some bankruptcy, defalcation or troubled area revealed or rumored, a sharp rise in the central bank discount rate to halt the hemorrhage of cash into domestic circulation or abroad. And then there is the interaction of falling prices—the crash—and its impact on the liquidity in the economy.

Domestic propagation of the mania and then the panic is the subject of Chapter 6. The inference from history is that a boom in one market spills over into other markets. 'A housing boom in Houston is an oil boom in drag.' Thus a financial crisis may be more serious if two or more assets are the subject of speculation. When and if a crash comes, the banking system may seize and banks may ration credit to reduce the likelihood of large loan losses even if the money supply is unchanged; indeed the money supply may be increasing. The connections between price changes in the stock and commodities markets were especially strong in New York in 1921 and the late 1920s, and those linking stocks and real estate were strong in the late 1980s in Japan and in Norway, Sweden and Finland.

The international contagion of manias and crises is highlighted in Chapter 7. There are many possible linkages among countries, including trade, capital markets, flows of hot money, changes in central bank reserves of gold or foreign exchange, fluctuations in prices of commodities, securities or national currencies, changes in interest rates, and direct contagion of speculators in euphoria or gloom. Some crises are local, others international. What constitutes the difference? Did, for example, the 1907 panic in New York precipitate the collapse of the Società Bancaria Italiana via pressure on Paris communicated to Turin by withdrawals of bank deposits? There is fundamental ambiguity here, too. Tight money in a given financial center can serve either to attract funds or to repel them, depending on the expectations that a rise in interest rates generates. With inelastic expectation—no fear of crisis or of currency depreciation—an increase in the discount rate attracts funds from abroad and helps provide the cash needed to ensure liquidity; with elastic expectations of change—of falling prices, bankruptcies, or exchange depreciation—raising the discount rate may suggest to foreigners the need to take more funds out rather than bring new funds in. The trouble is familiar in economic life generally. A rise in the price of a commodity may lead consumers to postpone purchases in anticipation of the decline, or to speed purchases before prices rise further. And even where expectations are inelastic, and the increased discount rate at the central bank sets in motion the right reactions, lags in responses may be so long that the crisis supervenes before the Marines arrive.

One complex but not unusual method of initiating financial crisis is a sudden halt to foreign lending because of a domestic boom; thus the boom in Germany and Austria in 1873 led to a decline in the capital outflows and contributed to the difficulties of Jay Cooke in the United States. Similar developments occurred with the Baring crisis in 1890, when troubles in Argentina led the British to halt lending to South Africa, Australia, the United States and the remainder of Latin America. The stock market boom in New York in the late 1920s led Americans in 1928 to buy far fewer of the new bond issues of Germany and various Latin American countries, which in turn caused them to slide into depression. A halt to foreign trading is likely to precipitate depression abroad, which may in turn feed back to the country that launched the process.[6]

The discussion in Chapter 8—a new chapter in this edition—highlights the relationships among the three asset price bubbles in the last fifteen years of the twentieth century. The first of the three bubbles was in Tokyo in the second half of the 1980s, the second was in Bangkok, Kuala Lumpur, and Jakarta and the other capitals in the region in the mid-1990s and the third was in New York in the second half of the 1990s. The likelihood that these three asset price bubbles were independent events is low; the theme of this chapter is that there was a systematic relationship among them. The bubble in Japan was *sui generis;* when that bubble imploded at the beginning of the 1990s, there was a surge in the flow of funds both to China and the various Asian countries and to the United States. The currency values and the asset prices in the countries that were receiving the money from Japan adjusted to an increase in the inflow of foreign savings. When the bubble in stock prices and real estate prices in Bangkok and the other Asian capitals imploded in 1997 and 1998, there was a surge in the flow of funds to New York as the borrowers in these Asian countries sought to reduce their indebtedness. The foreign exchange value of the U.S. dollar and U.S. asset prices increased in response to the increase in the inflow of foreign saving. The money had to go someplace, and the result was that the prices of U.S. stocks reached stratospheric levels.

Swindles that occur in the mania phase and then in the panic phase are reviewed in Chapter 9. The combination of failed thrift institutions and the rapid growth of junk bonds in the 1980s cost the American taxpayers $150 billion. Enron, MCIWorldCom, Tyco, Dynegy, Adelphia Cable are like a rogue's gallery of the 1990s. And then many of the large U.S. mutual fund families were exposed as providing favored treatment to hedge funds. Crashes and panics are often precipitated by the revelation of some misfeasance, malfeasance or malversation (the corruption of officials) that occurred during the mania. The inference from the historical record is that swindles are a response to the greedy appetite for wealth stimulated by the boom; the Smiths want to keep up with the Joneses and some Smiths engage in fraudulent behavior. As the monetary system gets stretched, institutions lose liquidity and unsuccessful swindles are about to be revealed, the temptation to take the money and run becomes virtually irresistible.

Jail time, fines and financial penalties: financial behavior in the 1990s U.S. economic boom

Enron was the poster-child of the 1990s boom; the company had transformed itself from the owner of regulated natural gas pipelines into a financial firm that traded natural gas, petroleum, electricity, and broadband width as well as owning water systems and an electrical power generating system. The top executives of Enron felt the need to show continued growth in profits to keep the stock price high, and in the late 1990s they began to use off-balance sheet financing vehicles to obtain the capital to grow the firm; they also put exceptionally high prices on some of their long trading positions so they could report that their trading profits were increasing. The collapse of Enron led to the failure of Arthur Andersen, which previously had been the most highly regarded of the global accounting firms.

MCIWorldCom was one of the most rapidly growing telecommunications firms. Again the need to show continued increases in profits led the managers to claim that several billion dollars of expenses should be regarded as investments. Jack Grubman had been one of the sages in Salomon Smith Barney (a unit of the Citibank Group); he was continually promoting MCIWorldCom stock. Henry Blodgett was a security analyst for Merrill Lynch who was privately writing scathing e-mails about the economic prospects of some of the firms that he was otherwise promoting to investors; Merrill Lynch paid $100 million to move the story off the front pages. Ten investment banking firms paid $1.4 billion to forestall trials. The chairman and chief executive officer of the New York Stock Exchange resigned soon after it became known that he had a compensation package of more than $150 million; the exchange served both as a tent for trading stocks and as a regulator and it appeared that the managers of some of the firms that were being regulated served as directors of the exchange and participated in determining the compensation package. Then a number of large U.S. mutual funds were revealed to have allowed firms to trade on stale news.

More individuals have already gone to prison than in the aftermath of any previous crisis, and a number are still awaiting trial. Six Enron senior managers already have been jailed. One Arthur Andersen partner who worked on the Enron account went to prison. Two of the senior financial officials of MCIWorldCom have gone to jail. Martha Stewart was found guilty of obstruction of justice and imprisoned for five months.

The subject of Chapters 10 and 11 is crisis management at the domestic level. The first of these two chapters considers the range of domestic responses to a crisis; at one extreme the government may take a hands-off position, at the other there is a range of miscellaneous measures. Those who believe that the market is rational and can take care of itself prefer the hands-off approach; according to one formulation, it is healthy for the economy to go through the purgative fires of deflation and bankruptcy to get rid of the mistakes and excesses of the boom. Among the miscellaneous devices are holidays, bank holidays, the issuance of scrip, guarantees of liabilities, issuance of government debt, deposit insurance and the formation of special institutions like the Reconstruction Finance Corporation in the United States (in 1932) or the Istituto per la

Ricostruzione Industriale (IRI) in Italy (in 1933). The Italian literature calls the process the 'salvage' of banks and companies; the British in 1974–1975 referred to saving the fringe banks as a 'lifeboat' operation.

The questions related to a domestic lender of last resort are the focus of Chapter 11—primarily whether there should be a lender of last resort, who this lender should be and how it should operate. A key topic is 'moral hazard'—if investors are confident that they will be 'bailed out' by a lender of last resort, their self-reliance may be weakened. But on the other hand, the priority may be to stop the panic, to 'save the system today' despite the adverse effects on the incentives of investors. If there is a lender of last resort, however, whom should it save? Insiders? Outsiders and insiders? Only the solvent, if illiquid? But solvency depends on the extent and duration of the panic. These are political questions, and they are raised in particular when it becomes necessary to legislate to increase the capital of the Federal Deposit Insurance Corporation (FDIC) or the Federal Savings and Loan Insurance Corporation (FSLIC) when one or the other runs out of funds to lend to banks in trouble in time of acute stress. The issue was particularly acute in the 1990s in Japan, where the collapse of the Nikkei stock bubble in 1990 uncovered all sorts of bad real estate loans by banks, credit unions, and other financial houses, confronting the government with the neuralgic question of how much of a burden to put on the taxpayer. Particularly troubling was the catatonic state of government in Japan in the 1990s, slow to decide how to meet the crisis and slower to act.

The penultimate chapter centers on the need for an international lender of last resort to provide global monetary stability even though there is no responsible government or agency of government with the *de jure* responsibility for providing this public good. U.S. government support for Mexico, first in 1982 and again in 1994 was justified on the grounds that countries of the North American Free Trade Agreement (NAFTA) should stick together and that assistance to Mexico would dampen or neutralize the contagion effect and prevent a collapse of lending to the 'emerging market' countries of Brazil and Argentina and other developing countries. The sharp depreciation of the Thai baht in the early summer of 1997 triggered crises in nearby Asian countries including Indonesia, Malaysia, and South Korea as well as in Singapore, Hong Kong, and Taiwan.

The last chapter seeks to answer two questions; the first is why there has been so much economic turmoil in the international financial economy in the last thirty years, and the second is whether an international

THE BOYS NEXT DOOR

FEB 20

Through February 20

Metropolis Performing Arts Center 111 W. Campbell St., Arlington Heights | 847-577-2121

In a month that's all about the heart, what better way to spend an evening than giving it a few tugs with an unforgettable story about four men with special needs and the caregiver that keeps it all together. This show is produced in partnership with several local organizations dedicated to supporting the lives of individuals with special needs, including Arlington Pediatric Therapy, Clearbrook, National Association for Down Syndrome and Northwest Special Recreation Association.

CHICAGO AUTO SHOW

FEB 11

February 11—20

McCormick Place | 2301 S. Lake Shore Dr., Chicago | chicagoautoshow.com

Rev your engines! A winter staple, the Chicago Auto Show is a great day trip downtown, with just about every car for any budget, entertainment and more.

LEWIS BLACK: IN GOD WE RUST

FEB 11

February 11

Centre East | 9501 Skokie Blvd. | 847-673-6

Daily Show aficionados will appreciate evening with Mr. Black—there's no w lender of last resort would have made a difference. The International Monetary Fund was established in the 1940s to act as an international lender of last resort and to fill an institutional vacuum; the view was that financial crises in the 1920s and the 1930s would have been less severe had there been an international lender of last resort. The large number of crises in the last thirty years leads to the question of whether the presence of the IMF as a supplier of national currencies to countries with financial crises encouraged profligate national financial policies.

Financial arrangements need a lender of last resort to prevent the escalation of the panics that are associated with crashes in asset prices. But the commitment that a lender is needed should be distinguished from the view that individual borrowers will be 'bailed out' if they become over-extended. For example, uncertainty about whether New York City would be helped, and by whom, may have proved just right in the long run, so long as help was finally provided, and so long as there was doubt right to the end as to whether it would be. This is a neat trick: always come to the rescue, in order to prevent needless deflation, but always leave it uncertain whether rescue will arrive in time or at all, so as to instill caution in other speculators, banks, cities, or countries. In Voltaire's *Candide,* the head of a general was cut off 'to encourage the others.' A sleight of hand may be necessary to 'encourage' the others (without, of course, cutting off actual heads) to participate in the lender of last resort activities because the alternative is likely to have very expensive consequences for the economic system.

2
Anatomy of a Typical Crisis

History vs economics

For historians each event is unique. In contrast economists maintain that there are patterns in the data and particular events are likely to induce similar responses. History is particular; economics is general. The business cycle is a standard feature of market economies; increases in investment in plant and equipment lead to increases in household income and the rate of growth of national income. Macroeconomics focuses on the explanations for the cyclical variations in the rate of growth of national income relative to its long-run trend rate of growth.

An economic model of a general financial crisis is presented in this chapter, while the various phases of the speculative manias that lead to crises are illustrated in the following chapters. This model of general financial crises covers the boom and the subsequent bust and centers on the episodic nature of the manias and the subsequent crises. This model differs from those that focus on the variations and the periodicity of economic expansions and contractions, including the Kitchin inventory cycle of thirty-nine months, the Juglar cycle of investment in plant and equipment that has a periodicity of seven or eight years and the Kuznets cycle of twenty years that highlights the rise and fall in housing construction.[1] In the first two-thirds of the nineteenth century, crises occurred regularly at ten-year intervals (1816, 1826, 1837, 1847, 1857, 1866), thereafter crises occurred less regularly (1873, 1907, 1921, 1929).

The model

A model developed by Hyman Minsky is used to interpret the financial crises in the United States, Great Britain, and other market economies. Minsky highlighted the pro-cyclical changes in the supply of credit, which increased when the economy was booming and decreased during economic slowdowns. During the expansion phase investors became more optimistic about the future and they revised upward their estimates of the profitability of a wide range of investments and so they became more eager to borrow. At the same time, both the lenders' assessments of the risk of individual investments and their risk averseness declined and so they became more willing to make loans, including some for investments that previously had seemed too risky.

When the economic conditions slowed, the investors became less optimistic and more cautious. At the same time, the loan losses of the lenders increased and they became much more cautious.

Minsky believed that the pro-cyclical increases in the supply of credit in good times and the decline in the supply of credit in less buoyant economic times led to fragility in financial arrangements and increased the likelihood of financial crisis.

This model is in the tradition of the classical economists, including John Stuart Mill, Alfred Marshall, Knut Wicksell, and Irving Fisher, who also focused on the instability in the supply of credit. Minsky followed Fisher and attached great importance to the behavior of heavily indebted borrowers, particularly those that increased their indebtedness in the expansion to finance the purchase of real estate or stocks or commodities for short-term capital gains. The motive for these transactions was that the anticipated rates of increase in the prices of these assets would exceed the interest rates on the funds borrowed to finance their purchases. When the economy slowed some of these borrowers might be disappointed because the rates of increase in the prices of the assets proved smaller than the interest rates on the borrowed money and so many would become distress sellers.

Minsky argued that the events that lead to a crisis start with a 'displacement,' some exogenous, outside shock to the macroeconomic system.[2] If the shock was sufficiently large and pervasive, the economic outlook and the anticipated profit opportunities would improve in at least one important sector of the economy. Business firms and individuals would borrow to take advantage of the increase in the anticipated profits associated with a wide range of investments. The rate of economic growth would accelerate and in turn there might be a feedback to even greater optimism. It's 'Japan as Number One' or the 'East Asian Miracle' or 'The New American Economy'—a new sense of more profound optimism about the economic environment. The words differ across the countries but the tune is the same.

The nature of the shock varies from one speculative boom to another. The shock in the United States in the 1920s was the rapid expansion of automobile production and associated development of highways together with the electrification of much of the country and the rapid expansion of the number of households with telephones. The shocks in Japan in the 1980s were financial liberalization and the surge in the foreign exchange value of the yen. The shock in the Nordic countries in the 1980s was financial liberalization.

The shock in the Asian countries in the 1990s was the implosion of the asset price bubble in Japan and the appreciation of the yen which led to increases in the inflows of money from Tokyo together with financial liberalization at home. The shock in the United States in the 1990s was the revolution in information technology and new and lower-cost forms of communication and control that involved the computer, wireless communication, and e-mail. At times the shock has been outbreak of war or the end of a war, a bumper harvest or crop failure, the widespread adoption of an invention with pervasive effects—canals, railroads. An unanticipated change of monetary policy has been a major shock.

If the shock is sufficiently large and pervasive, the anticipated profit opportunities improve in at least one important sector of the economy: the profit share of GDP increases. In the early 1980s, U.S. corporate profits were 3 percent of GDP; toward the end of the 1990s this ratio had increased to 10 percent. That corporate profits were increasing one-third more rapidly than U.S. GDP in turn contributed to the significant increase in stock prices.

The boom in the Minsky model is fueled by an expansion of credit. In the prebanking seventeenth and eighteenth centuries personal credit or vendor financing fueled the speculative boom. Once banks had been developed they expanded the supply of credit and their liabilities; in the first several decades of the nineteenth century they increased the supplies of bank notes and subsequently they added to the deposit balances of individual borrowers. In addition to the expansion of credit by the established banks, new banks may be formed; the efforts of these new banks to increase market share can lead to rapid growth of credit and money because the established banks have often been reluctant to accept a decline in market share that they would otherwise incur. In the 1970s the European banks were beginning to poach on the turf of the U.S. banks in making loans to the governments in Latin America.

Minsky argued that the growth of bank credit has been very unstable; at times the banks as lenders have become more euphoric and have lent freely and then at other times they have become extremely cautious and let the borrowers 'swing in the wind.'

One central policy issue centers on the control of credit from banks and from other suppliers of credit. Often the authorities in a country have applied strict controls to the ability of banks to make certain types of loans. The banks then set up wholly-owned subsidiaries that can make the loans the banks themselves are prohibited from making. Or the loans are made by the bank holding companies. Even if the instability of credits from the financial institutions were controlled, increases in the supply of personal credit could finance the boom.

Assume an increase in the effective demand for goods and services. After a time, the increase in demand presses against the capacity to produce goods. Market prices increase, and the more rapid increase in profits attracts both more investment and more firms. Positive feedback develops as the increase in investment leads to increases in the rate of growth of national income that in turn induce additional investment so the rate of growth of national income accelerates.

Minsky noted that 'euphoria' might develop at this stage. Investors buy goods and securities to profit from the capital gains associated with the anticipated increases in the prices of these goods and securities. The authorities recognize that something exceptional is happening in the economy and while they are mindful of earlier manias, 'this time it's different,' and they have extensive explanations for the difference. Chairman Greenspan discovered a surge in U.S. productivity about a year after he first became concerned about the high level of U.S. stock prices in 1996; the increase in productivity meant that profits would increase at a more rapid rate, and so the higher level of stock prices relative to corporate earnings did not seem unreasonable.

Minsky's three-part taxonomy

Minsky distinguished between three types of finance—hedge finance, speculative finance, and Ponzi finance—on the basis of the relation between the operating income and the debt service payments of individual borrowers. A firm is in the hedge finance group if its anticipated operating income is more than sufficient to pay both the interest and scheduled reduction in its indebtedness. A firm is in the speculative finance group if its anticipated operating income is sufficient so it can pay the interest on its indebtedness; however the firm must use cash from new loans to repay part or all of the amounts due on maturing loans. A firm is in the Ponzi group if its anticipated operating income is not likely to be sufficiently large to pay all of the interest on its indebtedness on the scheduled due dates; to get the cash the firm must either increase its indebtedness or sell some assets.

Minsky's hypothesis is that when the economy slows, some of the firms that had been involved in hedge finance are shunted to the group involved in speculative finance and that some of the firms that had been involved in the speculative finance group now find they are in the Ponzi finance group.

The term 'Ponzi finance' memorializes Carlos Ponzi, who operated a small loans company in one of the Boston suburbs in the early 1920s. Ponzi promised his depositors that he would pay interest at the rate of 30 percent a month and his financial transactions went smoothly for three months. In the fourth month however the inflow of cash from new depositors was smaller than the interest payments promised to the older borrowers and eventually Ponzi went to prison.

The term Ponzi finance is now a generic term for a nonsustainable pattern of finance. The borrowers can only meet their commitments to pay the high interest rates on their outstanding loans or deposits if they obtain the cash from new loans or deposits. Since in many arrangements the interest rates are very high, often 30 to 40 percent a year, the continuation of the arrangement requires that there be a continuous injection of new money and often at an accelerating rate. Initially many of the existing depositors are so pleased with their high returns that they allow their interest income to compound; the cliché is that they are 'earning interest on the interest.' As a result the inflow of new money can be below the promised interest rate for a few months. But to the extent that some depositors take some of their interest returns in cash, the arrangement can operate only as long as these withdrawals are smaller than the inflow of new money.

The result of the continuation of the process is what Adam Smith and his contemporaries called 'overtrading.' This term is less than precise and includes speculation about increases in the prices of assets or commodities, an overestimate of prospective returns, or 'excessive leverage.'[3] Speculation involves buying commodities for the capital gain from anticipated increases in their prices rather than for their use. Similarly speculation involves buying securities for resale rather than for investment income attached to these commodities. The euphoria leads to an increase in the optimism about the rate of economic growth and about the rate of increase in corporate profits and affects firms engaged in production and distribution. In the late 1990s Wall Street security analysts projected that U.S. corporate profits would increase at the rate of 15 percent a year for five years. (If their forecasts had been correct, then at the end of the fifth year the share of U.S. corporate profits in U.S. GDP would have been 40 percent higher than ever before.) Loan losses incurred by the lenders decline and they respond and become more optimistic and reduce the minimum down payments and the minimum margin requirements. Even though bank loans are increasing, the leverage—the ratio of debt to capital or to equity—of many of their borrowers may decline because the increase in the prices of the real estate or securities means that the net worth of the borrowers may be increasing at a rapid rate.

A follow-the-leader process develops as firms and households see that others are profiting from speculative purchases. 'There is nothing as disturbing to one's well-being and judgment as to see a friend get rich.'[4] Unless it is to see a nonfriend get rich. Similarly banks may increase their loans to various groups of borrowers because they are reluctant to lose market share to other lenders which are increasing their loans at a more rapid rate. More and more firms and households that previously had been aloof from these speculative ventures begin to participate in the scramble for high rates of return. Making money never seemed easier. Speculation for capital gains leads away from normal, rational behavior to what has been described as a 'mania' or a 'bubble.'

The word 'mania' emphasizes irrationality; 'bubble' foreshadows that some values will eventually burst. Economists use the term bubble to mean any deviation in the price of an asset or a security or a commodity that cannot be explained in terms of the 'fundamentals.' Small price variations based on fundamentals are called 'noise.' In this book, a bubble is an upward price movement over an extended period of fifteen to forty months that then implodes. Someone with 'perfect foresight' should have foreseen that the process was not sustainable and that an implosion was inevitable.

In the twentieth century most of the manias and bubbles have centered on real estate and stocks. There was a mania in land in Southeast Florida in the mid-1920s and an unprecedented bubble in U.S. stocks in the second half of the 1920s. In Japan in the 1980s the speculative purchases of real estate induced a boom in the stock market. Similarly the bubble in the Asian countries in the 1990s involved both real estate and stocks, and generally increases in real estate prices pulled up stock prices. The U.S. bubble in the late 1990s primarily involved stocks, although the increases in household wealth in Silicon Valley and several regions led to surges in real estate prices. The oil price shocks of the 1970s led to surges in real estate activity in Texas, Oklahoma, and Louisiana. Similarly the sharp increases in the prices of cereals in the inflationary 1970s led to surges in land prices in Iowa, Nebraska, and Kansas and other Midwest farm states.

International propagation

Minsky focused on the instability in the supply of credit in a single country. Historically euphoria has often spread from one country to others through one of several different channels. The bubble in Japan in the 1980s had significant impacts on South Korea, Taiwan, and the State of Hawaii. South Korea and Taiwan were parts of the Japanese supply chain; if Japan is doing well economically, its former colonies will do well. Hawaii is to Tokyo as Miami is to New York; Japanese travel to Hawaii for rest and recreation in the sun. Hawaii experienced a real estate boom in the 1980s as the Japanese bought second homes and golf courses and hotels.

One conduit from a shock in one country to its impacts in other countries is arbitrage which ensures that the changes in the price of a commodity in one national market will lead to comparable changes in the prices of the more or less identical commodity in other national markets. Thus changes in the price of gold in Zurich, Beirut, and Hong Kong are closely tied to changes in the price of gold in London. Similarly changes in the prices of securities in one national market will lead to nearly identical changes in the prices of the same securities in other national markets.

In addition increases in national income in one country induce increases in its demand for imports and hence increases in counterpart exports in other countries and in the national incomes in these countries. Capital flows constitute a third link; the increase in the exports of securities from one country will lead to increases in both the price of these securities and the value of its currency in the foreign exchange market.

Moreover there are psychological connections, as when investor euphoria or pessimism in one country affects investors in others. The declines in stock prices on October 19, 1987, were practically instantaneous in all national financial centers (except Tokyo), far faster than can be accounted for by arbitrage, income changes, capital flows, or money movements.

In the ideal textbook world an increase in the gold coins in circulation in one country because of the flow of gold to that country would be matched by a corresponding decline in the gold supplies in other countries, and the increase in the money supply and the credit expansion in the first country would be offset by the contraction of credit and the money supply in the second. In the real world, however, the increase in the credit expansion in the first country may not be followed by a contraction of credit in the second country, because investors in the second country may respond to rising prices and profits abroad by demanding more credit so they can buy the assets and securities whose prices they anticipate will increase. The potential contraction from the shrinkage in the monetary base in the second country may be overwhelmed by the increase in speculative interest and the increase in the demand for credit.

As the speculative boom continues, interest rates, the speed of payments and the commodity price level increase. The purchases of securities or real estate by 'outsiders' means that the insiders—those who owned or purchased these assets earlier—sell the same securities and real estate and take some profits. A few insiders take their profits and sell; indeed if newcomers to the market are buyers, then the insiders must be sellers. At every moment the purchases of real estate or stocks by the new investors or outsiders are necessarily balanced by sales by the insiders. In 1928 the market value of the stocks traded on the New York Stock Exchange increased at an annual rate of 36 percent, and in the first eight months of 1929 the market value increased at an annual rate of 53 percent. Similarly in 1998 the market value of the stocks traded on the NASDAQ increased at an annual rate of 41 percent; in the subsequent fifteen months they increased at the annual rate of 101 percent. Investors rush to get on the train before it leaves the station and accelerates. If the eagerness of the outsiders to buy is stronger than the eagerness of the insiders to sell, the prices of the assets or securities continue to increase. In contrast if the sellers become more eager than the buyers, then the prices will decline.

As the buyers become less eager and the sellers become more eager an uneasy period of 'financial distress' follows; the term is from corporate finance and reflects that a firm is unable to adhere to its debt servicing commitments. For the economy as a whole, the equivalent is the awareness on the part of a considerable segment of both firms and individual investors that it is time to become more liquid—to reduce holdings of real estate and stocks and to increase holdings of money. The prices of goods and securities may fall sharply. Some highly leveraged investors may go bankrupt because the decline in asset prices is so sharp that the value of their assets declines below the amounts borrowed to buy the same assets. Some investors continue to hold the assets despite the decline in price because they believe that the decline in prices is temporary, a hiccup. The prices of the securities may begin to increase again; in Tokyo in the 1990s there were six 'bear market rallies' that involved stock price increases of more than 20 percent even though the trend was that stock prices had been declining. But some investors believed that stock prices had declined too far, and so they wanted to be among the first to buy the stocks while they were still cheap.

As the decline in prices continues, more and more investors realize that prices are unlikely to increase and that they should sell before prices decline further; in some cases this realization occurs gradually and in others suddenly. The race out of real or long-term financial securities and into money may turn into a stampede.

The specific signal that precipitates the crisis may be the failure of a bank or of a firm, the revelation of a swindle or defalcation by an investor who sought to escape distress by dishonest means, or a sharp fall in the price of a security or a commodity. The rush is on—prices decline and bankruptcies increase. Liquidation sometimes is orderly but may degenerate into panic as the realization spreads that only a relatively few investors can sell while prices remain not far below their peak values. In the nineteenth century the word 'revulsion' was used to describe this behavior. The banks become much more cautious in their lending on the collateral of commodities and securities. In the early nineteenth century this condition was known as 'discredit.'

'Overtrading,' 'revulsion,' 'discredit' have a musty, old-fashioned flavor; they convey a graphic picture of the decline in investor optimism.

Revulsion and discredit may lead to panic (or as the Germans put it, *Torschlusspanik,* 'door-shut-panic') as investors crowd to get through the door before it slams shut. The panic feeds on itself until prices have declined so far and have become so low that investors are tempted to buy the less liquid assets, or until trade in the assets is stopped by setting limits on price declines, shutting down exchanges or otherwise closing trading, or a lender of last resort succeeds in convincing investors that money will be made available in the amounts needed to meet the demand for cash and that hence security prices will no longer decline because of a shortage of liquidity. Confidence may be restored even without a large increase in the volume of money because the confidence that one can get money may be sufficient to reduce the demand for liquidity.

Whether a lender of last resort should provide liquidity to forestall a panic and the decline in prices of real estate and stocks has been debated extensively. Those who oppose the provision of liquidity from a lender of last resort argue that the knowledge that such credits will be available encourages speculation. Those who want a lender of last resort worry more about coping with the current crisis and reducing the likelihood that a liquidity crisis will cascade into a solvency crisis than they do about forestalling a future crisis. In domestic crises, government or the central bank has responsibility to act as a lender of last resort. At the international level, there is neither a world government nor any world bank adequately equipped to serve as a lender of last resort. The International Monetary Fund has not met the expectations of its founders as a lender of last resort.

The validity of the model

Three types of criticism have been directed at the Minsky model. One criticism is that each crisis is unique so that a general model is not relevant. A second is that this type of model is no longer relevant because of changes in business and economic environments. A third is that asset price bubbles are highly improbable because 'all the information is in the price'—the mantra of the efficient market view of finance.

Each criticism merits its own response.

The first criticism is that each crisis is unique, a product of a unique set of circumstances, or that there are such wide differences among economic crises as a class that they should be broken down into various species, each with its own particular features. Financial crises were frequent in the first two-thirds of the nineteenth century and in the last third of the twentieth century. In this view, each unique crisis is a product of a specific series of historical accidents—which was said about 1848 and about 1929,[5] and may be inferred from the historical accounts of separate crises referred to throughout this book. Each crisis also has its unique individual features—the nature of the shock, the object of speculation, the form of credit expansion, the ingenuity of the swindlers, and the nature of the incident that touches off revulsion. But if one may borrow a French phrase, the more something changes, the more it remains the same. Details proliferate; structure abides.

More compelling is the suggestion that the genus 'crises' should be divided into commercial, industrial, monetary, banking, fiscal, and financial (in the sense of financial markets) species or into local, regional, national, and international groups. Taxonomies along such lines abound. This view is not accepted because the primary concern is with international financial crises that involve a number of critical elements—speculation, monetary expansion, an increase in the prices of securities or real estate or commodities followed by a sharp fall and a rush into money. The test is whether use of the Minsky model provides insights about the broad features of the crises.

The second criticism is that the Minsky model of the instability of the supply of credit is no longer relevant because of structural changes in the institutional underpinnings of the economy, including the rise of the corporation, the emergence of big labor unions and big government, modern banking and speedier communications. The financial debacles in Mexico, Brazil, Argentina, and more than ten other developing countries in the early 1980s are consistent with the Minsky model; the increases in the external indebtedness of these countries were much higher than the interest rates on their loans so the borrowers were obtaining all of the cash to pay the scheduled interest from the lenders. The bubble in real estate prices and stock prices in Japan in the second half of the 1980s and the subsequent implosion of asset prices is consistent with the Minsky model since the annual increases in the prices of stocks and real estate was three or four times higher than the interest rates on the funds borrowed to finance the purchases of these assets. The booms and the subsequent busts in Thailand and Hong Kong and Indonesia and then in Russia feature the same pattern of cash flows.

The third criticism is that there can be no bubbles because market prices always reflect the economic fundamentals, and that sharp declines in asset prices usually reflect 'policy switching' by government or central banks. Those who take this position suggest that the alleged bubble appears to be the result of herd behavior, positive feedback or bandwagon effects—credulous suckers following smart insiders. These critics suggest that the model is 'misspecified,' that is, that something was going on not taken into account by the theory, and that more research is called for.[6] Some of the research ignored by those with this belief is offered in this book.

A more cogent attack on the Minsky model was by Alvin Hansen who claimed that the model was relevant prior to the middle of the nineteenth century but ceased to be so because of changes in the institutional environment.

> Theories based on uncertainty of the market, on speculation in commodities, on 'overtrading,' on the excesses of bank credit, on the psychology of traders and merchants, did indeed reasonably fit the early 'mercantile' or commercial phase of modern capitalism. But as the nineteenth century wore on, captains of industry... became the main outlets for funds seeking a profitable return through savings and investments.[7]

Hansen—who was a foremost expositor of the Keynesian model of the business cycle and especially of persistent high levels of unemployment—sought to explain the business cycle and wanted to downplay the significance of alternative explanations for changes in the level of economic activity. Hansen's emphasis on the importance of the relation between savings and investment does not require the rejection of the view that changes in the supply of credit can have important impacts on the prices of securities and the level of economic activity.

The model's relevance today

The Minsky model can be readily applied to the foreign exchange market and to periods of overvaluation and undervaluation of national currencies that are associated with 'overshooting' and 'undershooting.' Changes in the foreign exchange values of national currencies have been large relative to long-run equilibrium values despite sizable intervention in the market by central banks. Speculation in foreign currencies has resulted in large losses for some firms and some banks while others have made substantial trading profits.[8]

Consider the growth in the external debt of Mexico, Brazil, Argentina, and the other developing countries from $125 billion in 1972 to $800 billion in 1982; bank loans to these countries increased at the rate of 30 percent a year and the total external debt of these countries was increasing at the rate of 20 percent a year. The bank loans generally had a maturity of eight years and interest rates were floating and set with a specified markup over the LIBOR, the London Interbank Offer Rate. An average of the interest rates was about 8 percent although they tended to increase throughout the decade. The cash that borrowers received from new loans was substantially larger than the interest payments on their outstanding loans, so in effect they incurred no burden or hardship in making their debt service payments on a timely basis.

The inflow of foreign funds led to a real appreciation of the currencies of the capital-importing countries which was necessary so that the increase in their trade and current account deficits would more or less match the increase in their capital account surpluses. Obviously at some future date the inflow of cash from new loans would decline below the interest payments on the outstanding loans, and at that time the foreign exchange value of their currencies would decline; the counterpart of the decline in the capital inflow was that these countries would need trade and current account surpluses to get some of the cash necessary to pay the interest to their foreign creditors. Most of these borrowers effectively defaulted on their loans when the lenders stopped making new loans. The cost to the lenders of these defaults has been estimated at $250 billion in the form of the reduction in the face value of the loans and what in effect was a reduction in the interest rates. The lenders had failed to ask the question 'Where will the borrowers get the cash to pay us the interest if we stop supplying them with the cash in the form of new loans?'

During the 1980s real estate prices in Japan increased by a factor of ten and stock prices by a factor of six or seven; in the second half of the decade Japan experienced an economic boom. The rates of return earned by real estate investors appeared to be about 30 percent a year. Business firms recognized that the profit rate on real estate investment was substantially higher than the profit rate from making steel or automobiles or TV sets and so they became large investors in real estate using money borrowed from the banks. Real estate prices were increasing many times more rapidly than rents. At some stage, the net rental income declined below the interest payments on the funds borrowed to buy the real estate and so the borrowers had a 'negative carry.' The borrowers might obtain the funds to make the interest payments by increasing their loans against some of the properties that they already owned. At the beginning of 1990, the incoming governor of the Bank of Japan instructed the banks to limit the growth in new real estate loans as a share of their total loans. Once the bank loans for real estate began to increase at 5 or 6 percent a year rather than 30 percent a year, some of the firms and investors that needed the cash from new loans to pay the interest on the outstanding loans were no longer able to obtain new loans. They sold real estate and the bubble began to implode.

The current U.S. international financial position in some ways parallels that of Mexico, Brazil, and Argentina in the 1970s. These countries had unsustainably large current account deficits and obtained the cash to pay the interest to their foreign creditors from the foreign creditors. The implication is that the U.S. external payments position is not sustainable.

This book is a study in financial history, not economic forecasting. Investors seem not to have learned from experience.

3
Speculative Manias

Rationality of markets

The word 'mania' in the chapter title suggests a loss of touch with rationality, something close to mass hysteria. Economic history is replete with canal manias, railroad manias, joint stock company manias, real estate manias, and stock price manias. Economic theory is based on the assumption that men are rational. Since the rationality assumption that underlies economic theory does not appear to be consistent with these different manias, the two views must be reconciled. The thrust of this chapter is with investor demand for a particular type of asset or security while the next chapter focuses on the supply of credit and changes in the supply.

The 'rational expectations' assumption used in economic models is that investors react to changes in economic variables as if they are always fully aware of the long-term implications of these changes, either because they are clairvoyant or because they have Superman-like kryptonic vision. Thus the cliché that 'all the information is in the price' reflects the view that prices in each market react immediately and fully to every bit of news so that no 'money is left on the table.'

Contrast the rational expectations assumption with the adaptive expectations assumption that the values of certain variables in the future are extensions of these values in the recent past. Thus the cliché that 'the trend is your friend,' reflecting the view that if prices have been increasing they will continue to increase. Instead the thrust of the rational expectations view is that the prices that are anticipated next week and next month determine the prices that prevail today, in effect a backward-looking view from the future to the present. Thus the price of gold in the spot market today is the anticipated price of gold at a distant future date discounted to the present by an appropriate interest rate, usually the interest rate on risk-free government securities. The price of the U.S. dollar in terms of the Canadian dollar in the foreign exchange market today is the anticipated price of the U.S. dollar in terms of the Canadian dollar for a distant future date discounted to the present by the difference between the U.S. and the Canadian interest rates. If a government reduces tax rates to stimulate consumption spending or investment spending, the conclusion of the rational expectations view is that the policy won't be successful because investors will immediately realize that a larger fiscal deficit today implies higher tax rates on their incomes tomorrow and so they will increase the amount they save in anticipation of the forthcoming increase in their tax bills.

What does it mean to say that investors are rational?[1] One assumption is that most investors behave rationally most of the time. A second is that all investors behave rationally most of the time. A third is that each and every participant in the markets has the same intelligence, the same information, the same purposes, and the same economic model in mind. A fourth is that all investors behave rationally all the time.

Each of these assumptions has different implications for the way that investors behave in financial markets. Obtaining agreement on the assumption that most investors behave rationally most of the time is easier than obtaining agreement on the assumption that each investor behaves rationally all of the time. Frequently the argument seems to be between two polar positions, one that holds that no investor is ever rational while the other asserts that all investors always are rational. Harry G. Johnson offered this description of the difference between an older group of economists and a younger group interested in international monetary reform:

> The difference can be encapsulated in the proposition that whereas the older generation of economists is inclined to say 'the floating rate system does not work the way I expected, therefore the theory is wrong, the world is irrational and we can only regain rationality by returning to some fixed rate system to be achieved by cooperation among national governments' while the younger group is inclined to say 'the floating rate system is a system that should be expected to operate rationally, like most markets; if it does not seem to work rationally by my standards, my understanding of how it ought to work is probably defective; and I must work harder at the theory of

> rational maximizing behavior and its empirical consequences if I am to achieve understanding.' This latter approach is the one that is being disseminated, and intellectually enforced, through the [younger] network.[2]

Rationality is thus an a priori assumption about the way the world should work rather than a description of the way the world has actually worked. The assumption that investors are rational in the long run is a useful hypothesis because it illuminates understanding of changes in prices in different markets; in the terminology of Karl Popper, it is a 'pregnant' hypothesis. Hence it is useful to assume that investors are rational in the long run and to analyze economic issues on the basis of this assumption.

One interpretation of the rationality assumption is that prices in a particular market today must be consistent with the prices in the same market one and two months from now and one and two years from now adjusted for the 'costs of storage'; otherwise there would be a profitable and relatively riskless arbitrage opportunity.

Ragnar Nurkse summarized his survey of changes in the foreign exchange values of the French franc and the German mark in the 1920s with the statement that speculation in the foreign exchange market had been destabilizing. Milton Friedman asserted in response that destabilizing speculation cannot occur in the foreign exchange market because any investors that bought as prices were increasing and sold as prices were declining 'would be buying high and selling low'; their continuing losses would lead them either to go out of business or to change their strategy. The Friedman view is that since in a Darwinian sense the destabilizing speculators would fail to survive, destabilizing speculation cannot occur.[3] One response might be that from time to time some investors may follow strategies that would lead to losses.

There have been many historic episodes of destabilizing speculation, although at times the language has been imprecise and at times possibly hyperbolic. Consider some of the phrases in the literature: *manias... insane land speculation... blind passion... financial orgies... frenzies... feverish speculation... epidemic desire to become rich quick... wishful thinking... intoxicated investors... turning a blind eye... people without ears to hear or eyes to see... investors living in a fool's paradise... easy credibility... overconfidence... overspeculation... overtrading... a raging appetite... a craze... a mad rush to expand.*

Fernand Braudel used the terms 'craze' and 'passion' when he discussed everyday life in Europe from the fifteenth to the eighteenth centuries, largely in connection with consumption but also extended to spices, styles of dress, craving for knowledge and purchases of land.[4]

The principals in the London banking firm of Overend, Gurney, which crashed on Black Friday in May 1866, were said to be 'sapient nincompoops.'[5] 'These losses,' said Bagehot, 'were made in a manner so reckless and so foolish that one would think a child who had lent money in the City of London would have lent it better.'[6]

Clapham's description of the Baring firm in 1890 is understated in a characteristic British fashion: 'They had not considered these enterprises or the expected investors in them coolly or wisely enough [but had] gone far beyond the limits of prudence.'[7]

Consider Adam Smith's comment on the South Sea Bubble: 'They had an immense capital dividend among an immense number of proprietors. It was naturally to be expected, therefore, that folly, negligence, and profusion should prevail in the whole management of their affairs. The knavery and extravagance of their stock-jobbing operations are sufficiently known [as are] the negligence, profusion and malversation of the servants of the company.'[8]

And finally in this parade of classical economists a description by the usually restrained Alfred Marshall:

> The evils of reckless trading are always apt to spread beyond the persons immediately concerned ... when rumors attach to a bank's credit, they make a wild stampede to exchange any of its notes which they may hold; their trust has been ignorant, their distrust was ignorance and fierce. Such a rush often caused a bank to fail which might have paid them gradually. The failure of one caused distrust to rage around others and to bring down banks that were really solid; as a fire spreads from one wooden house to another until even fireproof buildings succumb to the blaze of a great conflagration.[9]

Rationality of the individual, irrationality of the market

Manias are associated on occasion with general 'irrationality' or mob psychology. The relationship between rational individuals and an irrational group of individuals can be complex. A number of distinctions can be made. One assumption is mob psychology, a sort of 'group thinking' when virtually all of the participants in the market change their views at the same time and move as a 'herd.' Alternatively different individuals change their views about market developments at different stages as part of a continuing process; most start rationally and then more of them lose contact with reality, gradually at first and then more quickly. A third possible case is that rationality differs among different groups of traders, investors, and speculators, and that an increasing number of individuals in these groups succumb to the hysteria as asset prices increase. A fourth case is that all the market participants succumb to the 'fallacy of composition,' the view that from time to time the behavior of the group of individuals differs from the sum of the behaviors of each of the individuals in the group. The fifth is that there is a failure of a market with rational expectations as to the *quality* of a reaction to a given stimulus to estimate the appropriate *quantity,* especially when there are lags between the stimulus and the reaction. Finally irrationality may exist because investors and individuals choose the wrong model, or fail to consider a particular and crucial bit of information, or suppress information that does not conform to the model that they have implicitly adopted. The irrationality of the gullible and greedy in succumbing to swindlers is discussed in a later chapter.[10]

Mob psychology or hysteria is well established as an occasional deviation from rational behavior. Some economic models highlight the demonstration effect, which leads the Smiths to spend more than their incomes—at least for a while—as they seek to keep up with the Joneses. Another is the Duesenberry effect: both the Smiths and the Joneses increase their consumption expenditure when their incomes increase and both are reluctant to reduce their consumption spending when their incomes decline. Politics has its 'bandwagon effects' when individuals back the most probable winners (or 'rats desert the sinking ship' when they turn from losers—though if the ship is really sinking, the rational rats leave). The French historian Gustave LeBon discussed this subject in *The Crowd.*[11] Charles MacKay in his discussion of the South Sea Bubble[12] mentioned the case of a banker who purchased £500 worth of South Sea stock in the third subscription list of August 1720 saying, 'When the rest of the world are mad, we must imitate them in some measure.'[13]

Hyman Minsky highlighted a mild form of this type of irrationality in his discussion of 'euphoria' in markets. In an earlier day, such waves of excessive optimism perhaps followed by excessive pessimism might have been tied to sunspots[14] or the path through the heavens of Venus or Mars. In Minsky's formulation these waves of optimism start with a 'displacement' or shock to some structural characteristics of the system, which leads to an increase in optimism of investors and business firms and of the banks as lenders. More confident expectations of a steady stream of prosperity and of an increase in profits induce investors to buy riskier stocks. Banks make riskier loans in this more optimistic environment. The optimism increases and may become self-fulfilling until it evolves into a mania.

The 1970s surge in the price of gold

On January 1, 1970, the market price of gold was less than $40 an ounce, on December 31, 1979, the price was $970. Between 1934 and 1970, the market price of gold had been linked to the U.S. gold parity of $35 an ounce. Beginning in the early 1970s, the formal link between gold and the U.S. dollar was broken and gold seemingly became 'just another commodity' like petroleum or pork bellies or eggs, freely traded on one of the commodity exchanges. (Obviously gold had a very different history from these other commodities; very few books have been written about the monetary history of pork bellies or of eggs.) The decade of the 1970s was one of accelerating inflation although not in a linear way, the price of gold increased to $200 an ounce in 1973 and then declined to $110 and surged in the second half of the decade.

One of the clichés is that 'gold is a good inflation hedge;' for four hundred years the real price of gold or its purchasing power in terms of a market basket of commodities had been more or less 'constant' over the long run. In the 1970s, in contrast, the annual percentage increase in the market price of gold was many times greater than the annual percentage increase in the consumer price level. The prices of petroleum, copper, wheat, and most other primary commodities were increasing in this inflationary episode, but the price of gold increased much more rapidly.

At some stage in the late 1970s the market price of gold was increasing because the market price of gold was increasing. Investors were extrapolating from the increase in the market price from Monday to Tuesday to project the market price on Friday; they purchased gold on Wednesday in anticipation that they could sell at a higher price on Friday. The 'greater fool theory' may have been at work, some of the buyers of gold may have realized that the increase in price was a bubble and anticipated that they would be able to sell their gold at a profit before the bubble imploded.

At the end of the 1990s the market price of gold was a bit less than $300 an ounce, and once again the cliché that gold is a good inflation hedge seemed valid; the price of gold had increased by a factor of fifteen since 1900 and the price of a market basket of U.S. goods had increased by about the same amount.

Two earlier alternative explanations for this unsober upswing were provided by Irving Fisher and by Knut Wicksell who emphasized that the real rate of interest was too low.[15] Consumer prices increase in economic expansions and while interest rates increase, they increase less rapidly than the inflation rate so the real rate of interest declines. Lenders have 'money illusion' and ignore the decline in the real rate of interest. In contrast borrowers recognize that the real rate of interest has declined; they do not have money illusion. Rational investors buy more stocks or real estate in this environment of increases in anticipated profits and declines in real interest rates. (The Fisher and Wicksell explanations were effective descriptions of the changes in nominal and real interest rates in the 1970s.)

This model relies on the ad hoc assumption that two groups of market participants systematically differ in their susceptibility to money illusion.

Too low an interest rate is a special case of what is perhaps a wider phenomenon—the pricing of financial innovations. Initially these innovations may be underpriced as 'loss leaders' so they will be more readily accepted, but the low price also may lead to excess demand. Or undue risks may be taken by recent entrants in an industry as they reduce prices to increase their market share relative to those of their established competitors. One notable example is that of Jay Cooke, the last prominent banker of the early 1870s to back a railroad, the Northern Pacific.[16] Other examples include Rogers Caldwell in the municipal bond market of the late 1920s,[17] Bernard K. Marcus of the Bank of the United States in mortgages in the same era,[18] and Michele Sindona of the Franklin National Bank in the early 1970s.[19]

Speculation often develops in two stages. In the first, sober, stage households, firms and investors, respond to a shock in a limited and rational way; in the second, the anticipations of capital gains play an increasingly dominant role in their transactions. 'The first taste is for high interest, but that taste soon becomes secondary. There is a second appetite for large gains to be made by selling the principal.'[20] In the 1830s in the United States investors initially bought land to expand the area of the cultivation of high-priced cotton; thereafter they purchased land for the anticipated capital gains they would realize when they sold the land to others. In the 1850s farmers and planters both 'consumed' land and speculated in land. In ordinary times they bought more land than they cultivated as a hedge against the declining value of the acres they planted; in booms this more or less sound basis was discarded, and farms were heavily mortgaged to buy *more* land, which in turn was mortgaged so they could buy still more land to profit from anticipated increases in land prices.[21] The 1830s railway boom in Great

Britain also had two stages: the first prior to 1835 when the projects were not bubbles, and a second after 1835 when they were. In the first phase, shares were sold by promoters to local chambers of commerce, Quaker capitalists, and hard-headed Lancashire businessmen, both merchants and industrialists—that is, to men of substance who anticipated benefits from the construction of the railroads. These groups were in a position to meet both the initial 5 to 10 percent payment and any subsequent calls for payment as the construction progressed. In the second phase, professional company promoters—many of them rogues interested only in quick profits—tempted a different class of investors, including ladies and clergymen.[22] The same stages are observed for building sites in Vienna in the early 1870s; initially these sites were bought for construction and then later like speculative poker chips for profitable resale.[23] Ilse Mintz noted a two-stage process in the sale of foreign bonds in New York in the 1920s; these bonds were sound prior to 1924 and the Dawes loan (which touched off the boom) and inferior thereafter.[24] The loans to Mexico and Brazil in the early 1970s were based on the realistic assessments of the credit standing of the borrowers; thereafter the banks wanted to increase their loans to these borrowers and so their concern with the quality of the projects that were being financed declined.

Essentially there was a reversal between the objective and the process, and in the end the objective became the process. The lenders became so enthusiastic about the process that they failed to appreciate the end-game and provide an answer to the question of where the borrowers would get the cash to pay the interest if the lenders stopped providing them with the cash in the form of new loans. Initially the junk bond market may have been rational, but then the supply of junk bonds surged and the creditworthiness of the borrowers declined sharply.

The market in just-built and unfinished houses in southern California, sold from one person to another at ever-increasing prices with the help of an active market in second mortgages, peaked in 1981 and then collapsed, with price declines of 40 percent.[25] There was a condominium 'craze' in Boston in 1985 and 1986; 60 percent of the buyers intended to sell the units. The condo market turned soft in 1988,[26] in a pattern similar to the 'flat craze' in Chicago in 1881.[27] A similar boom and dip occurred in the apartment market in Chicago in 2003.

The analysis in terms of two stages suggests two groups of speculators, the insiders and the outsiders. The insiders destabilize by driving the price up and up and then sell at or near the top to the outsiders. The losses of the outsiders necessarily are equal to the gains of the insiders.

Johnson pointed out that for every destabilizing speculator there must be a stabilizing one.[28] But the professional insiders initially destabilize by exaggerating the upswings and the downswings; these insiders follow the mantra that the 'trend is my friend.' At one stage, these investors were known as 'tape watchers;' more recently they have been called 'momentum investors.' The outsider amateurs who buy high and sell low are the victims of euphoria that affects them late in the day. After they lose, they go back to their normal occupations to save for another splurge five or ten years in the future.

Although Larry Wimmer concluded that destabilizing speculation did not occur in the gold panic of 1869, the evidence is consistent with the hypothesis that Gould and Fisk first drove up the gold price and then sold at the top in a manner that is consistent with destabilizing speculation.[29] The information available to the two groups of speculators differed. In the early stage, Gould tried to persuade the U.S. government of the desirability of forcibly depreciating the U.S. dollar by driving up the 'agio' or premium on gold to increase grain prices, while the outsider speculators operated on the expectation derived from past performance that the U.S. government would seek to drive the agio down so that greenbacks would again be convertible into gold at the pre-Civil War parity. On September 16 the outsiders abandoned this expectation and adopted Gould's; they bought gold and the price went up. On September 22 Gould learned from his associate, President Grant's brother-in-law, that the outsiders had originally been right and that his plan was not going to be adopted; Gould then sold. Belatedly the outsiders saw they were wrong. The result was the Black Friday of September 23, 1869, when stock prices collapsed.

Another case that involves two sets of speculators, insiders, and outsiders, is the 'bucket shop.' This term has practically disappeared from the language since the Securities and Exchange Commission declared the practice illegal, but the men and women who run the boiler shops are the children of those who ran bucket shops in an earlier generation. Bucket shops are described in novels; a classic picture is given in Christina Stead's excellent *House of All Nations*.[30] The insiders in a bucket shop take orders from the public to buy and sell securities but do not execute these orders because they assume that the outsider's bet will prove to be wrong. And the bucket shop has the advantage of a hedge. If the outsiders should turn out to be right by 'buying low and selling high,' the bucket-shop operators decamp. In *House of All Nations,* Jules Bertillon in 1934 fled to Latvia; today the destination might be Brazil, Costa Rica, or Cuba.

Bucket shops evolved into boiler shops that hustled untutored investors with promises of quick sure-fire gains. The owners of the boiler shops had brought forth their own firms; initially they owned nearly all or all of the shares in the firm. Robert Brennan of First Jersey Securities owned and operated or was associated with a series of boiler shops; the names kept changing but the scam was always the same. They used their buddies to hustle the increases in the prices of the stocks; once the stock prices were increasing, they used telemarketing to sell the stocks to the dentists and the undertakers in all the small towns of America. They managed to increase the prices of the stock day by day until most of the shares in the firms had been sold to the gullible investors who were congratulating themselves on how much money they had made—on paper. When one or several of these investors tried to sell to realize their profits, they found there were no buyers.

For a further example of an outside destabilizing speculator who bought high and sold low, there is the story of the great Master of the Mint, Isaac Newton, a world-class scientist. In the spring of 1720 he stated: 'I can calculate the motions of the heavenly bodies, but not the madness of people.' On April 20, accordingly, he sold his shares in the South Sea Company at a 100 percent profit of £7000. Later an infection from the mania gripping the world that spring and summer caused him to buy a larger number of shares near the market top and he lost £20,000. In the irrational habit of so many who experience financial disaster, he put it out of his mind and never for the rest of his life could he bear to hear the name South Sea.[31]

Yet euphoric speculation with insiders and outsiders may also lead to manias and panics when the behavior of every participant seems rational in itself. Consider the fallacy of composition when the whole differs from the sum of its parts. The action of each individual is rational—or would be if many other individuals did not behave in the same way. If an investor is quick enough to get in and out ahead of the others, he may do well, as insiders generally do. Carswell quotes a rational participant on the South Sea Bubble:

> The additional rise above the true capital will only be imaginary; one added to one, by any stretch of vulgar arithmetic will never make three and a half, consequently all fictitious value must be a loss to some person or other first or last. The only way to prevent it to oneself must be to sell out betimes, and so let the Devil take the hindmost.[32]

'Devil take the hindmost,' *'sauve qui pent,' 'die Letzen beissen die Runde,'* ('dogs bite the laggards'), and the like are recipes for a panic. The analogy is someone yelling fire in a crowded theater. The chain letter is another analogy; because the chain cannot expand infinitely, only a few investors can sell before the prices start declining. It is rational for an individual to participate in the early stages of the chain and to believe that all others will think they are rational too.

Closely akin to the fallacy of composition is the standard 'cobweb' demonstration in elementary economics in which demand and supply are linked with a lag rather than simultaneously, as in an auction that clears the market at each moment of time. 'Displacement' consists of events that change the situation, extend the horizon, and alter expectations. In such cases, otherwise rational expectations of some investors fail to take recognizance of the strength of similar responses by others. When there appears to be a shortage of physicists or mathematicians or schoolteachers many young people enter graduate school to study for one of these professions; by the time they have finished their studies, there may be an 'excess supply' of individuals trained for careers in these fields. After the belated surge in supply, job opportunities suddenly become scarce. But the excess supply becomes known only after the gestation period of study. Responses to shortages of coffee, sugar, cotton, or some other commodity may be similarly excessive. The price increases sharply in response to the initial surge in demand and then declines even more rapidly as the new supply becomes available after an extended investment period.

The history of manias and panics is replete with examples of destabilizing 'cobweb' responses to exogenous shocks. When Brazil became open as a market for British goods in 1808, more Manchester goods were sent to the market in a few weeks than had been consumed there in the previous twenty years, including ice skates and warming pans that, as Clapham noted, proved to be the accepted illustration of commercial madness among nineteenth-century economists.[33] In the 1820s, independence for the Spanish colonies triggered a boom in lending to new Latin American governments, investing in mining shares, and exporting to the area; the surge in investment proved excessive. 'The demand is sudden, and as suddenly stops. But too many have acted as if it were likely to continue.'[34]

In the 1830s the cobweb fluctuation had a two-year periodicity. 'Each merchant would be ignorant of the amount other merchants would be bringing forward by the time his own merchandise was on the market.'[35] The same was true in the United States in the 1850s following the discovery of gold in California:

> The extraordinary and undue expectations entertained not only in the United States but in this country [Britain] as to the capability of California—after the 1849 gold discovery—unquestionably aided in multiplying and extending the disaster consequent on the American crisis. When it was again and again stated, both in London and in Boston, in regard to all shipments to San Francisco, that six, or at most eight, moderately-sized or assorted cargos per month were all that were required or could be consumed; instead of that eastern shippers dispatch twelve to fifteen first-class ships a month, fully laden.[36]

A rather far-fetched line of reasoning led from the phylloxera that ruined many vineyards and set back wine production in France to the 1880s boom in brewery shares in Great Britain, as one after another, private breweries sold shares to investors for the first time in the public-companies mania. Among them, Arthur Guinness and Co. was bought for £1.7 million and sold for £3.2 million.[37] 'The success of the issue was like the firing of a starting pistol; by November 1890, 86 other brewery companies had issued new shares to the public for the first time.'[38]

There was a boom in Great Britain at the end of World War I when businessmen thought victory would ensure the elimination of German competition in coal, steel, shipping, and cotton textiles. Prices of industrial assets, ships, equities, and even houses increased. Companies were merged; many of the mergers were financed with large amounts of credit. Then sober realization set in from the summer of 1920 to the coal strike of the second quarter of 1921.[39]

Three more cases are on the borderline of rationality. The first deals with target workers, so to speak—individuals who get used to a certain level of income and find it difficult to adjust their spending downward when their incomes decline. In consumption theory, this is the Duesenberry effect already referred to. In labor supply, it constitutes the 'backward-bending supply curve,' which suggests that higher wages or salaries produce not more work but less and that the way to increase effort is to lower the wage per unit of time. In economic history books, this principle is known as 'John Bull can stand many things but he cannot stand 2 percent.' John Stuart Mill put it thus:

> Such vicissitudes, beginning with irrational speculation and ending with a commercial crisis, have not hitherto become less frequent or less violent with the growth of capital and the extension of industry... Rather they may be said to have become more so: in consequence, it is often said, of increased competition; but, as I prefer to say, of a low rate of profit and interest, which makes the capitalists dissatisfied with the ordinary course of safe mercantile gains.[40]

In France at the end of the Restoration and the beginning of the July Monarchy—that is, between 1826 and 1832—speculation was rife despite the 'distrust that the French always feel toward ill-gotten money.' Landowners earned 2.25 to 3.75 percent on their assets; industrialists tried to do better than the long-run interest rate on their fixed investments by 2 to 4 percentage points and earn 7 to 9 percent. Merchants and speculators in raw materials sought returns in the range of 20 to 25 percent on their investments.[41] Charles Wilson noted that earlier the Dutch were converted from merchants into bankers (accused of idleness and greed); they developed habits of speculation because of the decline in the rate of interest in Amsterdam to 2.5 and 3 percent.[42] Large-scale conversions of public debt in 1822 and 1824 and again in 1888 led to a decline in the rate of interest and induced British investors to buy more foreign securities.[43] Andréadès observed that 'When interest goes down, the English commercial world, unable to reduce its mode of life, deserts its usual business in favour of the more profitable, but on that very account more risky undertakings... speculation leads to disaster and ultimately must be borne by the central bank.'[44]

The boom in Third World bank-syndicated loans in the 1970s followed a sharp decline in interest rates on U.S. dollar securities in the spring of 1970 as the Federal Reserve adopted a more expansive policy. Banks were highly liquid and looked for attractive borrowers which they found in Third World governments and government-owned firms, mostly in Latin America. The 1960s had been a decade of accelerating internationalization for the major U.S. banks and they had rapidly increased the numbers of their foreign branches. Because of the sharp increase in commodity prices, nominal incomes and real incomes in Mexico, Brazil, and most other developing countries were increasing at above-trend rates. Commodity prices declined sharply in the early 1980s in response to the surge in U.S. interest rates, and then nominal and real incomes declined in the developing countries. Should the banks have foreseen that the decline in commodity prices was inevitable?

The second borderline case involves hanging on in the hope of some improvement, or failing to take a specific type of action when changes in circumstances occur. On the first score, note the failures of the New York Warehouse and Security Company, of Kenyon, Cox & Co., and of Jay Cooke and Co. on September 8, 13, and 18, 1873, because of loans made to railroads (respectively, the Missouri, Kansas and Texas, the Canada Southern, and the Northern Pacific) with which they were associated. These railroads were unable to sell bonds to obtain the funds they needed to complete construction that was already under way because Berlin and Vienna had stopped lending to the United States.[45] Similarly, when U.S. long-term lending to Germany stopped in 1928, as U.S. investors turned to stocks and stopped buying bonds, New York banks and investment houses continued to make short-term loans to German borrowers. When riding a tiger or holding a bear by the tail, it seems rational to hang on—at least for a while.

For an error of omission, note the plight of Hamburg banks that had made large loans to Swedish banks during the Crimean War that were engaged in financing smuggled goods into Russia; the Hamburg banks failed to cancel these loans when peace came. The Swedes used the money to speculate in shipbuilding, factories, and mining, which helped embroil Hamburg in the world crisis of 1857.[46]

The third borderline case is to have a rational model in mind, but the wrong one. The most famous example in another field is the French 'Maginot Line psychology,' though this may be thought of less as a case of irrational expectations than one of an undistributed lag. '"When a man's vision is fixed on one thing," thought Ponzi, "he might as well be blind".'[47] Or Bagehot on Malthus: 'Scarcely any man who has evolved a striking and original conception ever gets rid of it.'[48] In the 1760s, Hamburg merchants were not hurt by the fall in commodity prices until the end of the Seven Years' War. Thus in 1799 while the Napoleonic Wars were continuing they were unprepared for the decline in prices that came with penetration of the blockade of Napoleon's 1798 Continental system.[49] Or take the French bankers and industrialists who formed the copper ring in 1888, patterned after the cartel movement in iron and steel, steel rails, coal, and sugar in the early part of the decade, attracted by the successes of the diamond syndicate in South Africa and of the Rothschilds' mercury monopoly in Spain. (Many economists and analysts extrapolated from the apparent success of the Organization of Petroleum Exporting Countries in increasing the price of petroleum in the 1970s to assume that successful price fixing cartels would reduce the output of practically every other raw material and foodstuff and lead to much higher prices for these products.) By 1890 the French syndicate owned 60,000 tons of high-priced copper plus contracts to buy more; the older mines were reworked and firms began to process scrap while the copper price was declining rapidly. The collapse of the copper price from £80 a ton to £38 a ton in 1889 almost took with it the Comptoir d'Escompte, which was saved by an advance of 140 million francs from the Bank of France, reluctantly guaranteed by the Paris banks.[50]

Financial innovation in the form of deregulation or liberalization has often been a shock. In the early 1970s Ronald McKinnon led an intellectual attack on 'financial repression,' that is, the segmentation of financial markets in developing countries that led to preferential treatment of government borrowers, borrowers that were involved in foreign trade, and large firms as borrowers.[51] The message appealed particularly to Latin American countries already influenced by the Chicago doctrine of liberalism. A number of countries deregulated their financial systems, which was followed by a rapid growth of new banks and a rapid growth of credit, inflation, and then the collapse of some of the new banks.[52] McKinnon felt that the lesson from this debacle was that the several steps in the process of deregulation should be staged carefully.[53]

The same questions surfaced again in Poland and in the former Soviet Union in the 1980s and early 1990s in fierce debates over whether the shift from command economies to market economies should be carried through rapidly or slowly. The success of a transition from a command economy seems to depend on the extent to which individuals in the socialist economy remember the institutional background of its early capitalism before it turned socialist. The memory of the market economy was far greater in Poland than in Russia; long years of socialism and corruption had eradicated the memory in Russia. Such memory is more important to transitional success than the speed of decontrols and of the privatization of state monopolies.

Charlie Ponzi was alive and well and living in Tirana

The transition from the command economies to the market economies in what had been Eastern Europe in the early 1990s meant that the financial structures were no longer regulated. Entrepreneurs—some of them former members of the army in Albania—started firms that promised high rates of return, often 30 percent a month. The public in these countries had accumulated lots of currency and lots of deposits in the state-owned banks; the interest rates on these deposits were extremely low. So the public was attracted to the high rates of returns promised by these newly established financial institutions. Competition among the several different 'banks' kept the promised interest rates high.

Some Albanians sold their homes to get the cash to buy these bank deposits and then rented the same properties from the buyers; the 'interest income' on their deposits was much higher than the rent they had to pay for the same homes. Often the buyers of the apartments were the same entrepreneurs who owned and managed the deposit banks. Albanians in its diaspora sent money from New York and Chicago and Frankfurt to their relatives in Tirana to be deposited in these new institutions. Some Albanians stopped working because the interest income on their deposits was so much higher than their wages and salaries.

Alas it was too good to be true and it wasn't.

One purely irrational case involves a society that pins its hopes on some outstanding event of limited relevance to its current economic circumstances and another is when a society ignores evidence that it would prefer not to think about. Many Austrian enterprises had invested extensively in anticipation of the increase in business activity that would follow from the opening of the World Exhibition in Vienna on May 1, 1873; their liquid liabilities greatly exceeded their liquid assets and so they had acute financial distress. The objective of these world's fairs and exhibitions is to increase business activity, so there is significant investment in facilities designed to accommodate the attendees at the fairs. The credit at banks was stretched to the limit; a move from commodities, land, shares, and debt back into money was under way and the chain of accommodation bills was extended as far as it would go. Nonetheless the banks and the firms hung on, waiting for the exhibition to open, because they thought or at least hoped that the increase in sales would save the situation. When the exhibition opened and the increase in sales was disappointing, on May 5 and 6 the market collapsed.[54]

As an illustration of repression of contradictory evidence—the cognitive-dissonance case—consider J.W. Beyen's analysis of the German failure to restrict short-term borrowing from abroad at the end of the 1920s. He suggested that the dangers were not faced, even by Schacht, the German finance minister, and added: 'It would not have been the first nor the last time . . . that consciousness was being "repressed."'[55]

These examples suggest that despite the general usefulness of the assumption of rationality, markets have on occasions—infrequent occasions—acted in ways that were irrational even when each participant in the market believed he or she was acting rationally.

Displacements

A displacement is an outside event or shock that changes horizons, expectations, anticipated profit opportunities, behavior—'some sudden advice many times unexpected.'[56] A surge in the oil price is a displacement. An unanticipated devaluation is another displacement—although most devaluations have been anticipated. The shock must be sufficiently large to have an impact on the economic outlook. Each day's events produce some changes in outlook, but few are significant enough to qualify as displacements.

War is a major displacement. Some crises occur immediately at the beginning or end of a war, or soon enough after the end to permit a few expectations to be falsified. For beginnings, the most notable is the crisis of August 1914. The displacements at the end of wars include the crises of 1713, 1763, 1783, 1816, 1857, 1864, 1873, and 1920. Moreover there have been an impressive series of crises seven to ten years after the end of a war, long enough for expectations formed at the end of the original crisis to be falsified; these included 1720, 1772, 1792, 1825, 1873 in the United States (if it be connected to the Civil War), and 1929.

Far-reaching political changes may also jar the system and change expectations. The Glorious Revolution of 1688 gave rise to a boom in company promotion. By 1695 there were 140 joint stock companies with a total capital of £4.5 million, more than 80 percent had been formed in the previous seven years. By 1717 total capitalization had reached £21 million.[57] In July 1720 the Bubble Act forbade formation of new joint-stock companies without explicit approval of parliament, a limitation that lasted until 1856. Although this regulation has normally been interpreted as a reaction against the South Sea Company speculation, Carswell asserts that it was undertaken in support of the South Sea Company, as king and parliament sought to repress the development of rival companies that might attract cash that was intensely needed by the South Sea promoters as the bubble expanded.[58]

The events of the French Revolution, Terror, Directorate, Consulate, and Empire, along with incidents of the Napoleonic Wars themselves, set in motion large-scale specie movements in 1792–1793 and 1797 and opening and closing markets in Europe and elsewhere for British and colonial goods. Further political events of the kind in France were the Restoration (1815), the July Monarchy (1830), the February 1848 revolution, and the Second Empire (1852). The Sepoy Mutiny in India in May 1857, followed by a Hindustan military revolution, contributed to the distress of London financial markets.[59] These events were a precedent for the Invergordon disorder of September 1931, when a contingent of British sailors came close to striking over reductions in pay decreed by the new national government. Continental Europeans interpreted this response as a mutiny on the part of one great British institution, the navy, and this interpretation contributed to the British decision to stop pegging the pound to gold.[60]

War, revolution, restoration, change of regime, and mutiny come largely from outside the system. Monetary and financial displacements are more difficult to describe as exogenous. But maladroit recoinage, tampering with gold/silver ratios under bimetallism, conversions undertaken to economize on government revenue that unexpectedly divert investor attention to other avenues, new lending that proves successful beyond all anticipation—these can also be regarded as displacements.

The Kipper- und Wipperzeit of 1619–1623 (noted earlier) got its name from the action of money-changers who took the debased coins that were coming from the rising number of princely mints and rigged their scales as they sought to exchange bad money for good with naive peasants, shopkeepers, and craftsmen. Rapidly rising debasement spread from state to state until the coins used in daily transactions became worthless.[61]

Two later German recoinages provide a study in contrast. In 1763, Frederick II of Prussia bought silver in Amsterdam on credit to provide for a new coinage to replace that which had been debased during the Seven Years' War. He withdrew the old debased money from circulation before the new money was issued, which precipitated a deflationary crisis and the collapse of a chain of discounted bills.[62] More than 100 years later, after the Franco-Prussian indemnity, the German authorities issued new money but this time before the old money was withdrawn to save on their interest payments. In three years the circulation of coins rose threefold from 254 million thalers (762 million marks). The result was inflation.[63]

The crisis of 1893 in the United States, arising from the threat to gold convertibility from the Sherman Silver Act of 1890, has already been noted. So have the British debt conversions of 1822, 1824, 1888, and 1932, although the last was associated with a boom in housing that did not lead to crisis. In France, conversion of the 5 percent *rente* was discussed after 1823 as the money supply expanded and the rate of interest would have fallen had investors not been reluctant to buy *rentes* at a premium. Each of three bankers had a different idea of the purpose of the conversion: Rothschild wanted to sell more *rentes;* Greffuhle (and Ouvrard) hoped to attract investors into canals while Laffitte wanted to ensure the development of industry. In the event, political obstacles prevented passage of the necessary legislation, and the market finally gave up its objection to maintaining the *rente* at a premium. This sharp decline in interest rates touched off speculation.[64] Canals were built by the government with private money,[65] and the faint glow of a railroad boom could be seen in France along the Loire, the Rhône, and the Seine. But the main object of speculation was building in and around the major cities—Paris, Mulhouse, Lyons, Marseilles, Le Havre.[66] Honoré de Balzac's novel *César Birotteau* was inspired by this experience. The novel, written in 1830, recounted the doleful story of a perfumier who was enticed into buying building lots in the vicinity of the Madeleine on borrowed money for 'one quarter of the value they were sure to have in three years.'[67]

The successes of loans in recycling reparations or indemnities after the Napoleonic and Franco-Prussian wars and World War I have been mentioned. Any surprising success of a security issue, with a large multiple oversubscription and a quick premium for subscribers, attracts borrowers, lenders, and especially investment bankers. The Baring loan of 1819—'the first important foreign loan contracted by a British bank'[68]—led quickly to a series of issues for France, Prussia, Austria, and, later, after independence, the countries that had been Spanish colonies. The Thiers *rente* made French banking houses salivate in the hope of foreign loans, a hunger that received a further fillip from the 1888 conversion loan for czarist Russia that bailed out German investors and sent French investors down a trail that was to end, after revolution in 1917, with a whimper rather than a bang. The Dawes loan in 1924 opened the eyes of American investors to the romance of buying foreign securities—at least for five years. The Thiers *rente* was oversubscribed fourteen times, and the Dawes loan eleven. Far more important than the size of the multiple, however, was its relation to expectation. Rosenberg described the three French loans of 1854 and 1855 as sensational, since they were oversubscribed almost two to one (468 million francs on an offering of 250 million), four to one (2,175 million francs for an issue of 500 million), and five to one (3,653 million against 750 million). In

Austria and Germany, however, when the speculative boom of the 1850s was under way, the Credit Anstalt opening stock sale was oversubscribed 43 times, largely by people who had stood in line all night; and when the Brunswick Bank sought 2 million thalers in May 1853, it was offered 112 times that amount in three hours.[69]

Among major recent displacements, as noted earlier, have been deregulation of bank and financial institutions; such innovations as derivatives (which existed earlier but only on a modest scale); mutual and hedge funds, offering new opportunities to acquire wealth, with however the risk of loss; REITs (Real Estate Investment Trusts); bank flotation of loans and mortgages as marketable securities; and initial public offerings (IPOs) of private companies.

The deregulation of financial institutions was a major contributory factor to the asset price bubble in Japan in the 1980s and especially the second half of that decade. Each Japanese bank was keenly interested in its position on the hit parade in terms of assets or deposits; each wanted to move to a higher position on the hit parade ladder—which meant that each had to 'grow its loans' more rapidly than the banks that were higher in the charts.

The technological revolution in the 1920s—the sharp increase in automobile production, the electrification of much of America, the rapid expansion of the telephone system, the increase in the number of movie theaters, and the beginning of radio—was a major shock. Investment surged. Similarly in the 1990s, especially in the second half of the decade, there was a major technological information revolution. The venture capital firms, especially those based in the San Francisco Bay area, were eager suppliers of finance to many of the engineers who had ideas. Then at a later stage these firms received 'mezzanine financing.' The next stage was that the firms had an initial public offering (IPO) arranged by one of the major investment banks like Merrill Lynch or Morgan Stanley or Credit Swiss First Boston. The investment banks would arrange 'road shows' for these firms as they were about to go public; the entrepreneurs would visit the mutual funds and the pension funds and the managers of other pools of cash. Based on the demand, the investment banks would price the shares at \$19 or \$23 or \$31 and perhaps 20 percent of the firms' outstanding shares would be sold. Often the price of the shares at the end of the first day's trading would be three or four times the IPO price.

The 'pop' in the share price on the first day's trading was an advertisement that stock prices only increase. During the late 1990s an extremely high proportion of new stock issues experienced these large price pops on the first day of trading. The price pops encouraged lots of new stock offerings.

'Dow at 36,000,' 'Dow at 40,000,' 'Dow at 100,000'*

Three books with nearly identical titles were published in 1999. Their themes were also almost identical—if interest rates remained low and corporate earnings continued to increase, then eventually the Dow Jones index of stock prices would reach much higher levels than ever before. The logic was irrefutable, more or less an extension of the Archimedes principle that he could move the world if he had a large enough lever. In the long run the level of stock prices reflects three factors: the rate of growth of GDP, the profit share of GDP and the relation of stock prices to corporate earnings or the price–earnings ratio. The profit share of U.S. GDP has been remarkably constant in the long run at about 8 percent and the price–earnings ratio has averaged about 18.

Investors continually choose between buying bonds and buying stocks. The interest rate on bonds has averaged about 5 percent; the earnings yield on bonds, the reciprocal of the interest rate, is thus 20.

Those who forecast the Dow at 36,000 believed that the price–earnings ratio should be much higher because stocks were no more risky than bonds.

*James K. Glassman and Kevin A. Hassett, *Dow 36,000: the New Strategy for Profiting from the Coming Rise in the Stock Market* (Random House, 1999); David Elias, *Dow 40,000: Strategies for Profiting from the Greatest Bull Market in History* (McGraw-Hill, 1999); Charles W. Kadlec, *Dow 100,000: Fact or Fiction* (Prentice Hall, 1999).

Objects of speculation

In the last several decades of the twentieth-century investors speculated primarily in real estate or stocks; in earlier periods the objects of speculation were more diverse. A stylized table of cycles is presented in the Appendix. The list shows the tendency for these objects to move from a few favored items at the beginning of our period to a wide variety of commodities and other assets and instruments at the end. The list is partial but suggestive.

How likely is it that a displacement will lead to a shock that induces individuals to invest for capital gains and especially capital gains in the near future? (Assume that destabilizing speculation can occur in a world of individuals whom it is convenient and fruitful to consider as normally rational. Then assume this world is disturbed by a shock largely from outside the system, giving rise to prospects that individuals misjudge, either for themselves or for others.) There are many shocks: only a relatively small proportion of shocks lead to a speculative mania.

One question is whether two or more objects of speculation such as real estate and stock are likely to be involved before 'overtrading' reaches sufficient dimensions to result in crisis. Consider a few occasions when there seem to have been two or more objects.

The 1720 South Sea and Mississippi bubbles were related, and stoked by monetary expansion in the two countries that supported a high head of speculative steam. Speculation starting in the securities of the South Sea Company and the Sword Blade Bank in England and in those of the Mississippi Company and John Law's *banques* in France spread rapidly to other ventures and to commodities and land; many of these other ventures were swindles. The South Sea Company was brought down by its attempt to suppress rival speculations, bringing proceedings under the Bubble Act of June 1720 against York Buildings, Lustrings, and Welsh Copper. The effort boomeranged.[70] The spread of speculation from one object to another, to generalize the rise of prices, occurred because the speculators that sold South Sea stock when prices were approaching their peak purchased banks and insurance stocks and country houses.[71] So closely linked were the several markets that in time the price of land began to move with the South Sea Bubble quotations.[72] In France land prices rose in the fall of 1719 as speculators started to take their profits from the Mississippi Bubble.[73]

The 1763 boom was based exclusively on government war expenditure and its finance through chains of discount bills. The DeNeufville Brothers, whose failure set off the panic, sold 'commodities, ships, and securities like so many Dutch firms,'[74] with hundreds of thousands of florins in acceptance liabilities against which they rarely kept more than a few thousand guilders in cash reserves. Some contribution to the downturn in business may have been brought on by an unparalleled drought in England in 1762, with a shortage of hay and scarcities of meat, butter, and cheese.[75]

The crisis of 1772 was precipitated by speculation in Amsterdam and London in the stock of the East India Company and by the collapse of the Ayr Bank (Douglas, Heron & Co.). Numerous complex details are involved, including the political reverses of the East India Company and restriction on its credit by the Bank of England; the practice of the thrusting new Ayr Bank (which was left bad loans by the established banks) in borrowing from London when its acceptances came due; and the flight in July 1772 of Alexander Fordyce, who had lost his firm's money selling East India Company stock prematurely. When the stock actually fell in the fall of the year, Clifford & Co., the Dutch bank that had headed a syndicate trying to push the price up, failed. These phenomena seem superficial, however. Heavy investment in Britain in houses, turnpikes, canals, and other public works had put a strain on resources and unleashed the excess credit.[76] One source relates the fall in coffee prices beginning in 1770 to the financial crisis of 1772–1773,[77] but this is not mentioned by Wilson, the standard source, or by Ashton, Clapham, or Buist.[78]

In 1793 there were several causes—country banks, canals, the Reign of Terror—that stimulated a flow of funds to Great Britain, as well as bad harvests. In 1799 there was one cause, the tightening and loosening of the blockade. Contrariwise, the crisis of 1809–1810 is said to have had 'two separate causes: a reaction from the speculation in South America; and a loosening and then tightening of the continental blockade.'[79] In 1815–1816 came a postwar boom in exports to Europe and the United States that exceeded all possibility of sales, plus a fall in the price of wheat. Canals and South American government bonds and mines combined in 1825; British exports, cotton, land sales in the United States, and the beginning of the railroad mania contributed to the crisis in the mid-1830s. The crisis of 1847 had as its cause the railway mania, the potato disease, a wheat crop failure one year and a bumper crop the next, followed by revolution in Europe.

Thus in most of the significant crises at least two objects of speculation were involved and at least two markets. Just as the national markets were connected, so the speculation was likely to be connected by the underlying credit conditions. But when a crisis like that of 1847 arises from objects as disparate as railroads and wheat, there is some basis for suggesting that the crisis is accidental in origin unless the monetary weakness that feeds it is systematic.

In Japan and in the Asian countries, bubbles in real estate and stocks have generally occurred together. In some countries, especially small countries, the market value of real estate companies is a relatively high proportion of the market value of all stocks as a group. When real estate prices increase, the value of the assets owned by real estate companies increases, and the market value of the real estate companies is likely to increase. Those investors who have sold the real estate stocks have cash to invest and much of their cash is likely to be invested in stocks of firms not involved in the real estate business. Moreover when the real estate prices increase, then the construction business is likely to boom and the market value of the construction companies is likely to increase. The bank loan losses are likely to be below trend at a time when real estate prices are increasing. And of course the symbiotic relationship is symmetric; when real estate prices decline, stock prices are likely to decline.

National differences in speculative temperament

One suggestion is that investors in some countries are more likely to speculate than those in other countries. Despite Ruth Benedict's distinction between cultures with Apollonian (balancing) and those with Dionysian (orgiastic) temperaments,[80] the proposition is dubious. And despite this implausibility, the opinion among historians seems general that the Brabanters had a strong gambling temperament in the sixteenth century, and that those tens of thousands who migrated to the United Provinces after the sack of Antwerp in November 1576 and its devastating siege in 1585 took it with them.[81] In the Dutch Republic, the gambling instinct of bankers, investors, and even common folk existed in great tension with Calvin and Lutheran frugality and abstemiousness.[82] There may then yet be something to the notion that banking institutions give more play to speculation in one country than in another. Juglar, for example, claims the French crises in the eighteenth century were less abrupt and less violent than those of Great Britain because (after the John Law affair) credit in France was less used and less abused.[83] A different view ascribes French experience to a severe bankruptcy law:

> Whether by the education forces of law and established institutions, or by tradition, a high standard of business honesty prevails in France. The act of sons in toiling for years to pay the debts of their fathers, and of notaries in paying for the defalcations of one of their number, for the sake of the profession, although without personal association with him, indicates a standard of compliance with business obligations which cannot be without influence upon the material prosperity of a people. It may be surprising that the nation whose soldiers are so noted for dash in war should furnish financiers and business men who are the embodiment of conservatism in their methods, but such is clearly the case.

This same author goes on to say: 'England is the country in which a spirit of adventure and speculation has done most to promote crises and depressions.'[84]

One historian has suggested that mining and sheep grazing contributed to a love of gambling, and that Australians, starting with the gold discoveries of 1851–1852, developed a particular love of gambling, expressed both through horse racing and speculation in land.[85]

A common view is that the United States is 'the classic home of commercial and financial panics,' presumably because of wildcat banking.[86] This was observed in the 1830s by Michel Chevalier who contrasted French moderation with American speculation (but who believed, however, that the latter was a stimulus to the production of canals, railroads, roads, factories, and villages).[87] Letter 25 of his letters from America to France is devoted entirely to a discussion of speculation: 'All the world speculates and it speculates on everything. From Maine to the Red River (in Arkansas) the United States has become an immense Rue Quincampoix [the Wall Street of the Mississippi Bubble].'[88] Partly the origins lie in permissive institutions. But it is easy to find abundant and contradictory views on the demand side for other countries as well. 'The French nation is prudent and economical, the English nation is enterprising and speculative.'[89] 'France has not shown proofs of prudence equal to those of Scotland; its nerves are extremely susceptible, impressionable in matters of credit.'[90] 'The character of this nation [Britain] is in carrying everything to excess... virtue, vice.'[91] After 1866, a new arrogance was said to have taken hold of the Germans, but they surpassed the French only in 'stock-market swindling and speculation horrors.'[92] Morgenstern finds ten panics in France, exceeding by two even the United States, which is 'not surprising, given the unstable character of French politics.'[93] (To be sure, this addresses displacements rather than love of speculation.) Contrast, however, the opinion of a French financier who claims that 'the French love money not for the possibilities of action which it opens, but for the income it assures.'[94] Or consider two views, at the level of a Harvard–Yale debate, from a fictional Frenchman and an Englishman in 1931:

> WILLIAM BERTILLION: England's such a Christmas tree for sharepushers. Noble lords will sit on the board of any company for a couple of quid a sitting. And the public. Loco or idiotic. God, I've never heard of such people, except perhaps some peasants in Bessarabia, or the niggers in the Cameroons, who believe in what they believe in. Magic. Put up any sort of business that sounds utterly impossible and they gulp it down.[95]

STEWART: England's the world's banker. Never failed yet, never failed yet. She keeps her word, that's why ... None of this—none of this speculation you get in the American stock market. Every Tom, Dick and Harry trying to make a pile-like in France.[96]

It's a stand-off. The speculative temperament may differ among countries. Levels of speculation may also differ from time to time for a given country, say, in moods of national elation or depression.

4
Fueling the Flames: The Expansion of Credit

> Axiom number one. Inflation depends on the growth of money. Axiom number two. Asset price bubbles depend on the growth of credit.

Speculative manias gather speed through expansion of money and credit. Most expansions of money and credit do not lead to a mania; there are many more economic expansions than there are manias. But every mania has been associated with the expansion of credit. In the last hundred or so years the expansion of credit has been almost exclusively through the banks and the financial system; earlier, nonbank lenders expanded the supply of credit. The tulip bubble mania of the seventeenth century developed with credits from sellers of the bulbs, a seventeenth-century version of 'vendor financing.'[1] John Law had his Banque Générale, later the Banque Royale, as his source of credit while the South Sea Company relied on the Sword Blade Bank. In 1763 credit expansion in Holland was financed by the *Wisselruiti,* or chains of accommodation bills from one merchant to another. The canal mania of 1793 in Great Britain was fed by spending facilitated by loans from many newly-established country banks to the entrepreneurs who were developing the canals.

In many cases the expansion of credit resulted from the development of substitutes for what previously had been the traditional monies. In the United States in the first part of the nineteenth century, the expansion of credit resulted from the substitution of bills of exchange for silver in triangular trade between the United States, China, and Great Britain. The United States had a bilateral trade deficit with China and China had a bilateral trade deficit with Great Britain. Previously the United

States bought silver from Mexico which was then shipped to China to finance the U.S. trade deficit; then the silver was shipped to Great Britain to finance China's trade deficit. The institutional innovation was that American merchants sent sterling bills of exchange to China in payment for goods, and the Chinese in turn then shipped these bills to Great Britain to finance its trade deficit. The transactions costs involved in making cross-border payments using bills of exchange were much smaller than those which involved the shipment of silver. The result of this innovation was that the silver stayed in the United States and was added to the U.S. money supply.[2]

The global boom of the 1850s followed from the combination of new gold discoveries, the formation of new banks in Great Britain, France, Germany, and the United States, the establishment of clearing-houses by the banks in New York and in Philadelphia and the expansion of the London bank clearinghouse. The expansion of the bank clearing-houses led to the increased use of credit in the transactions between the banks which were members of the clearing-house; payments imbalances between these banks were settled by transfer of clearing-house certificates—a new form of money. The expansion of credit in Great Britain in 1866 resulted from the increase in loans by the newly formed joint-stock discount houses. The boom in Central Europe in the 1870s was based on the gold reparations payments from France to Prussia and on the creation of *Maklerbanken* (brokers' banks) in Germany, which spread into Austria, and *Baubanken* (construction banks) in Austria, which expanded into Germany.

One of the many different institutional avenues for the expansion of credit that occurred in France in 1882 was based on a system of fortnightly clearing of stock exchange transactions which provided credit to speculators through a system of delayed payments called *reportage*. The buyers of stocks had up to fourteen days before they had to pay for their purchases, so in effect they got interest-free loans until the date of payment (although the value of the loans may have been reflected in the prices paid for the stocks).[3] Similarly the expansion of credit in the call-money market in New York helped finance the stock market boom in the late 1920s. The catalyst for the expansion of credit in the United States in 1893 was the addition of silver coins to the U.S. money supply; in 1907, the increase in the supply of credit resulted from the expansion of loans by the trust companies. In the years before and after World War I, the international credit base was expanded by the development of the gold-exchange standard that facilitated the financing of a much larger volume of international trade with the existing stock of monetary gold. The rapid increase in installment credit in the United States in the 1920s facilitated the surge in automobile ownership (although the dramatic increases in the number of automobiles and other consumer durables led to rapid growth in demand for staggered payments arrangements).

After World War II, the development of negotiable certificates of deposit (CDs) contributed to the expansion of credit. The Austrian banks had developed a new financial instrument similar to the negotiable CD in the 1870s (the so-called *Cassenscheine*) that paid interest; the expansion in the demand for these instruments led to an increase in credit and hence to an increase in spending on the same amount of high-powered money or reserves. In the 1950s and the 1960s the large U.S. banks adopted the practice of liability management which meant that the growth of their deposits depended on the pace at which they wanted to increase their loans; under the earlier practice of asset management the growth of their loans depended on the growth of their deposit liabilities. Liability management enabled the banks to be much more aggressive in managing the growth of their loans and their deposits.

One unique form of the expansion of 'bank credit' occurred in Kuwait between 1977 and 1982 when shares and real estate were bought and sold on the Kuwaiti Souk al-Manakh (stock exchange) with post-dated checks; eventually the value of these checks in circulation increased to billions of dinars—nearly U.S. $100 billion at its peak. The values of post-dated checks written by the buyers of the shares and real estate were much, much larger than their bank deposits. The sellers of the shares and real estate increased their spending as their wealth was increasing; they hoped that there would be money in the bank accounts of the payors when the due dates of the checks arrived. In July 1982 some sellers of stocks tried to collect on checks on the due dates; the checks bounced.[4]

The inference from these examples is that the expansion of credit is not a series of accidents but instead a systematic development that has continued for several hundred years as the participants in financial markets sought to reduce the costs both of transactions and of holding liquidity and money balances. The form each event takes may seem accidental—the substitution of bills of exchange for silver in payments to China, or the development of deposits in the Eurocurrency market because ceilings prevented U.S. banks from increasing the interest rates that they could pay on deposits in New York, Chicago, and Los Angeles.

The development of new substitutes for the existing monies seems to occur periodically in response to different changes in institutional arrangements but the process is a continuing one. Monetary expansion is systematic and endogenous rather than random and exogenous.

During economic booms the amount of money defined as means of payment has been continuously expanded and the existing money supply has been used more efficiently to finance both increases in economic activity and the purchases of real estate and securities and commodities in search of capital gains. The efforts of central bankers to limit and control the growth of the money supply have been offset in part by the development of new and very close substitutes for money. Such efforts have a long history, including the resumption of specie payments and the return to convertibility of national currencies into gold after the ends of wars. The demonetization of the lesser metallic monies—initially copper was displaced by silver and subsequently silver's monetary role was eclipsed by gold—was an effort to obtain greater control over the money supply. Central banks sought to obtain a monopoly of the issue of currency notes, which restricted and then eliminated the rights of private, country, and joint-stock (corporate) banks to issue currency notes. Legislation and custom limited the amounts of deposit money that could be issued against primary bank reserves, starting shortly after the Bank Act of 1844 and continuing through the application by the Federal Reserve System of reserve requirements against both demand and time deposits (as embodied in the Federal Reserve Act of 1913) and then against certificates of deposit and subsequently against the borrowings by U.S. banks from their branches in offshore financial centers including London, Zurich, and Luxembourg. The process is Sisyphean, a *perpetuum mobile*; the history of money is a story of continuing innovations so that the existing supply of money can be used more efficiently and the development of close substitutes for traditional money that circumvent the formal requirements applied to money. The Eurocurrency deposit market surged in the 1960s as an end-run around the costs of regulation imposed on U.S. banks by the Federal Reserve and the Federal Deposit Insurance Corporation; the U.S. dollar deposits produced by the branches of U.S. banks in London, Luxembourg, and Zurich were not subject to interest rate ceilings, reserve requirements, and deposit insurance premiums. The U.S. stock brokerage firms developed money market funds in the 1970s and paid interest on the deposits in these funds (the deposits were not guaranteed by any agency of the U.S. government).

Currency School vs Banking School

One aspect of the history of monetary theory is a continuing debate between two different views—the Currency School and the Banking School—about how best to manage the growth of the money supply. The proponents of the Currency School advocated a firm limit on the expansion of the money supply to avoid inflation. The adherents of the Banking School believed that increases in the supply of money would not lead to inflation as long as these increases were associated with business transactions. In the 1890s in the United States more or less the same breakdown in ideology and economic analysis separated the hard-money school, which was concerned about inflation, from the populists who did not believe that increases in the money supply would lead to increases in the price levels as long as these increases were associated with increases in economic activity. The debate between these two views of managing the growth in the money supply has continued for at least three hundred years.

The Currency School wanted a simple rule that would fix the growth rate of the money supply at 2, 4, or 5 percent, much like today's monetarists.[5] Viner's discussion of the nineteenth-century controversy is succinct:

> The currency school tended also to minimize or to deny the importance of bank credit in other forms than notes as a factor affecting prices, or as in the case of Torrens, to claim that the fluctuations in the deposits were governed closely by the fluctuations in the note issues. They had a hankering also for a simple automatic rule, and could find none suitable for governing the general credit operations of the Bank. They also had laissez faire objections to extending legislative control of the banking system any further than seemed absolutely necessary.[6]

Neither the Currency School nor the Banking School paid much attention to the expansion of nonbank credit. The Bank of Amsterdam, founded in 1609, was a giro-bank that issued notes against deposits of precious metals; in effect these notes were warehouse receipts and the amounts outstanding of these notes were tied to the deposits of the metal on a one-to-one basis. Initially the Bank of Amsterdam did not expand credit; subsequently in the eighteenth century the bank expanded its loans in the effort to rescue the Dutch East India Company during the fourth Anglo-Dutch War. The Bank of Amsterdam was also a *Wisselbank* where bills of exchange (*Wissel* in Dutch, *Wechsel* in German) were paid. Merchants kept deposits at the Bank of Amsterdam to meet bills presented for collection. Deposits of precious metals enabled the Bank of Amsterdam to earn seignorage on its minting operation so it was able to pay a low interest rate on deposits. In 1614 a Bank of Lending (*Huys van Leening*) was established by the Municipality of Amsterdam; this bank enabled merchants to establish their own credit efficiently but it was not an active lender.[7] This credit created by the merchants led to an excessive expansion of the *Wisselruiti;* when the chain of bills of exchange broke in 1763 because one of the merchants did not have the money to pay on a maturing bill, the DeNeufville bank failed.

The Swedish Riksbank, established in 1668, had two departments, a Bank of Exchange patterned after the Bank of Amsterdam (*Wisselbank*) and a Bank of Lending (*Liinebank*).[8] These two departments foreshadowed the Bank Act of 1844 in Great Britain, which was a compromise between the two schools; an Issue Department, which would provide bank notes against deposits of coin or bullion above a specified fiduciary issue that represented the Bank of England's holdings of British government debt, and a Banking Department that would make loans and discounts up to a multiple of its reserves of bank notes that had been produced by the Issue Department. The establishment of the Issue Department was a victory for the Currency School, which had criticized the Bank of England's granting of loans and issuance of bank notes after the suspension of the gold standard in 1797. (The Bank of England's defense of this practice was that the inflation rate did not increase when loans were made to finance trade.) The establishment of the Banking Department was a victory for the Banking School and for those who believed that an expansion of credit would help finance the initial upswing in the early stages of an economic recovery.

The Currency School's view that the expansion of credit based on the availability of attractive business opportunities would eventually lead to inflation was correct. The Banking School's view that an increase in the supply of credit was needed at the start of an economic expansion was also correct. The Currency School's view that the discounts be limited to acceptances that were related to actual commercial transactions became known as the 'real bills doctrine.' The larger the number of business opportunities, the greater the scope for discounting, and the greater the increase in the money supply and eventually the higher the inflation rate. The central policy questions, once an expansion of credit has started, are whether it is practicable to decree a stopping place and whether this limit could be determined by an automatic rule.

The core issue is that it is easier to define money than it is to measure the effective money supply. Walter Bagehot wrote 'Men of business in England do not . . . like the currency question. They are perplexed to define accurately what money is: *how* to count they know, but *what* to count they do not know.'[9]

The stylized historical fact is that every time the monetary authorities stabilize or control some quantity of money, M, either in absolute volume or at a predetermined rate of growth, more of the money and the near-money substitutes will be produced in periods of euphoria. If the definition of money is fixed in terms of designated liquid securities the euphoria may lead to the 'monetization' of credit in ways that are beyond the definition; the velocity of money (velocity is defined either as total spending or national income divided by the money supply) will increase even if the amount of money defined in the traditional way remains unchanged. The debate was over whether money should be defined as M_1, currency plus demand deposits adjusted; M_2, equal to M_1 plus time deposits; M_3, consisting of M_2 plus highly liquid government securities; or some other designation.

The process seemed endless; fix any M_i and in economic booms the market will create new forms of money and near-money substitutes to get around the limit.

The Radcliffe Commission in Great Britain in 1959 claimed that in a developed economy there is 'an indefinitely wide range of financial institutions' and 'many highly liquid assets which are close substitutes for money, as good to hold, and only inferior when the actual moment for a payment arrives.' The Radcliffe Commission did not use the concept of velocity of money because it 'could not find any reason for supposing, or any experience in monetary history indicating, that there is any limit to the velocity of circulation.'[10] The commission was primarily interested in the recommendation that a complex of controls of a wide range of financial institutions be developed as a substitute for the traditional control of the money supply: 'Such a prospect would be unwelcome except as a last resort, not mainly because of its administrative burdens, but because the further growth of new financial institutions would allow the situation continually to slip out from under the grip of the authorities.'[11]

Economists have debated the items that should be included in 'money' for two centuries. One view is that the most appropriate definition is the one that provides the strongest correlation with changes in economic activity. Measuring economic activity is relatively unambiguous. The identification of the monetary variables that have the highest correlation with the economic activity variable might change over time and differ across countries. 'In common parlance, *bank currency* means *circulating bank notes*—"paper money." Yet, it would seem that some writers include under the same head, checks and *promissory notes,* if not also loans and deposits' (italics in original).[12]

The debate was neatly summarized by John Stuart Mill:

> The purchasing power of an individual at any moment is not measured by the money actually in his pocket, whether we mean by money the metals, or include bank notes. It consists, first, of the money in his possession; secondly, of the money at his banker's, and all the other money due him and payable on demand; thirdly of whatever credit he happens to possess.[13]

A valiant attempt has been made to improve the concept of the quantity of money to include the total of all the credit or debt.[14] This approach gets away from defining exactly what money is although it may lead into other muddy waters when the need arrives to decide which credit items should be included and which should not be included. But in theory the analyst wants to know, with Mill, what credit a household, firm, or government would be able to command at a given time, and the amount is almost certain to vary over a wide range because the access to credit depends on satisfying certain conditions and the households and firms are better able to satisfy these conditions in euphoric periods. Banks and other lenders have often extended credit lines to firms and household borrowers, but the amount of credit available under the lines at each moment may require that the borrowers meet certain tests.

Consider the rapid growth of U.S. dollar deposits in London and other offshore banking centers in the 1960s, 1970s, and the 1980s, which was a response to the increases in interest rates on these deposits relative to interest rates on bank deposits produced in the United States which were subject to regulatory ceilings. The banks that sold these deposits in the offshore banking centers used the funds to make loans denominated in the U.S. dollar to American firms that they might otherwise have made loans to from one of their U.S. offices. The firms that borrowed U.S. dollar funds from the offshore banks in London were as likely to spend these funds in the United States as if they had had borrowed the U.S. dollar funds in New York, Chicago, or Los Angeles. Should the U.S. dollar deposits produced in London and other offshore banking centers be included in the measurement of the U.S. money supply?

The home-equity credit line is a recent financial innovation; banks and other lenders offer to lend homeowners an amount that may be equal to the value of the equity in their homes or in some cases an amount modestly in excess of the homeowner's equity. (At an earlier period the loans that used the equity in the home as collateral were known as second mortgages; a home-equity credit line represents potential borrowing until the homeowner draws on the line, while the second mortgage was an actual loan.) The availability of home equity credit lines means that homeowners economize on their holdings of money and near-monies, so the increase in the availability of these credit lines leads to increases in spending with the same money supply. Thus the development of the home-equity credit line permits households to engage in liability management of the type that banks developed thirty and forty years earlier.

The purchasing power of the individual cannot readily be extrapolated to that for a country since an increase in the amount of credit extended to one individual may or may not subtract from the amounts of credit available to others, depending on both banking institutions and on the scope of euphoria. One novelist wrote on credit:

> Beautiful credit! The foundation of modern society. Who shall say this is not the age of mutual trust, of unlimited reliance on human promises? That is a peculiar condition of modern society which enables a whole country to instantly recognize point and meaning to the familiar newspaper anecdote, which puts into the speculator in lands and mines this remark: 'I wasn't worth a cent two years ago, and now I owe two million dollars.'[15]

The basis for this generalization is the historical development of close substitutes for money that led to increases in the amount of credit and total spending. Consider only bills of exchange, call money, and the gold-exchange standard from a list that also includes bank notes, bank deposits, clearing-house certificates, the liabilities of specialized banks (e.g., *banques d'affaires, Maklerbanken,* or *Baubanken*), the liabilities of trust companies, negotiable CDs, the Eurocurrency deposits, installment credit, credit cards, and NOW accounts.

Quality of debt[16]

The credit-rating agencies were established to rank the quality of the debt of individual borrowers—firms, governments, and even households. Minsky's taxonomy of corporate debt used a three-part distinction based on the relationship between cash inflows to the borrowers from their operating activities and their projected cash outflows for debt-servicing payments. 'Hedge finance' occurred when the cash from the firm's operating activities would be larger than the cash needed for its scheduled debt-servicing payments. 'Speculative finance' occurred when the cash from the firm's operating activities would be large enough to enable the firm to pay the interest on its debt on a timely basis; however the firm would need to borrow the amount necessary to get the cash to pay some or all of the principal due on maturing loans. 'Ponzi finance' occurred when the cash from the firm's operating activities would not be large enough to pay all of the interest due on debt on a timely basis. The firms involved in Ponzi finance either will need to borrow to pay some or all of the interest or they will need a capital gain on some of their assets to get the cash to pay the interest.[17] (This distinction between Ponzi finance and speculative finance is comparable to that used in the public finance literature between a 'primary fiscal balance' which involves the relationship between the government's tax and other receipts and its total payments exclusive of those for interest. A government with a primary fiscal deficit needs to borrow more than the amount necessary to pay all of the scheduled interest.)

Minsky emphasized the 'quality' of debt to gauge the fragility of the credit structure; the terms 'speculative' and 'Ponzi' highlight this fragility. The implication of the term 'Ponzi finance' is that the firm may not be able to make a debt service payment on a timely basis unless there is a 'miracle.'[18] An edifice of debt contracted to finance risky ventures is inherently unstable.

The model set forth in the previous chapter emphasizes that in periods of economic euphoria the quantity of debt increases because the lenders and investors become less risk-averse and more willing—or less unwilling—to make loans that had previously seemed too risky. During economic slowdowns, many firms experience less rapid increases in their revenues than they had anticipated, with the result that some firms that had been in the hedge finance group are shunted into the speculative finance group while some firms that had been in the speculative finance group move into the Ponzi finance group.

Drexel Burnham Lambert, Michael Milken, and 'junk bonds'

One of the great financial innovations in the 1980s was the development of the 'junk bond' market—the bonds of firms that had not been ranked by one of the major credit-rating agencies. The interest rates on these bonds were generally 3 to 4 percentage points higher than interest rates on the bonds that had been ranked in one of the 'investment grades.' Many of these bonds had been 'fallen angels'—issued by firms when their economic circumstances were more favorable so they received a credit rating. A series of mishaps would lead to a reduction in the credit rating and eventually to the lowest investment grade, one more mishap and the credit-rating agencies would move the firm to the noninvestment grade or speculative ranking.

A large number of financial institutions are prohibited by the regulatory authorities from holding bonds that are below investment grade, and once this threshold was crossed, these banks and insurance companies would sell these bonds so the interest rates on the bonds would increase sharply.

The sales pitch was that the buyers of junk bonds—say of a diversified portfolio of these bonds—had a 'free lunch' because the additional interest income would be more than enough to cover the losses when one or several of these bonds tanked because the borrowers went bankrupt.

The innovation in the 1970s and 1980s was that Drexel Burnham Lambert, then a second-tier investment bank, began to issue junk bonds, known in more polite circles as high yield bonds; the mastermind of this innovation was Michael Milken. The firms that issued these high yield bonds had such low credit ratings that investors would buy their bonds only if the interest rates were high. Many firms issued junk bonds to get the cash to finance leverage buyouts; often the senior executives of a firm would seek to buy all of the publicly traded shares. Or Firm A might issue high yield bonds to get the cash to acquire Firm B before Firm B got the cash to buy Firm A.

Because the bonds had not been rated by one of the credit-rating agencies, the interest rates that borrowers paid on these bonds typically were 3 to 4 percentage points higher than the interest rates on the investment grade bonds that had been reviewed by one of the credit-rating agencies.

So much for the facts that are not in dispute. What is in dispute is whether some parts of the underwriting transactions by Milken were illegal or unethical. The polite critics note that many of the firms that were buyers of junk bonds were savings and loan associations and other thrift institutions and insurance companies; the managers and the owners of some of these firms had used Drexel Burnham Lambert as the underwriter to raise the money so they might buy ownership and control. The thrift institutions sold deposits based on the guarantee of the U.S. government, they offered very high interest rates on their deposits and they then used the cash from the sale of deposits to buy the junk bonds that Milken and Drexel Burnham Lambert had underwritten. About half of the firms that had issued the junk bonds through Drexel Burnham Lambert went bankrupt and as a consequence the thrift institutions incurred large losses; many of these institutions, that had provided the ready market for the high yield bonds, went bankrupt with losses to the American taxpayers of many tens of billions. But it was all legal.

In 1988 the Revco D.S., Inc. drugstore chain filed for bankruptcy, unable to pay the interest on the $1.3 billion borrowed to finance its 1987 buyout.[19] By the time the 1980s chapter in the junk bond story was over, more than half of the issues underwritten by Drexel Burnham Lambert had gone into default with losses to the bondholders—and the U.S. taxpayers—of tens of billions of dollars.

In a Cassandra-like book, Henry Kaufman decried the increase of all kinds of debt—consumer, government, mortgage, and corporate, including junk bonds; Kaufman argued that the quality of debt declined as the quantity of debt increased.[20] Felix Rohatyn, a distinguished investment banker and the head of the U.S. office of Lazard Frères, called the United States 'a junk-bond casino.'

Still the owners of junk bonds were earning much higher interest rates than the owners of traditional bonds—at least for a while.

In the economic slowdown of the late 1980s and early 1990s, many of the firms that had issued junk bonds went bankrupt. A new set of studies showed that the owners of junk bonds on average lost one-third of their money and that the additional 3 to 4 percentage points of interest income per year of these bonds was insufficient to compensate for the large number of defaults.

The large number of failures among the issuers of junk bonds was consistent with Minsky's taxonomy: many of these bonds might have been in his speculative group in the good economic times when they were initially issued. When the U.S. economy moved into a recession, the cash receipts of the firms issuing these bonds declined, and the bonds would have shifted to the Ponzi group. An economic miracle would have been necessary to avoid a default.

A very expensive free lunch.

Bills of exchange

Bills of exchange were claims for future payment made by a seller of goods and were initially developed because the supply of coin was inelastic; the bills were a form of vendor financing.[21] The seller of the goods provided credit to the buyers of the goods to facilitate the sale; the buyer would be obliged to repay the loan in 90 or 120 days. These bills of exchange were frequently discounted with banks that provided the holder of the bills with cash in the form of bank notes or coin and, in the nineteenth century, bank deposits. The bills of exchange were often used directly in payment, much like post-dated checks. Once the seller of the goods had received a bill of exchange from the buyer, the seller in turn transferred the bill to someone else in payment. Each recipient of a bill would add its name to the bill, much like endorsing a check; there might be five or ten endorsers on the bill. 'The bill was now money.' Ashton said that even if some of the parties in the chain of endorsers were of doubtful credit, the bill would still circulate as if it were a bank note.[22] In the first half of the nineteenth century, some bills for as little as £10 circulated with fifty or sixty names on them.

Payment practices differed. Bank notes were disliked in Lancashire, and at the beginning of the nineteenth century coins and bills of exchange were the primary items used for payments.[23] Because of the increase in the use of bills of exchange in payments, Bank of England note circulation declined by £9 million from 1852 to 1857, a period of economic expansion. The deposits of five banks in London rose from £17.7 million to £40 million. The average volume of bills of exchange in circulation, however, expanded during the same period from £66 million to £200 million, according to the contemporary estimates of Newmarch.[24]

Initially the bills of exchange were issued in connection with specific transactions and the amount of the bill more or less matched the exact value of the sale. Subsequently the link between the sale of goods and the issue of a bill of exchange was broken. In 1763 in Sweden, Carlos and Claes Grill bills on Lindegren in London could not be identified with particular shipments, which were often made in rapid succession, but were drawn when the firm needed money, generally for remittances to creditors.[25] Thus the credit of a house or individual was gradually separated from that of particular transactions and the bill had become 'accommodation paper' or a post-dated check or a promissory note.

Some economists were firmly opposed to 'accommodation paper' because it was believed to be of lower quality than self-liquidating commercial bills since there was less assurance that the firms that issued the bills would have the cash to pay the holders of the bills on the dates that the bills matured.[26] In a period of falling prices, however, the merits of the higher quality commercial bills were exaggerated, since the buyers of the goods might not have the cash to settle their obligations on the due dates because they might not be able to sell the goods at a profit.[27] The ratio of the debt to the debtor's income or wealth is a more meaningful measure of the quality of credit.

The bill of credit, as Franklin said:

> is found very convenient in Business; because a great Sum is more easily counted in them, lighter in Carriage, concealed in less Room, and therefore safer in Travelling or Laying Up, and on many other Accounts they are very much valued. The Banks are the General Cashiers of all Gentlemen, Merchants, and Great Traders... This gives Bills a Credit; so that in *England* they are never less valuable than Money, and in *Venice* and *Amsterdam* they are generally more so.[28]

The statement that in Great Britain bills were 'never less valuable than Money' is somewhat optimistic, but the efficiency of bills when they were as good as money is clear. During the first half of the nineteenth century there was a continuous debate as to whether bills of exchange were 'money,' 'means of payment,' or 'purchasing power.' The members of the Currency School agreed that only the supply of bank notes needed to be controlled, and that there was no need to control or limit the amounts of bills of exchange and of bank deposits.[29]

Problems were likely to arise when the ratio of the debt represented by the outstanding value of bills of exchange issued by a borrower became large relative to the borrower's wealth which often happened in periods of euphoria. Drawing of bills of exchange in chains was infectious. Described by Adam Smith as a normal business practice, it could easily be overdone.[30] A draws on B, B on C, C on D, and so on, which increases the supply of credit. The vice of the accommodation bill, according to Hawtrey, was its 'use for construction of fixed capital when the necessary supply of bona-fide long-run savings cannot be obtained from the investment market.' Hawtrey claimed the system was particularly abused in the London crisis of 1866 and the New York crisis of 1907.[31] The spectacular failure of the DeNeufvilles in Amsterdam in 1763 has been noted. This produced a panic in Hamburg, Berlin, and to a lesser extent in London as well as in Amsterdam because a particularly impressive chain of bills was unraveled. If one house in the chain of houses that had endorsed the bill failed, the chain collapsed and might bring down good names, those with a reasonable ratio of debt to capital as well as those with much higher ratios. Each endorser on the bill was liable for the full payment. Accommodation bills enabled traders with limited capital to borrow large amounts of money, and these short-term loans in effect stretched into longer-term loans because they were rolled over and over when they matured. During the period when the gold standard was suspended at the beginning of the nineteenth century, Sir Francis Baring knew of clerks not worth £100 who were allowed discounts of £5,000 to £10,000. The uniqueness of the period was that the suspension of the gold standard meant that there was no need to be concerned about the impacts of the expansion of credit on the foreign exchanges. The 'phrenzy of speculation' during this period strongly influenced the Currency School.[32] In 1857 John Ball, a London accountant, reported knowing firms with capital under £10,000 and obligations of £900,000 and claimed it was a fair illustration.[33] In Hamburg during the same boom, Schäffle reported a man with capital of £100 and £400,000 worth of acceptances outstanding.[34]

The Long-Term Capital Management hedge fund, started in 1994, had equity capital of $5 billion and borrowed more than $125 billion from banks, investment banks, and pension funds. This leverage ratio of 25 to 1 was much higher than the leverage ratios of other hedge funds, which generally were below 10 to 1. In the eighteenth century, however, many firms, according to Wirth, speculated for ten to twenty times their real capital during the boom of 1763 and many participated in this dangerous undertaking on pure credit with little if any capital.[35]

Finance or accommodation bills could lead to excessive credit expansion. From time to time fictitious names were introduced into the chain to improve the appearance of creditworthiness. Moreover such bills were written for odd amounts in order to suggest an underlying commercial transaction. Claims were sometimes made (e.g., by German banks drawing on Dutch and American banks after the halt in American lending) that the banks knew it was finance paper disguised as commercial bills.[36]

Call money

The expansion in the use of call money was important in the crashes of 1882 and 1929. The crash of 1882 in France is not well known and had limited repercussions but it was a classic mania and panic, financed by call money, or money lent to stockbrokers by banks 'on call' that is, for one day (in French, *reports*).[37] The stockbrokers used the money to finance their holdings of an inventory of stocks and they anticipated being able to renew the one-day loan day after day.

The Union Générale was a bank started by Eugène Bontoux, an engineer who had worked with Rothschild and then left to initiate rival operations in Austria, Serbia, and southeastern Europe. An earlier Union Générale, founded in 1875, did badly. Bontoux started his Union Générale in Paris in 1878 as France was entering a boom based on the expansion of the railroads, the construction of the Suez Canal, and the growth of banks. The boom peaked in December 1881 and the crash followed in the next month. Bouvier's interest was in whether Bontoux, a Catholic, failed because of his own mistakes as a lender or whether he was 'done in' by a conspiracy of establishment Jewish and Protestant bankers that resented an intruder. Bouvier concluded with a Scottish verdict of 'not proven.'

Bontoux's Union Générale was capitalized at 25 million francs, which was increased in the spring of 1879 to 50 million and increased again in January 1881 to 100 million; a third increase, planned for January 1882, would have raised the capital to 150 million. The initial capital was only one-fourth paid in.[38] With each increase in capital, the investors had to pay a premium above the par value of 500 francs into the reserves of the bank to take account of the increase in the market price of the stock. These premiums were 20, 175, and 250 francs, respectively. Shares were registered in the names of buyers because of the three-quarters of the par value they still owed for the purchases of shares; nevertheless, roughly half of the 200,000 original shares floated in the trading market.

Trading in securities was conducted through fortnightly settlements in both Paris and Lyon. A purchaser would pay 10 percent down, borrow 90 percent from an *agent de change* or broker who in turn borrowed the money in the call-money market. Money was invested in *reports* by banks, by special *caisses* (funds created especially by banks and other investors for this outlet) and by individuals. A bank and *caisse* moreover could favor brokers who specialized in trading in a particular stock. Thus banks such as the Union Générale and the Banque de Lyon et de la Loire—not to mention three or four less successful if less spectacular banks created during the boom—could support their own stock indirectly. When the market was steady, speculators made gains and losses, and brokers would typically pay out or receive very little net, assuming that speculators were working on roughly the same margin, for example 10 percent. If stock prices were increasing however more funds were needed to pay off profits that would be realized and withdrawn from the market. These funds were often reinvested in the market, but if they were not reinvested, the market needed more capital. Assume a speculator bought a share for 100 francs, paid 10 francs down and borrowed 90 francs. If the speculator sold the share at 110 francs and withdrew his

20 francs, 11 francs of the 20 francs withdrawn from the market would come from the new speculator, and 9 francs had to be new *report* and taken from the call market. As stock prices increased the interest rates on call money (*taux des reports*) increased to attract new money; the interest rate on call money increased from 4 to 5 percent at the end of 1880 to 8 to 10 percent in the spring of 1881, and reached a peak of 12 percent in the autumn of 1881.[39]

When the share prices declined new money was also required, this time from the speculators. If the speculator bought a share at 100 francs, again with 10 francs down and 90 francs in *reports,* and the share price then fell to 90 francs, the speculator had to produce 9 more francs to comply with the 10 percent requirement. If the speculator had been fully leveraged earlier and did not have the money to meet the margin call, the broker sold the speculator's position. If the price dropped below 90 francs, the broker, bank, or individual that had made the loan lost money. The stock of the Union Générale went from 1,250 francs in March 1881 to a peak of 3,040 on December 14, as the mania gathered speed. Thereafter a period of distress followed with quotations at 2,950 francs on January 10, 1882, and 2,800 francs on January 16. On January 19 the quotation declined to 1,300 francs. Brokers were 18 million francs short on that day, as speculators could not produce the cash needed to meet requirements, and 33 million short when it came to the month-end liquidation on January 31.[40]

The collapse of Banque de Lyon et de la Loire was more spectacular as the share price went from a peak of 1,765 francs on December 17, 1881, to 1,550 francs on December 28, when it was supporting its own stock, to 1,040 francs on January 4, 1882, 650 francs on January 10, and finally 400 francs on January 19, the day after it closed its doors.[41] The signal for the collapse of the Banque de Lyon et de la Loire was the approval given to Bontoux to establish a Banque de Crédit Maritime at Trieste, which was announced on January 4, 1882. The coup boomeranged.[42] Investors with losses on their holdings of shares in Banque de Lyon et de la Loire sold their Union Générale shares. The combination of highly leveraged speculation and a credit mechanism that rested on bank and personal credit cycled through the call loan market and spread collapse among banks, *caisses,* brokers, individuals, and businesses in a few days. Economic activity was adversely affected in advance of the stock market collapse, not because of a change in the money supply but because at the peak of the fever the business world of Lyons turned to speculation in Union Générale: 'silk merchants, cloth manufacturers, industrialists, tradesmen, dry-goods merchants, grocers, butchers, people with fixed incomes, janitors, shoemakers;' 'A lot of capital was diverted from regular business to stock market both in securities and in call money.'[43]

Some of the features of the U.S. stock market crash of 1929 were similar to those in the collapse of the French banks: a preoccupation with speculation and a decline in economic activity as the stock market approached its apex; the role of brokers' loans by banks and by individuals that provided the basis for the increase in the prices of stocks and then their decline even as the money supply did not change significantly. Another similarity is that as stock prices peaked, call loans of 'all others' as opposed to New York banks and banks outside New York, increased from just under $2 billion at the end of 1926 to nearly $4 billion on December 31, 1928, and to more than $6.6 billion on October 4, 1929. Margin credit was extensive. Brokerage firms might require that the buyers of stocks pay 10 percent down; the remaining 90 percent of the purchase price was borrowed. Meanwhile, brokers' loans of New York banks declined from $1.6 billion at their height at the end of 1928 to $1.1 billion on October 4, 1929.[44]

With the crash, 'all others' and banks outside New York took call funds from the market. They were fearful that the Stock Exchange might be closed as it had been in 1873, which would have frozen their hitherto liquid day-to-day loans.[45] At this stage, New York banks maintained and even slightly increased their brokers' loans. Similarly, in 1882, one consortium of Paris banks headed by the Banque de Paris et des Pays-Bas (Parisbas) advanced 18 million francs in five credits to the Union Générale directly, while another group headed by the Rothschild house loaned 80 million francs to the company of brokers to get them through the end of January settlement and to give them and their clients time to work out arrangements. In both crises many brokers, clients, and (in 1882) banks and their *caisses* went bankrupt. The central money market banks eased the adjustment, but in Paris in 1882 they did not save the Union Générale.

In the United States buying stocks on margin was curbed in the 1930s by a Federal Reserve regulation that ultimately fixed margin requirements at 50 percent. Financial institutions made an end run around this regulation. The regulation applied to organized exchanges for shares, including the New York Stock Exchange, but not to the Chicago Mercantile Exchange, which dealt in Standard and Poor's (S&P) 500 stock index futures and where there was a margin requirement of 10 percent on the value of futures positions. Arbitrageurs linked the two markets and so they were in effect one market. An investor who bought an S&P 500 futures contract in Chicago with a 10 percent margin was in effect buying stocks in New York with a 10 percent margin; as the price of futures contracts increased in Chicago, arbitrageurs would sell the futures contracts in Chicago and at the same time buy a representative basket of stocks of the companies that dominated the index.

In the aftermath of the October 19, 1987 collapse, there was some support for the idea of regulating the Chicago and New York markets by a single agency—the Federal Reserve Board or the Securities and Exchange Commission—some for tightening margin regulations in the futures market, and some for banning futures trading in stocks altogether.

The gold-exchange standard

A third illustration of the virtually infinite set of possibilities for expanding credit on a fixed money base is international in character. The gold-exchange standard involved central bank holdings of liquid securities denominated in the British pound, the U.S. dollar, and the German mark as central bank reserve assets along with their holdings of gold. The gold-exchange standard developed before World War I, although this arrangement was long thought to have been a post-World War I development based on the recommendations of the Genoa Conference of 1922 and the Gold Delegation of the League of Nations and pushed hard by Governor Montagu Norman of the Bank of England who sought to increase foreign holdings of British pound securities to provide relief for the British balance of payments.[46] The boom in world lending of 1913–1914 was financed by increases in central bank holdings of securities denominated in the British pound, the French franc and the German mark.

Just as bank notes and bills of exchange are more efficient monies than coin, so holding of international reserve assets in the form of securities denominated in the currency of a country with a large capital market dominate holdings of gold bullion as long as monetary conditions are stable. These assets are easier to use in transactions, free of the need for transport, safeguarding, and assay, and directly useful without conversion into national money. A country can increase its holdings of international reserve assets by selling bonds in London or in New York and then holding the money receipts either in British pounds or in U.S. dollars as part of its central bank reserves. If the British or U.S. monetary authorities do not regard the increase in the foreign holdings of liquid securities denominated in their currencies as a reason for contracting their own credit superstructure, this transaction leads to an expansion of credit.

International lending on the gold standard may have the same unstable character as the gold-exchange standard. Before countries borrowed foreign balances as reserves for domestic monetary expansion, they borrowed gold. During the nineteenth century, the United States borrowed in Great Britain during economic upswings both to acquire real capital in the form of imports and to increase the gold base of the U.S. banking system. Transactions in gold helped with the transfer of goods and services; gold loans enabled the borrowers to expand credit without inducing credit contractions in the lending countries.[47]

Instability of credit and the Great Depression

The notion that manias and crashes result from the instability of the supply of credit is an old one. Alvin Hansen, writing on business cycles, discussed it in a general survey of 'early concepts' and in a chapter on mid-nineteenth-century economists—John Stuart Mill and Alfred Marshall—entitled 'Confidence and Credit.'[48] In his judgment, these views had become obsolete because they neglected the investment and savings decisions of large firms. Perhaps. But theories that attach importance to the instability of credit persisted into the twentieth century. Hawtrey was a classic economist in this vein, and so was A.C. Pigou, whose book *Industrial Fluctuations* (1927) has a chapter dealing with panics.[49] The paradox is that the role of the instability of credit began to be neglected about the time of the Great Depression of the 1930s.

The monetarist view of the Great Depression is set out in a monumental work by Milton Friedman and Anna Schwartz; they maintained that the sharp decline in economic activity in the first half of the 1930s was the result of mistakes in monetary policy made by the Federal Reserve. For the most part, they focused on the decline in the money supply from August 1929 to March 1933. Whenever the question turns on the start of the depression, the point is made that the money supply did not increase in 1928 and 1929, or that it declined 2.6 percent from August 1929 to October 1930 when it should have been increased to offset the weakness in the economy. Friedman and Schwartz contend that the stock market crash of October 1929 had little or nothing to do with the intensity of the decline in output and that the depression was the consequence of U.S. domestic policies and had only a tangential connection with international capital movements, exchange rates, or deflation abroad.[50] Their monetarist view of the depression has held sway in the United States for an extended period.[51]

Peter Temin took issue with this monetarist view from a Keynesian point of view. He asked whether the decline in spending resulted from a decline in the money supply or whether instead the decline in the money supply followed from the decline in spending; he used sophisticated econometrics to choose between these two views. Much of Temin's argument ran in terms of how much actual consumption deviated from forecasts of the levels based on the relationships between consumption, income, wealth, and similar variables that should be specified in forecasting a 'normal' trend in consumption. In addition he examined the relationship between the timing of changes in the money supply and changes in interest rates; thus if the increases in spending preceded the increase in the money supply then interest rates should increase whereas if the increase in the money supply preceded the increase in spending then interest rates should have declined—and vice versa. Since interest rates declined sharply after the 1929 crash (except for interest rates on high risk bonds which increased because of the increase in concern with default risk) he concluded that the decline in spending preceded the decline in the money supply. Temin also examined the changes in real money balances (the nominal money supply adjusted for changes in the consumer price level) and concluded that real balances increased between 1929 and 1931 by varying amounts that ranged from 1 to 18 percent, depending on the choice between M_1 and M_2 and between a wholesale price deflator and a consumer price deflator. Annual averages further dampened the movement; on the basis of monthly figures, and averaging M_1 and M_2 expressed as percentages or relatives of a base year and of the two price indexes, the money supply actually increased 5 percent between August 1929 and August 1931, if the same month is used to minimize seasonal influences. Temin concluded that there is no evidence that changes in the money supply between the stock market crash and the British departure from the gold standard in September 1931 caused the depression.[52]

Temin's analysis did not provide an explanation of the depression even though it was a strong challenge to the monetarist view. One analyst claimed that the stock market crash led banks to ration credit to borrowers and thus started the depression without reducing the money supply.[53] Another suggested that the sharp decline in share prices reduced nominal wealth and household spending; the implicit assumption was that the real value of wealth was important in explaining changes in consumption.[54]

These arguments ignore both the speed of the decline in industrial production in 1929 and the fact that this decline began four or five months before the stock market crash. The industrial production index fell from 127 in June to 122 in September, 117 in October, 106 in November, and 99 in December; automobile production declined from 660,000 units in March 1929 to 440,000 in August, 319,000 in October, and 92,500 in December. These declines are much too large to be explained by changes in the money supply or by an autonomous shift in spending.

Instead these declines are best explained by the instability of the credit system. As the stock market moved toward its apex, funds were channeled to the call-money market from consumption and production; the volume of call money rose from $6.4 billion at the end of December 1928 to $8.5 billion in early October 1929. Moreover, first New York banks and then banks headquartered in other U.S. cities became more cautious lenders to the stock market participants and to others. When the stock market crashed, the credit system suddenly froze. Loans to finance imports declined sharply, in part because of the sharp decline in the prices of imports.

The debate between the monetarists and the Keynesians ignores the instability of credit and the fragility of the banking system and the negative impacts on production and prices when the credit system became paralyzed because declines in the prices of many commodities and goods caused many borrowers to default on their loans—which factors explain the events in the early stages of the 1929 depression. This view was largely ignored except by Hyman Minsky and Henry Simons, the Chicago economist who thought the Great Depression was caused by declines in business confidence that led through an unstable credit system to changes in liquidity and consequent effects on the money supply.[55]

Henry Simons's views were set forth in his *Economic Policy for a Free Society*,[56] written after World War II under the strong influence of the 1930's depression. He recommended a 100 percent currency reserve against bank deposits to prevent changes in deposits arising from changes in public willingness to hold currency and a vigorous effort to stamp out the variability of credit elsewhere in the system. He proposed restrictions on open-book credit and installment loans as well as limitation of government debt to non-interest-bearing money at one end of the spectrum and very long-term debt (ideally, perpetual obligations) at the other. Simons advocated a system in which all financial wealth would be held in equity form with no fixed money contracts so that no institution that was not a bank could create effective money substitutes. He was concerned about the speculative temper of the community and the ease with which short-term nonbank borrowing and lending made society vulnerable to changes in business confidence.

Simon's recommendations to limit the character of money and financial assets were sharply at variance with Friedman's liberal propensity to let market forces determine the demand and supply for different types of financial assets.[57] Friedman was confident that control of the growth of the money supply would prevent major business cycles and that instability of the credit mechanism is not to be feared. Even if Simons's positive proposals were desirable (and there is grave doubt on this score) they are surely inoperable because they are utopian. Nevertheless Simons's diagnosis of the tendency of the system toward unstable short-term borrowing and repayment is on target.

In the last several decades still another viewpoint on the relations of money and banking to economic stability has come into prominence from the neo-Austrian school that wants to decontrol money and banking entirely. This group, led by Friedrich Hayek in Britain, Roland Vaubel in Germany, Richard Timberlake, Leland Yeager, Lawrence White, and George Selgin in the United States, seeks to abolish an active monetary policy. Any bank, company, or person would be allowed to issue 'money;' they believe that market forces will determine which firms issue good money. The different firms that issue money will compete to ensure that their own money is accepted, and so good money will drive out bad. White defends the position on the basis of the experience of the Scottish banks that were unregulated between the failure of the Ayr Bank in 1772 and the Bank Act of 1845 which applied the Bank Act of 1844 to Scotland.[58]

During this period the leading commercial banks accumulated the notes of the lesser ones and were ready to convert them to specie if they thought the supply of currency notes issued by any bank was increasing too rapidly. The large banks served as informal controllers of the money supply. But several historical experiences—the country banks in England from 1745 to 1835, wildcat banking in Michigan in the 1830s, and the latest experience with bank deregulation in Latin America and especially in East Asia—do not support the view that 'good money drives out bad.'

The global inflation of the 1970s resulted from a combination of expansive U.S. monetary policy and expansive monetary policies of

Europe and Japan as their holdings of international reserve assets and their money supplies increased as a result of their balance of payments surpluses in their transactions with the United States. Central bank holdings of international reserve assets again increased rapidly in the mid-1990s and the late 1990s.[59] Three years later a French economist, Pascal Blanqué, wrote of a U.S. credit bubble.[60] In a similar view, Graciela Kaminsky and Carmen Reinhart blame foreign countries for printing money and the United States for running a continuous balance-of-payments deficit.[61]

The central question is whether a central bank can restrain the instability of credit and slow speculation to avoid its dangerous extension. If the monetary authorities fix some proxy for the money supply or for liquidity, or if they focus directly on the rate of interest itself, can the upswing and decline of the crisis be moderated or eliminated entirely? There is no a priori way to determine whether a central bank policy of holding the money supply constant, limiting the liquidity of the money market, or raising the discount rate at the first sign of euphoric speculation would prevent the manias that lead to crises. Economists cannot conduct carefully controlled experiments. In the fall of 1998, after the collapse of Long-Term Capital Management and the financial debacle in Russia, the Federal Reserve reduced short-term interest rates three times to forestall a budding crisis. But such experiments cannot be conclusive, since they are open to the objection that if the course of action had been somewhat altered, the outcome would have been different. Nevertheless, the weight of historical evidence favors the theory that a somewhat different monetary policy might have moderated booms but would not have eliminated them completely.

The Bank of England was severely attacked for its blindness to an approaching crisis in 1839 and its failure to raise interest rates sooner. The general view that it had been dilatory is said, in fact, to have been the proximate cause of the Bank Act of 1844.[62] In the 1850s the glut of gold led to declines in interest rates in 1852 and 1853. Thereafter interest rates increased although not by enough to forestall the severe crisis of 1857.[63] The number of bills of exchange in circulation kept on increasing as the discount rate rose, and declined as it fell, rather than responding to policy changes in the opposite direction; speculation based on bill creation seems to have been uninhibited by the increases in discount rates.[64] One mid-1850s proposal was that the bank rate should vary as a function of the Bank of England reserves to enable the public to have a clear idea of what to expect—a suggestion that Elmer Wood claims shows no grasp of Bank of England transactions.[65] In 1863 and 1864 the Bank of England twice raised the interest rate to 9 percent, which perhaps delayed but did not prevent the 1866 crash. Liquidation was completed in France in 1864; there were two shakeouts in Britain that year, but the main deflation was delayed.[66] In July 1869 the National Bank of Austria-Hungary raised interest rates but the increase came too late to forestall a crash in the fall of 1869 which was a pale forerunner of the Great Crash of 1873 in Vienna.[67] The Bank raised its discount rate again in 1872. At 5 percent for exchange and 6 percent for Lombard loans at the time of the last increase in March 1873, the rate was too low, according to Wirth.[68] In similar fashion, with the same timing and the same absence of result (unless it precipitated the crisis), the Federal Reserve Bank of New York raised its discount rate from 5 to 6 percent on August 9, 1929.

In 1873 the Bank of England changed its discount rate twenty-four times and avoided the financial crises that seized Austria and Germany in May and the United States in September. In November the rate was raised to 9 percent to prevent the Germans from drawing out the remaining sterling balances remaining from the Franco-Prussian indemnity.[69] Whether this represented successful fine-tuning against the possibility of crisis or merely increasing sensitivity to short-term capital movements, the secondary sources do not make clear.

In the panic of 1907, the preparatory expansion had involved lending in New York by outside banks in historically unknown amounts, along with heavy borrowing by New York in London on accommodation paper—a combination of two of the methods of expansion discussed earlier, if one equates out-of-town banks lending in New York to the gold-exchange standard. (The basis for doing so, of course, is that interbank deposits serve as reserves for the owner of the assets, but not necessarily as a one-for-one claim against the reserves of the bank receiving the deposit.) Lacking a central bank, New York could take no discretionary action to change interest rates. In London, gold exports as a result of American borrowing led to advances in the bank rate in October 1906, followed by the Bank of England's advice to the market that further acceptance of American finance bills was a menace to stability and unwelcome.[70] This slowed the boom but failed to prevent the 'rich man's panic' of March 1907 and the full-scale panic of October.

If central bankers were omniscient and omnipotent, they might be able to use central bank weapons to stabilize the credit system; they could then correct the instability implicit in the infinite expansibility of credit. But 'there are no positive limitations to the expansion of individual credit.'[71]

Central banking developed to impose control on the growth of credit and the instability in the supply of credit. The evolution of central banking from profit-oriented private banking is a remarkable achievement. There was implicit agreement on the division of labor between private banking and central banking by 1825; private bankers in London and the provinces would finance the boom while the Bank of England would 'finance the crisis' so it would not become self-justifying. In the United States, which was without a central bank after 1837, the major banks in New York were caught between the profitmaking role that led them to contribute to the instability of credit and their role as holders of deposits of banks from elsewhere in the country against whose instability they had to guard. There was a conflict between the short-run concern with profitability and the long-run concern with financial stability, the private good with the public. No one decreed that the New York banks should act responsibly in the public interest; it may or may not have been to their advantage to do so. The problem is a general one in politics and business and centers on who should look out for the public interest.

5
The Critical Stage

Changing expectations

The standard model of the sequence of events that leads to financial crises is that a shock leads to an economic expansion that then morphs into an economic boom; euphoria develops and then there is a pause in the increase in asset prices. Distress is likely to follow as asset prices begin to decline. The pattern is biological in its regularity. A panic is likely and then a crash may follow. Lord Overstone, the leading British banker of the middle of the nineteenth century, saw a similar pattern and was quoted with approval by Walter Bagehot: 'quiescence, improvement, confidence, prosperity, excitement, overtrading, CONVULSION [sic], pressure, stagnation, ending again in quiescence.'[1] Overstone identified five stages of euphoria before the financial crisis, or, in his words, the convulsion.

The theory of rational expectations assumes that investors' expectations change more or less instantaneously in response to each shock and that investors immediately see through to the impacts of each shock on the long-run equilibrium prices for real estate and stocks and commodities. In contrast the insight from financial history is that expectations in the real world change slowly at some times and rapidly at others as different groups realize—sometimes at different moments and at other times more or less simultaneously—that the current forecasts of prices and values in the distant future differ from earlier views of these same prices and values.

The change in the mind-sets of investors from confidence to pessimism is the source of instability in the credit markets as some borrowers—individuals as well as firms—realize that their indebtedness is too large relative to their incomes. These borrowers begin to adjust to their new perceptions about the economic future by reducing their spending so they will have the cash to pay down debt or to increase saving. Some firms may sell divisions and operating units to get the cash to pay down debt. The lenders recognize that they have too many risky loans and so they seek repayment of outstanding loans from the borrowers that they deem most risky; they become reluctant to renew these loans as they mature. The lenders also raise the credit standard for new loans.

The period of financial distress may last weeks, months, even years, or it may be concentrated into a few days. The economic downturn that followed the collapse of the U.S. stock market in 1929 continued for four years—until the change to a new, more interventionist government. Japan was in the economic doldrums for more than ten years after stock prices and real estate prices began to decline in January 1990. Korea recovered from its 1998 economic malaise by the beginning of 1999. The handover of sovereignty in Hong Kong in mid-1997 and its advent as a special economic region of China coincided with the Asian Financial Crisis. Hong Kong remained in a deflationary mode for five years and property prices declined by 40 to 50 percent. The United States experienced a massive decline in household wealth following the decline in stock prices that began in 2000 and yet the recession of 2001 was relatively mild.

Should a government intervene to moderate the cycle? Government policies play a vital role in the formation of expectations. Can the government head off a financial crisis by dampening the expectations that develop in the euphoria? Should the government seek to moderate the impacts of the decline in prices of stocks and real estate and commodities after the bubble has imploded?

Warnings

One proposal has been that if a government knows more than it thinks the speculators know, the appropriate solution is that the government make that knowledge available or publish its own forecast.[2] Thus the government might calm the concerns or fears of investors by making that knowledge publicly available.[3] Many individuals within government have views about the economic and financial outlook but these are often at variance with each other so that developing a 'government view' could occur only if someone—the prime minister, the head of the central bank, the minister of finance—succeeded in forging a consensus.

The historical record provides little support for the view that statements from government officials have much of an impact in dampening euphoria. In some cases 'a word to the wise' may be sufficient but in others the warnings are likely to be inadequate. The likelihood that investors and speculators would heed the warnings of a government official when asset prices are increasing at annual rates of 20 to 30 percent a year is not especially high.

The first such warnings on the record were made about 1825. Although many writers have viewed the Bubble Act of June 1720 as a warning by Robert Walpole and King George II against speculation, the primary objective of that legislation was to repress competitors of the South Sea Company because the other bubbles were draining cash subscriptions that the South Sea Company wanted and needed.[4] The Bubble Act, which had been strengthened in 1749, made swindles and starting a legitimate business more difficult and was not repealed until the nineteenth century.

The banking authorities began to warn about speculative booms in the nineteenth century. In the spring of 1825, Prime Minister Canning, the Chancellor of the Exchequer, Lord Liverpool, Sir Francis Baring, and W.R. McCulloch in *The Scotsman* warned against the excesses of speculation. The warning contributed to the crisis—but the crisis was probably inevitable. In the crash and panic of December 1825, Lord Liverpool did not rescue the speculators because nine months earlier he had said he would not.[5] In 1837 the President of the Board of Trade, J. Poulett Thompson, excoriated the prevalent spirit of speculation, which differed from that of 1825 in that individuals were investing at home rather than abroad.[6]

In the fall of 1837 the gambling spirit crossed the Channel, and the Belgian and French authorities attempted to repress speculation by forbidding the quotation of notes and shares of corporations. Their efforts were futile; speculation had gone beyond the narrow framework of the Bourse and nonprofessionals such as *rentiers* and even 'women and foreigners' were becoming involved. Chambers of Commerce in Liège, Vervier, and Antwerp condemned stock market speculation. The Belgian king refused to charter a proposed bank, the Mutualité Industrielle. Investment slowed as a result of a decline in economic activity rather than in response to the statements from the administration and business establishment.[7] In July 1839, Lamartine in the French Chamber of Deputies spoke against speculation and especially warned about the guarantees of railroad securities.[8]

The only suggestion that official condemnation of speculation may have been effective was from a French observer who commented on the 1857 crisis. In March 1856 the minister of the interior brought legal action against certain swindlers. Emperor Napoleon III congratulated O. de Vallée, the author of a book, *Les Manieurs d'argent,* which dealt sternly with dubious financial practices. The Senate passed laws. The Bank of France raised the discount rate to 10 percent. Napoleon III published a letter in *Le Moniteur* on December 11, that indicated that the government would provide support only for those catastrophes that were beyond human anticipation. According to d'Ormesson, speculative exuberance declined and the memory of the 1857 crisis reflected a certain glory on French commerce.[9] But Rosenberg concluded that the warnings had been too late.[10]

Restrictions by the Austrian National Bank in 1869 produced a 'great crash' that proved to be a mini-crash in comparison with the one that followed in 1873.[11] The warnings and revelations of Eduard Lasker, who was a member of the Diet and in February 1873 had exposed the scandalous connections between the Prussian government and its commerce ministry and the railroad concessionaires, had no significant impact in quelling speculative sentiment.[12]

More timely were warnings issued by *The Economist* in 1888 against commitments to buy *cedulas,* the Argentinean land bonds. In April *The Economist* said that 'the bonds . . . might . . . become a very inadequate security. Just at present all real estate at the River Plate commands inflated prices, but the occurrence of financial difficulties might easily render them unsaleable.'[13] Then in May 'A collapse of the "boom" in real estate, which is easily conceivable, would be sure to severely depress the value of the cedulas.'[14] The warnings proved ineffective.

More memorable is the Cassandra-like utterance of Paul Warburg, a partner of Kuhn, Loeb & Co. and one of the founders of the Federal Reserve System, who in February 1929 warned the American public that U.S. stock prices were too high and showed symptoms reminiscent of the 1907 panic; his statement followed a similar statement from the Chairman of the Federal Reserve Board. Investors paused briefly and then stock prices again increased. The ineffectiveness of Fed Chairman Greenspan's statement about 'irrational exuberance' in December 1996 about the level of U.S. stock prices was noted earlier. In August 1999 Greenspan stated that the Federal Reserve would consider the level of stock prices when it set interest rates after the Fed had increased the discount rate by 0.25 percent in August. Again the stock market barely noticed.

If prices of real estate and stocks continue to increase despite these warnings, then it appears that the warnings lack credibility. Economic forecasters may know—or at least think they know—the long-run equilibrium values for real estate and for stocks, but the ability to foretell when market prices will move back toward these long-run average values rather than away from them is modest. Roger Babson sold his clients' stocks in 1928 and he appeared foolish for more than a year as stock prices continued to increase.

The timing issue is complex. If the government authorities want their warnings to be effective, they need to provide their cautionary statements early enough to forestall some of the excesses of the euphoric period and late enough so the statements are credible. One metaphor from a former chairman of the Federal Reserve is that authorities are reluctant to take the 'punch bowl away from the party just as the party is getting going' because of the unfavorable public reactions.

The modern tradition is that the central banks are comfortable in developing their monetary policies to moderate the increases in the consumer price level or some other price level index; 'inflation targeting' is their new mantra. The policy question is whether the central bankers should ignore the increases in real estate prices and stock prices if these prices have moved far from their long-run equilibrium values. Attempting to convince the speculators through statements alone has generally been futile.

Financial distress

Distress has been widely used in discussions of financial crises. The term is imprecise: one meaning is a state of suffering and another is of a hazardous situation. Commercial distress reflects the first definition, financial distress the second. Commercial distress implies that prices and business activity and profitability have declined and that many mercantile and industrial firms have gone bankrupt. Financial distress for an individual firm means that its profitability has declined sharply so that it is incurring significant losses so there is a nontrivial probability that the firm will not be able to pay scheduled interest on its outstanding debt.[15] Financial distress for an economy also has a prospective significance and implies the need for economic adjustments; firms may be on the verge of bankruptcy and banks may need to be recapitalized. Many investment projects may be far from completion because the developers can no longer obtain the finance necessary to complete the construction.

Other words used to describe the interval between the end of euphoria and the onset of what classic writers called revulsion and discredit (or crash and panic) are *uneasiness, apprehension, tension, stringency, pressure, uncertainty, ominous conditions, fragility*. More colorful expressions include *an ugly drop in the market*[16] or *a thundery atmosphere*[17] Meteorological metaphors have been used frequently: 'One feels again the oppressive atmosphere that precedes a storm.'[18] And geological metaphors: two years before the panic of 1847 Lord Overstone wrote to his friend G.W. Norman (the grandfather of Montagu Norman, the Governor of the Bank of England in the 1920s): 'We have no crash at present, only a slight premonitory movement of the ground under our feet.'[19] The seismographic metaphor was also used by Michel Chevalier who wrote from America about President Jackson's war against the Second Bank of the United States: 'A general collapse of credit, however short the time it lasts, is more fearful than the most terrible earthquake.'[20] Another French writer noted the 'presentiment of disaster.'[21] A German metaphor spoke of the 'bow being so bent in the fall of 1782 that it threatened to snap.'[22]

Distress is not an easily measured condition for an economy. Investors may have become apprehensive when the values of certain variables diverged significantly from average values; some of these variables include the gold reserve ratios of a central bank, the ratio of debt to capital of a large number of firms or individuals, the losses of banks in relation to their capital, the ratio of external debt service payments to export earnings of a country, and the price–earnings ratios for stocks and the rental ratio for real estate. There may be contemporary awareness of the approach of some limit, such as the ceiling on note issues by the Bank of England stipulated in the Bank Act of 1844, the $100 million gold minimum requirement of the U.S. Treasury in 1893, the ceiling on advances from the Bank of France to the French Treasury in 1924, the gold reserve ratio of the Reichsbank under the Dawes Plan in June 1931, or the free gold available to the Federal Reserve System prior to the passage of the Glass-Steagall Act in February 1932. A ratio of external debt to GDP of 60 percent for a country has been viewed as a premonitory indicator by investors; the 'ice is thin' for a country when this ratio is much higher. Similarly a ratio of government debt to GDP of significantly more than

60 percent is viewed as too high. Limits excite, as one Chancellor of the Exchequer noted in 1857:

> Now when you impose a limit, there is no question that the existence of that limit, provided it makes itself felt at a time of crisis, must increase the alarm. People feel at the moment that a peril presses on them, they begin to calculate how much remains of that fund to which they look for assistance in times of commercial difficulty, and in whatever way you fix the limit, whether by Act of Parliament, or, as Mr. Thomas Tooke [a leader of the Banking School] proposed, by a sort of usage, or, as in France, by the discretion of the Government acting on the Bank of France, there is no doubt that in moments of crisis the limit must aggravate the alarm.[23]

A French official expressed the same idea two decades later when he defended the tradition that the Bank of France should maintain a specie reserve of about one-third of its demand liabilities but without a hard and fast legal requirement: 'A fixed ratio is not required. That would be unwise . . . the terror of a limit fixed and absolute.'[24] Overshooting of the limit may have psychological significance. In March 1924 although sophisticated bankers knew that a small increase in the French money supply would not be dangerous, the public had come to regard the ceiling on Bank of France advances to the Treasury as an index of economic health. As one minister put it, the French were close to the upper limit of elasticity of confidence in their own currency.[25]

Causes of distress and the symptoms of distress are observed at the same time and include sharply rising interest rates in some or all segments of the capital market, an increase in the interest rates paid by subprime borrowers relative to the interest rates paid by prime borrowers, a sharp depreciation of the currency in the foreign exchange market, an increase in bankruptcies, and an end of price increases in commodities, securities, and real estate. These developments are often related and show that the lenders have become over-extended and are trying to reduce their exposure to risks and especially to large risks.

Financial distress in the nineteenth century was compounded by the payments arrangements for purchases of newly issued stock that provided for a series of payments by the buyers in response to 'calls' from the issuers of stocks as construction work proceeded. In 1825 and 1847 in Britain and in 1882 in France some of the buyers of the stocks did not have the cash to meet the call; these may have counted on selling the security at a profit before the next call. Thomas Tooke describes this embarrassment in 1825 as acute because the call for cash payment was immediate and pressing while prospects for earnings on the stock were remote and uncertain.[26] Distress developed in January 1847 when railroad calls amounted to £6.5 million in a single month.[27]

The chain-letter aspect of security issues became evident in the finances of the South Sea Company in June, July, and August 1720 with repeated attempts to raise cash through new issues of stock. In 1881 more than 125 new issues with a market value of 5 billion francs were sold in Paris when France's annual savings were estimated at 2 billion francs.[28] Nor was this an era when private companies were going public in large numbers, as in the late 1880s in Great Britain and the late 1920s in the United States; in both cases there was no need for an increase in savings because the newly-issued publicly owned shares were exchanged for privately owned shares.

The end of a period of rising prices for assets leads to distress whenever a significant number of investors have based their purchases of these assets on the anticipation that their prices will continue to increase. Some of these investors may have a 'negative carry' in that the interest rates on the funds borrowed to buy the assets exceed the cash income on the assets; these investors anticipated that they would be able to use the increase in the value of the asset as collateral for new loans that would provide them with some of the cash that they would need to pay the interest on the outstanding loans. When asset prices stop increasing, these investors are shunted into distress mode since they have no ready way to get the cash they need to pay the interest on their outstanding indebtedness.

Distress may arise from an increase in the flow of funds from the country—a bad harvest may require an increase in imports and an increase in interest rates in a major international financial center may attract funds away from domestic financial markets. Credit in the domestic credit market might become less readily available—tighter—because of a reduction in the reserves of the banking system.

The capital outflow may be potential; there was distress in the London money market in 1872 when as a result of French payment of reparations to Prussia the Reichsbank acquired substantial money market securities denominated in the British pound that could be readily converted into gold. Similarly there was a flow of capital to London prior to April 1925 in anticipation that the British pound would appreciate to its prewar gold parity; once the pound was again pegged to gold, the owners of these deposits had modest incentive to keep them in London. The Bank of England's choice of policies was constrained because of the concern that some of these funds might leave London. The Bank of France acquired large British pound balances in the effort to limit the appreciation of the French franc after its successful monetary stabilization at the end of 1926; the likelihood that the French might use part or all of their British pound balances to buy gold was a bargaining chip that increased nervousness in London.

The essence of financial distress is loss of confidence. What comes next—slow recovery of belief in the future as various aspects of the economy are corrected, or collapse of prices, panic, runs on banks, and a rush to get out of illiquid assets and into money?

The issue is concisely posed by James S. Gibbons:

> Bank officers are not always insensible to alarm when respectable merchants, failing in their best endeavors, are driven into a corner and assume an air of desperation. They know the danger that hangs over the market. Credit is prodigiously extended; the public excitement is wrought up to a high pitch of apprehension, and there need be but a single failure of a 'great house' to explode the 'mighty bubble.' Who knows that it is a bubble? Who knows that the highest point of pressure is not reached today, and that tomorrow the waters will not begin to subside? And then gradually things fall into their old channels, confidence revives and it is proved that there was no bubble to burst after all.[29]

How long does distress last?

Financial distress may subside as in France in 1866 and in Great Britain in 1873 and 1907 or a panic may follow the distress. In the United States there were near-panics over the failed attempt by Bunker Hunt to corner the silver market in 1979, the failure of the Continental Illinois Bank in 1984, and the debacle of Long-Term Capital Management in 1998. There were extended periods of distress after August 1982 over bank loans to Mexico, Brazil, and other developing countries and over loans by the thrift institutions in Louisiana, Oklahoma, and Texas to borrowers who had based their exploration activities on the prospect that the oil price would increase to $80 per barrel. After the collapse of hundreds of U.S. banks and thrift institutions at the end of the 1980s, the U.S. Resolution Trust Corporation (RTC) acquired tens of billions of dollars worth of real estate that had been used as collateral for loans. Eventually these would be sold to the public; the uncertainty about the values of these properties depressed values.

Similarly there was distress in Tokyo for an extended period in the 1990s; in any 'mark to market' test most of the large Japanese banks were bankrupt and yet there were no runs on the banks because depositors understood that they would be made whole by the government if the banks were closed. The Japanese government's policies toward these failed institutions were a cause of distress: would the government close these failed banks or would the government provide new capital to them on favorable terms?

The sharp decline in stock prices on Monday, October 19, 1987, proved to be a correction rather than a panic because it did not spread to other U.S. markets, although there were nearly simultaneous sharp declines in most other national stock markets (the exception being Tokyo). Distress lasted for several weeks while investors waited to see whether the decline in stock prices would have significant impacts on other markets.

The debacle of Long-Term Capital Management (LTCM) in the summer of 1998 occurred at about the same time as the collapse of the finances in Russia; indeed the impact of the impending disaster in Russia induced changes in interest rate and yield relationships that contributed significantly to the collapse of LTCM. Although LTCM was usually considered a hedge fund, it was in effect an unregulated bank. LTCM was considered a 'very smart' financial institution; two Nobel laureates in finance were among its top officers. It had $5 billion of capital and $125 billion of debt so it was much more highly leveraged than traditional banks and most other hedge funds. Moreover LTCM had tens of billions of positions in derivatives contracts like futures and options that sometimes were hedges or offsets against its assets and liabilities. In its initial years, LTCM had been viewed as a money machine, and extremely clever in taking advantage of small deviations in prices of highly similar assets. For example, the thirty-year U.S. Treasury bond was extensively traded but the twenty-nine-year bond was not, so the interest rate on the twenty-nine-year bond was modestly higher than that on the thirty-year bond because the twenty-nine-year bond was less liquid. So LTCM would buy hundreds of millions of dollars worth of the twenty-nine-year bond and sell short more or less the same amount of the thirty-year bond, and profit from the interest rate differential. The excess of the interest rate earned on the bond with the twenty-nine-year maturity over the interest rate on the bond with the thirty-year maturity was modest, but the product of this small number and the position of hundreds of millions of dollars was large.

Some of the major banks that were large lenders to LTCM tended to mimic some of its portfolio positions. The positions of LTCM and its banks in some securities dominated the markets for these securities.

In the spring of 1998, LTCM had a long position in emerging market bonds that it hedged by shorting U.S. Treasury bonds. As investors became increasingly apprehensive about Russia's financial future, the prices of emerging market bonds declined as the contagion effect came into play. The Federal Reserve responded with greater monetary ease and the prices of U.S. Treasury bonds increased. LTCM lost money on both legs of its hedge, which eroded its capital base. As the prices of these emerging market bonds declined, LTCM was between the proverbial 'rock and a hard place'; if it sold any of its holdings of individual securities, their prices would fall further and its net worth would decline even more rapidly.

The Federal Reserve was concerned that if LTCM failed there would be an extended period of significant uncertainty—distress—in the capital markets while its positions were unwound and bond prices would fall further. The Fed used its muscle—more precisely the threat of its regulatory muscle—to induce the major banks that were lenders to LTCM to invest their own capital in LTCM and the banks then acquired 90 percent ownership of the firm.

The crash or panic that follows financial distress may do so immediately, in a matter of weeks, or with a delay of several years. John Law's system peaked in December 1719 and collapsed in May 1720—five or six months from glory to disaster. In the South Sea Bubble of 1720, the lunatic note sounded clearly at the end of April, the ugly drop in the market occurred in August, and collapse came in the first days of September. In 1763 distress developed in March while the actual crisis precipitated by the failure of DeNeufville in Amsterdam occurred in July. In 1772 the Bank of England raised its discount rate early in the year; the Ayr Bank cut back operations in May, but too late. Fordyce absconded on June 10 and the news precipitated a panic in Great Britain on June 22; the consequent distress in Amsterdam lasted until the failure of Clifford & Co. in December.

Timing of crises from 1789 to 1815 was dominated by individual apocalyptic events, including the guillotining of Louis XVI in January 1793 (losing one's head always is apocalyptic), the landing of the French army at Fishguard on the southwestern tip of Wales in February 1797, and the penetration of the continental blockade in 1799. The periods of distress on these occasions were short because the panic was virtually immediate. In 1809–1810 the setback arose from a tightening of the continental blockade and overtrading in exports to Brazil. Pressure mounted slowly from the middle of 1809, then more rapidly from mid-1810 to the climax of bankruptcies in January 1811.

Calls for further payments on subscriptions to the shares in railroads in January 1847 set the background of tension against which speculation in grain peaked in May, collapsed in August, and led to panic in November. The crisis of 1866 was the delayed result of the 1864 collapse of cotton prices that had brought panic to France in that year. Great Britain had two 'critical moments' in 1864, one in January—the real crisis that related to the collapse in cotton prices—and another in the last quarter.[30] British treatment of the period tends to look more to speculative expansion that affected the discount houses and started the previous year, and to a series of firms that resembled the Credit Mobilier and were using the funds from new share issues to buy back their own shares to pump up the investors. W.T.C. King wrote that one Albert Gottheimer used the name Albert Grant to float the imposing Credit Foncier and Mobilier of England, which ultimately achieved a paid-up or rather called-up capital of £1 million.[31] The conversion of the discounting house of Overend, Gurney & Co. to a public company in July 1865 at the peak of the boom and 'dividend race' led to a 100 percent premium on the stock in October. The Bank of England responded by raising its discount rate from 3 percent to 7 percent; the crash did not occur until May 1866. The distress in Great Britain lasted seven months, from October 1865 to May 1866, while the period of distress in France lasted nearly thirty months.

Periods of financial stringency and crisis 'and panic (in the United States) occurred in the autumn when western banks drew large sums of money from the East to pay for shipments of cereals.'[32] Credit demand peaked in the autumn when the grain dealers needed money to pay the farmers. Sprague noted that the crisis of 1873 came in September because of the early harvest, that the outbreak of a crisis invariably came as a surprise to the business community and that the crisis of 1873 was not an exception.[33] The seasonal tightness of money was well known and hence the puzzle is why it would have come as a surprise. The 'excessive tightness' of money from September 1872 to May 1873 caused the railroads to borrow short-term funds rather than issue bonds, which could have been seen as a sign of distress, and then the seasonal tightness precipitated the crash.[34]

Distress may be continuous or it may oscillate in its own rhythm. The crash of the Union Générale in January 1882 was preceded by three separate tense periods, in July, October, and December 1881.[35] The panic of October 1907 was anticipated (although Sprague indicated its exact timing was not foreseeable) and preceded by a 'rich man's panic' in March when Union Pacific stock, the security most widely used as collateral for finance bill operations, dropped 50 points.[36] Markets recovered from this blow and from the failure of an offering of New York City bonds in June (only $2 million was tendered for an offering of $29 million of 4 percent bonds) and from the collapse of the copper market in July, and from the $29 million fine levied against the Standard Oil Company for antitrust law violations in August—only to succumb to the failure of the Knickerbocker Trust Company in October.[37] In 1929 distress lasted from June to the last week in October.

Financial distress in Japan began at the start of the 1990s and continued throughout that decade and into the next one. Japanese industrial firms were extremely reluctant to downsize and make the other adjustments needed for their costs to decline below their current revenues; in the previous forty years these firms had been able to rely on the banks for the cash to finance their operating losses and investments. Japanese banks were extremely reluctant to stop making new loans, even to enterprises that would be considered bankrupt in any 'mark to market' test; and the regulatory authorities were reluctant to close banks that would be considered bankrupt. Traditionally the risk of financial losses in Japan has been 'socialized'; society prefers to distribute these losses among taxpayers as a group, rather than to impose the costs of adjustment associated with closing failed enterprises on the employees of these firms.

Argentina experienced an extended period of distress at the end of the 1990s and in 2000 before its currency collapsed in January 2001. At the end of the 1980s Argentina suffered through two years of hyperinflation. The incoming government of President Carlos Menem pegged the new Argentinean peso to the U.S. dollar at the rate of one Argentinean peso to one U.S. dollar; at the same time Argentina adopted a currency board arrangement that meant that its central bank would increase the supply of peso liabilities only if its holdings of U.S. dollars increased—more or less a very strict application of the Currency School doctrine. During the 1990s, the tax revenues of the Argentinean government were smaller than its expenditures and the excess of expenditures over tax revenues was financed partly with the receipts from privatization and partly by government borrowing. The hyperinflation of the 1980s had sharply reduced the real value of the Argentinean government debt and so investors purchased Argentinean government bonds denominated in the U.S. dollar because the government looked like a good credit risk. As the ratio of Argentinean government debt to the country's GDP increased, the interest rates that the Argentinean government had to pay to sell new bonds rose. There was a recession in Argentina toward the end of the decade, in part because the U.S. dollar (to which the peso was pegged) was appreciating; and the Argentinean fiscal deficit increased as its tax receipts declined relative to expenditures. The recession in Argentina was intensified by the depreciation of the Brazilian real in January 1998. Brazil was Argentina's major trading partner. The policy question was whether Argentina would be able to reduce its fiscal deficit while maintaining the established parity of one Argentinean peso to one U.S. dollar. (The Argentineans do not have an established tradition of paying taxes so tax rates tend to be high and tax collections low, while government salaries tend to be high and the performance of government officials low.) The efforts to raise taxes and cut government expenditures led to a series of political problems; Argentinean citizens were extremely reluctant to pay more taxes when the economy was doing poorly. The country was moving in slow motion toward a disaster. In the end Argentina both devalued and defaulted on the government debt.

Suppose the monetary authorities tighten credit to raise the cost of speculating. When commodity and asset markets move together, up or down, the direction that monetary policy should take is clear. But when share prices or real estate or both soar while commodity prices are stable or falling the authorities face a dilemma. The Federal Reserve encountered this dilemma in the 1920s; President Benjamin Strong had agonized over the appropriate policy in 1925 and again in 1927. The dilemma is that the policymakers cannot kill two birds with one stone, or more precisely they cannot achieve two policy targets with one policy instrument, or in what is perhaps a better metaphor, it is difficult to pick off a target if it is standing next to another one that one wants to leave untouched and the weapon is a shotgun rather than a rifle. The Japanese authorities encountered this problem in the real estate markets in the late 1980s; housing prices had soared to such a height that only those who qualified for one-hundred-year or three-generation mortgages could afford to buy. At the same time, any tightening of credit to dampen the boom in real estate would be likely to dampen a remarkable economic expansion.[38]

Chairman Greenspan was concerned that U.S. stock prices were too high or increasing too rapidly when he made his famous remark about 'irrational exuberance' in December 1996. The Fed proved reluctant to raise interest rates to dampen the increase in stock prices because of the negative impacts on economic growth and employment. In 1999 the Fed became concerned (obsessed??) with the Y2K problem, the likelihood that U.S. computer systems would collapse because so many software programs were not designed to recognize the transition to 2000. In the last several months of the year the Fed provided the monetary system with abundant liquidity to forestall any problems associated with the end-of-the-millennium transition and in the meantime the money had to go someplace so it fed stock market speculation.

Onset of a crisis

Students of logic have discussed the damp squib thrown by A that lands at B's feet, which is then thrown from B to C, and from C to D, and so on, only to explode after Y throws it in Z's face. Who is to blame? A, *causa remota*? Or Y, *causa proximal*? *Causa remota* of any crisis is the expansion of credit and speculation while *causa proxima* is some incident that saps the confidence of the system and induces investors to sell commodities, stocks, real estate, bills of exchange, or promissory notes and increase their money holdings. The *causa proxima* may be trivial: a bankruptcy, a suicide, a flight, a revelation of fraud, a refusal of credit to some borrowers, or some change of view that leads a market participant with a large position to sell. Prices fall. Expectations are reversed. The downward price movement accelerates. To the extent that investors have used borrowed money to finance their purchases of stocks and real estate the decline in prices is likely to lead to calls for more margin or cash and to further liquidation of stocks or real estate. As prices fall further, bank loan losses increase and one or more mercantile houses, banks, discount houses, or brokerages fail. The credit system appears shaky, and there is a race for liquidity.

Identifying the original sellers is difficult. Conspiracy theories abound. One can single out bear speculators like Joseph P. Kennedy, Sr, or Bernard Baruch in 1929; the Protestant–Jewish cartel that allegedly did for Eugène Bontoux in 1882; or Thomas Guy, who liquidated £54,000 of South Sea stock over six weeks between April and June 1720, never selling more than £1,000's worth at a time. (He used his fortune to endow Guy's Hospital in London, 'the best memorial of the Bubble.')[39]

Someone sells. Occasionally it is a foreigner. In 1847, for example, the French (according to one S. Saunders, quoted by Evans) bought up surplus wheat and sent it to Great Britain in June and July where it was sold at prices much below the then-prevailing market prices, which fell from 96 shillings to 56 shillings per quarter and brought about the bankruptcies of a large number of houses connected with the corn trade.[40] The story is not persuasive. The price of wheat had risen from 46 shillings in August 1846 to 93 shillings in May 1847 because of violent storms that ruined the crop and because of the potato disease in Ireland and on the Continent. The price dropped in July 1847 with favorable weather and the prospect of a good crop. Imports of wheat and flour rose from 2.3 million quarters (a quarter is equal to eight bushels) in 1846 to 4.4 million in 1847, aided by the repeal of the Corn Laws;[41] the 70,000 quarters are a trivial proportion of this sum. In 1846 France had its smallest crop of wheat in 100 years (a problem exacerbated by the potato crop failure); in 1847 the crop was the largest for 100 years. But the condition was general, and British wheat speculation had been excessive.

One view is that the Baring crisis of 1890 was triggered by the German sale of Argentinean bonds. German investors had stopped buying these bonds two years earlier either because of general uneasiness,[42] or because they were concerned about the instability in the foreign exchange value of the Argentinean currency,[43] or because the domestic boom led them to sell other foreign bonds including Russian bonds.[44] German sales of the Argentinean bonds contributed to distress rather than to a crisis, since British investors then acquired a higher proportion of the £200 million in bonds issued by Argentina. In November 1888 a £3.5 million offering of the Buenos Aires Drainage and Waterworks Company failed, and Baring felt obliged to lend to Argentina through acceptance credits. Declining primary product prices in 1890 meant that the Argentine government did not have the money to repay these loans as they came due. The Baring crisis of November 1890, after two years of distress, resulted from a warning from the Bank of England to Baring Brothers to limit the level of its acceptances (which stood at £30 million in the summer of 1890), from the crisis in New York in October, and from the maturing of £4 million of acceptances in November when Baring could no longer sell securities that it had acquired from underwriting or borrow further on short term.

New information may precipitate a crash, as when it was revealed that the Paris-Lyons-Marseilles railroad would cost 300 million francs instead of the projected 200 million.[45] *Causa remota,* and much more important, were the large balance of payments deficit from extensive imports of railroad materials and, especially, the crop failure of 1846 followed by the glut of 1847. The Granger movement helped precipitate the collapse in the United States in 1873. The Grangers, who in some ways resembled the environmentalists of today, started in the late 1860s and early 1870s as activists for legislation that would control intrastate transportation by prohibiting discriminatory charges, establishing regulatory commissions, and setting maximum freight rates.[46] A very large volume of railroad securities had been sold on credit—including a number of 'superfluous and ridiculous' enterprises like the Rockford, Rock Island and St Louis line which had been sold at par and then declined to 6 cents on the dollar—so the prospect of local control of freight rates put an end to optimism and triggered sales and then liquidation of these bonds.

One 'accidental' detonator of a crisis has been the sinking of a ship. In 1799, when interest rates ranged between 12 and 14 percent and the price of sugar was 35 percent below the peak before the convoy had broken through the blockade, British merchants shipped £1 million on the frigate *Lutine* destined for Texel in an attempt to assist in the Amsterdam crisis. The ship sank in a storm off the Dutch coast and the hope of alleviating the crisis was dashed.[47] During the 1857 crisis in New York the news that the steamer *Central America,* bound from Panama to New York with a cargo including $2 million in gold, was overdue came at the time of extreme distress in Philadelphia, Cincinnati, and Chicago. Two days later it was learned that the ship had gone down, uninsured, with heavy loss of life and cargo.[48]

An accident may precipitate a crisis, but so may action designed to prevent it—or action by the authorities adopted to achieve other objectives. The matter was well put by H.S. Foxwell apropos the crisis of 1808–1809:

> To refuse accommodation altogether is always held to be dangerous. To make personal reference is invidious, especially for a National Bank. It is just possible that the Bank might have resorted to the expedient used in 1795–1796, I mean the granting of pro rata discounts . . . [In seeking to contract the circulation] it must have put severe pressure on the market and risked the creation of a panic . . . The Bank was responsible for the solvency of this crowd of small, ill-managed institutions [country banks], but dared not call them to account, on peril of provoking a general collapse of credit.[49]

Foxwell posed the dilemma neatly. Not to apply discipline will let the credit market expand to dangerous levels; to apply discipline may prick the bubble and induce collapse.

The pinprick

The nature of the bubble is that eventually it will be pricked, and then as with a child's balloon the air may escape sharply. The bubble in Japanese real estate and stock prices was pricked by the incoming governor of the Bank of Japan who at the beginning of 1990 instructed the banks to limit the growth of real estate loans relative to their total loans, which might be expected to increase at the rate of 5 or 6 percent a year. The reduction in the rate of growth of real estate loans meant that some individuals and firms which had been using credit to buy real estate would no longer be able to get enough cash from new loans to pay the interest on old loans, and so they were obliged to sell some real estate to get the cash. But if it hadn't been this instruction, some other event would have pricked the bubble.

The late 1990s bubble in U.S. stock prices was pricked by the Federal Reserve in 2000 when it sought to withdraw some of the liquidity that it had provided to the financial system in the previous six months in anticipation of the Y2K problem—the expectation that computer systems would break down because some computers lacked the appropriate digits. The bias of the Fed is to adjust to the anticipated problems by providing the system with more liquidity. So toward the end of 1999 the Fed began to supply the system with liquidity. The money had to go someplace, and some of it went to higher stock prices. The millennium turned without a disaster and the withdrawal of liquidity led to higher interest rates.

The bubbles in many of the Asian countries burst in 1997 because of the 'contagion effect.' The devaluation of the Thai baht on July 2, 1997, was like a clarion call; each of the Asian countries (except Taiwan and Singapore) had trade deficits that were financed with money borrowed from abroad. Asian firms were eager to borrow dollars because the interest rates generally were significantly lower than the interest rates on loans in their own currencies. When the baht was devalued, the foreign lenders recognized that the Asian countries would no longer be able to maintain the foreign exchange value of their currencies if they were no longer able to borrow foreign money. So the capital inflow declined and a self-fulfilling prophecy was triggered.

Policies adopted to deal with a crisis often encounter lags. Raising the discount rate in the face of an external drain of cash may induce a return flow. An increase in the discount rate of the Bank of England to

10 percent can 'draw gold from the moon' in the folklore of the City, but how long would it take to produce that result? The issue was debated between the Banking and the Currency schools in the context of the Bank Act of 1844 and the need either to suspend the Act or for a lender of last resort. In 1825 and again in 1836, speculation in boom conditions led to an outflow of gold and financial stringency. On one interpretation, the boom broke before the Bank of England belatedly raised its discount rate in an effort to reduce its liabilities; thus, a combination of tight money and declining commodity prices produced the crisis and induced the Bank to reverse course and to lower interest rates.[50] The Banking School believed that the increase in the discount rate rather than the topping of the boom checked the drain of specie and produced an immediate return flow of money. The Currency School, on the other hand, had two wings; one believed there would be an immediate return flow and the other, represented by Lord Overstone, thought there would be lags in the operation of bank rate so that a lender of last resort would be required to fill the gap.[51]

Hawtrey pointed to a lag at the level of commercial banks and internal drains, based on backlogs:

> Bankers may take proper steps, but panic because they work slowly: They may have really checked the fundamental danger of the position . . . stopped the stress of new orders . . . and yet the demand for fresh credits and the drain of cash may go undiminished. The consequence may be a state of panic among the bankers, who, unaware of the cause of the apparent ineffectiveness of the measures they have taken [the working off of the backlog of old orders], despair of saving themselves from failure, call in existing loans regardless of the embarrassment of debtors, and precipitate a series of bankruptcies among their customers and themselves.
>
> The fact is that there is no golden rule for keeping the extension of credits within bounds.[52]

Apart from lags and mistakes in discount policy, the authorities may precipitate a panic by brusque action in the early stages of distress. In the summer of 1836, with credit extended in acceptances drawn by American houses on British joint-stock banks, the Bank of England refused to discount any bills that carried the name of a joint-stock bank and specifically instructed its Liverpool agent not to rediscount any paper of the three so-called 'W banks' (Wiggins, Wildes, and Wilson) among the seven American banks in Britain, an action that 'seemed vindictive'[53] and led immediately to panic.[54] The Bank of England had to reverse its policies. It had long conferences with the 'W banks' in October, extended lines of discount to them in the first quarter of 1837, but was unable to prevent their failure in June of that year. The Bank acted to dampen the extension of too large an amount of credit. But credit is delicate; expectations can quickly be altered.

Panic in the form of a run on a bank or banks has usually been started by small depositors as happened in the 1980s in Ohio and Maryland and Rhode Island, where some of the state-chartered banks had chosen not to participate in the FDIC insurance arrangement because the state-chartered insurance arrangements charged lower premiums. (All federally-chartered banks and thrifts were required to participate in the federal government's deposit insurance programs.) In contrast stock market panic often resulted from selling by big-money insider speculators or institutional investors such as mutual funds, pension funds, and insurance companies, perhaps severally following similar models of program trading. The run on Franklin National Bank was initiated by other banks, and especially the large-money banks in New York that refused to take the counterpart of Franklin's forward foreign exchange contracts or to lend it federal funds or to buy Franklin repurchase agreements, except at rates of interest that reflected deep distrust.[55] Similarly the run on the Continental Illinois Bank in 1984 was triggered by the reluctance of other large banks to renew maturing deposits in the federal funds market and in the offshore deposit market. Smaller depositors were protected by the FDIC deposit insurance. And in the stock market meltdown of October 1987, the Fidelity group of mutual funds of Boston was a large seller in the London market before the New York Stock Exchange opened on the nineteenth. These orders were communicated back to New York, where they had accumulated into a mountain of sell orders by the time the market opened for trading. Fidelity's sales were a response to the redemptions by the holders of its mutual funds rather than to its own position, although it may have wanted to raise cash in anticipation of future redemptions—and before stock prices fell further.

The clumsiness of the International Monetary Fund triggered a run on many of the banks in Indonesia during the early days of the Asian crisis in 1997. The IMF induced the government to take over and support fifteen of the large private banks, in effect guaranteeing their deposits. But the remaining fifty or so other private banks then were placed in a nether world position and were subject to runs as the depositors scrambled to withdraw funds before the banks collapsed.

Crashes and panics

A crash is a collapse of the prices of assets, or perhaps the failure of an important firm or bank. A panic, 'a sudden fright without cause' (from the god Pan, known for causing terror), may occur in asset markets or involve a rush from less liquid securities to money or government securities—in the belief that governments do not go bankrupt because they can always print more money. A financial crisis may involve one or both and in either order. The collapse of the stock of the South Sea Company and the Sword Blade Bank almost brought down the Bank of England. The 1929 crash and panic in the New York stock market had adverse consequences in both the commodity and real estate markets, and the seizure in the credit markets led to sharp declines in income and employment and output. But there was no panic in the money market; interest rates did not increase because the Federal Reserve was pumping funds into the market.[56] In 1893 lack of confidence in the ability of the United States to maintain the gold standard under pressure from the silver interests led to money market pressure, bank failures, and downward pressure on prices of securities.[57]

The system is one of positive feedback. The debt-deflation cycles involve a decline in prices of assets and commodities which leads to a reduction in the value of collateral and induces banks to call loans or refuse new ones; firms sell commodities and inventories because their prices are in decline, and the decline in prices causes more and more firms to fail. Households sell securities and firms postpone borrowing and investing and prices fall still further. Further declines in the value of loan collateral lead to further liquidation. The failure of firms means that the banks incur loan losses and fail. As banks fail, depositors withdraw their money (this was particularly true in the days before deposit insurance). Deposit withdrawals require more loans to be called, more securities to be sold. Merchant houses, industrial firms, investors, banks in need of ready cash—their riskiest securities cannot be sold at any price, they are forced to sell their best securities and so their prices decline. The banks may carry the firms, corporations, and households that are known to be in trouble for a time in the expectation or hope that prices will pick up again and refloat the frail bark of credit. Bank examiners may *in extremis* look the other way as banks continue to value loans and securities at cost rather than at market value, extend loans due, or add to loans of delinquent borrowers so they can pay some of the interest. But when bankruptcy occurs, the nettle of bad loans must be grasped. Prices, solvency, liquidity, and the demand for cash—in German *Bargeld,* in French *numéraire*— are related. Not only banking institutions: as Sprague stated, households, firms, and banks are 'very similar to a row of bricks, the fall of one endangering the stability of the rest.'[58] The metaphor is a cliché, but nonetheless appropriate.

At the height of the panic, money is said to be unavailable. Descriptions are frequently exaggerated, not least about 1825:

> Bankers in Lombard Street called on the Governor [of the Bank of England] on Sunday [after the panic of country banks had reached Pole, Thornton & Co. on December 12] to warn that if such a house, drawn on by 47 country banks, were allowed to stop, a run would take place on every bank in London.
>
> It was allowed to stop. A panic seized upon the public, such as had never been witnessed before: everybody begging for money—money—but money was hardly on any condition to be had. 'It was not the character of the security,' observes the *Times,* 'that was considered: but the impossibility of producing money at all.'[59]

This was the occasion when the failure of seventy-three banks brought Great Britain, according to Huskisson, within twenty-four hours of barter.[60] 'It was, as the Duke said of Waterloo, "a damned nice thing—the nearest run thing you ever saw in your life."'[61] Barter was avoided by exchanging silver for gold with the Bank of France, and by the luck of the Bank of England in finding, just as it ran out of £5 and £10 notes (which were then all it issued), a block of £1 notes left in the vault from 1797. With government approval these were issued on December 17 and 'worked wonders.'[62]

In 1857 New York Central stock went from 93 to 61, Reading from 96 to 36.[63] The price of pork fell from $24 a barrel to $13; flour, from $10 to $5 or $6.[64] In September interest rates rose from 15 to 24 percent, as 150 banks in Pennsylvania, Maryland, Rhode Island, and Virginia failed in the last four days of the month. The panic reached a peak in October, when 1,415 banks in the United States failed and interest rates rose from 60 to 100 percent per annum.[65] This, of course, was for monies borrowed for a few days.

Very high rates of interest, such as 4 percent a day, have sometimes been quoted for a particular kind of loan, as for call money in 1884, when commercial discounts continued at 4.5 to 5 percent a day for first-class endorsed paper;[66] or 5 percent a day at the peak as a premium for cash at the onset of the panic of 1907.[67] Perhaps the apogee of the liquidity squeeze was recorded in 1907, when one bank paid $48 per $1,000 for the cash gate receipts of the Harvard-Yale football game.[68] The mild and short recession in 2001 after the massive implosion in U.S. stock prices resulted from the abrupt change in the policy of the Federal Reserve and its rapid and aggressive move to reduce interest rates. The result was a mortgage refinancing boom; millions of individuals refinanced their mortgages at lower interest rates and used some of the cash obtained in the refinancing to buy autos and other consumer durables and to go on vacations. The Fed reduced short-term interest rates to 1 percent and since the inflation rate was nearer 2 percent, real short-term interest rates were negative. One result was a boom in the housing market; house prices increased sharply in New York, Boston, Washington, and Los Angeles. Skeptics wondered whether the deflationary effects of the implosion of the stock price bubble had been largely offset by a bubble in the housing market.

Will the storm subside, the flood crest and fall? Or will boom and crash spread from one market and country to another and the steps taken locally and internationally fail to halt panic and reverse the damage?

6
Euphoria and Economic Booms

Consider some of the tallest office buildings in the world. The Empire State Building in New York City was started in 1929. The Petronas Twin Towers in Kuala Lumpur were started in 1993. The Jailing Tower in the Pudong area of Shanghai was started in 1995. In the late 1980s it seemed like half of the building cranes used to construct tall structures were in Tokyo. By the mid-1990s many of these cranes had migrated to Shanghai and Beijing.

The association between super-skyscrapers and asset price bubbles is a strong one. These towers of eighty, ninety, or one hundred storeys became a visual manifestation of bubbles in the twentieth century. So, however, were the number of concert halls and the extension of art museums and even the student unions on college and university campuses. Many of these cultural centers are financed with gifts from wealthy individuals and families and these groups are much richer during periods of economic euphoria.

The association between asset price bubbles and economic euphoria is also strong. As we have seen, one of the best-selling books in Tokyo in the late 1980s was *Japan as Number One*. The World Bank published *The East Asian Miracle* several years before the bubble in real estate prices and stock prices in Thailand and Malaysia and their neighbors imploded. Less has been heard of the New American Economy since the implosion of stock prices and the surge in the U.S. fiscal deficit. Changes in household wealth associated with the increase in asset prices directly affect household consumption spending and business spending.

There are two feedback loops from the increases in real estate prices and stock prices to the rate of growth of national income. One link is from the increases in household wealth to the increases in household spending. Households have savings or wealth objectives; as their wealth increases from the surge in asset prices, households save less from earned income and their consumption spending increases. The second link is from the increase in stock prices to investment spending. When stock prices increase, firms can raise cash from existing and new investors at lower costs and can undertake new projects that would be less profitable. Thus, the 'cost of capital' to a firm varies inversely with the level of stock prices: the higher the stock prices relative to the earnings of these firms, the lower the cost of capital. The lower the cost of capital to firms, the larger their investments in plant and equipment, since higher stock prices mean that the firms can earn a lower rate of return and still be very profitable.

The cliché is that 'stock prices are a leading indicator' of changes in economic activity. But the response is that changes in stock prices have forecast six of the last three recessions. U.S. stock prices began to decline four to six months before the collapse of the economy at the beginning of the 1930s. The Japanese economy began to decline after stock prices and real estate prices began to fall at the beginning of 1990. The outlier to this small sample set is that the sharp decline in U.S. stock prices that began in 2000 and continued for the next two years was associated with only a relatively mild recession.

There is a symmetry between increases in economic activity in response to increases in asset prices and the declines in economic activity when asset prices decline. During the expansion phase, business firms increase the amounts borrowed in response to the increase in their net worth. Banks increase their loans and may relax their loan criteria. During the period when asset prices implode, the banks incur loan losses, and some banks may be decapitalized by these losses and be forced to close or to merge with a better capitalized institution or obtain new capital from the state.

The strong positive correlation between the increases in asset prices and economic expansions and the reverse leads to the question of whether the dominant influence is from asset prices and wealth to the economy or whether instead the dominant influence is from economic expansion to the asset prices.

Albania was one of several former communist countries that experienced a Ponzi-type deposit scheme soon after its transition from a command economy to what was to become a market economy.

Bank regulation was extremely lax during this transition. Entrepreneurs promised to pay interest at the rate of 30 or 40 percent a month. At such rates, wealth increased rapidly; for example, if the interest rate was 35 percent a month then 1,000 leks deposited at the beginning of the year would amount to 64,000 leks at the end of the year. Depositors in this scheme had every incentive to watch their deposits grow rather than to withdraw cash from the bank. Some Albanians dropped out of the active labor force because their incomes from the compounding interest were much larger than their wages and salaries. Others increased their spending because their financial wealth was growing so rapidly. The managers of the deposit arrangement always needed to attract new cash to offset the cash that was being withdrawn to manage the arrangement, in effect for the day-to-day living expenses of the managers.

When the deposit scheme unraveled there were lots of angry Albanians. And economic activity slowed rapidly because households went into a savings mode to compensate for the decline in their wealth.

Asset price bubbles—at least the large ones—are almost always associated with economic euphoria. In contrast, the bursting of the bubbles leads to a downturn in economic activity and is often associated with the failure of financial institutions, frequently on a large scale. The failure of these institutions disrupts the channels of credit that in turn can lead to a slowdown in economic activity.

The tulipmania

The price of Dutch tulips increased by several hundred percent in the autumn of 1636—and the increases in the prices of the more exotic species of bulbs were even larger. Some analysts, especially those with a strong commitment to rationality and market efficiency, have questioned whether the use of the term bubble is appropriate. Even then there were many different types of tulips; some exotic and some garden varieties. The tulip bulbs are subject to a cobweb-like growth behavior; once planted, a bulb may develop for six to eight months before it begins to bloom. And each bulb may produce many little bulbs.

Not only the exotic varieties of bulbs were affected; ordinary garden-variety tulips such as the Gouda, Switzer, or White Crown that were traded among the simple folk at so-called colleges or public houses also soared and fell in price.[1]

The excitement in tulips began in earnest after September 1636, when bulbs were no longer available for examination since they were in their normal cycle and had been planted to bloom the following spring. Some of the buyers of the bulbs committed to pay for the 'merchandise' that was buried in the ground and that they could not see at the time of purchase. The excited bidding of November and December 1636 and January 1637 was conducted with no specimens in evidence.

In the absence of bank credit at that early stage of financial development, down payments were frequently made in kind.[2] Simon Schama, the historian, provided examples; in one case, for a pound of White Crowns (*Witte Croon* in Dutch, sold by weight because of its ordinariness) Fl. 525 was to be paid on delivery (presumably the next June), but four cows at once. Other down payments consisted of tracts of land, houses, furniture, silver and gold vessels, paintings, a suit and a coat, a coach and dapple-gray pair; and for a single Viceroy (rare), valued at Fl. 2,500, two *lasts* (a measure that varied by commodity and locality) of wheat and four of rye, eight pigs, a dozen sheep, two oxheads of wine, four tons of butter, a thousand pounds of cheese, a bed, some clothing, and a silver beaker.[3]

The tulipmania was not isolated. The Dutch economy had been depressed during the 1620s when war with Spain was resumed after a twelve-year truce, but recovered impressively in the 1630s. Shares in the Amsterdam Chamber of the Dutch East India Company doubled between 1630 and 1639, mostly after early 1636, going from 229 in March 1636 to 412 in August 1639, and rising another 20 percent to 500 by 1640. Houses had fallen in price in the early 1630s but 'shot up' in the middle of the decade, and other surging investments were made in drainage schemes, in the West Indies Company and in canals.[4] Jan de Vries wrote of the *trekschuit,* a system of passenger barge canals which got under way in 1636 and reached a 'fever' in 1640. Construction was undertaken between pairs of towns to make the travel of merchants and officials more dependable than by sailing ships which have to wait on wind and weather. Two lines from Amsterdam to smaller towns were decided on in 1636, and one between Leiden and Delft. Building of the complex network reached a peak in 1659 and 1665, but de Vries connected the project to the tulipmania and to the explosive growth of the Dutch economy between 1622 and 1660.[5]

Jonathan Israel wrote that the tulipmania should be viewed against the background of the general boom and as a mania of 'small-town dealers, tavern-keepers and horticulturalists' with the wealthy for the most part making money in other ways.[6] This perspective undermines one of Garber's points that there could have been no tulipmania because there was no depressed aftermath.[7] The Dutch economy slowed in the

1640s before putting on a tremendous spurt from 1650 to 1672. This extended especially to luxury housing, civic buildings, and paintings, the market for the last of which collapsed with the French invasion of 1672.[8] At the height of the boom there was a 'mania' for clocks and clock towers. In Leiden a clock was installed in a tower at the top of the White Gate where the station of the *trekschuit* loaded and unloaded passengers, to assure the punctuality of the personal barges.[9]

Did the decline in the prices of tulip bulbs lead to a decline in economic activity? The answer is yes, and the causal connection is that households were less eager spenders as their wealth declined.

The stock market and real estate

Many bubbles in stock markets are related to bubbles in real estate. There are three different types of connections between these two asset markets. One is that in many countries, especially smaller countries and those in the early stages of industrialization, a substantial amount of the stock market valuation consists of real estate companies, construction companies, and firms in other industries that are closely associated with real estate, including banks. A second connection is that individuals whose wealth has increased sharply as a result of the increase in real estate values want to keep their wealth diversified and so they buy stocks; there aren't many other easy ways to diversify wealth. The third connection is the mirror-image of the second; the individual investors who have profited extensively from the increase in stock market valuations buy larger and more expensive first homes and second homes. The fluctuations in the Manhattan real estate market have been tied to the bonuses on Wall Street.

Homer Hoyt's *One Hundred Years of Land Values in Chicago*[10] traced five cycles of boom and relapse in real estate prices in Chicago to the growth of the city. The boom in the U.S. stock market in 1928–1929 was linked to increases in prices of raw land, residential sites, commercial buildings in both the central business district and in the suburbs, both when prices were increasing and when they were declining. Hoyt quotes from a *Chicago Tribune* editorial of April 1890:

> In the ruin of all collapsed booms is to be found the work of men who bought property at prices they knew perfectly well were fictitious, but who were willing to pay such prices simply because they knew that some still greater fool could be depended on to take the property off their hands and leave them with a profit.[11]

Chicago's reputation for real estate booms was such that Berlin, overindulging in real estate speculation in the euphoria of victory over France in 1870–1871, was called 'Chicago on the [river] Spree.'[12] The booms in Berlin and Vienna in 1873 were related to that in the New York stock market. One writer claimed that in Chicago in 1871, every other man and every fourth woman had an investment in house lots.[13] The bubbles expanded in parallel until the summer of 1873.

The spread of euphoria from one market to another is easily understood. When asset prices are increasing at a rapid rate, the widows and orphans climb onto the bandwagon. Capital gains can be made without any special skill. When asset prices collapse, shareholders know they are in trouble and have to reduce their indebtedness; those investors who have high leverage recognize that their wealth is declining much more rapidly than stock prices and so they sell—or their positions are sold by their brokers and lenders.

Speculators in real estate initially feel no such compunction. Their debts are not day-to-day brokers' loans, but come from banks on extended terms. They have real assets, not just paper claims. Most choose to wait for the recovery that they think is just over the horizon.

The economic downturn leads to a drying up of the demand for real estate to hold and for land to build on. Taxes and interest on loans, however, continue without interruption. Hoyt wrote that slowly but inexorably the speculators in real estate are ground down. The lenders to the real estate speculators, and especially the bank lenders, incur large loan losses. One hundred and sixty-three out of 200 banks in Chicago in 1933 suspended payment. Real estate loans in default, not failed stockbrokers' accounts, were the largest single element in the failure of 4,800 banks in the years from 1930 to 1933.[14]

Hoyt's analysis of the relation between the stock market and the real estate market can be readily applied to the Japan of the 1990s. The large decline in real estate values meant that many borrowers defaulted on their real estate loans. The bank loans to credit cooperatives and other types of financial firms declined sharply in value because these firms had made real estate loans that were also below water. And the decline in real estate values led to a sharp decline in banks' capital since they owned large amounts of real estate.

The stock market's troubles of October 1987 cleared up brilliantly as the monetary authorities rapidly increased bank liquidity to forestall any shortage of credit. Margin requirements of 50 percent helped. But the agony in real estate was drawn out. Construction slowed as buildings were completed, but new starts abandoned. Vacancy rates in office buildings rose sharply, varying according to location, whether downtown, midtown, or in the 'edge cities' built in the suburbs during the 1980s boom.

Rockefeller Center Properties, Inc., had a $1.3 billion mortgage on the Rockefeller Center in midtown Manhattan after the complex had been sold to Mitsubishi Real Estate. The mortgage was held in a Real Estate Investment Trust (REIT). In 1987 the trustees sought to increase the income of the trust by using the cash from short-term loans to buy back bonds that were selling at a discount. The gains were paid out as dividends. In 1989 as the deterioration in the real estate market progressed, the trustees borrowed, using a letter of credit to get the cash to pay off the short-term debt. The president of the REIT said, 'It was a prudent thing to do at the time.'[15] Hoyt's analysis suggested that there would be an extended downturn in real estate values following a stock market crash. After prolonged agony, the REIT crashed.

The story of the collapse of the bubble in the Japanese real estate market in the 1990s begins in the early 1950s when GDP began to increase rapidly in both nominal and real terms from the sharply depressed values immediately after World War II. (Only in 1951 did Japanese per capita incomes return to 1940 levels.) Exports increased rapidly in value, and the composition of exports shifted from cheap toys and textiles to bicycles and motorcycles and then steel and autos and electronics. The government began to deregulate financial controls throughout the first half of the 1980s, and extensive efforts by the Bank of Japan to limit the appreciation of the yen in the second half of the 1980s led to rapid growth in the supplies of money and of credit.

Real estate prices increased steadily, although with substantial year-on-year variability. Because of financial regulation, the real rate of return on bank deposits and other fixed price assets in the 1950s, the 1960s, and the 1970s was negative; the nominal interest rate was lower than the annual inflation rate. The price index for residential real estate in six large cities started at 100 in 1955 and reached 4,100 in the mid-1970s and 5,800 in 1980; the owners of real estate were one of the few groups with a positive real rate of return. During the 1980s the price of real estate increased by a factor of nine.[16] At its peak, the value of real estate in Japan was twice the value of real estate in the United States; the ratio of the value of real estate to GDP in Japan was four times that in the United States.[17]

The Nikkei stock market index, which started at 100 in May 1949, had reached 6,000 by the early 1980s. Stock prices surged in the second half of the 1980s and nearly reached 40,000 at the end of 1989. The volume of shares traded did not quite keep pace, going from 120 billion shares in 1983 to 280 billion in 1989.[18]

The increase in the price of real estate fed the boom in stock prices. Many of the firms listed on the stock market were real estate companies that owned substantial amounts of land in central Tokyo and the other major cities. The boom in real estate prices and financial deregulation led to a surge in construction activity. Banks owned large amounts of real estate and stocks so increases in the values of real estate and stocks led to increases in the value of bank stocks. Banks usually required that borrowers pledge real estate; the increases in the value of real estate meant that the value of the collateral for loans increased, and the banks were eager to make more loans because they wanted to increase their size—their total footings—relative to other Japanese banks and banks in the United States and Europe. Industrial firms were increasingly eager to borrow to buy real estate, since the profit rate from owning real estate was many times higher than the profit rates from producing steel and automobiles and TV sets.

The rapid expansion of bank loans was facilitated by financial deregulation which was largely a response to pressure from foreign authorities, especially those in the United States. In part U.S. officials were motivated by the unevenness of the regulatory framework, since U.S. firms found many regulations impeded their expansion in the Tokyo markets while Japanese firms found it much easier to expand in the United States. In part the U.S. Treasury wanted Japanese financial institutions as buyers for U.S. government securities at a time when the U.S. fiscal deficit was surging.

Deregulation proceeded slowly and deliberately.[19] Of perhaps particular significance was the deregulation of interest rates paid by banks on large deposits, with the minimum reduced by steps from ¥1 billion (for terms of three months to two years) to ¥500 million and ¥300 million in 1986, ¥100 million (and one month) in 1987, ¥50 million and then ¥30 million in 1988, and ¥10 million in 1989.[20] In the early stages of this process, the Bank of Japan reduced its discount rate from 5.5 percent in 1982 to 5 percent in 1983, 3.5 percent at the beginning of 1986 and 2.5 percent a year later. The 1986 reduction was taken simultaneously with similar action by the Federal Reserve System in the United States and the Bundesbank in the Federal Republic of Germany. In reverse, however, first the United States in the middle of 1987 and Germany in

1988 began increasing their interest rates. The Bank of Japan waited until a new governor, Yasuki Mieno, took over in December 1989, and began to restrict real estate loans. The crash began in January 1990 and then became more intense when it became known that some major banks had made good losses on loans to favored customers and hidden these actions by imaginative accounting.[21]

The euphoria in Japan was evident in many ways. There was a boom in corporate investments in plant and equipment. The vision in Herman Kahn's *The Emerging Japanese Superstate: Challenge and Response,* published in 1970, appeared to be becoming reality.[22] Japanese firms were preparing for a glorious global future. There was a real estate construction boom; a favorite game was to count the cranes from the twentieth or thirtieth floor of an office building or hotel. Golf course construction surged. A new office building next to the Tokyo railroad station was named 'The Pacific Century Building.'

Stock prices peaked on the last trading day of 1989 and then declined by 30 percent in 1990. The trough for stock prices occurred in 2002 at a level that was a bit more than 20 percent of their peak values. Real estate prices fell more slowly but almost as extensively.

The result of the decline in asset values was that many financial institutions were decapitalized and remained in business only because of the implicit support of the government. A few were allowed (or forced) to close, although no depositor incurred a loss. The banks became owners of thousands of French paintings. Many golf courses went bankrupt.

Economic growth plummeted. The inflation rate began to fall and then ten years later the price level began to fall. The banks took over ownership titles to much of the French art. There was no way to recover the gold leaf that had been sprinkled on the desserts. The failures of firms meant that the banks took over title to the properties and sold the inventories, putting further downward pressure on the price levels which complicated the business plans of other firms. So there was a downward spiral and concern about a debt deflation trap.[23] Commercial and industrial enterprises were going bankrupt at a steady rate of 1,000 a month. Three large credit unions were rescued by the government. The capital adequacy problems of the banks and insurance companies were compounded by losses on their portfolios of foreign assets, a topic reserved for the next chapter. Two economic experts on Japan have characterized the country's problems for the next decade as 'debt, deflation, default, demography and deregulation.'[24]

Commodity prices, asset prices and monetary policy

The reduction in the Bank of Japan's discount rate, especially from 1986, which touched off the bubble, was stimulated by pressures from the United States and other industrialized countries and rationalized because the price level in Japan was steady. Prices of goods and services in Japan had been held down by the appreciation of the yen, which moved up from almost 240 to the dollar in 1985 to 130 in 1988. Despite the appreciation of the yen, Japan continued to have a current account surplus, although a somewhat smaller one.[25]

A major question is whether central bankers should be concerned with asset prices. Most central bankers choose price stability as the main target of monetary policy,[26] whether it be wholesale prices, the consumer price index, or the gross domestic product deflator is not a critical issue. Most recently the policy mantra has been inflation targeting—central banks aim to achieve an inflation rate no higher than 2 percent. If, however, the implosion of a bubble in stocks and/or real estate leads to a significant decline in bank solvency, should the central banker be concerned with asset prices? In one view, asset prices should be incorporated into the general price level because, in a world of efficient markets, they hold a forecast of future prices and consumption.[27] But this view assumes that asset prices are determined by the economic fundamentals and are not affected by herd behavior that leads to a bubble.

Central bankers traditionally have not been reluctant to raise interest rates to prevent an increase in the inflation rate. They are exceedingly reluctant to attempt to deal with asset price bubbles or even to recognize that they exist or could have existed—although they appear to be recognized after the fact. The sharp decline in U.S. stock prices in 2000 and 2001 was evidence that there had been an asset price bubble. The question is why those outside the Federal Reserve found it easier to recognize that the increase in stock prices was nonsustainable. And in that sense the much younger Federal Reserve of the 1920s seems more heroic in its statements about asset price developments.

7
International Contagion

Allocating the blame for crisis

A widespread historical pastime is fixing the national location where a crisis starts. President Herbert Hoover insisted that Europe primarily was responsible for the 1930s depression because of its cartels and the 'European statesmen [who] did not have the courage to face these issues.'[1] There was global overproduction of wheat, rubber, coffee, sugar, silver, zinc, and cotton. Hoover accepted some U.S. responsibility for stock market speculation. Friedman and Schwartz asserted that the crisis originated in the United States, although the gold-exchange standard rendered the international financial system vulnerable. The initial climactic event—the stock market crash—was American, and the developments that led to a decline in the stock of money in late 1930 were predominantly domestic.[2]

In 1837 President Jackson had placed the blame for that year's crisis on both Great Britain and the United States:

> It would seem impossible for sincere inquiries after the truth to resist the conviction that the causes of the revulsion in both countries have been substantially the same. Two nations, the most commercial in the world, enjoying but recently the highest degree of apparent prosperity, are suddenly, without any great national calamity, arrested in that career, and plunged into embarrassment and distress. In both countries have we witnessed the same redundancy of paper money, and other facilities of credit, the same spirit of speculation, the same partial success, the same difficulties and reverses, and, at length, the same overwhelming catastrophe.[3]

Although observers in the 1850s called the panics of 1836–1837 the 'American panics' because they originated in and were confined to the banks that traded with the United States,[4] the conclusion of a modern economist that it was 'futile to try to draw any hard-and-fast line assigning to either country causal primacy in the cycle as a whole or in its individual phases'[5] can be viewed as a generic appraisal of many crises.

Friedman and Schwartz cited the pattern of gold movements to blame the United States for the recession of 1920–1921.[6]

Another observer disagreed:

> How was [the early postwar fall in economic activity] brought about? . . . I think the answer must be: It was a deliberate policy inaugurated by the two economically dominating countries, the U.K. and the U.S.A. It is impossible to give priority to any of them. The earliest official statement of the policy was undoubtedly made by England. On the other hand, causally U.S.A.'s policy must have the greater weight.[7]

A few crises are purely national—the gold agio crisis in the United States in 1869, the City of Glasgow Bank in 1878, the Union Générale in France in 1882. The Canadian financial crises that occurred in 1879, 1887, and 1908 seemed related to major financial currents that bound Western Europe, Scandinavia, and the United States together.[8]

Some countries may not be affected by international crises that impact neighboring countries and for obvious reasons. France was not affected in 1873 because it had undergone severe deflation in 1871 and 1872 in the effort to transfer reparations to Prussia. The United States was insulated from the European potato disease and the tumultuous European wheat situation in 1847 because U.S. railroads had not yet developed to the point where U.S. food markets were closely linked to those in Europe.

For the most part however financial crises ricochet from one country to another. Juglar,[9] Mitchell,[10] and Morgenstern[11] noted that financial crises tend to be international, and either affect a number of countries at the same time or alternatively spread from the centers where they originate to other countries.

One of the several different types of links between these countries is that arbitrage connects national markets; the implication of the law of one price is that the difference in the prices of identical or similar goods in various countries cannot exceed the costs of transport and trade barriers. The links between commodity markets in different countries may involve only a modest amount of trade. When the price of cotton soared in the 1830s in one country, the price increased in all other countries; similarly the decline in the price of cotton after 1864 was worldwide. A decline in the price of a given commodity—especially a widely-traded product like wheat or cotton—may produce bankruptcies and bank failures far from the source of the original change in demand or supply and price, depending on the vulnerability of markets and the amount of the leverage of speculators in each of these markets.

Similarly the security markets in the various countries are also linked, since the prices of internationally-traded securities available in different national markets must be virtually identical after a conversion of prices in one currency into the equivalent in other currencies at the prevailing exchange rates. The prices of internationally-traded securities that are listed on the stock exchanges in several different countries increase and decrease together. The prices of domestic securities often move in a synchronous fashion with internationally-traded securities even though there may be few actual trades as a result of psychological linkages or through impacts on interest rates transmitted through short-term capital movements.

In 1929 all stock markets crashed simultaneously and again in October 1987 virtually all of the stock markets declined at the same time (ironically the one exception was the Tokyo market which then seemed the most overvalued). Even though national financial markets generally were believed to be more fully integrated in the 1980s and the 1990s than in earlier periods, share prices in the 1920s were as strongly correlated as in later decades. Because of the strong correlation of the stock price movements in different countries, many of the investors who sought to reduce risk by diversification through ownership of stocks in different national markets obtained smaller reductions in risk than they had anticipated.

When changes in stock prices are small, the correlations between the stock price movements in different national markets are low. As the scope of the changes in stock prices increases, the correlations become larger.

The pattern in the correlation between changes in stock prices in different countries is somewhat asymmetric in that changes in U.S. stock prices have a much more powerful impact on stock prices in various foreign countries than changes in stock prices elsewhere have on the U.S. Stock prices in the U.S. continued to rise in the early 1990s despite the decline in stock prices in Tokyo—but when U.S. stock prices declined in 2001 stock prices in Tokyo, London, and Frankfurt declined. The Mexican financial crisis of 1994–1995 (which triggered the 'Tequila Crises') impacted both Brazil and Argentina; the mechanism was that U.S.-based investors became somewhat more cautious in buying both Latin American bonds and stocks. The devaluation of the Thai baht in early July 1997 triggered the 'contagion effect' and induced devaluations in nearby Asian countries in the following six months and then spread eventually to Russia and Brazil.

Transmission mechanisms

Booms and panics are transmitted from one country to another in several different ways, including arbitrage in commodities or securities and movements of money in various forms (specie, bank deposits, bills of exchange), cooperation among monetary authorities, and pure psychology.[12]

The security and asset markets in various countries are linked by movements of money. The inflation in the United States in the late 1960s and the early 1970s led to an increase in capital flows from the United States to Germany and Japan and other countries and the result was that the inflation rates in these countries increased as their monetary bases and their money supplies increased. Capital movements may respond to real causes, including wars and revolutions, technical innovations and the opening of new markets and new sources of raw materials, and to changes in the relationship between the growth rates in different countries, as well as to changes in monetary policy and fiscal policy. The privatization of government-owned firms in different countries often induces inflows of foreign buyers. The awareness that a currency may be 'mis-priced' in the foreign exchange market induces capital flows.

Consider the connections between the appreciation of a currency and deflation in that country's goods market (or the connections between the depreciation of a currency and inflation in that country's goods market); the increase in the foreign exchange value of the national currency leads to declines in the prices of internationally-traded goods and to bankruptcies and the decapitalization of financial firms. The appreciation of the Japanese yen has put downward pressure on the prices of internationally-traded goods in Japan. The depreciation of the Argentine, Uruguayan, Australian, and New Zealand currencies in the early 1930s contributed to the decline in wheat prices in the United States which in turn led to bankruptcies among farmers as well as failures of banks in farm communities, particularly in Missouri, Indiana, Illinois, Iowa, Arkansas, and North Carolina.[13]

Booms and busts are connected internationally and in several different ways. An economic boom in one country almost always attracts money from abroad. Similarly, a boom in one country may reduce the flow of money to others; thus in 1872 Berlin and Vienna stopped lending to New York, while the U.S. stock market boom in 1928 led to a sharp curtailment in loans to and bond purchases from Germany, Australia, and Latin America and tipped their economies downward before the October 1929 stock market crash in New York. Similarly in 1982 the collapse of syndicated bank loans to Mexico, Brazil, and Argentina led to a sharp decline in the foreign exchange value of their currencies.

Stock prices and real estate prices increased sharply in the Scandinavian countries in the late 1980s; with a three-fold increase in Norway in the second half of the 1980s and a five-fold increase in Sweden and Finland.[14]

The surge in real estate prices and stock prices in Tokyo in the 1980s had a major impact on the real estate market in Hawaii, which is to Tokyo as Miami is to New York. Japanese tourists visit Hawaii often, many Japanese are married there. Many Japanese have bought second homes in Hawaii. Japanese real estate firms bought land in Hawaii to develop golf courses around hotels; one expensive hotel property would have had to have charged $800 per room per night to cover its costs. When the boom in Tokyo ended, Hawaii entered an extended period of economic stagnation—a lost decade.

The *Kipper- und Wipperzeit*

This pathological financial episode is interesting because the financial crisis occurred with only metallic money and without bank credit. Princes, abbots, bishops, even the Holy Roman Emperor debased the subsidiary coinage used in daily transactions (but not gold and silver coin of large denominations) by raising the denomination of existing coins, substituting base for good metals, and reducing the metallic content of coins to extract more seignorage to prepare for the Thirty Years' War that broke out in 1618. Debasement was limited at first to their own territory. Some entrepreneurial spirit then found that it was more profitable to take bad coins across the borders into neighboring principalities to exchange them for good coins with ignorant common people; the good coins were then brought back to the home territory and debased. The territorial unit on which the original injury had been inflicted would debase its own coin in defense and turn to other neighbors to make good its losses and build its war chest. More and more mints were established to extract more seignorage.

Debasement accelerated in hyperfashion until the subsidiary coins became practically worthless, and children played with them in the street, much as recounted in Leo Tolstoy's short story, 'Ivan the Fool.'

Some local sources set forth the view that the first invasion of debased money came from Italy and from there to southern Germany through the Bishop of Chur on Lake Constance. The same source at Ulm, however, claimed that the counterfeiting of the Upper Rhine Circle that included Strasbourg was especially outrageous. Beginning on a small scale around 1600, debasement slowly picked up speed after 1618 and spread over Germany and Austria and to what became Hungary and Czechoslovakia and into Poland and, according to some sources, to the Near and Far East by way of Lvov in Russia.[15]

South Sea and Mississippi bubbles

Åkerman called the crisis of 1720 the first international crisis, because the speculation of 1717 to 1720 in France and Great Britain affected the cities of the Netherlands and northern Italy as well as Hamburg.[16] The South Sea and Mississippi bubbles were connected in several ways. As early as 1717 British investors began to follow trading in the shares of John Law's banks and companies on the Rue de Quincampoix in Paris. In May 1719 the British ambassador in Paris had received letters from friends and relatives in Scotland begging him to buy stock for them in the Compagnie des Indes. Thirty thousand foreigners, including British nobility, traveled to Paris to subscribe in person. In May, Ambassador Stair urged his government to do something to compete with John Law and slow the flow of money from Great Britain into Paris. As Law's system peaked in December 1719, some speculators, including the Duke of Chandos, sold South Sea stock and bought Mississippi stock.[17]

While British speculators were buying Mississippi stock in Paris, many continentals were buying South Sea stock in London. Sir Theodore Janssen had a long list of subscribers from Geneva, Paris, Amsterdam, and the Hague. One of the French investors was the banker Martin, who as already noted was recorded by Charles McKay as subscribing £500 with the remark: 'When the rest of the world are mad, we must imitate them in some measure.' When the early birds liquidated in July, the Canton of Berne, which had speculated with £200,000 of public funds, sold for a profit of £2 million.[18]

Amsterdam profited from its position between Paris and London. The Dutch sold their stock in Mississippi Compagnie des Indes at the right psychological moment and lost little in the crash. In April 1720, a bit prematurely perhaps, David Leeuw liquidated his South Sea stock and bought Bank of England and East India Company stock. By the end of that month, the Dutch banker Crellius observed coolly that Exchange Alley resembled 'nothing so much as if all the Lunatics had escaped out of the Madhouse at once.'[19] In June and July there were twelve-hour relays by ship between Great Britain and Amsterdam, and on July 16 some eighty Jews, Presbyterians, and Anabaptists, speculators from Exchange Alley, were off to Holland and Hamburg to enhance their fortunes by speculating in continental insurance stocks.[20]

By the autumn of 1720 London and the Continent were sharing the financial disaster. Samuel Bernard, a French banker, was sent to London to sell South Sea stock against gold, to be brought back to France in revulsion against Law's system. Dutch banks 'shortened sail, recalling advances, refusing further credit, selling stocks held as collateral.'[21] The price of the British pound in terms of the guilder in Amsterdam, which had risen from 35.4 guilders to the pound to 36.1 when the first increase in South Sea stock took place in April and 'France, Holland and to some extent Denmark, Spain and Portugal' were buying, declined to 33.9 on September 1 as 'foreigners lost their taste for English securities.' At the height of the panic it recovered to 35.2.[22]

1763 to 1819

The crisis of 1763 involved mainly Holland, Hamburg, Prussia, and Scandinavia, with repercussions on, and help from, London. France was not involved; the Seven Years' War had been directed against France. George Chalmers, a perceptive contemporary observer, claimed that speculation in land in the United States was a factor in the crisis although the statement is not supported in other writings.[23] Amsterdam had been the entrepôt center for the payment of money to British allies, and the Dutch had been expanding credit by investing both in British government stock and in *Wisselruiti* (chains of accommodation bills) that led to a giddy credit edifice on a small base (the proverbial 'house of cards') with bills drawn on merchant houses in Stockholm, Hamburg, Bremen, Leipzig,

Altona, Lubeck, Copenhagen, and St Petersburg. Bills of exchange drawn with the security of goods shipped also circulated in Amsterdam in addition to the accommodation paper. When prices of commodities fell after the war—especially sugar as imports from the French West Indies were resumed—the bills could not be paid.[24] Hamburg warned Amsterdam houses that they would suspend payment unless support was furnished to the DeNeufvilles. In one account, the letter arrived too late.[25] Another stated that a plan to save the firm failed because its reputation was too bad.[26] In the long run, the DeNeufvilles would have been able to pay 70 percent of their obligations, but they settled with creditors for 60 percent before that became known. In the end, the Hamburg creditors had to wait thirty-six years to collect even that much.[27] The *coup de grâce* occurred when King Frederick II of Prussia who had debased the silver coins in 1759 to help fight the war recalled the old coins and had new ones minted in Amsterdam on the basis of credits from the Dutch bankers.[28] Withdrawing the old coins before issuing new ones put deflationary pressure on credit because the money supply declined.

London came to the rescue of Amsterdam and took over a considerable portion of Dutch trade and finance with Scandinavia and Russia. Very much against his will, King Frederick had to assist Berlin merchants that were caught in the crisis as their bills were protested.[29] Swedish houses complained early in the fall of 1762 that bills they drew were protested and not paid in Amsterdam while remittances sent to cover the bills were retained. Whether Amsterdam tried to save itself by selling its British securities is debatable. Wilson claimed that in this way Amsterdam exported the crisis to London. Carter insisted she cannot find evidence of sales in the transfer books.[30]

The 1772 crisis spread from Scotland and London to Amsterdam and thence to Stockholm and St Petersburg. Heavy outflows of specie from Paris to London fed the canal and country bank mania during the Reign of Terror in 1792 that peaked with the guillotining of Louis XVI in January 1793; the direction of flow of precious metals reversed itself in 1797 when monetary order had been more or less restored under the Consulate after the Assignats.

The British crisis of 1810 was highly localized: British exporters first overdid sales to Brazil and then were cut off from their Baltic outlets by the blockade. There were echoes of this crisis in Hamburg and in New York.

The international aspects of the crises of 1816 and 1819 resulted because the prospect of the end of war in 1814 led to large British sales of manufactures on the Continent. Smart called this an exporting frenzy that soon broke like the South Sea and Mississippi bubbles. When prices collapsed, the goods were sent to North America which led to the tariff of 1816 in the United States. The result was a deep depression without a panic or even a crisis.[31] In 1818 and 1819 there were panics on both sides of the Atlantic that were connected in a nonobvious way. The 1819 crisis in Britain followed the collapse of commodity speculation in 1818, the discredit and distress 'originating clearly in great previous overtrading.'[32] The year 1819 was marked by the resumption of specie payments and by the Peterloo massacre, when protesting Manchester workers and their families were charged by cavalry who killed at least eight protesters; Smart called it a 'disastrous year.'[33] In America, the Second Bank of the United States precipitated a panic by having its branches call on state banks to redeem large balances and notes in its holdings. The purpose was to assemble $4 million in specie to repay the borrowing undertaken in Europe in 1803 to pay for the Louisiana Purchase.[34] But the Second Bank itself was a bubble, having been reestablished in 1817 after dissolution in 1811. The bank was run by greedy and corrupt directors who accepted promissory notes in payment of stock, registered stock in different names to get around the law limiting concentration of ownership, voted loans on the security of bank stock, permitted other loans without collateral, and allowed accounts to be overdrawn. Hammond observed that the sober pace of eighteenth-century business had given way to a democratic passion to get rich quick, and that men imbued with this passion and unscrupulousness had gained control of the Second Bank.[35]

1825 to 1896

The 1825 crisis involved Great Britain and South America, although there was a distinct spillover to Paris that stretched out until panic struck there in January 1828. With the panic in London in December 1825, continental sales halted, impacting banks in Paris, Lyons, Leipzig, and Vienna and obliging Italy and other markets that depended on these centers for finance to reduce their purchases. Distress from burdensome stocks in the textile-producing area of Alsace was general; firms were low on money and circulated between 9 million francs and 16 million francs in promissory notes as a substitute for money. When this edifice was toppled in December 1827 by Parisian banks' refusal to renew the Alsatian paper, the London crisis that resulted from overtrading in South American stocks had arrived on the Continent.[36]

Åkerman calls the crises of 1825 and 1836 'Anglo-American' in contrast to the one in 1847 that was Anglo-French.[37] The first two were Anglo-American in different ways: the 1825 crisis was Anglo-South American, the 1836 crisis Anglo-United States. In addition, the situation in 1836 was more complex than the one in 1825.

As noted earlier, President Jackson considered that responsibility for the crisis of 1836 to 1839 should be divided equally between Great Britain and the United States, while Matthews thought it futile to assign causal primacy. Monetary expansion in the two countries was vastly different. Wildcat banking aided by silver imports had started in the United States while new joint-stock banks had been established in Great Britain following new legislation in 1826 and 1833. British speculation was in cotton, cotton textiles, and railroads; American speculation was in cotton and land, especially land that could grow cotton. Moreover, Anglo-American houses in Great Britain financed British exports to the United States.

The crisis was by no means a purely Anglo-U.S. affair, although it is often discussed in these terms with emphasis on its impact on the evolution of the Bank of England's discount policy.[38] Hawtrey states that it started in Great Britain in 1836 and 1837, spread to the United States, and then in May 1838, when Great Britain was quietly recuperating, erupted in Belgium, France, and Germany to spread back again to Great Britain and to the United States in 1839.[39] The crisis in the United States also affected France and Germany directly through the decline in the volume of imports, price declines and a series of financial connections. Lyons felt the loss of outlets for silk immediately. American purchases were important to the success of the fairs in Frankfurt and in Leipzig. American commission houses in Paris, which financed their purchases largely in London, and the American banker Samuel Welles, who also relied on London for finance, were threatened with failure as early as the spring of 1837.[40] The Maison Hottinguer, a French bank, helped Nicholas Biddle of the Bank of the United States underwrite the corner in cotton, which strangled cotton spinners in Manchester, Rouen, and Alsace in the summer and fall of 1838 before the collapse of the corner in November of that year that followed from an Anglo-French boycott.[41] Moreover the Bank of France provided assistance to the Bank of England. By the 1830s, the financial world had complex transatlantic relations in trade, commodity prices, and capital flows between Great Britain, the United States and France.

In January 1847 distress developed in London in response to railroad calls and the crisis came late in the summer. Åkerman stated that the

Table 7.1 Reported Failures in the Crisis of 1847–1848, by Cities (Number of Failures)

	1847					1848								
City	**Aug**	**Sept**	**Oct**	**Nov**	**Dec**	**Jan**	**Feb**	**Mar**	**Apr**	**May**	**June**	**July**	**Aug**	**Oct–Dec**
London	11	19	21	25	7	3	7	3	1	8	2	1	1	1
Liverpool	5	4	28	10	4		3						1	
Manchester		6	11	8	1				1					
Glasgow	2	4	6	9	7	6				1				
Other U.K.	2	4	16	7	7	2		1	1					1
Calcutta					1	11	5		1	2				1
Other British Empire											1	2	1	4
Paris		1				2	1	14	2					
Le Havre				1			1	5	2					
Marseilles		1			1	1		2	13					
Other France			2			1		1		1	1			
Amsterdam				3	1	1		14	4		1			
Other Low Countries	1		1	4				4		1	1			
Hamburg	1			2		1			7	4	3	1		
Frankfurt					3	1			1					
Berlin								3	4	1				
Other Germany		2			1		1		6					
Italy		3		7	1									
Other Europe		1		3	2	1	1		1	1				
New York		1		3	1				1	5				4
Other U.S.														7
Elsewhere		1			1					2	1			2

Source: Derived from names of firms and banks listed by D. Morier Evans, *The Commercial Crisis, 1847–48* (1849; reprint edn, New York: Augustus M. Keliey, 1969), pp. 69, 74, 91–2, 103–4, 105–6, 112–13, 118–20, 123, 127.

distress was Anglo-French, but it had echoes in British-Indian trade, in Amsterdam and the Low Countries, and to a certain extent in Germany and even New York. Some sense of the spread of the crisis can be gained from the record of bankruptcies collected by Evans that listed the number of bankruptcies but not the value of the assets of failed banks and firms. The data are likely to be more complete for Great Britain than for other countries since Evans reported only the 'principal foreign failures.' Despite its serious deficiencies a table showing the monthly failures provides a useful impression of how the shock wave of the crisis spread. The British crisis is seen to have almost died away, except for London, when revolution in France and Germany produced the reactions of March and April 1848 that are probably under-recorded in Evans's data.[42]

The failure of the A. Schaaffhausen Bank of Cologne on March 29, 1848, played a role in the development of German banking. The Prussian government allowed the bank to be saved via conversion into a joint-stock company, despite its standing policy of opposition to credit expansion; this precedent paved the way for the substantial expansion of German banks in the 1850s with important consequences for German economic growth.[43] Since Cologne had been a Hanseatic city, the bank was probably tied into the merchant banking network of London-Antwerp-Hamburg-Bremen-Le Havre-Marseilles featured so prominently by Evans. A local source claimed that Cologne was at the crossroads of trade between Holland, Brabant, France, and eastern and upper Germany and that the city suffered many bankruptcies as a consequence of the British crisis of 1825. The source admitted that apart from some financing of leather imports from Latin America, most banking finance was local and undertaken for heavy industry. Johann Wolter and Abraham Schaaffhausen got their start as leather merchants, purchasing Latin American hides from Spain, first through Amsterdam and then directly. Abraham, the son, was a merchant, commission agent, forwarder, and banker with international connections. The trouble in 1848 however came largely from financing real estate investments in Cologne. Almost one-quarter of the portfolio of the bank consisted of owned land and loans to a single builder that together amounted to 1.6 million thalers compared to the bank's capital of 1.5 million. As social unrest increased and depositors sought cash, the bank first took on a Dutch partner and then received help from the Prussian Bank's branch in Cologne, the same bank's branch in Münster, the Prussian Seehandlung (another state financial agency), and the Prussian lottery. Permission for A. Schaaffhausen to convert into *A. Schaaffhausen'scher Bankverein* may have been related to the fact that joint-stock banks were forbidden to invest in building sites and all other forms of speculation.[44]

The boom leading up to the panic of 1857 was worldwide. Gold discoveries in California (1849) and Australia (1851) led to export spurts to those countries and enlarged the credit bases in Europe and the United States. It would have done so to a greater extent had it not been for the fact that India was exporting far more than it was importing and beginning to receive, along with the United States, the capital flow from Britain which had been discouraged from investing on the Continent by the revolutions of 1848. The balance of payments surplus was taken in silver, replaced in Europe by newly-mined gold. Both Europe and the United States had railroad and banking booms. Expansion also came from joint-stock banks in Great Britain and Germany and from the *Crédit Mobilier, Crédit Foncier,* and *Crédit Agricole* in France which made large loans to trade and industry. Scandinavia in particular had been stimulated by the boom in trade generated by the repeal of the British Corn Laws, timber duties, and Navigation Acts.[45] Bad harvests and the Crimean War, which cut off Russian exports, raised the price of grain for farmers worldwide. These were, in fact, golden years for British farmers, despite the repeal of the Corn Laws in 1846. After the war, grain prices sank as Russian supplies came back on the market, and railroad building declined. The dominoes started their collapse in Ohio—or, rather, the New York branch of an Ohio bank—and fell in New York, Ohio, Pennsylvania, Maryland, Rhode Island, and Virginia, and then in Liverpool, London, Paris, Hamburg, Oslo, and Stockholm. Evans's data on bankruptcies for 1857 are sketchier than those for 1847 and so the path of failures cannot be traced. The failure of the New York branch of the Ohio Life and Trust Company occurred around the same time as British withdrawals of funds from the United States in response to increases in interest rates in London.

The concentrated nature of the crisis from the Ohio Life revelation on August 24 to suspension of the Bank Act in London on November 12 through Hamburg's loan from Austria (the *Silberzug*) on December 10 is striking. Clapham observed that the crisis appeared at almost the same moment in the United States, Great Britain, and Central Europe and was felt in South America, South Africa, and the Far East.[46] Rosenberg calls it 'the first worldwide crisis.' The chamber of commerce of Elberfeld asserted: 'The world is a unit; industry and trade have made it so.'[47]

The crisis of 1866 is the tail end of one that began in 1864. Åkerman said that it parallels the 1857 crisis, insofar as it followed the Civil War as 1857 followed the Crimean War, and as the collapse of cotton in 1866 paralleled the collapse of wheat a decade earlier.[48] The inclusion of 1864 eliminates a general view that the crisis was strictly British.[49] The timing of the panic on Black Friday, May 11, 1866, was intimately tied to the Prussian-Austrian war, largely through stock market collapses attributable to rumors of war and then the advent of the war, and then to the *corso forzoso* of May 11, 1866, when the Italian government suspended convertibility of the lira into gold and in return for this privilege borrowed 250 million lire from the national bank.[50] Like the Overend, Gurney collapse, the *corso forzoso* had been triggered by an internal run on notes against gold, stimulated by capital withdrawals toward Paris that in turn had suffered from sales of foreign securities. The London market was shaky in mid-April because of rumors of war. The Berlin bourse panicked on May 2 with mobilization and again on May 12 when war broke out. The Prussian Bank raised its discount rate to 9 percent on May 11. The panic in London that same day was part of a general rush for liquidity against a vulnerable company at a time of acute financial distress. Alfred André, a Parisian banker with major interests in Egypt, spent 'an exhausting week' in London looking after the interests of his firm at the time of the Overend, Gurney crisis. He returned to Paris on May 17, having concluded that the finance companies were ruined and that business was paralyzed in Italy, Prussia, Austria, and Russia, with France standing up pretty well, but only for a moment.[51]

There is no obvious connection between the U.S. gold crisis of September 1869 and the Austrian crisis of the same month. Both national currencies were floating. Both countries had had investment booms following their wars, although the devastation from the conflict had been much greater in the United States. Wirth prefaced his brief discussion of the 'great crash of 1869,' which preceded the real great crash of 1873, with some remarks about German and Austrian investments in the United States, the invasion of European markets by U.S. goods, and the extension of shipping and banking connections across the Atlantic.[52] Since Wirth did not mention the U.S. gold crisis, however, it seems unlikely that he was suggesting a connection. The accounts of the 1869 gold crisis in the United States ignore Austria.[53] A possible link may run through the price of wheat, which Jay Gould and Jim Fisk were trying to raise when they bid up the gold premium (e.g., the discount on the greenback dollar). The difficulties following the September 1869 'crash' were concentrated in Hungary which was a wheat-growing country.[54] Gould states that the United States could sell wheat to Great Britain in competition with the low-priced labor and water transportation from the Mediterranean with the gold agio at 45, but the United States could not sell wheat with gold below 40.[55] The decline in the gold agio in the United States in September should have assisted Hungarian economic prospects.

The 1873 story begins with the Franco-Prussian indemnity that was one-tenth paid in gold in 1871 and led to substantial speculation in Germany which then spilled over into Austria.[56] Jay Cooke, a latecomer to railroad finance and seeking capital for railroads in Europe, overextended himself with the Northern Pacific; he tried to borrow in Frankfurt but could not compete with the German and Austrian building booms.[57] Other shocks included the opening of the Suez Canal in 1869, the mistake of the German authorities in paying out new coin before withdrawing the old silver coins, the Chicago fire of October 9, 1871,[58] and especially the excitement generated by German unification under the leadership of Prussia's Bismarck. German acquisition of £90 million from the indemnity endangered stability in Great Britain because of the threat of conversion into gold. France deflated to pay the indemnity and was not affected by the inflation that occurred elsewhere in Europe.

A major question is the connection between the collapse in May 1873 in Austria and Germany after some months of distress and that in the United States in September. One linkage is through the changes in German investments in American railroads; initially German investors speculated in the railroads and western lands and then there was an abrupt halt to further investment. McCartney stated that 1873 is generally accepted as the first significant international crisis. The crisis erupted in Austria and Germany in May; spread to Italy, Holland, and Belgium and then to the United States in September; and then later involved Great Britain, France, and Russia. A second panic indeed hit Vienna on November 1 but was shortlived.[59] Morgenstern noted 'clear evidence of transmission throughout the year, extended to Amsterdam and Zurich' in his table of international stock exchange panics.[60] In the fall of 1875, Baron Carl Meyer von Rothschild wrote to Gerson von Bleichröder and commented on the low state of stock market prices everywhere, noting that 'the whole world has become a city.'[61]

A series of less intimately related failures and panics followed, including the City of Glasgow in 1878, Union Générale in 1882, and the New York stock market in 1884; the European-wide stock market panics in 1887 over the threat of war between Russia and Turkey; the copper corner in 1888 in Paris with the failure of the Comptoir d'Escompte; and the Baring crisis of 1890, the Panama scandal of 1892, and the New York panic of 1893. Their propagation was studied in detail by Morgenstern[62] and

Pressnell who focused especially on the Baring crisis and attached particular importance to its impact on the Bank of England's gold reserves.[63] The 1890 Baring crisis produced financial stringency rather than panic in New York as British investors sold good U.S. stocks to carry bad Latin American loans.[64] One view is that the financial crisis in New York in October 1890 precipitated the Baring Brothers collapse in November by producing a number of failures in London, which made it more difficult for Baring to continue in a period of acute distress. The Baring crisis, induced by difficulties in Argentina, brought a sharp decline in British lending worldwide and precipitated or contributed strongly to economic crises in South Africa, Australia, and the United States down to 1893.[65]

1907

The crisis of 1907 began several years earlier in Italy.[66] Italy had participated in the upswing of the first several years of the century. Speculation fed by credit had been rife. There were fictitious ventures and a steel trust that used funds ostensibly borrowed for real investment to speculate in its own securities; high dividends were paid with the cash from borrowings to stimulate investor interest. Distress set in in May 1905 with the collapse of many new companies. A second relapse occurred on the Genoa stock market in October 1906. By April and May 1907 lending from Paris and London had slowed and the distress became more acute. The Società Bancaria Italiana had started in 1898 with capital of 4 million lire, which was raised to 5 million in 1899, 9 million in 1900, 20 million in 1904, 30 million in 1905, and 50 million in March 1906. New personnel and old and often troubled banks were acquired as the capital was increased at each stage.[67] The head office of the bank in Milan did not know the risks that had been acquired by its branch in Genoa.[68] In particular, the bank was deeply involved in advances on securities (*riporti*). Governor Stringher of the Banca d'ltalia was worried because of the poor quality of its loans and the large amount it had borrowed from the central bank by December 1906. When Paris and London cut off new credits to Italy and to the United States in the spring of 1907, the upstart, marginal bank was doomed. Direct connections between Turin-Milan-Genoa and New York were limited. But Italian centers were connected to Paris; New York was connected mainly to London; and Paris and London to each other. Bonelli asserted that when Paris sold its British securities, and Paris and London both stopped lending, the colonial countries suddenly found themselves deprived of capital and were obliged to halt ongoing investment projects with consequent downward pressure on demand and output and employment and prices. The analogy between Italy in 1907 and a colonial territory is striking. Bonelli asserted that the Paris cut-off of loans to Italy would have had much more serious consequences if it not been for emigrant remittances, largely from the United States.[69] There was a direct connection across the Atlantic, largely New York to Naples. Bonelli's account focused on the narrow direct connections and contrasted with that of a contemporary observer, a New York banker named Frank Vanderlip, in a paper called 'The Panic as a World Phenomenon.' Vanderlip asserted that the basic causes of the panic were the Boer War, the Russo-Japanese War, and the San Francisco earthquake. But after such a grandiose beginning, he discussed overtrading by newly formed trust companies and the need for an expansive currency.[70]

The international ramifications of 1929

President Hoover stated that some part of the real cause of the depression was expansion of production outside of Europe during World War I, expansion that proved excessive at 1925 prices when European production recovered after that year. In addition, there were the financial complications of reparations and war debts; an overvalued British pound and an undervalued French franc, and the recycling of German reparations after the Dawes Plan by American private purchases of the bonds of German corporations and public bodies. Some blame attaches to the reduction of interest rates in New York in the summer of 1927 to assist Great Britain to maintain the overvalued parity for the pound when U.S. domestic purposes might have been better served by an increase. When prices in the New York stock market began to increase in March 1928 and especially after June, U.S. purchases of foreign bonds came to a halt. For a time, Germany, the Latin American countries and Australia shifted to short-term borrowing. Germany responded to the reduced inflow of capital by deflating its economy so it would have the cash to make reparations payments abroad. Argentina, Australia, Uruguay, and Brazil found their balances of payments turning sharply adverse. Unable to fund their accumulations of short-term indebtedness or to borrow more, the currencies of these countries began to depreciate shortly after the stock market crash of October 1929, as the prices of such items as wheat, coffee, rubber, sugar, silk, and cotton fell sharply. Prices and business in the United States were strongly affected by the liquidity seizure noted in Chapter 4.

An open-market program undertaken by the Federal Reserve Bank of New York on its own initiative, over the protest of the Federal Reserve

Board in Washington, alleviated the credit squeeze early in 1929. There was an increase in international lending in the first half of 1930; the volume of international lending in the April–June quarter was larger than in any other quarter in the 1920s and the 1930s. However, the lowered level of prices and the loss of confidence in Germany, especially after the National Socialist gains in the September 1930 elections, meant that the world remained in distress. Banks in Central Europe, largely Austria and Germany, tried to improve their positions by bidding up the prices of their own stocks. Two private banks, the Banque Adam and the Banque Oustric, failed in Paris, the latter unleashing a scandal that implicated three government officials and led to the fall of the government. The deflationary Laval government came to power early in 1931. And then the rolling deflation started: the failure of the Credit Anstalt in Vienna in May, the failure of the Danatbank in Germany in July, the German standstill agreement of July, a series of withdrawals from London in August, culminating in the decision of the British in September 1931 to break the link between the pound and gold. At this stage the gold bloc of France, Belgium, the Netherlands, and Switzerland started buying gold with U.S. dollars and the withdrawal of gold from the United States reduced the reserves of U.S. banks. Japan went off gold in December 1931. Deflation in the United States came from appreciation of the U.S. dollar (that is, the depreciation of the British pound and the currencies of the sterling area countries that were pegged to the pound) and from the reduction of bank reserves. In February 1932 the Glass-Steagall Act made it possible to reflate through open-market operations, but it was too late. Bank failures continued to spread in a positive feedback debt deflation process of declining goods prices, bankruptcies, and bank failures. The economy reached the bottom with the general Bank Holiday that began in March 1933 and the depreciation of the dollar in the spring of that year.

This history does not lead to the conclusion that the 1930s depression originated in the United States.

Contagion and the East Asian crisis

The East Asian crisis that spread halfway round the world had its proximate origin on July 2, 1997 when Thailand declared its inability to service its foreign debt. The blame for the rolling crisis was divided by most observers between the countries in trouble—especially Thailand, Indonesia, Malaysia, and South Korea—the experts, governmental and private, who urged deregulation on them, and the borrowers and lenders themselves, especially, among the latter, the bankers and investment houses that rushed to lend foreign currencies and then halted the lending abruptly. The Asian crisis seemed particularly surprising because the East Asian Tigers had grown so rapidly in the 1980s and 1990s. Herd behavior among the Tigers took the form of large borrowings in foreign currencies, speculative investments in real estate and pegging their currencies to the U.S. dollar, which led to overvaluation of their currencies as their domestic price levels increased. The Hong Kong authorities retained control of interest rates by lowering the limit permitted for loans on construction—from 90 percent at the start of the 1990s to 60 percent in the mid-1990s—so that interest rates could be raised without imposing large losses on bank mortgages. There were differences between countries; the Thai government, for example, was honest, weak, and indecisive; the Indonesian, corrupt, strong, and decisive.[71] Policies differed as well. Thailand lost $24 billion of reserve assets while defending the baht against speculators, and then it allowed the baht to depreciate. In contrast Indonesia permitted the rupiah to float soon after the development of speculative pressure. Dr Mahathir of Malaysia blamed foreign speculators, including George Soros of the Quantum hedge fund, who denied selling the rupiah short; Mahathir imposed a limited moratorium on repayment of foreign debt.

The spread of the crisis to Russia and Brazil was largely psychological as financial markets recognized that those countries also had large amounts of debt and their currencies were overvalued, and in the case of Russia that the government was remarkably corrupt. The displacement leading to the Russian boom in the early 1990s was abandonment of the Communist system and widespread privatization. In due course, euphoria produced overtrading and excessive capital investment, with corruption leading to large outflows of dubiously acquired monies. The stock market collapsed on August 11, 1998, followed by flotation of the ruble six days later.[72]

Brazil's troubles were the product of deregulation, a large fiscal dificit, a sudden halt in inward capital flows, and loss of export markets in Asia, especially of woodpulp for paper. A second depreciation and floating of the real in early 1999 led to an increase in stock prices and appreciation of the real.[73]

8

Bubble Contagion: Tokyo to Bangkok to New York

The first of the four distinct asset price bubbles in the last fifteen years of the twentieth century was in real estate and stocks in Tokyo in the second half of the 1980s, and the second, at about the same time, was in real estate and stocks of three of the Nordic countries—Finland, Norway, and Sweden. The third was in Bangkok, Kuala Lumpur, Jakarta, and Hong Kong and nearby national financial centers in the mid-1990s, and the fourth was in U.S. stocks and especially those traded in the over-the-counter markets in the second half of the 1990s.

Asset price bubbles in major industrial countries are rare; the previous bubble in the United States had been in the late 1920s. Japan had never had an asset price bubble before and neither had the Asian countries. A bubble in six or eight countries at the same time is an extraordinary phenomenon; nothing like it had ever happened before. But then four distinct asset price bubbles in a fifteen-year period was also unprecedented.

These asset price bubbles were systematically related. The bubble in the Nordic countries resulted from a surge in the loans of the offshore branches of banks headquartered in Tokyo and Osaka; the coincidence was that the Japanese banking regulators relaxed the restrictions on the foreign activities of Japanese banks at the same time that the regulatory authorities in the Nordic countries were relaxing restrictions on borrowing abroad by their domestic banks. The surge in the flow of loans from the offices of the Japanese banks based in London and Zurich and offshore centers to the borrowers in the three Nordic countries led to rapid increases in the prices of real estate and stocks. The bubble in Thailand and the other Asian countries was triggered by the inflow of funds from Tokyo in the several years following the implosion of the asset price bubble in Japan. The bubble in U.S. stocks began in the mid-1990s and accelerated rapidly following the implosion of the bubbles in Thailand, Malaysia, and Indonesia and their neighbors in the second half of 1997, which led to a surge in the flow of funds from the Asian countries to the United States. In 1998 the Federal Reserve provided more liquidity to the U.S. financial system to cope with the uncertainty triggered by the collapse of Long-Term Capital Management and in 1999 the Federal Reserve provided additional liquidity again in anticipation of Y2K transition.

The link between these asset price bubbles is that 'monies sloshed' from Tokyo to Bangkok and the other Asian countries after the implosion of the bubble in Japan, which led to an appreciation of the yen and a decline in Japanese competitiveness. Japanese firms began to outsource production to China and the countries in Southeast Asia in the effort to reduce their production costs. The implosion of the bubbles in Thailand and other Asian countries led to a sharp reversal in their external financial positions; the currencies of most of these countries (with the exceptions of the Chinese yuan and the Hong Kong dollar) depreciated sharply and there was a rapid turnabout in their trade positions that had a mirror-image counterpart in the surge in the U.S. trade deficit. There was a dramatic increase in the flow of funds from these countries to the United States that contributed significantly to the increases in the prices of U.S. securities; U.S. residents who sold securities to foreign residents then used a very large part of their sales receipts to buy other securities from other U.S. residents. The prices of these U.S. securities increased further; in turn the sellers of these securities used most of their sales receipts to buy other securities from other U.S. residents. The money became like the proverbial 'hot potato,' passed from investor to investor at ever-increasing prices.

The invisible hand is always at work when money flows from one country to another and adjustments automatically occur both in the countries that receive these funds and in the countries that are the sources of them. One adjustment in the former group of countries is that their currencies appreciate in the foreign exchange market and another is that asset prices almost always increase. The increase in the inflow of funds from abroad is almost always associated with economic booms. There is a bit of a chicken and egg problem: buoyant economic activity attracts foreign funds and the inflow of foreign funds leads to increases in business investment because higher stock prices mean a lower cost of capital for domestic firms; a wider range of investment projects becomes profitable as the costs of capital reduce. The increase in household wealth induces an increase in consumption or, what is same thing, a decline in the saving rate as increases in asset prices mean that more and more households achieve their savings objectives.

Thus the expansion of the asset price bubbles in the Asian capitals followed from the implosion of the asset price bubble in Tokyo and the surge in the outflow of money from Japan at the beginning of the 1990s. Most of these funds were Japanese-owned; some had been owned by foreigners who sold Japanese stocks as their prices declined. The flow of funds from Tokyo to Thailand and Indonesia and the other Asian countries led to increases in the foreign exchange value of their currencies if they were floating in the foreign exchange market and to increases in the international reserve assets and the money supplies if these currencies were pegged. The rates of growth of domestic income in these countries increased in response to the increases in investment spending and in consumption spending that followed from the increases in the prices of real estate and stocks. The residents in these countries who sold their securities and assets to the Japanese used most of their receipts to buy other domestic securities and real estate.

The term 'overshooting' describes the increase in the value of a currency in the foreign exchange market relative to the value inferred from the differences between the domestic inflation rate and the inflation rates in the country's major trading partners. In contrast 'undershooting' involves a real depreciation. Overshooting and undershooting are inevitable responses to the changes in the amount of cross-border capital flows from one period to the next. Thus the exchange market transactions of the investors which change the currency composition of their assets and liabilities at an increasing rate appear to be destabilizing in that they cause the value of the currency in the foreign exchange market to diverge from the value inferred from the difference in national inflation rates.

In the 1980s the global index stock funds bought Japanese stocks as the stock prices in Tokyo were increasing and their transactions contributed both to the appreciation of the yen and to the increase in the prices of Japanese stocks. The mantra of these index funds was that the share of Japanese stocks in their portfolios should be directly proportional to the ratio of the market value of Japanese stocks as a group to the market value of stocks in all national markets. When the prices of Japanese stocks declined with the implosion of the bubble, the global index funds sold Japanese stocks and moved their money from Tokyo.

One similarity between the asset price bubbles in Japan, Thailand, and the other Asian countries, and the United States was that market participants began to forecast the prices of assets and securities by extrapolating from recent increases in their prices. Most of the time the prices of assets and securities are based on their earning power—the price of an office building reflects the estimate of its rental income and the prices of shares in Sony and in General Electric reflect their anticipated profitability. Occasionally some investors begin to estimate stock prices and real estate prices in the future by extrapolating from the recent increases in their prices. These investors—at times they've been called tape watchers, and at other times momentum investors or day traders—extrapolate the recent changes in the prices of individual securities as the basis of the forecasts of prices in the near future. These investors bought the currencies that were appreciating in the foreign exchange market and so the currencies appreciated even further. Real estate prices ceased to be based primarily on current and projected rents and stock prices ceased to be based on anticipated profitability; instead these prices were based on extrapolation from the recent increases in prices; it's as if the increases in the prices from Monday to Tuesday are used on Wednesday to forecast the levels of the prices on Friday. Since many newly-established firms are not profitable in their first several years of operations, investors project the value of the shares of these firms on the basis of their revenues—or, in some cases, on their projected revenues.

The asset price bubbles in Japan and the Asian countries involved real estate and stocks; the increase in real estate prices 'pulled up' stock prices. In contrast the bubble in the United States exclusively involved stocks, although real estate prices surged in Silicon Valley and in several cities where large numbers of individuals were employed in financial services or were experiencing sharp increases in household wealth. The bubbles in the Asian countries were similar to those in Japan and reflect that stocks were a much smaller share of national wealth than in the United States.

Asset price bubbles in Tokyo and Osaka

The 1980s real estate bubble in Japan was so massive that by the end of the decade the chatter in Tokyo was that the market value of the land under the Imperial Palace was greater than the market value of all of the real estate in California. The land area in California is several billion times larger than the grounds of the Imperial Palace, which meant that there was an enormous difference in the price per acre or hectare. Not that there had been an auction or even a pseudo-auction for the Imperial Palace grounds. The analyst who first made this comparison estimated the value of the palace grounds by multiplying the hundred or so hectares by the recent price per hectare paid for a small plot of land in the nearby Ginza entertainment neighborhood, which was much the most valuable land in Tokyo. The value of Californian real estate was obtained from Federal Reserve data on U.S. household wealth.

All of the financial values in Tokyo were sky high at the end of the 1980s. The market value of Japanese stocks was twice the market value of U.S. stocks, even though Japanese GDP was less than half of U.S. GDP. The comparison between Japanese and U.S. firms in terms of the ratios of the market value of stocks to profitability was even more skewed. The market value of Japanese real estate was twice the market value of U.S. real estate, even though the land area in Japan is 5 percent that in the United States and 80 percent of Japan is mountainous. The market value of land per capita in Japan was more than four times that in the United States even though per capita income in Japan was only 60 or 70 percent that of the United States.

The Japanese banks were at the top of the hit parades of the world's banks as measured by assets and by deposits (but not by profits); usually seven of the ten largest banks on this list were Japanese. Similarly the capital of Nomura, Japan's largest investment bank, was larger than the capital of the five largest U.S. banks.

Business investment surged in Japan in the 1980s because the cost of capital was declining as stock prices increased rapidly. Many Japanese firms issued convertible bonds denominated in U.S. dollars, which could be exchanged for a specified number of yen-denominated shares in each of the firms that issued the bonds. Because investors were so enthusiastic about the continued increase in prices of Japanese stocks, the interest rates on these bonds were low—often about 2 percent. The low interest rate meant that the cost of capital to Japanese firms was low and their investment spending surged, both in building new factories and in acquiring established U.S. and European firms.

As we have detailed in the first chapter, the Mitsui Real Estate Company paid $625 million for the Exxon building on Sixth Avenue in New York City against an asking price of $310 million because the company wanted to get into the *Guinness Book of World Records*. Other Japanese firms were also acquiring trophy properties and buildings in the United

States. Mitsubishi Real Estate bought 50 percent of the Rockefeller Center, and a group related to Sumitomo Bank bought the Pebble Beach Golf Course in Northern California. Sony bought Columbia Records and then Columbia Pictures, and Matsushita, its dominant rival in the electronics industry, acquired MGM Universal.

Consumption spending surged in Japan and Japanese bidders bought at auctions of French Impressionist paintings at Sotheby's and Christie's and other art auction firms. As we have seen, Vincent van Gogh's *Portrait of Dr Guichet* went to a racetrack entrepreneur from the Osaka area for the highest price ever paid for one work of art.

Golf courses mushroomed. Land was very expensive in Japan and so were the golf club memberships.

The Japanese had all the money—and they were spending it to buy all kinds of assets both at home and abroad. The paradox was that the Japanese were spending as if they were very rich and yet there didn't seem to be that many rich Japanese, much of the spending was by Japanese corporations.

Japan had begun to industrialize in the last third of the nineteenth century at the same time as the country decided to open to foreigners (because of the fear that if they didn't Western countries would establish outposts in Japan much as they had along China's seacoast). The emperor sent groups of travelers to the United States, Germany, Great Britain, Belgium, and other countries in Western Europe to bring back models of how Japan should develop its government, its civil service, its banking system, its central bank, and its economy. The central railroad station in Tokyo was modeled on the central station in Amsterdam, the building of the Bank of Japan was based on that of the National Bank of Belgium, the civil service followed the French model, and the railroad system was patterned on the British model (which is why the Japanese drive on the left side of the road). The industrial economy in Japan developed around feudal families; the classic names included Mitsui, Mitsubishi, Sumitomo, and Yamoto and live on today in the names of some of the banks and trading companies and industrial firms. Each of these families formed an industrial group, or *'Zaibatsu,'* with a trading company, a steamship company, and a steel mill all under the umbrella of a bank holding company which owned many of the shares in these operating companies and provided them with both long-term capital and short-term loans for operating capital—more or less on the German model.

Competition among these industrial groups for market share was intense.

These bank holding companies were outlawed in the late 1940s by General Douglas MacArthur who had succeeded Emperor Hirohito as Japan's supreme ruler. The industrial groups responded by developing a pattern of cross-shareholding; the steamship company would hold shares in the trading company, the bank and the steel company, and each of these companies would own shares in the steamship company and in every other company in the group. Each group was like a mutual protection and advancement society and provided the funds, the leadership and even the markets for firms that had been established to produce the new technologies. The Mitsui Steamship Company purchased its steel from the Mitsui Steel Company and its insurance from the Mitsui Insurance Company.

Japanese economic accomplishments in the forty or more years after the bombing of Hiroshima and Nagasaki in the summer of 1945 were phenomenal. The industrial structure of the country had been devastated in the last several years of World War II. Japan had lost what had been its economic colonies in Korea, Formosa (subsequently Taiwan), and Manchuria, and was bereft of commercial links with other countries. The country was viewed as an economic pariah and its meager exports brought forth derisive laughter because of their inferior quality and because they were rip-offs of the design and engineering of American and European firms.

In the 1950s and the 1960s Japan began to catch up and achieved rates of economic growth of more than 10 percent a year. These two high decades of growth led Herman Kahn to write *Japan: the First Superstate* in 1971. Kahn's arithmetic was straightforward—if the rate of economic growth in Japan continued to be 2 to 4 percentage points higher a year than the rates of growth in the United States and in Germany and France and other industrial countries then in a relatively few years per capita income in Japan would exceed per capita incomes in these other industrial countries.

By the 1980s Japan was the second leading industrial power, more economically powerful than Germany. Toyota, Nissan, and Honda were leaders in the global automobile industry. Sony, Matsushita, and Sharp and a seemingly endless list of firms dominated the global electronics industry. Nikon and Canon 'owned' the world's photo-optics industry. Japanese-built computers were among the most powerful in the world.

The economic success of Japan led to extensive analysis both in Tokyo and Washington and in other foreign capitals about its unique advantages. The 'Japan Inc.' story was that there was a master plan formulated by the bureaucrats in the Ministry of Finance and the Ministry of International Trade and Investment, who had identified the 'winners and losers' among the firms in different industries and especially the industries that would be the winners in global competition. These agencies encouraged the growth of the 'winners' through low-cost loans and favored government procurement and tariff protection from foreign competitors, at least until the firms had perfected their products and reduced their unit production costs to such low levels that they could challenge established American and European firms.

Foreign firms found it difficult to sell their goods in the Japanese market and to establish subsidiaries in Japan because of complex regulatory procedures. American and European firms found it difficult to buy seats on the Tokyo Stock Exchange. The Japanese claimed that skis manufactured in the United States and Europe were not suitable for Japanese snow and that the stomachs of the Japanese could not tolerate rice produced in California.

The mandarins in the Ministry of Finance maintained low interest rate ceilings on both bank deposits and bank lending rates; the interest rates on deposits were below the inflation rate so households had to save a high proportion of their incomes or else their wealth would have declined. The demand for loans from business firms at these low interest rates was much greater than the supply; government officials provided 'window guidance' to the banks identifying the firms that were to be given preference.

One result of extensive financial regulation was that the real rates of return on bank deposits and most other securities were negative. One exception was that the real rate of return on real estate was positive and high, and another was that the real rate of return on stocks was also positive and high.

In the first half of the 1980s Japan began to undergo financial liberalization, in large part because of pressure from the Americans to 'open up' the financial markets in Tokyo so U.S. firms would have access to clients and customers and trading opportunities in Japan comparable to those that Japanese firms had in New York and other U.S. financial centers. The Japanese recognized—very, very reluctantly—that if Japanese firms were to expand abroad, foreign firms would have to be allowed to expand in Japan. Interest rate ceilings on deposits and on loans were raised. Window guidance became much less extensive. The restrictions on the foreign investments of Japanese firms were relaxed. Japanese banks were permitted to increase their foreign branches and subsidiaries.

Japanese banks established branches in New York, Chicago, and Los Angeles, London and Zurich and Frankfurt, both to lend to the local branches and subsidiaries of Japanese firms and to lend to non-Japanese firms; the offshore bank branches obtained funds for these loans by borrowing in the local interbank market and in the offshore deposit market from non-Japanese banks. Japanese purchases of U.S. real estate surged. Japan was booming. Presidents of U.S. universities went to Tokyo seeking funds for chairs in Japanese studies. MIT was among the institutions that obtained university professorships in Japan from these harvesting activities.

Financial liberalization meant that the banks could increase their loans to borrowers who wanted to buy real estate and to build new office buildings and apartment buildings and shopping centers. The increase in the funds available for real estate loans led to more rapid increases in real estate prices.

Firms involved in the real estate business accounted for a significant proportion of the market value of all of the firms listed on the Tokyo Stock Exchange. These real estate holding companies were somewhat like mutual funds; when the prices of the properties they owned increased, investors rushed to buy more of their shares, and so the share prices of the real estate companies increased. Increases in real estate prices led to a construction boom as new skyscrapers were constructed. The Japanese banks owned large amounts of real estate and of stocks, and the contribution of the increase in the value of both real estate and stocks to the capital of the banks was much greater than their operating profits. As their capital increased, the banks were able to increase their loans.

Japan appeared to have developed the financial equivalent of a 'perpetual motion machine.' The increases in real estate prices led to increases in stock prices; the increases in both real estate prices and stock prices led to increases in bank capital. As bank capital increased, banks were in a position to increase their loans, and because of financial liberalization, they were much better positioned to increase their loans to groups that had been restricted in their ability to borrow in earlier periods. Because most bank loans were collateralized by real estate, bank loan losses were trivially small as long as real estate prices continued to increase. As real estate prices increased, the profits of the firms that invested in real estate were increasing, and so many of these firms borrowed more in their search for larger profits.

The structure of cross share-holding meant that the increase in share prices had a magnified impact in increasing the market value of the stocks traded on the Tokyo Stock Exchange. Industrial firms began to borrow to obtain the funds to buy real estate and shares in other firms because the rates of return were so much higher than the rates of return from producing automobiles and electronics and steel.

Dating the onset of the Japanese bubble

Dating the onset of an asset price bubble is always complex because asset prices will already be increasing rapidly before the transition to the bubble period. In Japan, the rate of increase in real estate prices and stock prices accelerated in 1985, at about the time of the beginning of a period of rapid appreciation of the Japanese yen.

The bubble in Japanese real estate prices resulted from three factors—one was that for more than thirty years the real rate of return on real estate in Japan had been positive at a time when the real rates of return on most other securities were negative. One of the great clichés in finance is 'Land is a good investment, the price of land always increases.' A derivative cliché is 'Land is a good investment, they aren't making any more of it.' Japanese investors believed in both clichés—and from the late 1940s the increases in the price of real estate confirmed their beliefs.

The second factor was the liberalization of financial regulations that had previously limited loans by Japanese banks to borrowers who wanted to purchase real estate; banks became free to increase their real estate loans as a share of their total loans—another process of catch-up. Investors in real estate could build upwards, and in the late 1980s it seemed like half of the world's construction cranes were in Tokyo. Investors in real estate could only with great difficulty acquire farmland.

The third factor was the rapid growth in the money supply in the second half of the 1980s as a result of the intervention of the Bank of Japan to limit the appreciation of the yen in the foreign exchange market. In the first half of the 1980s the Japanese yen had depreciated sharply relative to the U.S. dollar; the competitive position of Japanese firms in world markets greatly improved. In the second half of the 1980s the yen began to appreciate, and the Bank of Japan sought to limit and moderate the appreciation because of the adverse impacts on the values of the investments in plant and equipment that had been made in the first part of the decade. The result of extensive intervention was that the money supply in Japan began to increase at an exceptional rate—that is, the monetary base was increasing. The increase in the reserves of the Japanese banks meant that they were able to increase their loans at a rapid rate because their reserves at the central bank were also increasing fast.

Economic growth remained rapid because the banks were able and ready to lend and firms and investors were eager to borrow. Real estate prices began to increase at a rate of 30 percent a year.

Traditionally Japanese firms had not been concerned with profitability. Their aims were to grow the firm and to expand the product line and to provide lifetime employment for a large number of employees. Each firm wanted to maintain its position on the hit parade in its industry. Many firms increased the amounts borrowed in efforts to improve product lines and increase market share.

Japanese banks owned large amounts of real estate and of stocks. When the prices of real estate and stocks increased, bank capital increased; as their capital increased, they were able to increase their loans. The borrowers increased their real estate purchases, but since the supply of real estate increases very slowly, these purchases had the effect of increasing real estate prices. Increases in the prices of real estate also led to increases in the prices of stocks.

In the early 1980s the banks established a new set of intermediaries, '*jusen*,' to make housing loans, which traditionally Japanese banks had been reluctant to make. The *jusen* would get the funds for housing loans by borrowing from the banks—in effect seven of the large banks established these specialized lenders. About the same time the Ministry of Finance established public sector lending institutions that would also make housing loans. The banks then decided to make housing loans on their own.

The surge in stock prices meant that firms were able to raise cash at very little cost. One innovation was the development of convertible bonds; firms would sell bonds that offered a very low interest rate and the opportunity to invest them into shares at a stipulated price. In effect the bond was like a call option to buy shares; however the owner of the bonds received an interest rate that was larger than the dividend on the stocks. There were three ways in which firms could use the cash obtained from the sale of these bonds: they could place the funds on deposit in the banks and earn an interest rate two to three times that which they were paying, they could buy stocks, or they could invest in plant and equipment to expand their productive capacity and upgrade their product lines.

The practice in Japan was that loans were collateralized by real estate; traditionally the banks would lend up to 70 percent of the appraised value of these properties. Some of the loans made by the *jusen* went to *'yakuza,'* organized criminal groups. These groups used their connections to secure exceptionally high property appraisals. Since property prices were increasing at the rate of 30 percent a year, a modest 'error' made by an appraiser in putting too high a value on the property would soon be corrected by the market.

Real estate prices increased much more rapidly than rents, with the consequence that the rental rate of return declined significantly below the interest rate on the borrowed funds. Investors who had bought properties in the last several years of the 1980s had a negative cash flow—the rental income on their properties after the payment of the operating costs was below the interest payments due to the lenders—but because property prices were increasing so fast, they could raise cash to make the interest payments either by increasing the amounts borrowed against a property in earlier years or by selling.

The surge in real estate prices and stock prices led to a surge in household wealth—Japanese households owned currency and bank deposits, real estate, and stocks. While many of the stocks in Japanese firms were owned by other firms in the same *'Keiretsu'* (successors to the *Zaibatsu*), one-third of the stocks were owned by individuals. In effect each firm was a combination of an operating company and a mutual fund.

As the market value of Japanese stocks increased, investors resident in the United States and Western Europe bought more Japanese stocks. Global stock index funds wanted to own Japanese shares. The rates of return to non-Japanese investors on their purchases of shares in Japanese firms were high since these investors benefited from the combination of the increase in the price of the stocks and the increase in the foreign exchange value of the Japanese yen.

Why and when the Tokyo bubble imploded

The bubble in Japan reached its crescendo at the end of 1989. Real estate prices seemed so high that the quip by the much quoted baseball star Yogi Berra that 'It's so expensive that no one can afford to live there' seemed applicable. Banks developed one-hundred-year, three-generation mortgages. The incoming governor of the Bank of Japan was concerned that such high prices for homes would erode social harmony. A new central bank regulation instructed Japanese banks to limit the rate of growth of their real estate loans so that it would be no greater than the rate of growth of their total loans.

Once the rate of growth of bank loans slowed, some recent buyers of real estate developed a cash bind; their rental income was still smaller than the interest payments on their mortgages, but they could no longer obtain the cash needed to pay the interest on their outstanding loans from new bank loans. Some of these investors then become distress sellers of their properties because of the high carrying costs. The combination of the sharp reduction in the rate of growth of credit for real estate and these distress sales caused real estate prices to decline; the cliché that the price of land always rises was tested and found to be false.

Stock prices and real estate prices began to decline at the beginning of 1990; stock prices declined by 30 percent in 1990 and an additional 30 percent in 1991. The stock price trend in Japan was downward although there were four significant rallies. At the beginning of 2003, stock prices in Japan were at the same level they had been at twenty years earlier, even though the real economy was much larger. Real economic growth averaged only slightly more than 1 percent.

The consumer price level began to decline in 1999 at a rate of 1 to 2 percent a year, and there was concern that a classic debt deflation might develop, with the decline in prices leading to an exceptionally large number of bankruptcies, which in turn resulted in large loan losses by the banks and hence sales of distressed assets which led to lower prices.

Now the perpetual motion machine began to work in reverse. Property sales led to declines in property prices. The decline in real estate prices and stock prices meant that bank capital was declining; banks were now much more constrained in making loans. Because the value of Japanese stocks was declining while that of U.S. stocks was increasing, the global stock equity funds sold Japanese stocks and bought U.S. stocks.

One of the stylized facts in monetary economics is that the implosion of an asset price bubble is deflationary, the flip-side of the economic boom that occurred during the expansion phase of the cycle. Investment spending in Japan declined in part because the cost of capital had surged and the anticipated growth of profits had been revised downward, and in part because the splurge in investment spending during the expansion phase had resulted in significant excess capacity. Household spending increased much more slowly as millions of families increased their saving from their earned incomes to compensate for the decline in their wealth that followed from the fall in stock prices and real estate prices.

Bankruptcies increased, and the banks and other financial institutions incurred large loan losses. Those nonbank financial institutions that specialized in making real estate loans were in great distress.

Despite the large number of bankruptcies and the large loan losses by the banks, depositors in the Japanese banks did not withdraw their money. Individuals and firms alike were convinced that the Japanese government would make depositors whole even if a bank failed, although there was no formal deposit insurance. That the share prices of the banks remained significantly above zero for an extended period reflected investors' belief that the banks were 'too big to fail,' even if they had a negative net worth, because the market value of their loans was smaller than their deposit liabilities.

Many of the banks now were super-cautious when making new loans—they had learned that what they had thought was a conservative policy of using real estate as collateral for loans had become highly risky because the price of real estate could decline. For the first time the banks began to ask, 'If we make this loan, what is the likelihood that we will be repaid?' Because of the new hard-nosed attitude of the banks, their borrowers began to ask 'Will this new investment be profitable and enhance our market value?'

Foreign investors and foreign banks became increasingly concerned about the solvency of the Japanese banks. The foreign branches and subsidiaries of the Japanese banks had been large 'takers' or borrowers in the offshore money market; they made loans to both the foreign subsidiaries of Japanese firms and to non-Japanese firms with funds obtained from non-Japanese banks in the offshore deposit market. The offshore branches of Japanese banks had increased their loans at a very rapid rate because in the traditional style these banks had operated on a very small spread between their own costs of funds and the interest rates that they charged on their loans.

The foreign banks that were lenders to the Japanese banks were not convinced that they would be 'made whole' by a Japanese government agency if one of the Japanese banks failed. So the foreign banks increased the interest rates they charged the Japanese banks. One immediate impact was that many of the loans made by the offshore branches of Japanese banks were no longer profitable, and so the Japanese banks began to call these loans as rapidly as they conveniently could, so they would no longer be required to pay the penalty interest rate.

The increase in the Japan premium was a warning signal to risk-sensitive investors. More and more Japanese firms and individuals shifted funds from Japanese banks in Tokyo to non-Japanese banks in Tokyo, and from Tokyo to foreign financial centers. Interest rates in Tokyo declined significantly and the capital outflow from Japan increased as Japanese investors sought higher yields available abroad.

The recession in Japan in 1991 meant that import growth slowed markedly while exports surged; some Japanese firms greatly increased their efforts to sell abroad because the domestic market for their products was growing slowly relative to the growth in their supply capabilities. The result of the slowdown in the growth of imports and the surge in the growth of exports was that Japan's trade surplus increased. This increase was larger than the increase in the capital outflow from Japan and resulted in the appreciation of the yen, which became a handicap to export-oriented Japanese firms. Many increased their investments in China, Malaysia, and Thailand to take advantage of lower labor costs. The increase in investment spending for firms in the export industries stimulated income growth.

The East Asian economic miracle and the Asian financial crisis

In 1992 the World Bank published *The East Asian Miracle,* an expressively descriptive title for the economic performance for the countries in the arc from Thailand to South Korea; the increases in their GDPs were in some ways comparable to the gains that Japan had made in the 1950s and the 1960s. The Korean peninsula had been fractured in the war in the early 1950s; in the mid-1960s South Korea began a remarkable period of economic growth. Singapore had been a fortified swamp in the 1950s and by the 1990s had achieved a first-world standard of living. The change in political leadership in China from Mao Tse Tung to Dien Xao Ping in 1978 led to a dramatic change from a self-contained, isolated country to one that was open and eager for international trade and international investment; the annual rate of growth averaged nearly 10 percent for more than twenty years and the increase was even more dramatic in the provinces that bordered the seacoast and in the major cities like Beijing, Shanghai, and Shenzen. Hong Kong had evolved from an outpost for peeking into China in the 1950s, the 1960s, and the 1970s into an entrepôt center for the prepping of Chinese goods for world markets.

In Thailand, Malaysia, and Indonesia in the first half of the 1990s stock prices increased by between 300 and 500 percent and manufacturing activity surged. Stock prices doubled in most of the East Asian countries in 1993 and continued to increase in 1994. Real estate prices soared. The economies boomed. Trade deficits grew. Since the asset price bubbles across these countries were pervasive despite marked differences in economic structures, per capita incomes, exchange rate arrangements, and whether they were international creditor countries like Singapore, Taiwan, and Hong Kong or international debtors like Thailand and Malaysia, there is a strong presumption that the bubbles had a common origin and that it was external.

China, Thailand, and the other East Asian countries were on the receiving end of outsourcing by American, Japanese, and European firms that wanted cheaper sources of supply for established domestic markets. Rapid economic growth was both the result and the cause of the inflow of foreign capital, especially from Japan. Japanese investment initially took the form of the construction of manufacturing plants to take advantage of lower labor costs; high valued-added components would be produced in Japan and shipped to the affiliated plants for assembly. From there a large part of the production would be exported, some to the United States, some to Japan, and some to third countries. The direct foreign investment by Japanese firms pulled supplier firms and the banks from Japan. The buzzword was export-led growth, which was almost always based on a low value for the country's currency in the foreign exchange market. Many of these exports were produced by major firms headquartered in the United States, Japan, and Taiwan. Firms headquartered in South Korea began to invest in China and Indonesia because the wage rates were so much lower than their domestic wage rates.

Then in the winter of 1996 the consumer finance companies in Thailand—many of which had been established by the large Thai banks to circumvent the regulations that limited their ability to make consumer loans—began to experience large losses on their loans. Foreign lenders to Thailand became increasingly concerned about the value of their loans to Thai borrowers, and the flow of foreign funds to the country declined. The Bank of Thailand's ability to support the baht at its existing value was quickly exhausted, and in early July 1997 the baht depreciated sharply.

The depreciation of the baht triggered the contagion effect and within six months the foreign exchange values of each of the currencies on the Asian arc, with the exception of the Chinese yuan and the Hong Kong dollar, had lost 30 percent or more of their value in the foreign exchange markets. Stock prices declined by 30 to 60 percent, partly because foreign investors were seeking to cash out, partly because the domestic firms were no longer profitable. Real estate prices declined sharply. Most banks, with the exception of those in Singapore and Hong Kong, failed. The closing of many banks in Indonesia triggered racial strife, and an immense run on the currency which lost more than 70 percent of its value.

When the crises occurred, the play script was a reprise of similar events in Japan in the previous decade. The chatter about the East Asian miracle disappeared and new buzzwords arose—crony capitalism, spontaneous privatization, and destabilizing speculation.

The sharp depreciation of the currencies led to significant losses for those firms that had borrowed U.S. dollars or Japanese yen or some other foreign currency. The banks that had lent to these firms also incurred losses; the banks in most of the Asian countries toppled into bankruptcy because of their own revaluation losses and the losses of the firms to which they had made loans. The depreciation also resulted in a very quick reversal of the Asian countries' trade balances, from large deficits to large surpluses.

The counterpart of the large swings in the trade and current account balances of the Asian countries was the mirror-image increase in the U.S. trade deficit; in effect the appreciation of the U.S. dollar reflected the depreciation of the Thai baht, the Malaysian ringgit, the Indonesian rupiah, and the other Asian currencies that were not pegged to the U.S. dollar—basically the Chinese yuan and the Hong Kong dollar.

Rational exuberance and irrational exuberance

Between 1982 and 1999 U.S. stock prices increased by a factor of thirteen—the most remarkable run of annual increases in stock prices in the two hundred years of the American republic. In the very long run, U.S. stock prices have declined every third year; in the last two decades of the last century, stock prices fell in only one year, and then only by 5 percent. The market value of U.S. stocks increased from 60 percent of U.S. GDP in 1982 to 300 percent of GDP in 1999.

The increase in U.S. real estate prices during this period was modest for the country as a whole, although there were significant regional increases in areas that were experiencing large increases in per capita income or in the number of employed individuals, including Silicon Valley and the broader San Francisco Bay area, Washington DC, and Boston and New York.

The U.S. economy boomed in the 1990s. The inflation rate declined from above 6 percent at the beginning of the 1990s to less than 2 percent at the end of the 1990s, the unemployment rate declined from 8 percent to less than 4 percent, the rate of economic growth increased from about 2.5 percent to 3.5 percent, and there was a remarkable increase in U.S. productivity. The U.S. Treasury's annual fiscal balance changed by more than 5 percent—from a deficit of nearly $300 billion at the beginning of the 1990s to a surplus of nearly $200 billion at the end of the decade.

One of the 'negatives' in terms of U.S. economic performance was that the annual U.S. trade deficit surged to $500 billion. Another was that the household saving rate declined to a new low.

The remarkable aspect of the boom was the focus on the 'new economy' and especially the role of information technology, the computer, the dot.coms, and the firms that provided both the hardware and the software or exploited these developments to serve traditional needs. These technological developments led to sharp declines in the cost of sending and storing information. E-bay provided a nationwide auction market for tens of thousands of different products. Amazon developed the technology for sale of books and electronic products. Peapod allowed individuals to shop for most of their groceries at home. Millions of accounts were established at the discount broker Charles Schwab and at its competitors. Firms were established that enabled investors to trade stocks using the computer at extremely low transactions costs. 'Day traders' emerged: individuals who quit their regular jobs to trade stocks either from their computers at home or from desks in specially designed shops. Priceline enabled airlines and hotels to sell seats and rooms at sharply discounted prices.

Entrepreneurs were able to get the cash to develop these ideas from venture capitalists (VCs) who provided seed money. The VCs developed a portfolio of investments in different firms in the hope that within three to five years they would be able to sell these shares—and make their profit—when the firms made their first public offerings of stock. The VCs' rates of return would depend on whether the firms in which they had invested were successful in their technological challenges and on the selling prices of their shares and the lengths of the holding periods.

As stock prices increased, the high rates of return earned by the VCs attracted lots of money, and the capital available to the VCs as a group surged by a factor of five. No investors wanted to be left behind. This capital was there, so a large number of ideas were funded; money was chasing ideas and concepts. Three or four years on, the new firms would have an Initial Public Offering (IPO). The IPO would follow the traditional road-show, the occasion on which the investment banks would parade the company to asset managers around the country seeking to induce them to buy the shares.

At the end of the road-show, the investment bankers would estimate the amount of the shares that they might sell at the IPO, and set both the price and the quantity. In 99.46 percent of the cases, the share price at the end of the first day of trading was significantly higher than the IPO price, and those fortunate enough to be able to buy at the share price would make a significant capital gain.

One impact of this price pop is that more and more investors clamored to buy at the IPO price. The second impact was that the demonstration of the strength of the demand meant that more and more people wanted to get a piece of the action—the entrepreneurs were attracted to the immense wealth they might earn with a successful innovation, the VCs were attracted to the large profits they could gain by identifying the entrepreneurs that were likely to be successful, and the investment bankers wanted the fees from bringing a large number of firms to the public. The investors wanted the large capital gains associated with the pop between the IPO price and the price of the same shares at the end of the first day of trading, the first week of trading, and the first month of trading.

The size of the price pop was like dynamite or nitroglycerine or maybe even fusion. The investment bankers appeared to set the price for the IPOs so as to maximize the price pop on the first day of trading—and not maximize the cash received by the shareholders who were selling. From this point of view, a lower price for the IPO might be preferable to a higher price, for the demand for the stock would increase—at least for a while—as the pop increased. The entrepreneurs sold only a small part of their total shares at the IPO; they calculated that the larger the pop, the greater their wealth. They were more interested in the apparent value of the shares they owned at the end of the first day's trading than they were with the amount of cash they might obtain from the IPO.

On some IPO days the number of shares traded was three or four times the number of shares that had been sold at the IPO. Since many of the buyers at the IPO had been told to hold their shares, the float was much smaller than the number of shares sold, and so these shares in the float might have been traded five or six times in the course of the day.

The United States seemed to have its own perpetual motion machine, one designed to enrich the fortunes of hundreds of thousands of families. The larger the price pop on the first day of trading, the greater the number of investors that were attracted to IPOs. The stronger the demand for IPOs, the larger the number of venture capitalists that were willing to back the entrepreneurs. The more capital that the entrepreneurs were willing to put in play, the larger the number of entrepreneurs that would seek their fortunes by breaking away from established firms.

In December 1996 Chairman Greenspan of the Federal Reserve Board first used the term 'irrational exuberance;' the Dow Jones was at 6,300 and the NASDAQ was at 1300. Greenspan is cautious and careful with data; it seems highly unlikely that he would have commented on stock prices unless he believed they were then over-valued by a minimum of 15 or 20 percent. At the end of December 1999 the Dow Jones was at 11,700 and the NASDAQ was at 5,400, and the market value of NASDAQ stocks was 80 percent of the market value of stocks traded on the New York Stock Exchange.

In the late 1990s the prices of stocks representing the new economy—the dot.coms, e-commerce, fiber optics, servers, chips, software, IT, telecom—which were traded on the NASDAQ had increased much more rapidly than the prices of old economy stocks, those of firms such as GE and GM, AT&T and Time-Life, that were traded on the New York Stock Exchange. But there was more than a spillover effect, for the enthusiasm about the future that was characterizing the new economy stocks was infectious and also led to increases in the prices of the old economy stocks.

It seemed as though developments in information technology were driving finance. Computers were becoming much more powerful and less expensive. The costs of transmitting and storing information and data were declining rapidly. Moore's Law came into play, and the cost of a unit of computing power declined by 30 percent a year. The World Wide Web was developing fast, and markets in separate centers were becoming linked. Computers were replacing humans in trading stocks. Individuals could order their airline tickets over the web. Fiber optics were linking the east coast and the west coast and the prices of long-distance phone calls were declining to the level of local calls. Servers were big, and so was storage capacity. Thousands—tens of thousands—of new firms had been established to move information or data, or to store information or data, and the profits earned by the venture capitalists that had funded them were so high that further money flooded in from pension funds, university and charitable endowments, and wealthy families. The outstripping of supply for newly issued shares at the IPO price led the investment bankers to engage in the process of 'spinning'—of allocating a goodly number of shares to the heads of the major firms that would bring them investment banking business. The investment banks grew rich; they had a lot of product to sell and a public convinced that share ownership would bring them a profit.

There is no easy answer to the question of when rational exuberance morphed into irrational exuberance. The idea that there might be an asset price bubble in U.S. stocks occurred to different investors at different dates. The first date for the onset of the bubble in U.S. stocks is the spring of 1995, eighteen or twenty months before Greenspan's 'irrational exuberance' comment. Stock prices had increased at an annual rate of 34 percent in 1995, and at 25 percent a year in the first eleven months of 1996; in 1994 in contrast stocks declined by 2 percent.

The surge in stock prices in 1995 and 1996 can be attributed to two different aspects of the Mexican financial crisis of 1994; one was direct and one was indirect. The direct effect was the sharp depreciation of the Mexican peso which resulted in a sudden shift in the Mexican trade balance from a deficit of $20 billion in 1994 to a surplus of $7 billion in the next year; the mirror image of this was that the U.S. trade deficit probably increased by about $25 billion since the United States was much the largest trading partner for Mexico. The counterpart of this change in the Mexican trade balance was that there was a capital inflow to the United States (a modest preview of the events that would occur in 1997 following the Asian Financial Crisis and the massive turnaround in the trade balances of the Asian countries). In effect the flow of money from Mexico to the United States led to an increase in the prices of U.S. securities. The second aspect was that the Federal Reserve eased its monetary policy and reversed its tightening policy of 1994.

An alternative starting date for the onset of the bubble is the summer of 1998, following the Asian Financial Crisis, the financial debacle in Moscow, and the collapse of Long-Term Capital Management. The sharp depreciation of the Asian currencies led to an increase in the U.S. trade deficit of more than $150 billion. Moreover, the Federal Reserve again eased policy, partly because of concern with the fragility of the monetary arrangements following the crisis in Long-Term Capital Management, until then the most professional and sophisticated of the many U.S. hedge funds.

In the twelve months after the end of June 1998 the market value of the stock traded on the New York Stock Exchange increased from $9,005 billion to $12,671 billion, an increase of 40 percent. The comparable increase in the market value of NASDAQ stocks was from $1,777 billion to $3,209 billion, an increase of 90 percent.

The surge in the inflow of capital to the United States—which otherwise can be considered an inflow of savings—initially led to an appreciation of the U.S. dollar. It brought about an increase in domestic investment and a dramatic decline in the domestic saving rate (which is identical with an increase in domestic consumption).

The counterpart of the flow of savings is that the U.S. trade deficit increased. The flow of savings from abroad to the United States led to an increase in the foreign exchange value of the U.S. dollar; the price of foreign goods declined in terms of the U.S. dollar, and this had the effect of dampening the U.S. inflation rate. Those who moved funds to the United States then bought U.S. dollar securities, which had the effect of increasing their prices; the Americans who sold some of the securities they owned to foreign investors then had to decide what to do with the money they received from the sale. They used most of the money to buy more securities from other Americans, but they also increased their purchases of U.S. goods as their wealth objectives were achieved. The decline in the U.S. saving rate and the increase in the U.S. trade deficit were inevitable outcomes of the increase in the flow of savings to the United States.

The data suggest that between 95 and 97 percent of the increase in household wealth that followed from the flow of savings from other countries to the United States was used to buy other U.S. securities and only 3 to 5 percent was used to buy consumption goods. Yet to the extent each of the sellers of the securities spent some of the money receipts on consumption goods, the domestic saving rate declined.

The spending on consumption goods is like a 'leakage.' The smaller the amount spent on consumption goods, the larger the amount spent to buy other securities and real assets and hence the larger the increase in the price of these assets.

During 1999 the Federal Reserve, the banks and the country at large became obsessed with the Y2K problem—a neurosis that the economy would break down because some computers would not be able to change the date. Precautionary behavior by the Federal Reserve led to an expansion of bank liquidity. Once again banks increased their loans in response to the increase in liquidity.

The increase in stock prices attracted European investors, and the U.S. dollar appreciated against the euro. Because of the real appreciation of the U.S. dollar and the surge in the trade deficit, inflationary pressures declined in the United States. Consequently, the Federal Reserve felt no need to adopt more contractive monetary policies.

With the advent of the new millennium, the Fed began to withdraw liquidity. Stock prices began to decline. The aggregate decline in the stock market was 40 percent and the decline in the market value of stocks traded on the NASDAQ was 80 percent.

Sloshing money and asset bubbles

The sequence of the three asset price bubbles in fifteen years—in Japan in the second half of the 1980s, in Thailand and Malaysia in the first half of the 1990s, and in the United States in the second half of the 1990s—was a unique monetary event. Japan's bubble followed from three decades of rapid increases in real estate prices, the liberalization of financial regulation that enabled the Japanese banks to increase their real estate loans at a rapid rate, and the rapid growth in the monetary base as the Bank of Japan intervened in the foreign exchange market to dampen the appreciation of the yen. When the bubble in Japan imploded, there was a surge in the flow of funds from Tokyo to Thailand and the other Asian countries; real estate prices and stock prices in these countries increased, in some cases as rapidly as they had in Japan, and their economies boomed—much as the Japanese economy boomed in the 1980s. When the bubbles in the Asian countries expanded, the money sloshed to the United States; the U.S. dollar appreciated and U.S. stock prices surged into an asset price bubble much larger than the one in the 1920s.

Japan, Thailand, and the other Asian countries, and then the United States experienced remarkable economic booms. Growth rates increased and yet inflation rates remained modest, perhaps because the currencies were appreciating and the declines in the prices of imported goods dampened upward pressure on the domestic price levels. The pattern of cash flows in each of these episodes was Ponzi-like—thus the real estate investors in Japan in the 1980s obtained all the money they needed to pay the interest to the bank lenders from these banks in the form of new loans. This pattern of cash flows wasn't sustainable and it wasn't sustained. Similarly Thailand and most of the other Asian countries had large trade deficits and were international debtors; they obtained the funds to pay the interest on their international indebtedness from their lenders in the form of new loans. In the same way the buyers of U.S. stocks in the second half of the 1990s were implicitly betting that there was a large supply of greater fools to whom the stocks could be sold. There were many greater fools but not so many that the investors that otherwise would be thought of as being rational and conservative could avoid large losses when stock prices tumbled.

9
Frauds, Swindles, and the Credit Cycle

The implosion of an asset price bubble always leads to the discovery of fraud and swindles. Enron began its tumble into bankruptcy within a few months of the peak in U.S. stock prices. At about the same time MCI-WorldCom began a series of announcements about some financial accounting mishaps that eventually culminated in the largest bankruptcy ever; the firm had overstated investments and understated expenses by $10 billion. The junk bond market collapsed after the increase in interest rates toward the end of the 1980s and the sharp decline in stock prices in October 1987.

The supply of corruption increases in a procyclical way much like the supply of credit. Soon after a recession appears likely the loans to firms that were fueling their growth with credit declines as the lenders became more cautious about the indebtedness of individual borrowers and their total credit exposure. In the absence of more credit, the fraud sprouts from the woodwork like mushrooms in a soggy forest.

Much of the fraudulent behavior is illegal, but some hovers on the borderline between what is legal and what is not. Should the award of options to senior management and employees be considered a cost, like wages, or should the award be buried in a footnote so that costs and profits are not affected? The answer determines how rapidly profits will increase and presumably how rapidly the stock prices will increase. Should Henry Blodgett, Mary Meeker, and Jack Grubman, the gurus of the telecom firms in the 1990s, have been obliged to inform the investing public of the rationale for their forecasts of prices of individual stocks, or was it sufficient for them to announce the price targets for individual firms at the end of the next six and twelve months? Should the governmental authorities establish 'truth police' to prevent the investing public from being misled, or should this public be on its own in determining which statements made by the stock sales personnel are not strictly true? Some business practices are legal, yet those engaged in the activity would be reluctant or embarrassed to have their transactions reported on the front pages of the *New York Times*, the *Wall Street Journal*, the *Chicago Tribune*, or the London *Telegraph* because the sunshine would awaken the victims to the con.

Consider Enron, MCIWorldCom, Adelphia, Tyco, HealthSouth, Global Crossing—the poster children of some of the financial excesses of the 1990s stock price bubble. Much of the fraudulent behavior initially had occurred in the mania phase as stock prices were increasing but was obscured in the froth of the bubble; high-risk borrowers were able to refinance their maturing loans because the lenders were eager to increase their total loans and assets. The investment banks believed in caveat emptor; customers old enough to vote presumably were capable of looking out for their own financial interests.

The CPA firms—the certified public accounting firms, Arthur Andersen and the like—had been established to protect investors from miscounts of the number of beans that might be reported by corporate firms; the CPAs were supposed to verify the count of the number of beans provided by the corporate firms. Some of the 'Big Five' global accounting firms were captured by the firms that they were auditing—the firms that were paying their bills—and colluded in deluding investors. Questions can be raised about whether the law firms that provided legal advice to the Enrons and the MCIWorldComs had any obligations to the investors.

Swindles, fraudulent behavior, defalcations, and elaborate hustles are part of life in market economies, more so in some countries than in others. Transparency International publishes an annual corruption index of countries; Finland has a lock on the number one position in terms of virtue and Iceland is close behind, for many years Bangladesh, the Congo, and Nigeria have competed for the bottom position in terms of the supply of corruption. The United States is much nearer the top of this hit parade than the bottom, although it may have slipped several places in the rankings because of the extensive fraud and deception that occurred in corporate America during the stock price bubble of the 1990s.

A traditional form of swindling involves overstating the value of commodities held as inventories. The McKesson Robbins scandal of the late 1930s involved the use of forged warehouse receipts as collateral for loans. Billie Sol Estes, the Texas plunger of the 1960s, falsified the number of fertilizer tanks he had under lease and borrowed against the fictitious larger number. Tino De Angelis stung American Express by using tanks of 'salad oil' in the 1960s as collateral for loans; Tino knew that that oil was less dense than water and he floated a six-inch layer of salad oil on top of twenty feet of water.[1]

Swindles that involve falsified statements about the value of inventories can be tested when the promises are made. Eventually the lenders wised up to Billie Sol Estes; someone went out and counted the fertilizer tanks. The lenders are taken in by the falsified values of the collateral offered by the borrowers, and initially the lender's accountants don't catch the deception. Swindles in financial markets may involve statements about the growth of corporate earnings or about the 'warranted' prices of shares of individual firms. A typical statement is that the 'price of Amazon stock' will climb to $400 a share by July 4; or the wording might be 'Our price target is $400 a share.' Another statement might be 'Corporate profits will increase at the rate of 15 percent a year for the next five years.' Some of the swindles in the financial markets involve 'excessive optimism' about the earnings of firms or future stock prices that those making the statements know are not likely to be true.

Wall Street makes a lot of its money selling stocks, and it prospers by having a set of highly paid individuals whose primary role is to make public statements to the effect that the prices of the shares of individual firms will increase; they're like the shills in front of the side-shows at carnivals whose role is to persuade the public to buy tickets to see the sword swallowers and the hermaphrodites. Stocks increase in price twice as often as they fall in price, so that even without any special skills the odds are that the 'market strategists' will be right twice as often as they are wrong. The market strategists typically are reluctant to indicate that stock prices as a group will decline and very rarely suggest that the price of the stock of an individual firm will decline (because the top executives of that firm would become furious and threaten never to bring any underwriting business to the investment bank ever again). If stock prices decline when the pitch has been that they will increase and the touts become an embarrassment to their employers, well they've been well paid and they're expendable and, hey, it's business. It's not hard to find replacements.

Corruption can't be measured unless an economy or a society has laws, norms, or rules that distinguish permissible from illegal or immoral behavior. Anything would be permissible and acceptable in a society without rules or norms, corruption would not occur because there would be no perceptible boundary between acceptable and nonacceptable behavior. Virtually every society has rules or norms; the implication is that these codes about what is and what isn't acceptable behavior were adopted to reduce the costs of doing business.

Laws differ among countries, what is legal in some countries may be illegal in others. Moreover within a country the laws and the norms about nonacceptable behavior change over time; some financial practices that were legal in the United States in the 1870s were illegal a hundred years later. Despite these differences across countries and over the years, there is a broader, more universal sense of acceptable financial behavior that is based on the Eighth Commandment: 'Thou Shalt not Steal.'

Corrupt behavior is part of virtually every economy. The number of transactions that overstep both moral and legal norms increases in euphoric periods like the 1990s. Paradoxically, increases in personal wealth as the prices of stocks and real estate and commodities increase at 30 or 40 percent a year for several years appear to trigger an increase in fraudulent behavior by individuals who want even more rapid increases in their wealth. Some individuals wish to keep up with the Joneses, and they may blur the truth and cut a few corners to do so.

Some entrepreneurs and managers may skate close to the edge of fraudulent behavior because of an apparent increase in the reward–risk ratio; the potential increase in their wealth from cutting the corners and bending the rules and deceiving the public may seem extremely large relative to the risk of being caught and fined or exposed to public embarrassment. Some may have calculated that they can make a big fortune and keep it if the rule-breaking is undetected; they may still get to keep half of it if they're caught. The odds on going to jail are low, and the prisons for white-collar crime are like modest country clubs with drab clothing.

Crash and panic, with their motto of *sauve qui peut,* induce many to cheat in the effort to forestall bankruptcy or some other financial disaster. A little cheating today may avert catastrophe tomorrow. When the boom ends and the losses become apparent, there is a tendency to make a big bet in the hope that a successful outcome will enable escape from what otherwise would be a disaster.

Nick Leeson was a modest functionary—one of five or six employees—in the Singapore office of Baring Brothers, the venerable London merchant bank. Leeson traded options on stocks and especially options on the Nikkei, the primary stock price index in Tokyo. The London office of Barings had set a limit on his position, the maximum amount of the firm's capital that he could risk. Leeson bought and sold call and put options on the Nikkei; the purchase of a call option was a bet that Japanese stocks would increase in price, and the purchase of a put option was a bet that Japanese stocks would decline in price. The sale of a call option was a bet that the Nikkei would not increase significantly in price, and the sale of a put option was a bet that the Nikkei would not decrease significantly in price. When Leeson bought either call options or put options, he had to pay a premium to the sellers of the options who were acquiring the price risk; when he sold put options or call options, he earned the premium from the buyers of the options because he was acquiring the price risk.

Someone in Leeson's office apparently made an error in a trade which showed a loss in his trading account. Rather than acknowledge the error to the head office of Barings in London, Leeson sold some put options on the Nikkei; his plan was to use the cash income from the premium to offset the loss due to the trading error. Instead, a big decline in the price of Tokyo stocks because of the Kobe earthquake meant that he incurred a loss on the options contract that was much larger than the premium income; the loss in his trading account increased. He then doubled his bet in the hope that a profit on the new contract would offset the previous losses, the position would be closed and no one in the head office would be any the wiser. Unfortunately for Leeson he lost on the second bet. Each time that his position incurred a loss, he made another 'double up' bet in the hope that it was his turn to win. So it went, until the losses in Leeson's error account were more or less equal to all of Baring's capital.

Leeson probably made four or five losing bets in a row. Consider the probability that he could have made five successive losing calls on the traditional coin-flip—a run of five heads in a row is a 1 in 32 chance. If he had won just one of the bets, his misadventure would not have made the front pages of the newspapers and he would not have spent two years in a Singapore jail.

There is a gallery of rogue traders. John Rusnak in the Baltimore office of the Allied Irish Bank lost $750 million of the firm's money trading foreign exchange before the head office in Dublin awoke and realized how large the losses were. Mr. Hamanaka of the New York office of Sumitomo Bank lost several billion dollars trading in the copper market. Five traders for the National Australian Bank in Sydney lost several hundred million dollars of the firm's money trading foreign currencies.

Leeson and Rusnak and the Aussies made an extended series of losing bets before being uncovered. In these cases, the problem became known because they were unable to come up with the cash to pay off on their losing bets.

The likelihood is high—very high—that there have been other rogue traders who started like Leeson and Rusnak and incurred losses on two or three or four of their 'double or nothing' bets before winning again. The bank's capital would have remained unaffected and their illegal and fraudulent behavior would have gone undetected.

The approach toward financial fraud in this chapter is descriptive and anecdotal. The *Guinness Book of World Records* does not yet have a chapter on the magnitude of financial swindles and fraud. Financial chicanery occurred in the U.S. economic expansion following the Civil War, and fraud was widespread in the Gilded Age of the 1880s. In the late 1920s a few bankers continued to sell the bonds of several Latin American countries after they had been told that the countries had stopped paying interest.

BCCI—the Bank of Credit and Commerce International—was a major financial beneficiary of the oil price shocks of the 1970s. The original BCCI had been chartered in Pakistan; the firm then established a network of branches and subsidiaries throughout the Middle East and in London and subsequently in some of the major cities in Europe and Africa. BCCI prospered greatly following the surges in the oil prices in the 1970s; the Middle East was awash with money and some of its early depositors were rich sheiks from the Persian Gulf states. BCCI's subtle appeal was to Muslim depositors. BCCI made large loans to rulers for political reasons which both helped the bank expand and eased its regulatory problems. The interest rates that it paid on its deposits were high.

It is probable that BCCI was one of the largest-ever Ponzi schemes and was never profitable. Nonperforming loans were refinanced, in effect delaying the recognition of losses. Some of BCCI's loans to a shipping magnate went sour, and the bank used fraudulent accounting to hide the losses; the auditors were bribed. BCCI then dealt extensively in options to make good the loan losses, and the firm recognized 'in the money' options at their market value and valued 'out of the money' options, on which it had losses, at zero. BCCI continued to expand as long as it could continue to sell its deposits to its 'captive clientele.'

When the bubble imploded in Japan at the beginning of the 1990s, the large banks headquartered in Tokyo and Osaka incurred massive losses on their loans, especially those that had been made to finance the purchases of real estate and stocks; these banks also incurred large losses on their loans to various credit cooperatives in rural Japan that had made real estate loans. Some of the regional banks in Japan had incurred even larger loan losses. Many of their loans for golf courses, hotels, and amusement parks were undertaken primarily to promote the development of local economies. The tradition that loans would be repaid was not well established in Japan; instead the practice was that the borrowers would use the cash from new loans to pay the interest on the outstanding loans so that the amounts of the loans outstanding would increase at the rate of interest. This practice of 'evergreen finance' was safe because property values were increasing three or four times as rapidly as the interest rate. The standard practice was that the banks required that borrowers pledge real estate as collateral for loans and the maximum loan was about 70 percent of the appraised value of the real estate. As long as real estate prices continued to increase the value of the collateral would increase and the banks would be well protected.

Once real estate prices began to decline some of the hanky-panky in the loan approval process became known. A woman who owned a small restaurant in Osaka had borrowed the yen equivalent of several billion dollars from the local branch of Sumitomo Bank; she had a 'friendly relationship' with the local banker. Some of the real estate appraisers for the banks had been bribed—or perhaps frightened—by the *yakuza,* who had figured out that the low-risk way to rob banks was to secure loans based on highly inflated appraisal values of the real estate that was being pledged as collateral. The senior officers of several of the large regional banks made loans to real estate developers so that they could buy land that was owned by the bank officials. Several senior officials of the august Ministry of Finance were entertained at a 'pantyless shabu-shabu restaurant' that had a mirrored floor; the suspicion was that these officials provided advance information to their hosts about impending changes in financial regulations.

When the real estate bubbles in Thailand and Malaysia and the other nearby Asian countries imploded and the banks incurred large losses, 'crony capitalism' suddenly appeared—favored treatments for certain borrowers that somehow had not been evident in the earlier years of exuberant economic growth. Indonesia had been a 'Suharto family business' for more than thirty years—and a remarkably successful one judged by the increase in the country's GDP. When Indonesia was doing well, the banks were happy to make loans to the many business enterprises headed by President Suharto's children—and indeed some of the banks were also headed by the president's children. The banks were not especially concerned with whether the projects that would be financed with these loans would be profitable.

One of the persistent U.S. financial headlines in the early 1980s was the impending financial disaster of the U.S. savings and loan associations and the U.S. mutual savings banks—thrift institutions that had been established to help Americans of limited means to finance the purchase of their first home. The thrifts used the funds obtained from the sale of deposits with short-term maturities to buy fixed interest rate mortgages with long-term maturities. Because the maturities of the deposit liabilities were so much shorter than the maturities of the mortgages, the thrifts acquired a 'transformation risk' that short-term interest rates could increase relative to long-term interest rates and so the excess of the interest rates they earned on their loans over the interest they paid on their deposits would decline, and perhaps even become negative. The thrifts had lived with this transformation risk for fifty years without any major problem because the interest rates on short-term deposits had been regulated by U.S. government agencies to limit 'excessive' price competition among the banks and thrifts for deposits. In the second half of the 1970s, however, interest rates on U.S. dollar securities surged, and many individuals withdrew their money from the thrifts so they could buy U.S. Treasury bills and money market funds that offered much higher interest rates than the thrifts then were allowed to pay.

The thrifts were between the proverbial rock and the hard place; if they raised interest rates on their deposits to levels that were competitive with interest rates on U.S. Treasury bills (assuming that they could get the regulators to raise the interest rate ceilings) then the interest payments on their deposits would be higher than the interest rates they were earning on their mortgages and so their capital would erode and eventually disappear. If instead the thrifts sold mortgages to reduce the excess of their interest payments over their interest income, they would incur large and immediate capital losses because the sale prices of the mortgages would be below—probably far below—the prices they had paid for them.

Most thrifts decided to pay the higher interest rates on deposits; slow death was preferable to sudden death. Each thrift could estimate the monthly rate of depletion of its capital and project the date when its capital would be fully exhausted.

Hundreds, then thousands of these thrift institutions failed. Initially a failed thrift was taken over by the Federal Savings and Loan Insurance

Corporation or the Federal Deposit Insurance Corporation, which were the U.S. government's deposit insurance guarantee agencies. These government agencies would sell the good loans of the failed thrifts to some other thrifts, and the agencies would use the cash from these loan sales and cash from their accumulated reserves to pay the depositors 100 cents for each dollar of deposits.

In a relatively few years, the accumulated reserves and the capital of both the FSLIC and the FDIC, which had been built up over nearly fifty years, were exhausted. The deposit insurance agencies found themselves between the rock and the hard place. Since they could no longer afford to close those thrifts with negative net worth because they didn't have enough money to honor their deposit insurance guarantee, they needed a subterfuge to enable the failed thrifts to remain open. They discovered the policy of 'forbearance;' they allowed these bankrupt thrifts to continue in business.

Inevitably the losses of the FSLIC and the FDIC would have to be made good, either by a transfer of taxpayer money from the U.S. Treasury or by increases in the deposit insurance premiums charged to the surviving banks and thrifts. These banks and thrifts were vehemently opposed to paying higher premiums to cover the losses of their failed competitors.

Several members of the U.S. Congress stalled the efforts to obtain funds from the U.S. Treasury so the FSLIC and the FDIC could pay off the depositors and close the failed institutions; these elected officials wanted to use this financial disaster to force a deregulation of the financial services industry. Some of the failed thrifts were 'recapitalized' as phoenix institutions; one failed thrift would acquire another and the asset side of the acquiring institution would be credited with a large entry for 'good will' and there would be a corresponding entry into its capital account. The idea—more precisely the hope—was that over the next twenty or thirty years the profits of the acquiring institution would be sufficient for them to amortize the good will and their negative net worth.

Some entrepreneurs had the bright idea that the way to save the failed thrifts was to help them rapidly to increase their deposits and loans so that their profits on new mortgages and loans would be larger than their losses on the older low interest rate mortgages. In 1982 the U.S. Congress reduced the regulations applied to the thrifts; the thrifts would be allowed to buy almost any type of security. At the same time the ceiling on the maximum amount of the insured deposit that any individual might have in a single thrift was increased to $100,000 from $40,000. (However, individuals could easily circumvent this ceiling by acquiring deposits under slightly different versions of the same name; Mr. Jones might have an insured deposit of $100,000, Mrs. Jones might have an insured deposit of $100,000, and Mr. and Mrs. Jones together might have a third insured account of $100,000. And the Jones family could buy separate deposit accounts for each child as well as a series of deposits in joint child accounts.)

These failed thrifts were eager to buy any loan or security that offered relatively high interest rates—and so they became one of the 'natural markets' for junk bonds. Initially the supply of junk bonds had been limited to those of the 'fallen angels'; bonds that had lost their investment grade rating because the firms that had issued them had fallen on tough times. The loss of the investment grade rating meant that some financial institutions could no longer hold these bonds, so the interest rates increased sharply.

Michael Milken of Drexel Burnham Lambert developed some market innovations that greatly increased both the demand for and the supply of junk bonds. The decline in interest rates and the increase in the rate of economic growth of the 1980s created an encouraging environment for the growth of the junk bond market. The Milken/Drexel sales pitch was that the excess of the interest rates on the junk bonds over the interest rates on investment grade bonds was more than adequate reward for the occasional failure of a firm and the losses the owners of its bonds then would incur.

Milken provided the financing for some of his friends and associates to gain control of thrift institutions and insurance companies and other firms that would be 'natural' buyers of the junk bonds. Milken provided 'comfort letters' to entrepreneurs contemplating a takeover of an established firm, assuring them that Drexel could raise the money they would need. Once his friends had ownership of these industrial companies, the firms would issue junk bonds that would be underwritten by Drexel, and Milken would place these bonds with the thrifts and the insurance companies that were also controlled by his friends. Drexel established its own mutual funds that would buy the junk bonds underwritten by Drexel.

Milken had a money machine. Drexel earned underwriting fees when its client firms issued new junk bonds, fees for selling the bonds to the mutual funds, sales fees for selling the shares in the mutual funds to the American public, and management fees for operating the mutual funds.

Merrill Lynch—ubiquitous Merrill—began to broker deposits for thrifts; the thrifts in California and the Southwest began to offer much higher interest rates and Merrill's army of thousands of brokers became the channel for moving money from around the country to the thrifts controlled by Milken's friends. The deposits that the thrifts were selling were guaranteed by the U.S. Treasury—which was all that the buyers wanted to know.

Few of the corporate raiders financed by Milken had much industrial experience. They used Uncle Sam's money—money obtained from the sale of deposits guaranteed by the U.S. government—to acquire more than fifty firms. They often 'overpaid' for these firms, but then they were paying with Sam's money rather than their own.

Many of the firms were unable to earn enough to pay the interest on the outstanding junk bonds. Not to worry, these firms issued some new securities that relieved them of the obligation to pay the interest on their outstanding bonds and the Milken-friendly thrifts bought these securities too. A money machine that worked as long as the junk bond market remained vibrant.

However, the junk bond market collapsed at the end of the 1980s, after the Federal regulators changed the rules so that the thrifts could no longer buy them. Junk bond prices declined sharply; the bondholders incurred large losses; the liquidity disappeared from the junk bond market. Drexel incurred large losses on its inventories of these bonds and went bankrupt in 1992.

In the end the debacle of the thrifts cost the Federal government around $150 billion. If the U.S. Congress had supplied the deposit insurance agencies with the money to close down the failed thrifts in the early 1980s when their capital was depleted, the cost to the American taxpayers would have been in the range of $20 to $30 billion. A large part of the difference between the actual costs and the costs that would have been incurred if the failed thrifts had been closed in a timely manner when their capital had become exhausted, resulted from the costs of closing down failed thrifts that had become major buyers of junk bonds. Most of the junk bonds that came to the market in the 1980s had been underwritten by Drexel, and about half of these junk bond issues went into default.

Milken and his family became billionaires and he probably remained one even after paying a fine or penalty of $550 million and spending thirty months in a federal country club.

Fiction and nonfiction about junk bonds

Corporate takeovers and junk bonds led to an interesting literature. Consider the titles of both the fiction and the nonfiction. Tom Wolfe's *Bonfire of the Vanities* is a remarkable description of the values of New York's financial elite. *Predator's Ball* by Connie Bruck is a description of an annual party for the buyers and sellers of junk bonds. *Barbarians at the Gate* is a tale about the would-be takeover of RJR Nabisco; it is hard to decide whether the would-be acquirers or the target was less attractive. The title of James Stewart's *Den of Thieves* offers a clue to the story of Milken and his friends. Ben Stein's *A License to Steal* provides a record of large corporate failures in the 1980s and 1990s and the number that had had their securities underwritten by Drexel Burnham Lambert.

There was a bumper crop of scams, swindles, and frauds in the United States in the second half of the 1990s. As outlined earlier, Enron was at the top of the hit parade of firms that were involved in the fraud and chicanery associated with the stock market boom; the firm was born from the merger of two regulated natural gas pipelines. 'Enron Heavy' made massive investments in an electrical generating plant in India and water systems in Great Britain and in Mexico. 'Enron Light' began to expand rapidly in the production and trading of electricity, natural gas, broadband, and anything else that could be traded in a wholesale market; the press hyped Enron as the single most important firm in the move toward the deregulation of the market for electricity.

The rapid expansion of both arms of Enron required large amounts of money for investment in plant and equipment, trading facilities, and software. Enron sold a lot of bonds and provided substantial revenues for its primary investment bankers, Merrill Lynch and Salomon Smith Barney. At its peak, the market capitalization of the firm was $250 billion, the market value of Enron's stock at $100 a share was over $200 billion and the market value of its publicly-owned bonds was $40 billion. Not as much as GE or Microsoft but very large numbers.

Soon after U.S. stock prices began to fall sharply in 2000, Enron—at one time touted (by its own public relations flacks) as the seventh largest firm in the United States and described by *Fortune* magazine as one of the most innovative firms in the United States—filed for bankruptcy. The market value of the stock was zip, and the market value of the bonds declined sharply.

One of the intriguing questions is when the top managers at Enron came to the proverbial 'fork in the road' and started on their elaborate path of financial chicanery. And a related question involves the roles of the accounting firms and the legal firms which were hired by Enron for professional advice and whether they were aware of its illegal practices.

A large part of the total compensation of the senior managers of Enron would come from selling the stock options they had received from the company as a form of incentive. The more rapid the rate of growth of Enron's profits, the higher the price of Enron stock; the more valuable the options, the wealthier the owners of the options. So Enron's senior officers had a powerful incentive to keep profits growing. Moreover their bonuses were geared to the stock price.

Enron was responding to the challenges presented by the stock market analysts on Wall Street. Quarter by quarter, the analysts were predicting the earnings per share to the penny. There were plenty of examples of firms that failed to make their earnings estimates; their stock prices declined by 10 or 20 percent. So the chief financial officers of Enron (and other companies) had a strong incentive to 'smooth' earnings so they met the estimates of the Wall Street analysts.

Enron had entered into sale-and-leaseback arrangements with Merrill Lynch and JP Morgan for some electrical generating barges in Nigeria. Merrill and Morgan paid above market prices for the barges so that Enron could realize a profit from their sale, which would contribute to Enron's reported profits for the year. Merrill and Morgan are not charities; because they paid above market prices for barges, the annual lease payments that they were charging were correspondingly higher. From Enron's point of view, the increase in profits in year one would be at the expense of profits in the next few years.

Enron was scrambling to increase this year's profits regardless of the negative impact on next year's profits. Next year's problem in growing earnings could be solved next year.

Enron had placed very high values on some esoteric futures contracts that were due to mature in five and ten years and which had no ready-reference market prices. Enron increased the value placed on these contracts from one year to the next and the increase in these values contributed to Enron's reported profits for the year; a sort of 1990s counterpart to Billie Sol Estes overestimating the number of fertilizer tanks that he had leased.

Enron's financial finagling led to increases in its reported profits of more than $1 billion at a time when the firm was concealing substantial debt, which had been buried in off-balance sheet financing partnerships, so-called special financing facilities or vehicles (SFVs). Many banks and industrial firms used these SFVs to remove debt from their balance sheets so they would be better positioned to increase the amounts they could borrow. The accounting rules provided that these SFVs could be considered independent entities as long as 3 percent of the equity in the SFV was owned by 'unrelated individuals.' Enron owned 97 percent of the partnerships and the private individuals who owned the remaining 3 percent were senior employees; some of the 3 percent was owned by Enron's bankers. Some of these partnerships had names taken from *Star Wars*—JEDI, Chewco, and so on. The partnerships would borrow from the banks and other lenders as if they were independent from Enron and then invest the funds with Enron.

Enron was using the cash obtained from the SFVs borrowings to support the price of its own stock. That's more or less a Nick Leeson go-for-broke strategy. If the stock price should fall, then the value of the partnerships would decline and they would be 'under water.' But that's the traditional practice and it had been used by American railroads in the nineteenth century. Firms borrowed using the value of their stock as collateral and then when the stock price declined, they scrambled to get the cash to support the stock price; if the stock price declined too far, the value of the collateral would fall below the amount of the loan and they would be asked to come up with additional collateral.

The major investment banks were eager to lend to these partnerships because Enron was such a good customer and a source of underwriting income.

The collapse of Enron led to the demise of Arthur Andersen, formerly the most respected of the large U.S. accounting firms—although in the previous few years Andersen had been sued by the creditors of the Baptist Hospital of Arizona, Waste Management, and several other audit clients that had bellied-up. Andersen was accused of shredding documents after the Securities and Exchange Commission had started its investigation into Enron's finances.

Andersen had been selling $2 million a year of auditing services to Enron and $25 million of consulting services. The implication was that Andersen's desire to retain the consulting income clouded its judgment about the appropriateness of how Enron should measure its profits—and that's a charitable statement. Andersen was only one of the outside groups that had been co-opted by Enron; Enron's board had multiple conflicts of interests since some of the board members received consulting income from the firm. Enron had established several groups of advisers, usually from the media, on a $25,000 a year retainer for one meeting a year. Enron's chair, Kenneth Lay ('Kenny boy' in some political circles in Washington) was a major contributor to politicians. In the end Andersen was convicted of obstruction of justice in June 2002. The firm subsequently folded, losing hundreds of clients who did not want to be associated with its tarnished reputation.

Criminal charges were filed against more than thirty Enron officials. There were three principal types of financial chicanery; the thrust was to overstate income and understate the growth of indebtedness. Some of the top officials also under-reported their taxable incomes to the Internal Revenue Service. Ken Lay and others have been charged with providing misleading information about the financial well-being of the firm. Five were found guilty after trials and one was acquitted; fifteen have pleaded guilty and several have been sentenced to prison. Most have not yet been sentenced. Eight are still awaiting trial. Jeffrey Skilling, the number two at Enron, was charged with thirty-five violations of the law, including conspiracy, securities fraud, wire fraud, and insider trading. Andrew Fastow, the chief financial officer, pleaded guilty to the conspiracy to commit securities fraud and will be imprisoned for a minimum of ten years without the possibility of parole; Lea Fastow, his wife, pleaded guilty to tax fraud and will be jailed for six months. Ben Glisan, the corporate treasurer, pleaded guilty to wire and securities fraud and received a five-year sentence. Michael Kopper, a finance executive, pleaded guilty to fraud and money-laundering. The former directors of Enron agreed to a $168 million settlement of a lawsuit brought by the shareholders; $13 million of this amount will come from their own pockets and the rest from the proceeds of an insurance policy. Lehman Brothers paid $222 million as part of this settlement and Bank of America paid $69 million.

WorldCom had been one of the most rapidly growing telecommunications firms in the 1990s, with more than sixty acquisitions. Bernie Ebbers, a former high school history teacher from Jackson, Mississippi, was the maestro of its rapid expansion. WorldCom's earnings per share increased at a rapid rate which meant that the ratio of its stock price to its earnings was higher than the stock prices of the firms that were being acquired. WorldCom paid for its acquisitions by exchanging newly issued shares in WorldCom for the shares in the firms being acquired.

WorldCom's earnings per share were increasing so fast because it was buying the earnings of other firms that had lower stock prices rather than because of its superior performance as a telecommunications firm. (WorldCom could not afford to buy a firm with a stock price higher than its own because that would lead to decline in the rate of growth of its earnings.)

Ebbers was riding the proverbial tiger: to keep WorldCom's stock price high, the firm had to continue to acquire other firms that had lower stock prices. As WorldCom increased in size as a result of its acquisitions, the only way it could maintain the rate of growth of earnings was to acquire larger and larger firms. The problem—the generic problem for firms that grow their earnings per share by acquisition—is that the number of telecom firms that remained attractive takeover targets was declining as WorldCom continued to grow.

WorldCom's last acquisition was MCI, one of the most innovative firms in the U.S. telecommunications industry; through the use of microwave towers it had broken AT&T's monopoly on long-distance phone services. MCI was so large that the firm was renamed MCIWorldCom. In the effort to maintain its growth of earnings, MCIWorldCom then attempted a merger with U.S. Sprint, but the proposal was blocked by the U.S. regulatory authorities.

Soon thereafter MCIWorldCom filed for bankruptcy—the largest bankruptcy in U.S. history. Subsequent investigation revealed that the chief financial officers in the firm had overstated earnings by claiming that $4.8 billion of everyday expenses were 'investments'—eventually the fudged numbers amounted to $10 billion. The major reason for this accounting fraud was to maintain the rate of growth of earnings because otherwise the stock price would have declined. Two of WorldCom's senior officials were arrested and pleaded guilty and have gone to prison.

Later it became known that MCI had lent Bernie Ebbers more than $400 million in off-the-books loans. Ebbers had used WorldCom stock as collateral for the loan—and he used some of the cash obtained from the loan to buy more WorldCom stock. Ebbers flunked the first lesson in investing—diversification of assets.

Enron and WorldCom had become victims of their own success. The stock market analysts on Wall Street had developed the practice of forecasting each firm's quarterly earnings. If the firm failed to meet the earnings targets, the stock price would decline by 15 or 20 percent. A big hit. So the senior financial officials began to play the game, and in two ways. If the prospective earnings were likely to be much higher than anticipated, then they had an incentive to prepay expenses or delay receipts, in effect postponing the recognition of earnings. The rationale was that the Wall Street analysts would raise the bar, and what might have been a one-time surge in earnings could become the new and higher benchmark. Conversely if earnings reported by the firm came in below estimates, they had a strong incentive to 'borrow' earnings from the future by delaying payments or advancing receipts. The problem would become more intense the next quarter.

Bernie Ebbers's trial on the charge of misleading the public about the financial condition of the firm began in January 2005. His lawyers claimed he was misinformed by Scott Sullivan, WorldCom's chief financial officer, and that Sullivan claimed that Ebbers directed the fraud to obtain a reduction in his own prison time. Ten of the former directors of WorldCom agreed to pay $18 million from their own pockets as part of a $54 million settlement with the shareholders.

Dennis Kozlowski, head of Tyco, a $200 billion dollar conglomerate, and Mark Swartz its chief financial officer were accused by the Federal government of looting Tyco of hundreds of millions of dollars in two ways: they awarded themselves options to buy Tyco stock without the approval of Tyco's directors and they tapped into Tyco's treasury to pay their personal living expenses. The Feds made a big deal of the $6,000 shower curtain and the $2 million birthday party for the second Mrs. Kozlowski in Sardinia; Tyco picked up 50 percent of the costs of the party. The press reported that one of the highlights of the party was an ice sculpture reproduction of Michelangelo's *David* that dispensed vodka from a vital body part.

Tyco had acquired several hundred firms in a wide variety of industries, mostly paid for with its stock but occasionally with the cash obtained by selling bonds and by borrowing from banks. Tyco massaged the earnings of the firms being acquired. After these firms had agreed to the acquisition, their earnings would be squeezed or otherwise temporarily depressed so that they would appear to surge when they were integrated into the Tyco family. This contributed to the rapid growth in Tyco's earnings.

Tyco was also sensitive about its costs and, especially, taxes; the firm's operating headquarters were in New Hampshire (a state with neither an income tax or a sales tax) and its legal headquarters were in Bermuda, enabling the firm to avoid paying U.S. corporate income taxes.

The State of New York alleged that Kozlowski had failed to pay the appropriate sales tax of $1 million on paintings that he purchased in New York City by asserting that the paintings would be shipped to New Hampshire; the empty crates that had contained the paintings were shipped there after the paintings had been removed to Kozlowski's New York apartment.

The first trial ended with a hung jury. Unlike Enron and MCIWorldCom, Tyco did not go bankrupt.

The Rigas family was charged by the Federal government with looting Adelphia Communications, the sixth largest cable system in the United States, of $2.3 billion; the family's transgressions combined elements of the misbehavior of both Enron and WorldCom. The family collected more than $3 billion in off-balance sheet loans; the company inflated capital expenses and hid debt. Adelphia had started as a small family-owned firm; and the boundary between personal accounts and business accounts is often blurred in such situations. Many of the borrowings by the firm were guaranteed by the family, and many of the Rigas family borrowings were guaranteed by the firm. The family borrowed in large part to use the cash to support the firm's stock. The former director of finance and the former vice president have pleaded guilty. Two of the Rigas family members were convicted.

The founder and chair of HealthSouth, Richard Scrushy, was charged with an accounting fraud of nearly $3 billion; the trial began in January 2005. There is agreement that fraud was committed. Scrushy has claimed—much like Bernie Ebbers at WorldCom and Ken Lay at Enron—that the fraud was committed by his subordinates and that they are now suggesting that he managed the fraud so their own prison time will be reduced.

Sam Waksal the founder and promoter of ImClone was committed to a federal prison after pleading guilty to six federal charges. Waksal had told his father and his daughter to sell their shares in the firm because an adverse statement from the Food and Drug Administration that would be released the next day would lead to a decline in the share price.

Martha Stewart's five-month stay in a federal prison may have been related to Sam Waksal's decision to sell shares in ImClone. Stewart sold her shares but denied that she had received any information from Waksal. An interesting coincidence. The Federal government indicted Stewart on an 'obstruction of justice' charge. She was found guilty.

Richard Grasso, the chairman and chief executive officer of the New York Stock Exchange, made it to the front pages of the nation's newspaper with the news that his retirement benefit package would be $150 million. The exchange is owned by its members and both provides them with a trading floor and regulates their trading practices. In this, it is an arbiter of what is permissible and what isn't. Most of the directors of the stock exchange are senior officers of the firms that are regulated by the exchange—or perhaps more precisely, are supposed to be regulated by the exchange. The retirement compensation package of Grasso seemed high—very high—relative both to the revenues of the exchange and to the retirement benefits packages of other leaders on Wall Street.

The suspicion was that Grasso was soft on the regulatory front because he did not want to offend the directors who determined his salary and bonuses. Grasso's successor and the new board have sued Grasso and the previous board.

Global Crossing swapped network capacity with other carriers to inflate its revenues. The company shredded documents and went bankrupt, but before it did, Gary Winnick received $800 million from the sales of his shares.

Shell Oil agreed to pay a fine of $150 million to the U.S. and the British regulatory authorities for overstating the volume of oil in its reserves in the ground. Harder to count the oil reserves than to count Billie Sol Estes's fertilizer tanks. As well as the fine, several Shell officials were bounced from the firm, but none went to jail.

Mutual fund scandals of 2003

In 2003 a number of the large U.S. mutual fund families—maybe half of the twenty largest firms that manage mutual funds—were accused of providing exceptional trading privileges to several hedge funds, enabling the hedge funds to earn large profits at the expense of the other owners of shares in the mutual funds. Some of these transactions were legal, most were not, and all violated the implicit contract between the mutual fund and its shareholders that each shareholder would be treated equally. Each U.S. mutual fund is required to file a contract with the U.S. Securities and Exchange Commission that stipulates its own rules for transactions—a description of what is permissible behavior and what isn't. A feature of most such contracts is that investors will not be allowed to make 'in-and-out' transactions—to sell the shares in the fund a day or two after the shares were purchased. The contract generally provides that if an investor does undertake an in-and-out transaction, the investor will be charged an additional 1 percent or the request to sell may be delayed. Another standard boiler-plate paragraph in the offering agreement is that the officers of the fund will not buy shares in a firm if the fund is buying shares in the same firm—or that if the officers do buy shares in the firm, they will not 'front-run,' that is, buy the shares in a firm for their own private accounts before the mutual fund buys the shares in the same company. Moreover the funds' standard practice was to disclose information about the securities that each fund owned only at the end of the quarter and not to provide any information on purchases and sales of individual securities between these end-of-quarter dates.

A number of hedge funds engaged in market timing transactions with the mutual funds; the hedge funds would buy the shares in the mutual fund if they thought it likely that the news would lead to increases in the prices of the stocks owned by the mutual funds and increases in the funds' net asset value per share. The hedge funds would trade on 'stale prices,' like shooting fish in the proverbial barrel; the opportunity to trade on stale prices arose because some of the mutual funds owned foreign securities, and the markets in which these foreign securities were traded closed before the U.S. market closed. The Japanese market closed before the U.S. market opened. The mutual funds would inform some of the hedge funds about the stocks they were buying and selling during the quarter, although they would not provide the same information to the rest of their shareholders. Some mutual fund managers would trade the shares of their own funds on an in-and-out basis; some would front-run the purchases of the mutual fund.

Why did the mutual funds break their commitments to their shareholders?

Because a lot of business is quid pro quo, and the hedge funds might make purchases of shares in some mutual funds owned by one of the mutual fund management companies that needed a bit of a boost.

Canary Capital, a family-owned hedge fund, agreed to pay restitution of $20 million to the mutual funds and a penalty of $10 million to the Securities and Exchange Commission for its transgressions.

Massachusetts Financial Services, the oldest U.S. mutual fund, agreed to a $200 million settlement. Alliance Capital agreed to pay a $250 million penalty and to cut its fees by $350 million over several years. The founder and the major owner of the Strong Funds in Milwaukee resigned his management positions, sold his ownership interest and paid a penalty in the tens of millions. Morgan Stanley instructed its brokers to hustle its own mutual funds rather than funds in general in a form of payola; the clients of Morgan Stanley were not made aware that the advice of the brokers was not impartial.

The increase in the number of swindles and the scope of fraudulent behavior has attracted the economic theorists. Many of the swindles—often the low class ones—involve 'Ponzi finance,' defined by Minsky as a pattern of financial transactions when a firm's interest payments are larger than its cash flows from operations.[2] Another theorist noted that those borrowers who can set the interest rates on their personal debts engage in Ponzi finance and use the cash obtained from new loans to make the debt service payments on their outstanding loans.[3]

Most of the entrepreneurs who establish a Ponzi finance operation appear to know and understand what they are doing; they live high for a few months or years before the authorities catch up with them.

Occasionally an innocent becomes involved and seems unable to understand the pattern of finance.

Henry Blodgett, Mary Meeker, and Jack Grubman

In a good year in the late 1990s Henry Blodgett earned $10 million, Mary Meeker $15 million, and Jack Grubman $20 million. Henry, Mary, and Jack were the apostles of the dot.coms and the telecommunications firms in the bubble years of the 1990s. They earned these rock-star incomes because they brought a lot of underwriting and trading business to their firms. There is no rule of thumb that relates their incomes to the profits they generated for their employers, but it's a safe bet that their employers had calculated that the profits were two to three times larger than their salaries.

Henry Blodgett of Merrill Lynch became famous for setting price targets for the stocks of individual dot.com firms, and some of these targets were achieved; in the heyday of the bull market these achievements could be seen as testimony to his success as a forecaster or to the self-fulfilling prophecy. Henry got a lot of attention because in some internal e-mails within Merrill he was deriding the attractiveness of some of the same stocks that he was promoting to the American public. Henry has left the security business never to return.

Jack Grubman of Salomon Smith Barney, part of the Citigroup family, became famous because he changed his recommendation on AT&T stock after a polite request from his boss Sandy Weill. The apparent quid pro quo was that Jack wanted Sandy's help in getting Jack's twin daughters admitted to the kindergarten class at the 92nd Street YMHA. About the same time Citigroup made a contribution of $lm to the Y, Jack left Salomon Smith Barney with a $20 million golden handshake. Jack paid a penalty of $20 million and agreed not to work in the securities business again.

Parmalat (the name combines that of the city of Parma and *latte* or milk) the Italian dairy and food products company headquartered in Parma, Italy, used fabricated certificates of deposits to overstate its assets by $4 billion; the fraudulent CDs were prepared by superimposing one document on another in a copying machine. This fraud—the deception of the investing public and the investment banks—appears to have continued for more than ten years.

Boiler shops are one form of a swindle. Robert Brennan of First Jersey Securities was a high profile boiler shop operator. The broker in a boiler shop specializes in making cold calls to individuals about a stock, say Shazam Rockets. Shazam's share price is usually low, perhaps between

$2 and $5 a share, and initially many of the shares in Shazam are owned by insiders—those who own the boiler shop. The insiders trade with each other and manage increases in the price of the stock say from $2 to $3 a share, and they then begin to make their cold calls, pointing to the 50 percent increase in the price of Shazam's stock in the last six weeks; they've learned that the gullible are much more willing to buy a stock whose price has increased rapidly. They also know that the unwashed investors have a preference for low price stocks.

Swindles differ from ordinary robbery in that they abuse a trust. Daniel Defoe thought the stock-jobber cheat 10,000 times worse than the highwayman because the swindler robbed people he knew—often his friends and relatives—and ran no physical 'risque.'[4]

Swindles should be distinguished from bribery, both of government officials and of the employees of one business by those of another. These illegal and/or immoral transactions involve both misrepresentation and the violation of an explicit or implicit trust between particular groups. Was Arthur Andersen corrupted by the $25 million a year in consulting fees from Enron? Was Bernie Ebbers bribed by Jack Grubman because Jack arranged for Bernie to be able to buy shares in twenty or thirty firms on the days when these stocks would be sold to the public for the first time? In the bubble euphoria, the odds were extremely high that the share prices would double on the first day of trading. Or did Bernie bribe Jack Grubman with the implicit threat that unless he was provided with favored treatment in buying newly issued stock he would take WorldCom's underwriting business across the street to Merrill Lynch or Morgan Stanley? The rules of the stock exchanges and the rules of the futures exchanges are like a 'code of purity' to instill confidence in the public that they will be treated fairly—so the rules are really designed to protect some of the members of the exchanges from the adverse consequences for the industry of recognition of cheating by others.

The National Association of Security Dealers (NASD) pursues disciplinary actions against those of its members who have violated the rules. In recent years, hundreds of its members have been at the receiving end of disciplinary actions.

Corruption has been discussed historically by Jacob van Klavaren, who was especially interested in corruption as a form of market transaction that facilitated getting things done that were profitable but forbidden, as in black markets, or simply dishonest, such as the looting of India by Clive or Hastings.[5] Van Klavaren also discussed the systematic embezzlement from the Royal African Company and the East India Company by insiders who skimmed the profits due to stockholders through contracts with companies that they themselves controlled. In a similar manner, the Credit Mobilier in the United States in 1873 diverted profits from Union Pacific stockholders to the inside group run by Oakes Ames, a congressman from Massachusetts, and his congressional and business cronies. Drew, Fisk, and Gould milked the Erie Railroad in similar fashion.[6]

Swindling in financial markets is many-faceted—the directors swindle the stockholders, the senior management swindles the directors, the security underwriters swindle both the owners of the firms that they are bringing to the public and the stockholders, borrowers swindle their bank lenders, and one group of employees may swindle another. Some swindlers issue fraudulent bills of exchange to the cost of those who own these bills when the fraud is discovered and who only then discover that they are holding counterfeit securities.

The line separating moral from immoral acts is now less fuzzy than it once was. One way that modernity is distinguished from backwardness is morality. In early stages of development, codes provided for honor and trust only within the family. Nepotism was efficient in these circumstances since strangers virtually had a license to steal. In 1720 a firm could buy a man's services but not his loyalty; to be a clerk was an invitation to start a new and competitive business at a time when embezzlement and fraudulent conversion were not regarded as crimes.[7] Lines between business and theft, commerce and piracy were not precise.[8] Hammond noted that it was not until 1799 that the borrowing of bank funds by bank officials was definitively ruled illegal,[9] although the 1720 House of Commons investigation of the South Sea Bubble ruled that the directors of the South Sea Company, having been guilty of a breach of trust in lending money of the company on its own stock, should use their own wealth to make good investor losses.[10]

A financial journalist writing a preface to a fictionalized biography of Ponzi drew a parallel between the 1920s and the 1970s and suggested that swindles were a product of inflation; his view was that when increases in the cost of living pinched family budgets, the heads of some households took additional risks to increase their incomes.[11] A somewhat different view held that destabilizing speculation in the absence of 'avoidable ignorance' is gambling, which provides utility to the participants even when they know they are likely to lose, in much the same way as participating in a lottery.[12]

Whether swindles should be included in the category of 'avoidable ignorance' is debatable. Cynics may share the belief of W.C. Fields that 'You can't cheat an honest man' and conclude that victims of swindles mainly have themselves to blame. *Mundus vult decipi—ergo decipitatur.* 'the world wants to be deceived, let it therefore be deceived.'[13] Some psychiatrists believe that the swindler and his victims are bound together in a symbiotic, love-hate relationship that provides satisfaction to both.

Fraud and euphoria

Fraudulent behavior increases in economic booms. Fortunes are made in a boom, individuals become greedy for a share of the increase in wealth and swindlers come forward to exploit that greed. The number of sheep waiting to be shorn increases in booms and an increasing number offer themselves as sacrifices to the swindlers. 'There's a sucker born every minute.' In *Little Dorrit,* Ferdinand Barnacle of the Circumlocution Office tells Arthur Clennam, who had hoped that the exposure of Mr. Merdle's swindles would serve as a warning to dupes that 'the next man who has as large a capacity and as genuine a taste for swindling will succeed as well.'

Greed also induces some of the amateurs to commit fraud, embezzlement, defalcation, and similar misfeasance. The demise of Overend, Gurney and Company, the well-established 'Corner House,' after the original partners had retired and the firm had gone public, was brought about by a pleasure-loving gallant inside the firm who had appointed an outsider as adviser for £5,000 a year, paid in advance and returned to the insider. D.W. Chapman, the insider, kept ten horses and entertained lavishly at Prince's Gate, Hyde Park. His outside adviser, Edward Watkins Edwards, a former accountant, recommended that many new activities be added to the bread-and-butter discount business: speculation in grain, production of iron, shipbuilding, shipping, and railroad finance. The firm became 'partners in every sort of lock-up and speculative business,' and Edwards drew commissions on each. By the end of 1860 the firm was losing £500,000 a year net even though it was earning £200,000 a year on its discount business. The bubble was pricked by the failure of an unrelated firm of railway contractors, Watson, Overend, and Company.[14]

From the world of fiction—in this case, *Melmoth réconcilié,* by Honoré de Balzac—the comparable figure to Chapman is Castanier, a bank cashier, whose mistress, Mme Aquilinia de la Garde, has expensive tastes in silver, linen, crystal, and rugs, passions that prove his undoing. For a time he survives by issuing promissory notes. At the point of no return, when he finally calculates his debts, he might have been saved by leaving Mme de la Garde, but he cannot give her up. Finally, because of the impossibility of continuing his financial maneuvers, given the growth of his debts and the very large interest payments it is clear that he is bankrupt. But he prefers fraud to honest bankruptcy and dips into the bank's till.[15]

Swindling increases in economic booms because greed appears to grow more rapidly than wealth; it's as if the increase in wealth triggers an increase in greed. Kozlowski was one of the richest people in America; yet the funds to pay for the $6,000 shower curtain and the other furnishings in his apartment were taken from Tyco—without the knowledge of the firm's directors. Swindling also increases in times of financial distress as a result of a taut credit system which induces declines in asset prices; at that stage the fraudulent behavior is undertaken to avoid a financial disaster. Ponzi resisted the suggestions of his associates that he should take the money and run and they in their turn swindled him.[16] The London banker Henry Fauntleroy forged conveyances of estates to use as collateral for loans. These men served as models for Augustus Melmotte, the swindler of Trollope's *The Way We Live Now,* who forged both a conveyance and a deed when the price of his Mexican railroad stock declined and he could no longer sell stock to raise cash.[17] John Blunt of the South Sea Company, Eugène Bontoux of the Union Générate, Jacob Wasserman of the Darmstäder und Nationalbank (Danatbank), and the directors of the Credit Anstalt all bought the shares of their firms in the open market to support their prices so they might sell more stock later. A bank that buys its own stock to keep the price high reduces its own liquidity since the ratio of its cash holdings to its deposits declines as it pays out cash to obtain the stock. In 1720 the Bank of England borrowed using its own stock as collateral. Clapham noted that the Bank of England did not penetrate into the far wilder and 'absolutely dishonest' finance of the South Sea Company.[18]

The revelation of a swindle or embezzlement increases distress which in turn often precipitates a crash and panic. In 1772 Alexander Fordyce absconded from London to the Continent, leaving his associates to meet obligations of £550,000, largely in dubious acceptances of the Ayr Bank, if they could—but they could not. Fordyce had personally been short of East India stock, whose price had risen enough to wipe him out.[19] On August 24, 1857, it became known that a cashier in the New York office of the Ohio Life Insurance and Trust Company had embezzled almost all the assets of that highly reputed enterprise to sustain his stock market transactions, which then triggered a series of failures that reverberated in Liverpool, London, Paris, Hamburg, and Stockholm.[20] A kind of mid-nineteenth-century version of Nick Leeson.

In September 1929 the Hatry empire in London, a set of investment trusts and operating companies in photographic supplies, cameras, slot machines, and small loans, collapsed. Hatry wanted to expand into the steel business. He was caught using fraudulent collateral in an attempt to borrow £8 million to buy United Steel, and his failure led to tightening of the British money market, withdrawal of call loans from the New York market, and a topping out of the stock market.

Bubbles and swindles

Some bubbles are swindles, some are not. The Mississippi Bubble was not a swindle; the South Sea Bubble was. A bubble generally starts with an apparently legitimate or at least legal purpose. What became the Mississippi Bubble initially started as the Compagnie d'Occident, to which the Law system added the farming-out of national tax collections and the Banque. John Law owned about one-third of the Place Vendôme and other valuable real estate in Paris and at least a dozen magnificent rural estates. His activities were not a swindle, but his financial demise reflected a mistake that was based on two fallacies: (1) that stocks and bonds were money and (2) that issuing more money as demand increased was not inflationary.[21]

In the South Sea Bubble, the monopoly of trade in the South Atlantic was purely incidental.[22] Very quickly, consolidation of British government debt overwhelmed the South Atlantic trade aspects of the enterprise, and stockjobbing overwhelmed government debt shortly thereafter. John Blunt and his insiders sought to profit on stock issued to themselves against loans secured by the stock as collateral. As they realized the capital gains from the increases in the price of the stock, they used the cash to buy estates; Blunt had six contracts to buy estates at the time of the collapse and a man named Surman had *four* contracts to buy real estate on which he owed £100,000. To get the cash to pay profits, the South Sea Company both needed to increase its capital and to have the price of its stock increase continuously. And it needed both increases at an accelerating rate as in a chain letter or in a Ponzi scheme.

Ponzi promised to pay 40 percent interest on the deposits for forty-five days. He said that the extraordinary rate of return reflected that he was buying foreign currencies at depreciated market values and then using the foreign currencies to buy International Postal Union coupons that could be redeemed for U.S. postage stamps at the official exchange rate which could then be resold at their face value. Ponzi might have been able to profit from this type of arbitrage, but his story was window-dressing; when he was arrested in August 1922, he had taken in $7.9 million and had only $61 worth of stamps and postal coupons on the premises.[23]

History has given less immortality to certain of Ponzi's forerunners. The former Munich actress Spitzeder paid 20 percent a year interest on the funds received from Bavarian farmers. She received 3 million guilden from these farmers. She and her helpers drew a long jail sentence at the end of 1872. Placht, a dismissed officer, promised to pay 40 percent a year and borrowed the pennies of 1,600 widows and orphans to get the money to play the stock market. His stock purchases were not profitable and he spent six years in jail.[24]

As economic booms progress, greed mounts and the excuses become thinner, more nearly gossamer bubbles. In 1720 and again in 1847 (two occasions when lists were compiled), such swindles were numerous, although they have been embroidered with hoaxes perpetrated by and on later historians.[25] In 1720, for example, there was one proposal for carrying on an undertaking of great advantage that would be revealed only in due time. The perpetrator charged two guineas a share and made off with £2,000, keeping his secret intact by failing to attend a meeting with the investors.[26] Another scheme was for the 'nitvender,' or selling of nothing.[27] But in the late 1990s stock market boom, some firms were able to raise money from the public before they had any business plans.

A project of modest current interest offers a premature example of women's liberation:

> A proposal by several ladies and others to make, print and stain calicos in England and also fine linen as fine as any Holland to be made of British flax ... They were resolved as one man [sic] to admit no man but will themselves subscribe to a joint-stock to carry on said trade.[28]

In later periods, both historians and novelists noted that stock promotions had little connection with reality. 'Many companies were founded without undertaking operations, railroads without way or traffic.'[29] 'Construction companies grew like mushrooms. Many of these companies speculated in building sites rather than in construction.'[30] 'Limehouse and Rotherhithe bridge ... It was not at all necessary for them that the bridge should ever be built; that, probably, was out of the question ... But if a committee of the House of Commons could be got to say that it ought to be built, they might safely calculate on selling out at a large profit.'[31]

Financial distress leads to fraud in the effort to dump the losses on others before they cascade into ever larger losses. If the market goes decisively the wrong way, for example, bucket-shop operators abscond. When new cash subscriptions failed to meet profits paid out to greedy insiders, Blunt borrowed the cash of the South Sea Company for his own use;[32] a preview of the story of the Rigas family and Adelphia. In 1861 Bleichröder characterized Bethel Henry Strousberg as 'clever but his manner of undertaking new ventures in order to mend old holes is dangerous, and if he should encounter a [sudden] obstacle his whole structure may collapse and under its ruins bury millions of gullible shareholders.'[33] Bleichröder was right. Another German financier, the Hamburg banker Gustav Goddefroy, lost heavily in railroad and mining shares in 1873 and then bled his overseas trading company to support his position in the stock market.[34]

These incurable optimists, who know they are going to win the first time, but lose, frequently try again, often doubling their bets and increasing their risks by transactions that either are of dubious morality or clearly illegal. In the late 1920s, when U.S. banks were still allowed to underwrite securities (before the Glass-Steagall Act of 1932), Albert Wiggins of the Chase Bank and Charles Mitchell of National City continued to sell Chilean and Peruvian bonds at the old prices after they had learned by cable from those governments that they had stopped paying interest.[35] Horace understood the position, if Sprague quotes and translates him accurately: 'Make money; make it honestly if you can; at all events, make money.'[36] Equally cynical is Jonathan Swift over the South Sea Bubble:

> Get money, money still
> And then let virtu follow, if she will.[37]

On this topic, Balzac has the last word: 'The most virtuous merchants tell you with the most candid air this word of the most unrestrained immorality: "One gets out of a bad affair as one can."'[38]

Noble gamblers

The literature abounds in condemnation of noble gamblers and insiders, who might have been thought to regard financial obligations as debts of honor but are better at promising than at paying their subscriptions.[39] The Austrian nobility was worse than the Junkers, who at least ostensibly disdained money. Eduard Lasker maintained that 'when the dilettantes enter, they make it even worse than the professional swindlers.'[40] Daigremont in Zola's *L'Argent* sends Saccard to the Marquis de Bohain to help launch his Banque Universelle: 'If he wins, he pockets it; if he loses, he does not pay. That is known, People are resigned to it.'[41] Again in novels and in real life, nobles seek seats on boards of directors. Wirth enumerates Austrian princes, Landgrafs, counts, barons, Freiherren, and other nobles on the boards of railroads, banks, and other industrial firms 'for which they have no capacity.'[42] To control the accounts of the Banque Universelle, Saccard appoints a *sieur* Rousseau and a *sieur* Lavignière, the first completely subservient to the second, who is tall, blond, very polite, approving always, devoured by ambition to come on the board.[43] *L'Argent* is a *roman à clef* based on Eugène Bontoux and the Union Générate, whose subscribers included the Pretender, royalists, notables, and country squires.[44] In Britain the *Economist* in October 1848 included the nobility and aristocracy at the head of a list of dishonor:

> Present prostration and dejection is [sic] but a necessary retribution for the folly, the avarice, the insufferable arrogance, the headlong, desperate and unprincipled gambling and jobbing which disgraced nobility and aristocracy, polluted senators and senate houses, and traders of all kinds.[45]

Rosenberg claims that while the Austrian and French aristocracy led the other estates in pursuit of the golden calf, Berlin bureaucrats successfully opposed a similar movement in Prussia, noting an abortive attempt by Mevissen to get some counts on the board of a 50 million thaler bank. Junkers speculated in spirits and land products, he admits, but shied away from urban developments.[46] Perhaps this was so in 1857. In the following decade, the perception of money as evil had weakened. Railroad finance, both inside Germany and in Strousberg's maneuvers in Romania, was tinged with scandal, reaching up to the peaks of the aristocracy and virtually into the Prussian court itself.[47]

Venal journalism

Speculation generally was helped by the press. Some members of the press were for sale, some were critical, and some were both. Daniel Defoe excoriated stockbrokers in November 1719 when the South Sea stock sold at 120 yet turned around to defend them at the peak of 1,000 in August 1720.[48] He expressed his 'just contempt' for people who claimed he wrote for the Royal African Company, stating he had sold his stock; but a modern critic concluded that he either continued to hold the stock or was hired by the company to attack individual traders who competed with the monopoly.[49] The press was still in an underdeveloped stage in France in the early nineteenth century; in 1837 a journalist wrote: 'Give me 30,000 francs of advertising and I will take responsibility for placing all the shares of the worst possible company that it is possible to imagine.'[50] Laffitte financed newspapers.[51] Charles Savary of the Banque de Lyon et de la Loire had 500 journalists singing the praises of his operations, using releases, largely paid for, as if they were stories created by the journal's staff.[52] Journals often sought favor with banks, the stock exchange, and the public by whipping up the speculative fever.[53] Bleichröder was cautious in avoiding speculation and outright misrepresentation, but he owned general and financial newspapers and used journalists to hype his financial interests. In 1890–1891 he financed a trip to Mexico for one Paul Lindau, who wrote thirty-four articles and a book on the country without mentioning his connection with Bleichröder who at the time was selling Mexican bonds on the Berlin market.[54] A critical press developed slowly during the nineteenth century on the Continent.

In the 1890s in the United States, on the other hand, a financier closer to the line was pursued by the press and lived in fear of it, at least this is the inference from Theodore Dreiser's fictionalized biography of Charles Tyson Yerkes, the Chicago streetcar tycoon who operated along, and sometimes over, the knife-edge that separates legitimate from illegitimate transactions. Yerkes needed favorable publicity to sell securities, which he sought and won through his gift of an observatory to the newly formed University of Chicago. The well-publicized gift helped restore his reputation and enabled him to sell his streetcar bonds in Europe.[55] But later the press drove him from Chicago.[56]

Tipping off friends before hawking a stock to the world in an investor column may be an old trick, but it is more readily detected today, along with all buying and selling of shares based on insider information.

Suspicious trades in a stock and in options to buy and sell the stock before the news that affects its price is made public are now analyzed by computer programs. The technique led to the arrests of investment columnist R. Foster Winans of the *Wall Street Journal,* who fed his tips in advance to a friend, and of former Undersecretary of Defense Thayer, who told a friend of forthcoming events in a company of which he was a director. (Thayer's friend speculated on the basis of the information; Winans capitalized on his experience by writing *Trading Secrets: Seduction and Scandal at the Wall Street Journal,* published by St Martin's Press, 1986.) Similarly a young Merrill Lynch broker in New London, Connecticut bought information from the local printers of *Business Week* before the magazine appeared on the newsstands. Once the ease of tracing trading on insider information became known, some miscreants with advance information would call a broker in, say, Zurich, instead of their local broker. The Zurich bank would place a massive order in London or New York before brokerage houses there became wary and would delay execution for a couple of days to see if a large and suspicious order was based on breaking news.

Most recently the internet has become the vehicle for manipulating stock prices. Jonathan Lebeck, aged seventeen, posted 'news' about particular thinly-traded stocks (which he owned) on internet chat rooms. The stock prices would increase and Jonathan would sell his shares. The Securities and Exchange Commission made Jonathan pay a penalty of $500,000.

MSNBC is a business news TV channel. Many of the commentators on the programs are promoting stocks that they own.

Enron had several committees of outsider advisers, including journalists, that met once or twice a year to provide advice on the firm's approach to the media. The honorarium of $50,000 a year seems high for such slight responsibilities.

Dubious practices

There are many forms of financial felony. In addition to stealing, misrepresentation, and lying, other dubious practices include diversion of funds from the stated use to another, paying dividends out of capital or with borrowed funds, dealing in company stock on inside knowledge, selling securities without full disclosure of new knowledge, using company funds for noncompetitive purchases from or loans to insider interests, taking orders but not executing them, altering the company's books.

George Hudson, who may have been the greatest figure in British railroad history, practiced nearly all of these at the same time in the 1846 railway mania. At one time he was chairman of four railways, and he mistakenly believed he was above the law that applied to his less powerful competitors. His accounts were muddled, and he may not have understood that he had appropriated shares or funds belonging to the York and North Midland railway. As a private individual he made contracts with various companies of which he was an officer, in direct violation of the Companies Clauses Consolidation Act. He raised the dividend of the Eastern Counties railway from 2 to 6 percent just before preparing the financial statements and then altered the accounts to justify the payments. Dividends of the York and North Midland were paid out of capital. He defended his actions against similar accusations in the case of the Yorkshire, Newcastle, and Berwick by noting that he had personally advanced funds to the railway to extend its network. The risk was his, and he was entitled to the advantages that ultimately developed from the expansion of the rail system. He embarked, on his own authority, on transactions that he deemed advantageous to the company, but that were nevertheless of doubtful legality. Still he had a career of great brilliance that greatly benefited the British railway network.[57]

A less interesting and imposing character in the United States in the 1850s was Robert Schuyler, who was president of the New York and New Haven, the New York and Harlem, and for a time the Illinois Central. Called the 'genteel swindler' by one author, he absconded to Europe in 1854 with almost $2 million obtained from fraudulently selling New York and New Haven stock and keeping the proceeds. Van Vleck suggests that the crisis of 1857 in the United States was precipitated by British withdrawals of funds following the publication of the news of Schuyler's defalcation. Schuyler had resigned from the presidency of the Illinois Central in 1853, but his fraud perpetrated on the New York and New Haven led to a massive sale of Illinois Central stock and bonds. The stock fell drastically, and the bonds declined to 62 from par by August 1855. British investors had been looking for this opportunity and they bought large amounts of these bonds; by February 1856 the bonds were back to 90. European investors owned more than 40,000 shares of the stock and 85 percent of the $12 million in bonds.[58] Schuyler was connected with a panic in September 1854 but not with the one in 1857.[59]

The 1920s in the United States has been called 'the greatest era of crooked high finance the world has ever known'—but that was before the 1990s.[60] Notorious swindlers of the period include Harold Russell

Snyder, who stole to extricate himself from losses incurred from the stock market crash (a precursor of the Rigas family, but on a smaller scale, even after adjusting for inflation). Arthur H. Montgomery paid the sincerest form of flattery to Ponzi by organizing a foreign-exchange investment scheme that promised a 400 percent return in sixty days. Charles V. Bob sought and obtained favorable publicity by a $100,000 gift to the Byrd Antarctic Polar Expedition and won the right to call the admiral 'Dick,' which presumably helped promote his aviation stocks, which enjoyed a boomlet after Lindbergh's 1927 flight to Paris.[61]

The 1930s produced many memorable examples of fraud and alleged fraud, led by the bankruptcies of the Bank of the United States, of Ivar Kreuger, and of Samuel Insull's Middle West Utilities holding company. In his riveting account of the New York stock market from 1929 to 1933, Barrie Wigmore observed that Insull's reputation was irreparably damaged when he fled the United States to escape trial before what he considered would be inflamed juries for crimes of which he was later acquitted. Wigmore asserted that Insull was a brilliant manager of operating utilities who went on a buying binge, acquiring badly-run companies for multiples of their net worth. Insull's purchases burdened his holding company with a mountain of debt, and the interest payments on the debt wiped out the equity of those who owned the common stock when the utilities got into trouble in the 1930s depression.[62] Wigmore treads warily in assessing the marketing practices of New York banks and their security affiliates. Albert Wiggins of the Chase Bank had a reputation as 'the most popular man on Wall Street' but his reputation was shattered when a Senate investigation exposed a picture of self-dealing at the expense of his bank, its subsidiaries, and its clients. Charles E. Mitchell of the National City Bank and its security affiliate, the National City Company, also marketed securities intensely, even though he had the inside information that the profits of the companies concerned were declining rapidly.[63]

The 1920s and the 1990s

The supply of corruption seems greater in the 1980s and the 1990s than in the 1920s. One explanation is that there has been a decline in adherence to moral norms. A second is that the risk–reward trade-off has been skewed; stock options have provided a much greater pay-off from financial success. Finance has been democratized. A third is the rise of certified public accountants, which can be traced to the legislation that led to the Securities and Exchange Commission of the 1930s. The initial role of the accounting firms was to protect the public from the financial chicanery of corporate managers who might have had a tendency to overstate the value of inventories and of accounts receivable. The accounting firms were paid to verify or certify the data on financial performance presented by the firms' financial managers. The accountants may have been the guardians of the public interest but the fees for their services were paid by the financial managers. Some of the firms being audited leaned on their accountants; the accounting firms were then forced to choose between agreeing to the firm's demands or walking away from the account.

The temptation of banks

There are no firm data that permit comparisons of financial chicanery and fraudulent behavior across several centuries. The development of journalism as a profession may mean that any untoward activities are much more likely to be exposed (although the activities themselves may not have changed). Exposure is the risk side of the equation; the reward is that the gains in wealth can be much greater. Martin Mayer's *The Bankers* does not dwell on safeguards against defalcation in the same way that James S. Gibbons did in 1859: 'There is perhaps no record of a bank fraud extant of which the perpetrator was not honest yesterday.'[64] Gibbons added, with emphasis, 'It will occur to the reader that there is one peculiar feature running through the whole system; and that is *the apprehension of fraud.*'[65]

What Gibbons said in 1859 is still true. The tendency is to believe that the banks and the bankers are 'paragons of integrity' and perhaps some of them are. A large number of banks lent extensively to Long-Term Capital Management in the 1990s, at the time believed to be one of the most innovative of the 'hedge funds.' (The term 'hedge funds' is a Madison Avenue home run, since the impression conveyed is that the firm has arranged its portfolio to reduce risk while in fact these firms rely extensively on borrowed funds to increase the return to their shareholders and investors.) LTCM had been remarkably profitable—at least until its collapse. The banks were eager to lend to LTCM because they hoped to mimic its trades and profit accordingly. In the spring and summer of 1998, LTCM encountered financial difficulties.

The awkward handling of derivatives and unclaimed deposits by Bankers Trust and the money laundering for Russia by the Bank of New

York suggest that standards are not much higher today than, say, in the 1920s.

In the boom years of the second half of the 1990s, everyone—well, nearly everyone—was getting rich. The major investment banks had very high incomes from the fees associated with underwriting new issues of stocks and bonds, especially those of firms associated with information technologies and biogenetics. The traditional 'Chinese wall' between the investment banking activities of these firms and their asset management activities was supposed to be retained after the repeal of the Glass-Steagall Act, which had become law in the early 1930s to force the separation of the traditional commercial banking activities of firms from their investment banking activities. The law had been adopted in response to the abuses of the 1920s. The firms 'promised' that they would maintain a Chinese wall and that the statements made by their security analysts would not be influenced by the desire of their investment bankers to sell more securities.

But consider the scorecard of Merrill Lynch. The firm was extensively involved in brokering deposits to the rogue thrift institutions in the 1980s. Henry Blodgett hustled information that he knew was misleading. Merrill helped Enron falsify its income by paying an above market price for the Enron barges in Nigeria.

Consider the scorecard of Citibank/Citigroup. The tale of Jack Grubman's hustles for the telecom firms has been noted; Citibank/Citigroup paid a settlement of $150 million. Citibank was obliged to close its private banking activities in Tokyo because of the failure of bank officials to deal fairly with customers by repeatedly buying inappropriate securities for them after ignoring the warning from the Japanese authorities to stop the practice. Several of the top managers of Citibank 'were resigned'—a Park Avenue euphemism for being fired. Citibank's traders in London dumped a lot of German government bonds on the market and caused the prices to dive; they then repurchased these bonds at much lower prices. Several of the managers of Citibank's mutual funds took rebates into the revenues of the bank rather than of the funds.

The wages of sin—in the 1920s and 1990s

What happens when a swindler is found out? Charles Blunt, the brother of John Blunt and himself an insider in the South Sea Company, in early September 1720 cut his throat 'upon some discontent' as contemporary newspapers put it; Charles Bouchard, the retired manager of

LeClerc, a small Geneva bank that lost money in unauthorized real estate investments, was found dead in Lac Léman, an apparent suicide, in May 1977. Psychiatry holds that suicide in these circumstances comes from an intolerable loss of self-esteem, stemming from the realization of the irrationality of past behavior. The picture of stockbrokers jumping from Wall Street windows in October 1929 as they faced bankruptcy is now believed to be a myth.[66] An upswing in suicides is also part of the legend of the Austrian *krach* of 1873.[67] Nonetheless, the response does occur: 'Thus died by his own hand [having taken poison on Hampton Heath], at the early age of forty-two, John Sadleir, one of the greatest, if not the greatest, and at the same time the most successful swindler that this [Britain] or any other country has produced.'[68] (Greatness and success seem curious as characterizations in the circumstances.) Denfert-Rocherau of 1888, and Ivar Kreuger, the 'match-king' of the 1920s, both committed suicide;[69] one of the senior officials of Enron took his own life. But suicide may be more usual in fiction. Mr. Merdle cut his throat in a public bath with a tortoiseshell penknife in Dickens's *Little Dorrit,* and Augustus Melmotte in Trollope's *The Way We Live Now* took prussic acid at his club.

Flight is a less final form of exit than suicide. The prize case is Robert Knight, who doctored the books of the South Sea Company and then escaped to the Continent, there to make another fortune in Paris after breaking out of an Antwerp jail.[70] Robert Vesco fled to Costa Rica and then Cuba with an embezzled fortune. Charles Savary, who swindled the Banque de Lyon et de la Loire, died in Canada. Eugène Bontoux returned to France after five years of self-imposed exile to take advantage of a loophole in French law that held that prison terms not begun within five years of sentencing had to be dropped.[71] The analogous case roughly a century earlier was that of Arend Joseph, whose failure in January 1763 initiated the financial distress that culminated in the bankruptcy of the brothers DeNeufville on July 25, touching off the panic of the same year. Arend Joseph left Amsterdam with 600,000 guilders, in a coach-and-six, for the free city of Kruilenburg in Holland, where he was immune from further process. He left a million guilders of debt in Amsterdam.[72]

Comparisons can be made across the cycles in terms of the number of individuals who were indicted and the number who did jail time. Consider several episodes, from the 1920s, 1980s, and the 1990s. In the 1920s two individuals went to jail for hustling the purchases of securities in a market that already had turned bearish. Eight or ten of the participants in the junk bond transactions of the 1980s including Michael Milken, Ivan

Boesky, Dennis Levine, and Charles Keating were jailed for crimes that included insider trading, 'parking' of securities, and collusion to defraud; among those who served the longest sentences were heads of the thrifts that had been large buyers of the junk bonds. The number of those who will have served jail sentences for their transgressions in the 1990s is still expanding and includes five individuals who had received paychecks from Enron and two who had been involved with MCIWorldCom. Thus far most of the Enron officers who have been indicted have gone to jail, although a large number remain to be sentenced; it seems likely that more than twenty-five individuals will serve prison time before this chapter is closed. Several of the individuals involved with HealthSouth have gone to jail. Two executives associated with Rite-Aid went to jail. Two members of the Rigas family are on trial. Sam Waksal and his good friend Martha Stewart have gone to jail. Very few Wall Street bankers have been jailed. Frank Quattrone, one of the star investment bankers for Credit Swiss First Boston, was found guilty in a second trial of obstruction of justice by destroying e-mails and is likely to go to prison unless his appeal is successful. One Arthur Andersen partner involved with the Enron account did jail time.

Hundreds of Andersen partners and former partners implicitly paid large fines when the firm was forced to close and the value of partnerships and former partnerships collapsed. (Thousands of Enron employees lost their pensions and much of their financial wealth as well as their jobs when the firm went bankrupt.)

The Milken family probably had $2 billion in the bank when Michael Milken was released from prison. It would be impossible to figure out how much of the fortune was earned legally from innovation and how much was earned from illegal behavior. But assume that half of the family fortune could be tracked to transactions that were illegal. Consider how Milken might answer the charge, 'You were in the jail for 1,000 days, you graduated with $1 billion so you were paid $100,000 for each day in the jail.'

Economists are not qualified to discuss the appropriate punishment for the white-collar crime of swindling. At the time of the South Sea Bubble, Molesworth, then a member of the House of Commons, suggested that parliament should declare the directors of the South Sea Company guilty of parricide and subject them to the ancient Roman punishment for that transgression—to be sewn into sacks, each with a monkey and a snake, and drowned.[73] The suggestion is echoed in Dreiser's novel *The Titan*. 'Here the punishment consists of strangling first, then being sewn into a sack, without company, and thrown into the Bosphorus, a punishment reserved for cheating girl friends.'[74] In *House of All Nations,* written a quarter of a century later, a character suggests that old sultans used to punish a faithless wife by tying her into a sack with two wildcats and sinking her in the Bosphorus.[75] These suggested punishments seem excessively harsh. Still those who commit white-collar crimes seem to get off lightly, and most keep most of their ill-earned fortunes. The fines paid by the Wall Street firms are a tax on the wealth of their shareholders and not a real burden on the malfeasants except in as much as they are shareholders.

Whether swindlers are punished or live out their days in indulgent luxury is a more appropriate topic for corporate governance and business ethics than financial history. The revelation of swindles, frauds, and defalcation, and the arrests and punishment of those who violate trust are important signals that economic euphoria has been overdone and that there will be significant social consequences.

10
Policy Responses: Letting It Burn Out, and Other Devices

If many financial crises have a stylized form, should there be a standard policy response? Assume plethora, speculation, panic; what then? Should the governmental authorities intervene to cope with a crisis and if so at what stage? Should they seek to forestall increases in real estate prices and stock prices as the bubble expands so the subsequent crash will be less severe? Should they prick the bubble once it is evident that asset prices are so high that it is extremely unlikely that increases in rents and in corporate earnings will be sufficiently rapid and large so as to 'ratify' these lofty prices? When asset prices begin to fall, should the authorities adopt any measures to dampen the decline and ameliorate the consequences?

Virtually every country has established a central bank to prevent or minimize shortages of liquidity, especially during a financial crisis. Many countries have some type of deposit insurance arrangement to reduce the likelihood that there might be a run on their domestic banks, and to forestall what otherwise could be a self-fulfilling prophecy that a shortage of liquidity would trigger a solvency crisis. Even when there is no formal insurance for bank deposits, the citizens of many countries believe that their governments have become committed to ensuring that they will not incur losses if the banks should fail.

This chapter and the next two center on the management of financial crises. This chapter initially considers the view that the best remedy for panic is to 'leave it alone'—to let it run its course, and to allow the economy to adjust to the decrease in household wealth that follows from the declines in prices of real estate, stocks, and commodities.

The primary rationale for noninterference is the moral hazard that the more interventionist the authorities are with respect to the current crisis, the more intense the next bubble will be, because many of the market participants will believe that their possible losses will be limited by government measures. The moral hazard argument is that intervention skews the risk and reward trade-off in the minds of many investors by reducing both the likelihood and the scope of future losses.

A variety of policy measures that have been used to minimize the impacts of the decline in asset prices are considered, followed by a discussion of the measures that might be adopted to forestall the panic by dampening the development of the mania. The next chapter focuses on the lender of last resort in a domestic context and the following one on the lender of last resort in an international context.

Benign neglect

Many economists take the view that the panic will work its own cure, and that 'the fire can be left to burn itself out.'[1] 'Cool if not very imaginative heads in the Bank [of England] parlour thought it in the nature of panics to exhaust themselves.'[2] Lord Overstone maintained that support of the financial system in crisis is not really necessary because the resources of the system are so great that even in times of the utmost stringency those that offer a sufficiently high rate of interest could borrow a large amount of money.[3] In 1847 an increase in the private rate of discount to 10 and 12 percent in London stopped the flow of gold to the United States; a small sloop was sent to overtake a ship that had already sailed for New York and got it to turn around and unload £100,000 in gold.[4] Testifying before the 1865 French *Enquête* (inquiry) into monetary circulation, Baron James de Rothschild stated that increases in interest rates could be relied upon to reduce speculation in commodities and securities. He added: 'If speculators could find unlimited credit, one can't tell what crises would ensue.'[5]

The moral hazard problem is that policy measures undertaken to provide stability to the system may encourage speculation by those who seek exceptionally high returns and who have become somewhat convinced that there is a strong likelihood that government measures will be adopted to prevent the economy from imploding—and so their losses on the downside will be limited. A 'free lunch' for the speculators today means that they are likely to be less prudent in the future. Hence the next several financial crises could be more severe. The moral hazard problem is a strong argument for nonintervention as a financial crisis develops, to reduce the likelihood and severity of crises in the future. Will the policymakers be able to devise approaches that penalize individual speculators while minimizing the adverse impacts of their imprudent behavior on the other 99 percent of the country? Even then the cost-benefit question is whether the benefit to the economy from not allowing the panic to run its course is worthwhile in terms of the undeserved reward to the speculators.

The view that a panic should be allowed to pursue its course has two elements. One element takes pleasure, or *schadenfreude,* in the troubles that the investors or speculators encounter as retribution for their excesses; this somewhat puritanical view welcomes hellfire as the just deserts for the excessively greedy. The other sees panic as a thunderstorm 'in a mephitic and unhealthy tropical atmosphere' that clears the air. 'It purified the commercial and financial elements, and tended to restore vitality and health, alike conducive to regular trade, sound progress and permanent prosperity.'[6] One powerful statement of this position was made by Herbert Hoover as he characterized—without approval—the view of Andrew Mellon:

> The 'leave-it-alone liquidationists' headed by Secretary of the Treasury Mellon felt that government must keep its hands off and let the slump liquidate itself. Mr. Mellon had only one formula: 'Liquidate labor, liquidate stocks, liquidate the farmers, liquidate real estate.' He insisted that when the people get an inflationary brainstorm, the only way to get it out of their blood is to let it collapse. He held that even panic was not altogether a bad thing. He said: 'It will purge the rottenness out of the system. High costs of living and high living will come down. People will work harder, live a moral life. Values will be adjusted, and enterprising people will pickup the wrecks from less competent people.'[7]

The neo-Austrian economic historian Murray Rothbard added: 'While phrased somewhat luridly, this was the sound and proper course for the administration to follow.'[8] The conservative historian Paul Johnson commented: 'It was the only sensible advice Hoover received during his presidency.'[9]

The opposing view conceded that while it is desirable to purge the system of bubbles and manic investments there is the risk that a deflationary panic would spread and wipe out sound investments by the nonspeculators who would not be able to obtain the credit they need to survive.

One feature of many liquidity crises is that interest rates seem extremely high, especially because they are always expressed as a percentage per annum when they are really premiums for liquidity for one, two, or at most a few days. The more fundamental question is whether money is available at these high interest rates or whether the market for credit is cleared by nonprice rationing. The evidence from a number of crises is that borrowing in a panic is difficult and sometimes impossible and that the quoted interest rates are irrelevant because money is not available at any price.

- After first Arend Joseph and then DeNeufville failed in 1763, and panic broke out on July 22, a succinct, not very informative or convincing report commented: 'Panic even on securities and on goods, no money was to be had.'[10] The statement in 1825 was 'A panic seized upon the public, such as had never been witnessed before: everybody begging for money—money—but money was hardly on any condition to be had. "It was not the character of the security," observes the *Times,* "that was considered, but the impossibility of producing money at all."'[11]
- The interrogation of Thomas Tooke before the Select Committee on the Commercial Crisis in 1847: Question 5421: 'For several days, if not some weeks, the Bank of England was the only establishment that was discounting?' Answer: 'Yes.' Question 5472: 'The Governor of the Bank of England said he could not sell £1 million of stock [English government bonds] in the week after October 14, if there had been no letter. Do you think possible?' Answer: 'No, perfectly impossible, taking the word impossible to signify with the exception of such a reduction in price as could not be contemplated.'[12]
- The evidence of Mr. Glyn in the same inquiry: Question: 'Are you aware that it was the opinion of the Bank broker that a very large sum might have been sold without materially affecting the prices of Consols [English perpetual bonds]?' Answer: I was not aware that the Bank broker had stated that. I should say, from what I saw at the time, that a sale of a million or two million, which were the figures talked of, would have been almost impossible without knocking down the funds to such a price as would have created a further panic.'
- Mr. Browne, MP, did not think such sales could have been effected, unless at a great sacrifice, adding that 'if the panic had been equal to what we might suppose it might have been, under such circumstances, I doubt whether they could have been sold at all.'[13]

- Then in 1857 'At one stage during the crisis it was impossible to negotiate paper at all, the charge under the most favorable circumstances being 12 and 15 percent.'[14]
- A letter from Liverpool: 'Bills of exchange of the first Quality in themselves, and to which this and other Banks were willing to add their Endorsement, were absolutely inconvertible into Cash, and it is my Belief that many Houses, who were not merely solvent but able to pay 40s and 60s to the Pound, must have stopped had not the Government letter been issued.'[15]
- 'Commercial confidence in Hamburg is entirely at an end. Bills of only three or four of the first houses are negotiable at the highest rate of interest ... A government bond advance of 15 million marks banco payable by banks failed to help. The panic was so great that government bonds could not be discounted, and on no security whatsoever would capitalists part with their money ... When it was known on December 12 that assistance would help all, the panic ceased. Government bonds which had not been discountable at 15 percent on the first of the month were readily taken at 2 and 3 percent.'[16]
- Edward Clark in New York wrote to Jay Cooke in Philadelphia before Cooke left Clark's firm to start his own firm: 'Money is *not tight—it is not to be had at all.* There is no money, no confidence & value to anything. A week more of such times and the Bks [sic] will fail.'[17]
- Then in 1866 'The Bank court raised the discount rate to 9 percent and intimated that loans on Government securities were available at 10 percent. Before that announcement it was impossible to sell either Consols or Exchequer bills. Jobbers in other securities refused to deal.'[18]
- During the 1873 crisis in New York the 'National Trust Company of New York had eight hundred thousand dollars worth of government securities in its vaults, but not a dollar could be borrowed on them; and it suspended.'[19]
- And finally in 1883 'The growing demand for money finally led to a money famine. Time loans were unobtainable, call loans were 72 percent in June, 72 percent on July 28th, 51 percent on August 4. First-class commercial paper was quoted 8 to 12 percent nominal, with a very small amount of money available.'[20]

The evidence is not unambiguous, since the sale of government bonds is some what qualified by such remarks as 'with the exception of such a reduction in price (i.e., increase in the rate of interest) as could not be contemplated.' Moreover, there is occasional information on the other side of the argument, especially in the United States under the national banking system, in which a lender of last resort was unavailable. In 1884:

> To add further to the discomfiture of dealers, money became exceedingly stringent, and at one time commanded as much as 4 percent for 24 hours use. This caused a further sacrifice of stocks since few could afford to pay the high rate asked. The exorbitant charge was, of course, the direct result of the distrust prevailing, since there was no actual scarcity . . . It was to . . . the desire to realize and obtain cash that the large decline on Thursday and Friday of nearly 7 percent on United States Government bonds is to be attributed. There was no loss in confidence in these, nor was there in good railroad bonds and stocks.
>
> One result of the phenomenal and temporary rise in rates for money was to bring a vast amount of foreign capital to the market. Some of it was sent here to buy stocks at their depressed prices, and more to loan on stocks or on any other good securities at the high rates of interest. The effect of this was to completely turn the foreign exchanges which had been running so heavily against the U.S.[21]

This statement in its turn is not unambiguous, since the panic started before an acute liquidity shortage had developed.

The International Monetary Fund acted as a lender of last resort in the Asian crisis of 1997—although long after the currencies had depreciated sharply—and insisted that the government in each of the Asian countries balance its budget and that the central bank in each of these countries increase its interest rates. A number of economists objected to these measures because they would be deflationary and lead to an increase in unemployment especially among the poor, while the financial problems had been set in motion by comfortable officials and well-to-do bankers.

Some support for orthodoxy, however, came from the Japanese experience in the 1990s when the combination of an expansive monetary policy and the depreciation of the yen in the foreign exchange market produced a 'liquidity trap.' Both Japanese interest rates and bank loans decreased after the 1990 declines in stock prices and real estate prices, and the inference was that there was a 'credit crunch.' Banks were reluctant to lend because their loan losses had eroded their capital and firms were reluctant to borrow because of the sluggish growth in the demand for their products.

The decline in short-term interest rates in Tokyo to 1 percent and below led to a surge in the 'carry-trade;' U.S. hedge funds would borrow yen in Tokyo, sell the yen to buy U.S. dollars in the foreign exchange market and then invest the U.S. dollars at an interest rate of 3 or 4 percent in New York. The 'carry trade' transactions led to an increase in the flow of funds from Tokyo to New York and to a decline in the foreign exchange value for the yen that in turn led to an increase in the Japanese trade surplus and increases in output and employment in Japan. The increase in the Japanese trade surplus was a useful response to the liquidity trap and an effective supplement to expansive Japanese fiscal and monetary policies. The carry trade transactions would remain profitable for the U.S. hedge funds as long as any appreciation of the yen in the foreign exchange market was smaller than the excess of the interest rates on U.S. dollar securities over the interest rates they were paying on their Japanese yen loans.

Moral suasion and other exhortatory devices

The dominant argument against the a priori view that panics can be cured by being left alone is that they almost never *are* left alone. The authorities feel compelled to intervene. In panic after panic, crash after crash, crisis after crisis, the authorities or some 'responsible citizens' try to halt the panic by one device or another. The authorities may be unduly alarmed and the position might correct itself without serious harm. The authorities may be stupid and unable to learn. (The Chicago School assumes that the market participants are always more intelligent than the authorities, in large part because the authorities are motivated by short-term political objectives.) The uneven distribution of intelligence cannot be tested against crisis management because authorities and leading figures in the marketplace both exert themselves in the same direction to halt the spread of falling prices, bankruptcy, and bank failures. If there is a learning process at work—and the assumption of rationality requires one—the lesson has been that a lender of last resort is more desirable and less costly than relying exclusively on the competitive forces of the market.

One insight from the historical record is that there are many examples when the authorities initially were resolved not to intervene but eventually reluctantly did so. Lord Liverpool threatened to resign as Chancellor of the Exchequer in December 1825 if an issue of Exchequer bills was provided to rescue the market after he had warned against excessive speculation six months earlier.[22] William Lidderdale, Governor of the Bank of England at the time of the Baring crisis, refused categorically to accept a 'letter of indemnity' to permit the Bank to exceed its lending limit.[23] On both occasions face was saved by finding some other approach to avert the panic. The initial strong moral stand not to intervene was reversed on many other occasions as the panic escalated. These included the intervention of Frederick II in the Berlin crisis of 1763,[24] the Bank of England's refusal to discount for the 'W banks'[25] and the U.S. Treasury's decision in 1869.[26]

Stalling and bank holidays

In a run, each depositor rushes to get his or her money from the bank before the bank is forced to close because its money holdings have been exhausted. Banks are often reluctant to pay the depositors because their money holdings are always much smaller than their short-term deposit liabilities. During the Great Depression, banks took their time to pay off depositors, hoping, like Micawber, for something to turn up. The technique goes back to the eighteenth century.

Mcleod's *Theory and Practice of Banking* describes how the Bank of England defended itself in September 1720 against a run brought on by its reversal of a promise to absorb the bonds of the South Sea Company at £400. The Bank organized its friends in the front of the line and paid them off slowly in sixpence coins. These friends brought the cash back to the Bank through another door. The money was deposited, again slowly counted, and then again paid out. The run was staved off until the feast of Michaelmas (September 29). When the holidays were over, so was the run, and the Bank remained open.[27]

A second story, which may well have the same origin and is likely to be more accurate, is that the Sword Blade Bank, a supporter of the South Sea Company, resisted attempts to redeem its paper with silver coins. When the run started on September 19, the bank brought up wagonloads of silver that it paid out 'slowly in small change.' One depositor is reported to have received £8,000 in shillings and sixpences before the bank closed its doors on Saturday September 24.[28] The circumstances suggest one story; the dates, two. Since the Sword Blade Bank and the Bank of England were mortal enemies, it is unlikely they cooperated.

The lessons of 1720 were not lost on the Bank of England a quarter century later. The Young Pretender (Charles Edward, grandson of James II) landed in Scotland in July 1745, unfurled his banner in September, invaded England in November, arrived in Carlisle on November 15, and reached Derby on December 4. Panic broke out on Black Friday, December 5, 1745. British consols fell to 45, the lowest price on record, and a run began on the Bank of England. The Bank resisted, partly by paying off its notes in sixpence coins. The time gained was used to induce London merchants to proclaim their loyalty and readiness to accept Bank of England notes. The second half of the prescription, collecting pledges of faith in notes, was used again in similar circumstances when the French landed at Fishguard in 1797. On that occasion, 1,140 signatures of merchants and investors in government stock were collected in a single day.[29] The time gained in 1745 by both the slow payout and the petition of support enabled the government to organize the army that defeated the Young Pretender at Culloden in April 1746.

Complete shutdown and bank holidays

One way to stop a panic is to stop trading by closing the market. Trading on the New York Stock Exchange was halted in 1873, and in London and many other cities at the outbreak of war in 1914. In both cases the motivation was to stop a run by providing the market participants with more time to think through whether it was necessary or desirable to sell at what were almost certainly depressed prices.

However, shutdowns may drive the trading underground and intensify the panic. Moreover, short-run and long-run goals are in conflict. Closing the stock market during one panic may exacerbate the next, as investors sell their stocks or withdraw their money from the call money market because they are fearful that trading will be halted. The New York Stock Exchange was closed in a panic in September 1873, but a financial editor suggested that fear that trading on the exchange might be halted in October 1929 was a factor in hastening the withdrawal of call money by out-of-town banks and other market participants.[30] The closing of local stock exchanges in Pittsburgh and New Orleans for two months in 1873 had fewer serious consequences, since they traded only the securities of the local firms that had brought on their difficulties.[31]

The New York Stock Exchange and the other stock exchanges in the United States were closed for a week after the bombing of the World Trade Center towers on September 11, 2001 because the communications and the technical support systems were inoperative. Many of the same securities could have been traded on the regional stock exchanges in the United States but these exchanges would have been overwhelmed.

The declaration of a legal holiday by the government is another technique for closing the market, which was used during the panic of 1907 in Oklahoma, Nevada, Washington, Oregon, and California.[32] The device was the forerunner of the bank holidays that started at the local level in the fall of 1932 and were generalized throughout the country on March 3, 1933, the day that Franklin D. Roosevelt was inaugurated as president. (A bank holiday closes only the banks, while a legal holiday shuts down all business.)

Another device is to suspend the publication of bank statements, as in 1873, in the hope that 'what you don't know won't hurt you.' The technique was designed to hide the large losses of reserves of a few banks since the fear was that accurate news would further reduce depositor confidence.[33]

Some commodity and financial markets set daily limits on the maximum change in prices; when the limit is reached, trading is suspended for the rest of the day. Specialists in individual stocks have often taken a 'time out' whenever the imbalance between the buy orders and the sell orders has been exceptionally large. This 'circuit breaker' was recommended for U.S. stock markets after the meltdown of Black Monday, October 19, 1987. The proposal for the New York Stock Exchange was to postpone trading for a stated interval—such as twenty minutes—in those stocks whose prices increased above or declined below the limit.

Time has been gained by moratoriums on payment of all debts or on particular types of obligations, such as bills of exchange that have less than two weeks to run. The most ubiquitous measure of this sort is that the bank examiners ignore bad loans in the portfolios of banks as long as they can, an implicit moratorium on marking the loans to their market value. Regulatory forbearance was used in the U.S. savings and loan debacle in the 1980s. The International Monetary Fund and the World Bank continued to allow the indebtedness of many of the poor African countries to increase by the amount of the interest that was due; if these institutions had declared the loans in default, they would have had to recognize the losses on the loans. The banks that were the lenders to the Real Estate Investment Trusts (REITs), landlords of mortgaged shopping centers and the owners of mothballed Boeing 747s allowed the interest due on their bank loans to compound because they wanted to delay the recognition of the losses on these loans to a more propitious moment when their own capital would be larger. But the lenders need forbearance from the bank examiners.

Official moratoriums may be less effective than informal ones, however. A moratorium on the settlement of differences in payments due on the 1873 Vienna Stock Exchange lasted a week, from the stock market collapse to May 15. A guarantee fund of 20 million guilden was put together by the Austrian National Bank and the solid commercial banks; these imitations of earlier measures were of little assistance.[34] Another moratorium was noted in Paris after the July Monarchy when the municipal council decreed that all bills payable in Paris between July 25 and August 15 should be extended by ten days. This moratorium sterilized the commercial paper in banking portfolios and did nothing to discourage a run by holders of notes, who demanded coin.[35]

Clearinghouse certificates

The major device used in the United States to cope with bank runs prior to the creation of the Federal Reserve System was the clearinghouse certificate, which is a near-money substitute that was the liability of a group of large local banks. A bank subject to a run could pay the departing depositors with these clearinghouse certificates rather than with coin. The New York clearinghouse was established in 1853 and the one in Philadelphia in 1858 after the panic of 1857. During the panic of 1857, New York banks failed to cooperate to halt the run. The Mercantile Agency of New York took the position that if four or five of the strongest banks had come to the assistance of the Ohio Life and Trust Company, enabling it to meet its obligations, the business and credit of the country would have been preserved.[36] By 1873 the New York banks were ready to accept payment on cleared checks in clearinghouse certificates rather than in currency or bank notes. The advantage of the use of these certificates was that the incentive for any bank to bid deposits away from its competitors was reduced. Sprague insisted that this system had to be accompanied by an agreement to pool bank reserves; otherwise, a bank that was not subject to a net drain might be forced to suspend payments after it paid cash to its own depositors if it had not received cash in settlements from other banks.[37] In 1873 reserves were pooled.

One serious drawback of clearinghouse certificates was that they were acceptable only in the local area—New York, Philadelphia, Baltimore. Thus these certificates helped maintain domestic payments such as payrolls and retail sales within a city but they dampened the effective flow of payments between cities. In the 1907 panic, 60 of the 160 clearinghouses in the United States adopted clearinghouse certificates to facilitate local payments. Nevertheless Sprague claimed that the dislocations of the domestic exchanges were no less complete and disturbing than on previous occasions. The prices of New York funds in Boston, Philadelphia, Chicago, St. Louis, Cincinnati, Kansas City, and New Orleans between October 26 and December 15, 1907 varied from a discount of 1.25 percent in Chicago on November 2 to a 7 percent premium in St. Louis on November 26, an increase from 1.5 percent the previous week.[38] In December 1907 Jacob H. Schiff wrote: 'The one lesson we should learn from recent experience is that the issuing of clearinghouse certificates in the different bank centers has also worked considerable harm. It has broken down domestic exchange and paralyzed to a large extent the business of the country.'[39]

Other devices of the same general character were clearinghouse checks and certified checks that were both close substitutes for money and increased the means of payment in circulation.

Nonbank groups can also organize to mitigate a panic. Consider, for example, the stock market consortium. On October 24, 1907, a bankers' pool, headed by J.P. Morgan, loaned $25 million at 10 percent in call money in an attempt to stem the collapse of the stock market.[40] Twenty-two years to the day later, on Black Thursday in 1929, Richard Whitney went from post to post on the floor of the New York Stock Exchange and placed bids to buy stocks on behalf of a syndicate headed once again by J.P. Morgan and Company.[41]

Bank collaboration

Banks have also collaborated through rescue committees (as in Vienna in May 1873 and earlier), loan funds, funds for guarantees of liabilities, arranged mergers of weak banks and firms, and other devices whereby the strong banks support the weak and failing banks.[42] Three examples include the role of the Paris banks in the 1828 crisis in Alsace, various devices employed by Hamburg in meeting the difficulties of 1857, and the Baring Brothers loan guarantee of 1890.

The Alsatian crisis of 1828

Three firms in textiles failed in December 1827 at Mulhouse. The Paris banks then refused to accept any Alsatian paper, and the Bank of France set a limit of 6 million francs on the amount it would support, a figure 'scarcely the fortune of two Alsatian houses.' The Bank of France then decided against accepting any paper with Mulhouse or Basel endorsements and that decision precipitated a panic. On January 19 two more Mulhouse merchants failed. On January 22 in Paris there were rumors of the failure of two Schlumberger firms. The Paris banks sent Jacques Laffitte as an emissary to Mulhouse; he arrived on January 26 and offered to lend 1 million francs on the consignment of merchandise. Before he came, however, two textile merchants, Nicholas Koechlin and Jean Dollfuss, had left Mulhouse for Paris. To raise cash, these merchants had been selling inventories on the market at discounts of 30 to 40 percent from the traditional market prices for these goods. Nine houses failed from January 26 to February 15. Lévy-Leboyer wrote that it could have been worse. At the last minute a syndicate of twenty-six Paris banks, presided over by J.-C. Davillier, extended a credit of 5 million francs to Koechlin and Dollfuss, who returned to Alsace on February 3 and distributed 1 million francs to those of their colleagues who offered guarantees and kept 4 million for themselves. These measures restored confidence.[43] Those who qualified for neither the Koechlin-Dollfuss fund nor Basel money failed.[44]

The Hamburg crisis of 1857

The background of the crisis of 1857 in Hamburg was that trade had expanded, particularly because the Crimean War had led to an expansion of credit. Hamburg was the 'all-English' city of Germany, but had close relations with the United States in sugar, tobacco, coffee, and cotton, and with Scandinavia. When the deflationary tidal wave swept across the Atlantic, Hamburg was inundated. The panic touched off by the failure of Ohio Life on August 24 arrived in Hamburg three months later (following price declines of 30 percent) with the suspension of Winterhoff and Piper, a firm that was engaged in the American trade.[45] Daily dispatches from the British consulate in Hamburg by date tell the story:

November 21: Some of the leading merchant houses and two banks plan for relief.

November 23: Two major houses engaged in the London trade fail, and the Discount Guarantee Association grows more cautious in endorsing Hamburg bills.[46] On one authority the Discount Guarantee Association is exhausted in three days.[47]

November 24: A Discount Guarantee Association (Garantie-Diskontverein) is formed, initially with a capital of 10 million marks banco, later raised to 13 million (about £1 million), of which the sum of 1 million marks is to be paid in immediately.

November 28: The chamber of commerce and leading merchants induce the senate to call parliament (Bürgerschaft) to arrange to issue government bonds in order to lend 50 to $66^2/_3$ percent of the value of hypothecated goods, bonds, and shares to merchants in distress.

December 1: With the suspension of Ullberg and Cremer, ten to twelve houses in the Swedish trade have gone down. The Discount Guarantee Association will not issue any more guarantees. Business is at a standstill.

December 2: A suggestion is made to change the laws of bankruptcy to enable creditors to share in attachment of goods.

December 7: A proposal is made to establish a state bank for discounting good bills to the amount of 30 million marks banco (about £2.4 million). The bank would advance government bills bearing $6\frac{2}{3}$ percent interest on mercantile bills of exchange. Parliament rejects this, wanting instead to issue 30 million marks banco of paper currency as legal tender. The senate rejects this, insisting on clinging to the silver standard.

In the end, a compromise was reached for a State Loan Institute fund of 15 million marks that included 5 million marks banco of Hamburg government bonds and 10 million in silver to be borrowed abroad.[48] The story of the silver train (Silberzug) is recounted in Chapter 12 as an example of an international lender of last resort.

One observer totaled the sums available for rescue operations to 35 million marks banco, which included 15 million in the Discount Guarantee Association, 15 million in the State Loan Institute, and 5 million from the chamber of commerce. He compared this amount with 100 million marks banco of protested bills and noted that if merchants speculated with capital equal only to one-sixth the value of their goods, a 17 percent decline in prices of these goods would be sufficient to wipe out their capital position. To the suggestion that the senate was 300 years behind the times, he reported with approval the senate's answer: The merchants have been 300 years ahead of the times in issuing debt. State help in these cases, he insisted, merely means assistance for speculation and perpetuation of higher prices at the cost of the consumer.[49]

Guarantees of liabilities: the Baring crisis

The most famous guarantee of liabilities was that worked out by William Lidderdale when he was Governor of the Bank of England during the Baring crisis of 1890. Similar guarantees had occurred earlier in Great Britain. In December 1836 the private bank Esdailes, Grenfell, Thomas and Company, which served as London agents for seventy-two country banks, was in financial difficulties. The view was that this firm could not be allowed to fail because of its relationships with the country banks; moreover, its paper included all the best names in the City. The assets of the bank far exceeded its liabilities, and the London bankers offered guarantees. The Bank of England led the list with £150,000. Esdailes survived, but only for two years.[50]

The guarantee was worked out as an alternative to a letter of indemnity that permitted suspension of the Bank Act of 1844. The letter was offered by the Chancellor of the Exchequer, Lord Goschen, to Lidderdale, who refused on the ground that 'reliance on such letters was the cause of a great deal of bad banking in England.'

If Lidderdale refused to quiet the market by the usual means that had been employed in 1847, 1857, and 1866, he was not one to let the market take its medicine. In August 1890 he warned Baring Brothers that the firm would have to moderate its acceptances for its Argentine agent, S.B. Hales. Baring Brothers revealed its acute distress to Lidderdale on Saturday, November 8. Fearful of a panic when Barings' condition was made public, the Bank of England met with the Exchequer on Monday, November 10, turned down the letter of indemnity, prepared for the problem by seeking assistance from foreign countries (a subject for Chapter 12), and formed a committee headed by Lord Rothschild to address the question of the large overhang of Argentinean securities in the market.

As the days passed, the rumors circulated and Barings' bills were increasingly discounted at the Bank of England. By Wednesday Lidderdale had learned that although Baring was solvent it would still need £8 to £9 million. On Friday John Daniell, the leading man at Mullens and Co., used by the Bank of England in open-market operations, came to Lidderdale, crying 'Can't you do something, or say something, to relieve people's minds: they have made up their minds that something awful is up, and they are talking of the very highest names—the *very highest—!*'[51]

On November 14 Lidderdale met with two cabinet ministers who represented the Exchequer, Lords Smith and Salisbury. They agreed that the government would increase its balance at the Bank immediately and that the government would share with the Bank in any losses suffered on Baring Brothers's paper discounted by the Bank between 2 p.m. Friday and 2 p.m. Saturday. On the basis of this agreement, Lidderdale met with eleven private banks to get them to contribute to a fund that would guarantee Barings' liabilities, and he got the State Bank of Russia to agree not to withdraw its £2.4 million deposit at Baring. The private banks as a group contributed £3,250,000, but this included £1 million from the Bank of England as well as £500,000 from each of three lenders, Glyn, Mills & Co., Currie and Co., and Rothschilds. Lidderdale than used these commitments to obtain the agreement of the five London joint-stock banks to join the guarantee fund for another £3,250,000. On the basis of these assurances, *The Times* of November 15 announced that Baring Brothers would fail but that there would be no loss. The work of the guarantee fund continued on Saturday because the directors of the joint-stock banks had to meet to approve their subscriptions, which was done by 11 a.m. Then other banks and financial institutions raised the fund from £7.5 million in the morning to £10 million by 4 p.m.; the guarantee fund eventually reached £17 million and was taken as a measure of the strength of the London financial system. Martin's Bank was in distress over its loans to Barings and to Murriettas, another bank involved in Argentina. Martin's Bank joined the guarantee fund for £100,000 on November 18 (Tuesday), too late to afford much help to Barings, but early enough to demonstrate to the world its own strength.[52] In summarizing the episode, Powell stated: 'The Bank is not a single combatant who must fight or retire, but the leader of the most colossal agglomeration of financial power which the world has so far witnessed.'[53]

On November 25 a new firm, Baring Brothers and Co., Ltd, was formed as a joint-stock company with a capital of £1 million. The form of the guarantee may be of interest.

Guarantee Fund
Bank of England, November, 1890

In consideration of advances which the Bank of England have agreed to make to Messrs. Baring Brothers and Co., to enable them to discharge at maturity their liabilities existing on the night of the 15th of November, 1890, or arising out of business initiated on or prior to the 15th of November, 1890.

We, the undersigned, hereby agree, each individual, firm, or company, for himself or themselves alone, and to the amount only set opposite to his or their names respectively, to make good to the Bank of England any loss which may appear whenever the Bank of England shall determine that the final liquidation of the liabilities of Messrs. Baring Brothers and Co. has been completed so far in the opinion of the Governors as practicable.

All the guarantors shall contribute rateably, and no one individual, firm, or company, shall be called on for his or their contribution without the like call being made on the others.

The maximum period over which the liquidation may extend is three years, commencing the 15th of November, 1890.[54]

The rescue of the Long-Term Capital Management hedge fund in September 1998 is a contrast to the rescue of Barings. William McDonough, the president of the Federal Reserve Bank of New York, induced fourteen large banks and investment banks, including Merrill Lynch, Morgan Stanley Dean Witter, J.P. Morgan, Chase Manhattan Bank, and the Union Bank of Switzerland to provide $3.6 billion of capital to prevent the collapse of LTCM; in exchange they acquired 90 percent of LTCM's equity.[55] These banks and investment banks were large creditors of LTCM so the 'bailout' involved a change in the legal nature of their claim on LTCM. The Federal Reserve was concerned that if LTCM failed the markets would be paralyzed by the need to unwind its massive position in futures and options contracts and other types of derivatives.

Deposit insurance

Since 1934, federal deposit insurance in the United States has prevented bank runs by providing an ex ante guarantee of deposits, limited originally to $10,000 but gradually increased to $100,000. The increase in the upper limit on the amount of insurance on each deposit was said by a knowledgeable bureaucrat to have been reached as a compromise between a proposal in the U.S. House of Representatives to increase the upper limit from $40,000 to $50,000 and a proposal in the U.S. Senate for an increase from $40,000 to $60,000. When large banks, including the Continental Illinois Bank in 1984 and the First Republic of Dallas in 1988, got into trouble, the FDIC deliberately removed all limits on the amounts of deposits covered by the guarantees to halt imminent runs and so in practice it established that banks with significant deposits over $100,000 were 'too big to fail' (although the shareholders of these banks would probably lose all of their investments in the bank's shares; similarly the owners of the subordinated debt of these banks might lose their investments). The deposits of the foreign branches of these banks had implicitly become insured even though the banks had paid deposit insurance premiums only against their domestic deposits. Although deposit insurance was designed to prevent bank runs by taking care of the 'little man,' with a deposit initially less than $10,000, this ceiling had in practice been raised to the sky.[56]

The formal $100,000 maximum on the amount of a deposit that would be insured gave rise to 'deposit brokers' who would arrange for the placement of larger amounts of money into deposits of $100,000 or less, ensuring that the depositor would be fully insured. John Doe could have an insured deposit of $100,000, his wife Mary could also have an insured deposit of $100,000, and together John and Mary could have a third insured deposit of $100,000. And the Does could follow the same strategy with the bank across the street. The effect of this innovation was that it provided a guarantee to wealthy individuals and hence circumvented one purpose of the ceiling. Moreover it encouraged banks to make riskier loans since they were confident that they were protected against runs—if these riskier loans proved profitable, the owners of the banks would benefit and if the loans went into default, the owners would not have to worry about bank runs (although the market value of their own shares might decline and even become worthless).

The implosion of the bubble in Japan in the 1990s caused the value of the loans of the banks headquartered in Tokyo and Osaka and various regional centers to decline sharply below the value of their liabilities. Nevertheless, there were no bank runs, the depositors were confident that they would be made whole by the government if any of the banks were closed.

Deposit insurance has limited both bank runs and contagion in the runs from one troubled bank to other banks in a neighborhood. What accounts for the reluctance to provide insurance at an earlier date?

In the long tradition of the United States, free banking, even wildcat banking, was the rule. Anyone could start a bank, and many did. Risks were large, banker turnover rapid. A guarantee of bankers' deposits would have constituted a license to speculate, if not embezzle, and would have removed the threat of withdrawal of deposits, which was the major check on the irresponsibility of bankers. Deposit guarantees were rejected as conducive to bad banking as late as March 2, 1933, when the Board of

Governors of the Federal Reserve was not prepared to recommend such a guarantee, or any other measures, on the eve of the national bank holiday.[57]

The Federal Deposit Insurance Corporation had an excellent financial record until the 1970s; the deposit insurance premiums that it collected were much higher than the amount it paid out on bank failures. From the beginning in 1934 through 1970, only one bank with deposits of more than $50 million had failed, and most failures were of banks with deposits of less than $5 million. The FDIC had in most cases arranged for takeovers of the failed banks so that the few depositors with deposits above the maximum insured amounts did not incur losses.

Beginning in the late 1970s the problems of the FDIC and those of the Federal Savings and Loan Insurance Corporation (FSLIC) mounted sharply. The FDIC rescued a considerable number of banks including two giants, the Continental Illinois of Chicago and the First Republic Bank of Dallas; honoring the deposit insurance guarantee cost these agencies billions of dollars. The usual operating procedure was to close the bank or the thrift institution when its capital had been depleted, and then to carve a 'good bank' from the rescued institution while the remaining assets of the failed institution would be retained for eventual sale by another newly-created government agency, the Resolution Trust Corporation (RTC). Both the insurance agencies incurred large losses in honoring their guarantees; eventually they would obtain the funds to pay for these losses by borrowing from the U.S. Treasury. In the early 1990s, the estimates were that the total losses to the U.S. taxpayers would amount to $150 billion but the pick up in the growth rate of the U.S. economy meant that the RTC received more money than anticipated from the sale of collateral and bad loans so the losses totaled about $100 billion.[58] There was some question whether a portion of this cost to the taxpayers could be reduced by increasing the insurance premiums on bank deposits—a suggestion resoundingly opposed by sound banks.[59]

Exchequer bills

One ancient device short of lending money to a firm in trouble was to issue marketable securities to the firm against appropriate collateral. (Of course, as the first part of this chapter indicated, when markets break down, even the most liquid securities may not be sold readily.) The securities have been private and public; both types were part of the complex package put together by Hamburg in 1857. In 1763 and 1799, in an equally complex and jerry-built system of support, admiralty bills were an integral feature.[60] The widest development, however, concerned the Exchequer bills issued in Britain in 1793, 1799, and (without enthusiasm) 1811, but sternly rejected in 1825.

The Exchequer bill was widely thought to have been the idea of Sir John Sinclair, although it may have originated with the Bank of England. On April 22, 1793, City leaders met with the Prime Minister, William Pitt, to devise means to combat the crisis that arose from the failure of 100 of the 300 country banks and the calamitous decline in commodity prices. The next day, eleven of their number met at the Mansion House to formulate a scheme for state assistance. According to Clapham, there was no clear guide to what ought to be done. In due course, the idea emerged of having the government issue £3 million in Exchequer bills, a total that was later raised by parliament to £5 million, to be issued to merchants on the collateral of goods that they would deposit in the customs houses. An additional feature of the plan was to issue £5 notes—the previous minimum was £10—to economize on the use of gold and silver coin. The Exchequer bills were issued by special commissioners rather than the Bank of England. Some £70,000 worth of these bills was immediately sent to Manchester and an equal amount to Glasgow. The device worked like a charm, according to MacPherson. Three hundred thirty-eight firms applied for only £3 million of the total amount. A total of £2.2 million was granted to 228 firms, only two of which subsequently went bankrupt. Applications for more than £1.2 million were withdrawn after the panic abated.[61]

In 1799 the panic in Hamburg had an echo in Liverpool, and Exchequer bills again were used. Parliament provided £500,000 in Exchequer bills, used solely in Liverpool, against £2 million of goods stored in warehouses.[62]

In 1811 the question arose again. A Select Committee on the State of Commercial Credit was appointed. Among its members were Henry Thornton, Sir John Sinclair, Sir Thomas Baring, and Alexander Baring. The committee's report, completed in a week, recorded the distress of exporters to and importers from the West Indies and South America, as well as the piles of goods bound for the Baltic that had been cut off and stored in London warehouses, and recommended a new issue of £6 million of Exchequer bills. Support was moderate in the House of Commons because of the overtrading in Latin America; the opposition, while sympathetic to the distress, doubted the wisdom of bailing out the speculators. Huskisson, who later made his mark as the president of the Board of Trade, claimed that the evil came from too easy credit:

> Did gentlemen not see that the race of old English merchants, who never could persuade themselves to go beyond their capital, was superseded by a set of mad and extravagant speculators, who never stopped so long as they could get credit, and that persons of notoriously small capital had now eclipsed those of the greatest consequence; so that speculations now took place even in the lowest articles of commerce ... If the relief given was used for further speculation, it would only aggravate the evil—and he feared that this might be done—in which case the present measure would go only to add six million to the circulation and to raise the prices of all our commodities.[63]

Smart gave the fullest account of the debate and noted that many criticized the measure, though few were bold enough to deny it. In the end the proposal passed, but few applications were made and only £2 million was advanced. 'Not many of those who were in embarrassed circumstances were able to furnish the desired security, and it is difficult to see what remedy there was in being enabled, by advances, to produce more goods when the radical evil was that there was no market for them.'[64]

Bank regulation and supervision

Can financial crisis be forestalled by strict regulation and supervision? Some observers advocate such an approach. Others recommend deregulation. Most of the rules for sound banking are already incorporated in the regulations or are implicit in banking tradition. Many of the rules are ignored by banks and regulators alike. Banks are supposed to 'mark to market,' that is, value their loans and investments each day (or week or month) at the price that would be realized if they were sold in the market rather than at their historic cost. Reserves should be established against 'problem loans' and write-offs against 'doubtful' ones. As a bank's capital declines as its loan losses increase, the bank might be required to raise more capital or be closed under the traditional rules. As an illustration of the unusual character of banks following these rules, the press was full of the news in the spring of 1987 when Citicorp wrote down the value of its Third World debt and the FSLIC allowed 500 insolvent banks to remain open in the hope that they would become sufficiently profitable to rebuild their capital. As part of the regulation process, the

Federal Reserve Board began to collaborate with other central banks in the Group of Ten to strengthen bank structures worldwide by gradually approaching uniform capital requirements and then risk-based capital requirements.

Emphasis on capital requirements as a percentage of assets or other liabilities has led some banks to switch to 'off-balance sheet' operations. These transactions generate fees or commissions for the banks, but the asset or liability is contingent or committed so that it is not shown on the balance sheet except as a footnote. These off-balance sheet transactions include interest rate and currency swaps, futures contracts, options, underwriting risks, 'repos' (sales of securities with a guarantee to repurchase them at a later date), and note-issuing facilities. Each of these can perhaps be valued as an option or warrant and included among assets or liabilities when calculating the appropriate amount of required capital,[65] but significant financial sophistication is required.

A strong case can be made for stricter regulations and supervision of banks to forestall lending in euphoric periods that may end in financial crisis. Historical fact suggests that such a case rests on a counsel of perfection. The bank examining system in the United States divides responsibility among the Comptroller of the Currency, the Federal Reserve Banks, and the state banking commissioners. In one view there is competition not in deregulation but in reregulation.[66] 'Divided responsibility,' said a famous German banker-politician, 'is no responsibility.'[67] The astute personnel needed in time of emergency are unwilling to submit to the boredom of long periods of calm. The mismanagement of banks is hard to detect before a crisis. In boom, entropy in regulation and supervision builds up danger spots that burst into view when the boom subsides. The question then is whether to liquidate, stall, guarantee, bail out, take over, or rely on other means of last-resort lending.

Luck: a tailpiece

Lady Luck once worked effectively to assist a bank in distress. Wirth wrote that the Brothers Kauffmann in Hamburg were failing during the crisis of 1799 when one of the brothers sent his bride a Hamburg city lottery ticket, which carried a first prize of 100,000 marks banco. She bought the same number in another lottery in the Duchy of Mecklenburg, the prize for which was an estate worth 50,000 Prussian thalers, then equal to 100,000 marks banco. She won both, and the Brothers Kauffmann were fully rehabilitated.[68] The odds at Las Vegas may be higher for the solution to a global crisis.

11
The Domestic Lender of Last Resort

The hallmark in the development of 'the Art of Central Banking' over the last two hundred years has been the evolution of the concept of a lender of last resort. The expression comes from the French *dernier ressort,* and centers on the last legal jurisdiction to which a petitioner can take an appeal. The term now has become thoroughly anglicized, and in central-banking English places the emphasis on the responsibilities of the lender rather than the rights of the borrower or petitioner.

The lender of last resort stands ready to halt a run out of real assets and illiquid financial assets into money by supplying as much money as may be necessary to forestall the run; the concept is of an 'elastic supply of money' that expands to meet the demand in panics. How much money? To whom? On what terms? When?

These questions are those faced by the lender of last resort and follow from the dilemma that if investors believe that banks and perhaps other selected borrowers will be supported in moments of distress by a lender of last resort, they will be less cautious in the extension of loans during the next boom. The public good of the lender of last resort weakens the responsibility of private lenders to ensure that they make 'sound' loans. If, however, in a panic the rush from the sales of securities and commodities into money cannot be halted, the fallacy of composition takes center stage. The sale of these assets by investors in the effort to minimize losses leads to declines in the asset prices, with the consequence that a large number of otherwise previously solvent and well-capitalized firms may become bankrupt.

The case for the opposition to a lender of last resort has been made continuously. Napoleon's minister of the public treasury, François Nicholas Mollien, wrote strongly against the interventionist instincts of his mentor, who wanted to save the failing manufacturers damaged by the Continental System (blockade); he asserted that a start in this direction would only get the Treasury in deeper and deeper.[1] Louis Antoine Garnier-Pagès, French minister of finance in 1848, claimed later that it was useful to precipitate a crisis to render it less durable: 'Do nothing to save the *rente,* clean out stocks; sell merchandise.' The policy, he asserted, contributed to the brilliance of the French recovery from 1850 to 1852.[2] Murray Rothbard asserted that 'any propping up of shaky positions postpones liquidation and aggravates unsound conditions.'[3] The most trenchant formulation is that of Herbert Spencer: 'The ultimate result of shielding man from the effects of folly is to people the world with fools.'[4] Such a view is understandable in a Darwinian age.

Origin of the concept

The development of the lender of last resort evolved from the practice of the market rather than from the minds of economists. Ashton asserted that the Bank of England was already the lender of last resort in the eighteenth century,[5] although this pronouncement does not entirely square with his statement that 'long before the rules for the treatment of crises were laid down by economists, it was recognized that the remedy [for a financial crisis] was for the monetary authority (the Bank of England or the government itself) to make an emergency issue of some kind of paper which bankers, merchants and the general public would accept. When this was done the panic was allayed.'[6]

The indecision as to whether the central bank or the government was the final monetary authority remains to this day and qualifies the statement that the Bank of England emerged as the lender of last resort in the 1700s. E.V. Morgan maintained that the Bank of England's realization of its responsibility was delayed by the government's action in issuing Exchequer bills in 1793, 1799, and 1811, and that the Bank assumed the role as lender of last resort only gradually during the first half of the nineteenth century 'in spite of the opposition of theorists.'[7] The same evolutionary process can be seen in the Bank of France. In 1833 the majority of the Conseil General overrode Hottinguer's idea for a policy on the English model as well as Odier's plea for an entirely new policy and concluded that the major function of the Bank of France was to defend the French franc. Capital outflows were not to be feared. Interest rates should not be held artificially low or speculation will be encouraged and crises intensified. When a crisis occurred, however, the Bank should provide abundant and cheap discounts to moderate the intensity of the crisis and shorten its duration.[8]

The role of the lender of last resort was not respectable among theorists until Bagehot's *Lombard Street* appeared in 1873, although Sir Francis Baring called attention to the idea at the end of the eighteenth century [9] and Thornton's classic, *Paper Credit,* developed both the doctrine and the counter-arguments in his discussion of the financial problems of the English country banks.[10] Bagehot traced the origin of the doctrine to David Ricardo rather than to Baring and Thornton in his statement before the Parliamentary Select Committee on Banks of Issue in 1875: 'The orthodox doctrine laid down by Ricardo is that there is a period in a panic at which restrictions upon the issue of legal tender must be removed.'[11] Bagehot himself had articulated the doctrine in his first published article, written in 1848, when he commented upon the suspension of the 1844 Bank Act in the panic of 1847:

> It is a great defect of a purely metallic circulation that the quantity of it cannot be readily suited to any sudden demand... Now as paper money can be supplied in unlimited quantities, however sudden the demand may be, it does not appear to us that there is any objection on principle to sudden issues of paper money to meet sudden and large extensions of demand... This power of issuing notes is one excessively liable to abuse... It should only be used in rare and exceptional cases.[12]

Some analysts continue to reject the doctrine and some powerful minds have argued both sides of the issue. Should one worry about the present panic or the next boom, the condition or the principle? 'There are times when rules and precedents cannot be broken; others when they cannot be adhered to with safety.'[13] The dilemma is that breaking the rule creates a new precedent and a new rule. Lord Overstone, the distinguished Currency School theorist, strongly opposed expansion of the money supply in a crisis but reluctantly admitted that a panic may require 'that power, which all governments must necessarily possess, of exercising special interference in cases of unforeseen emergency and great state necessity.'[14] On one occasion he produced a ringing metaphoric defense: 'There is an old Eastern proverb which says, you may stop with a bodkin a fountain, which if suffered to flow, will sweep away whole cities in its course.'[15]

Friedman and Schwartz similarly and metaphorically flirted with lender-of-last-resort doctrine:

> The detailed story of every banking crisis in our history shows how much depends on the presence of one or more outstanding individuals willing to assume responsibility and leadership... Economic collapse often has the characteristics of a cumulative process. Let it go beyond a certain point, and it will tend for a time to gain strength from its own development... Because no great strength would be required to hold back the rock that starts a landslide, it does not follow that the landslide will not be of major proportions.[16]

The paradox is equivalent to the prisoner's dilemma. Central banks should lend freely to halt the panic, but leave the market to its own devices to reduce the likelihood of future panics. A dilemma: actuality inevitably dominates contingency, today wins over tomorrow.

The Bank Act of 1844 represented a victory for the Currency School, which stood for a fixed supply of money, over the Banking School, which thought it useful for the money supply to grow as output and trade grew. Both schools were concerned with the long run rather than the short run, and neither approved of increasing the money supply as a temporary expedient to meet a crisis. When the Bank Act was being considered, the idea that there be power to suspend its provisions in an emergency was rejected. After 1847 and again after 1857, when it proved necessary to suspend the Bank Act and issue more money as a last resort, parliament conducted inquiries to determine whether the legislation needed to be changed. Both inquiries concluded that it was not desirable to have built-in provision for suspending the act even though the suspension had been useful and necessary. To limit precedent-setting, the bill brokers who had been sudden borrowers 'wanting incalculable advances in 1857 were told not to expect the like again.'[17] The principle of having a rule but breaking it if one had to was so widely accepted that after the suspension in 1866 there was no demand for a new investigation.

In the 1850s Jellico and Chapman had proposed rules for adjusting the discount rate of the Bank of England to the state of its reserves by a mathematical formula written into the legislation. Wood criticized them as having no real grasp of Bank transactions and methods of procedure.[18] Robert Love, Chancellor of the Exchequer in June 1875, introduced a bill to provide for authorizing a temporary increase in Bank of England notes in exchange for securities (under certain contingencies, including panic), a bank rate above 12 percent, and the foreign exchanges favorable. The bill was tabled and given a first reading on June 12 but it never received a second reading and was withdrawn in July.[19] Hard-and-fast rules were agreed not to be workable. *The Economist* and Walter Bagehot thought it proper that the Bank of England rather than the banks themselves should hold the reserves necessary to get the country through a panic. Mr Hankey, a former governor of the Bank, called this 'the most mischievous doctrine ever broached in the monetary or banking world in this country; viz. that is the proper function of the Bank of England to keep money available at all times to supply the demands of bankers who have rendered their own assets unavailable.'[20] The public, however, sided with Bagehot and practice against Hankey and theory. If the expansion of credit in boom periods cannot be controlled, then measures should be adopted to halt the contraction of credit in crisis.

Who is the lender of last resort?

The lack of clear agreement in Great Britain about whether the Treasury should relieve panics through the issue of Exchequer bills or whether instead the Bank of England should discount freely at a penalty rate, even if it is necessary to suspend the limits imposed by the Bank Act of 1844 has already been noted. Uncertainty about the answers to these questions may be optimal, along with the question of whether the governmental authorities will come to the rescue and whether they will arrive in time if they decide to come. Thus there was no explicit provision for a lender of last resort in Great Britain and no fixed rule as to which agency should fill this role. In 1825 the Exchequer was not the selected agency. The task was given resolutely to the Bank of England whose reluctant acceptance was 'the sulky answer of driven men.'[21] In 1890 guarantees were used rather than the Bank or the Exchequer. Gradually the responsibility devolved on the Bank, which led Alfred Marshall to write that 'its directorate came to be regarded at home and abroad as a committee of safety of English business generally.'[22]

The Bank of France had agreed by the 1830s that it had responsibilities in a crisis but it thought it had other responsibilities as well, such as to ensure monopoly of the bank note circulation which permitted it to let the regional banks fail in 1848 and then to convert them into subsidiaries (*comptoirs*). The provinces had been fearful of Paris; they wanted the privilege of note issue for their own regional banks because of the concern that in a crisis Paris would take care of its own needs at the expense of the regions. But after Le Havre acquired a bank, the mistake was making too many illiquid industrial loans, including those to shipyards and to importers of cotton when its price was falling. In February 1848 the Banque du Havre made a trip to Paris. 'The return was not glorious. The Bank of France had been impitiable.'[23] It refused to lend on mortgages, saying, 'The statutes forbid it, and you have refused to accept a *comptoir.*'[24]

The Bank of France wavered over this question even as it wanted to destroy the regional banks. From America, Chevalier observed that the Bank of France had discounted freely in 1810, 1818, and 1826—with Jacques Laffitte as governor for the first two years—making great efforts to sustain commerce; but it lacked the same courage in the crisis of 1831–1832.[25] In 1830, after the revolution, the task was left to local authorities. A regional bank, conducted with honesty but not prudence, threatened a provincial crisis. The local receiver general undertook to discount its doubtful paper, apparently after consulting Paris, where, Thiers testified, after 'mature reflection the public interest was put above that of the Finance Minister, M. Louis,' 'with happy results,' that is, the avoidance of the collapse of the bank and a resultant disturbance.[26]

After it achieved its monopoly of the note issue and the conversion of the banks in the regions into branches of the Bank of France, the Bank began to act as a lender of last resort. Its statutes required it to discount only three-name paper; the task became one of producing acceptable names. Sixty *comptoirs d'escompte* were established throughout France, as well as a number of *sous-comptoirs* organized by various branches of trade to hold stocks of goods and issue paper against them. With the names of the merchant, the *sous-comptoir,* and a *comptoir,* the Bank of France could discount the paper and relieve the liquidity crisis. Louis Raphael Bischoffsheim of Bischoffsheim & Goldschmidt mocked the requirement of three names: 'The number is not important. With bad signatures one can collect 10 instead of three. I prefer one good to 20 bad.'[27] After the crisis was over, a number of the *comptoirs* were taken over by bankers, merchants, and industrialists and became regular banks. The most famous of this group the Comptoir d'Escompte de Paris took its place among the leading banks in the country.[28]

The Crédit Mobilier of the Pereire brothers was not saved in 1868: on this occasion, the Bank of France refused to discount its paper, which might be interpreted as the revenge of the establishment on an outsider, the Rothschilds against the Pereires who had once worked for them;[29] as punishment for not conceding the Banque de Savoie note issue to the Bank of France when the Pereires took over the Savoy bank after the region had been ceded to France by Italy in 1860; or as the entirely normal refusal of a lender of last resort to bail out an insolvent institution.[30] Cameron accuses the Bank of France of conducting guerrilla warfare against the Pereire brothers in the interest of a Rothschild-Pereire quarrel that went back to the 1830s.[31]

The Bank of France and Paris bankers again did not come to the rescue of the Union Générale in 1882 but seven years later they rescued the Comptoir d'Escompte de Paris. Critics of the Bank of France ascribe the difference in outcomes to venality. A less emotional position asserts that a second large bank failure in seven years might have completely destroyed the French banking system and that on this account Rouvier, the minister of finance, took the necessary measures to have the Bank of France and the Paris banks advance 140 million to the Comptoir d'Escompte.[32] In the Union Générale operation, as was noted in an earlier chapter, the Paris banks withdrew from the speculative activity when it began to peak in August 1881 and advanced 18.1 million francs to the Union Générale after the crash the following January to permit its more orderly liquidation rather than to save the bank.[33] Led by the Rothschilds and Hottinguer, and including the Comptoir d'Escompte and the Société Générale (but not the Lyons rival of Bontoux, the Crédit Lyonnais), the consortium represented the establishment, in which it was not really necessary to distinguish the Bank of France from the leading private banks (*hautes banques*) and deposit banks.

In Prussia the king was the lender of last resort in 1763. In 1848 various state agencies, including the Prussian Bank, the Seehandlung, and the Prussian lottery vainly tried to help the Cologne bank, A. Schaaffhausen, before it was allowed to reorganize as a joint-stock bank. In the absence of a central bank in 1763, 1799, and 1857 the Hamburg city government, the chamber of commerce, and the banks—any and all leading agencies took part in the rescue operation.

The experience of the United States is especially pertinent to the question of the identity of the lender of last resort. There was some ambiguity as to whether the First Bank of the United States and then the Second Bank of the United States were lenders of last resort despite the designation of the Bank in each case as a chosen instrument. On various occasions, the U.S. Treasury came to the aid of the banks by accepting customs receipts in post-dated thirty-day notes (1792), by making special deposits of government funds in the banks that were in trouble (1801,1818, and 1819), and by relaxing the requirement that a commercial bank pay the Bank of the United States in specie (1801).[34] After the failure to renew the charter of the Second Bank of the United States in 1833, the U.S. Treasury was even busier, both before and after passage of the 1845 law that required the Treasury to keep its funds out of the banks. In times of crisis and in periods of stringency caused by crop movements, the U.S. Treasury would pay interest and/or principal on its debt in advance, make deposits in banks despite the law, offer to accept securities other than government bonds as collateral for deposits of government funds, or buy and sell gold and silver. Banks began to look to the Secretary of the Treasury for help in an emergency and to relieve seasonal tightness. In the fall of 1872, Secretary of the Treasury George S. Boutwell served as a lender of last resort by reissuing retired greenbacks—which may have been illegal. His successor, William A. Richardson, did the same thing a year later.[35]

The U.S. Treasury could absorb money in deposits and pay out cash surpluses it had acquired in previous periods but apart from the greenback period it could not create money. For this reason, the Treasury was unsatisfactory as a lender of last resort, unless it had previously had budget surpluses and built up its holdings of cash. In 1907, when its cash holdings were low, the Treasury issued new bonds—$50 million of Panama Canal bonds, which were eligible for collateral for national bank notes, and $100 million of 3 percent certificates of indebtedness—that it hoped would entice existing cash and specie from hoards. In the end, the crisis was averted by a capital inflow from Great Britain of more than $100 million.[36] Moreover, the devices used to cope with a crisis were ad hoc. An analysis of the crisis of 1857 suggested that the Federal government was incapable of intervening effectively and that the public, including the banks, was left without guidance to stem the crisis.[37] In fact intervention proved to be too much and too early.

The complex record of interference by the U.S. Treasury raises the question of whether the market should not have regulated itself and, if so, how. O.M.W. Sprague, the historian of the crises under the National Banking System for the 1910 Aldrich Commission, believed that the banks should have taken responsibility to ensure that they had enough reserves to meet all needs.[38] But Sprague was vague on which banks should take this responsibility or why the duty fell on them in the absence of responsibility embodied in legislation. Noblesse oblige? Duty? Several statements by Sprague indicate why a limited number of New

York banks had the obligation to stabilize the system and behave differently from other banks:

> During the period before the crisis of 1873 some 15 of the 50 New York banks held practically all the bankers' deposits in the city, and 7 of them held between 70 and 80 percent of these deposits. These 7 banks were directly responsible for the satisfactory working of the credit machinery of the country. (p. 15)
>
> It must always be remembered that in the absence of any important central institution, such as exists in other commercial nations, the associated banks are the last resort in this country, in times of financial extremity, and upon their stability and sound conduct the national prosperity greatly depends. (From the New York Clearing House report of November 11, 1873, p. 95)
>
> The fundamental characteristic of our banking system was illustrated [in 1890], that for any extraordinary cash requirements the reserves of the country banks are an unused asset. Evidence was again given which should have brought home to city institutions the heavy responsibility which they have incurred in attracting the reserves of other banks. (p. 147)
>
> The New York banks did not normally maintain the large reserves which the responsibilities of their position demanded. (p. 153)
>
> ... there was the possibility that the contraction of loans by outside banks, trust companies and foreign lenders might come together, creating a situation ... well nigh impossible if in normal times the important clearing house banks failed to exercise great caution and maintain large reserves. (p. 230)
>
> The failure of the banks holding the ultimate reserve of the country to live up to the responsibilities of their positions is evident in still another direction. While the exact moment of the outbreak of the crisis of 1907 could not be foreseen, the imminence of a period of trade reaction had for many months been so probable that precautionary measures might reasonably have been expected from these banks if not from banks and the public in general. (pp. 236–7)
>
> The outside banks feel no responsibility for the course of the market. They will naturally withdraw from it when affairs at home require more of their funds or when they come to distrust its future. It

> therefore becomes necessary for the local banks to be able at all times to shoulder at least a part of the loans that may be liquidated by outside banks, and also to supply the cash which they thus secure the power to draw away. (p. 239)
>
> It is certainly an element of weakness in our central money market that influential credit institutions should have to be dragooned into doing what is after all in their own interest as well as to the general advantage. (p. 255)
>
> ...feeling common among New York bankers that they cannot reasonably be expected to remit funds which are the proceeds of loans made in the New York money market by outside banks and liquidated in an emergency...It should be remembered, however, that responsibilities are incurred in return for the advantages which accrue to the New York banks from their peculiar position. London holds its commanding position because it is known that money lent there can be instantly recalled. Similarly, New York is not meeting the obligations of its position as our domestic money center, to say nothing of living up to future international responsibilities, so long as it is unable or unwilling to respond to any demand, however unreasonable, that can lawfully be made upon it for cash. (pp. 273–4)

Sprague obviously believed that the market needed a stabilizer and that the banks could not depend on the U.S. Treasury to help supply the seasonal needs for cash, but neither did he believe that the biggest and most profitable U.S. banks rather than the U.S. Treasury should take on the responsibility. These banks should be aware of seasonal currency requirements, the prospect that the out-of-town banks may withdraw deposits, and the state of the international balance of payments. Not all New York banks should take on this responsibility but only those that charged interest on out-of-town deposits, or the largest, or those with intimate connections with the stock exchange, or the leading members of the New York Clearing House.

The leading bankers of New York drew a different conclusion; they believed that the difficulties arose from lack of elasticity of the money supply and thus they fell into the trap of the Banking School. This was the real-bills doctrine, the idea that a money supply expanding and contracting on the basis of trade bills, representing goods moving in domestic and foreign trade, could not be inflationary, and would have the necessary elasticity through discounting at banks and rediscounting at a central bank. There could be no doubt about it: 'The laws of finance are as well known, and as sure in their operation as the laws of physics.'[39] The lesson that Frank Vanderlip, Myron T. Herrick, William Barret Ridgely, George E. Roberts, Isaac N. Seligman, and Jacob H. Schiff drew from the panic of 1907 was that there should be a central bank with an elastic currency.[40]

Some ambiguity as to location of ultimate responsibility may be helpful to the extent that it leaves some uncertainty so that the bankers are more self-reliant—provided there is not so much uncertainty as to disorient the market. In London it was vaguely understood that there should be no formal provision for a lender of last resort but that there should be in time of crisis. The intuitive politicians in the British government and the merchant bankers who ran the Bank of England thought it best to give power to grant relief neither wholly to the Bank nor wholly to the government, but to leave it uncertain.[41] If the giving of relief were formally within the power of either the Bank or the government, pressure from the public would be difficult to resist.[42]

No one would bear the responsibility in too large a group. If only one entity were responsible, pressure for action might become irresistible. The optimum may be a small number of actors, closely attuned to one another in an oligarchic relation, like-minded, who apply strong pressure to keep down the chiselers and free-riders and who are prepared ultimately to accept responsibility. To give a more up-to-date example, tension in 1975 and 1976 among New York City officials, the unions, bankers, the state, and the Federal government as to who would be the lender of last resort for New York may have been enough to ensure uncertainty at a high level, and to encourage Yonkers, Buffalo, Boston, Philadelphia, et al., not to slacken in their efforts to right themselves; yet action to save New York was finally taken.

Bonelli's statements about the 1907 crisis in Italy offer a moving account of muddle. The Società Bancaria Italiana was failing, and dragging down a host of small financial, mercantile, and industrial firms. A consortium of the larger banks put together a support fund. The Bank of Italy was involved early and deeply, and almost became too heavily committed. The Treasury finally came to the rescue, at the insistence of Stringher, governor of the Bank of Italy, and paid the interest on the national debt early and thus relieved the liquidity crisis. Bonelli saw that the episode inevitably involved both the Bank of Italy and the government and suggested that this indecision might develop when the economy works for more than ten years with no one in charge.[43] Part of the difficulty may have lain in the lack of sufficient cohesion among Turin, Genoa, Milan, and Rome and the resulting uncertainty, buck-passing and indecision.

Some uncertainty was inevitable because as a House of Commons committee noted in 1846 'looking to the impossibility of foreseeing what the precise character of the circumstances might be' it was thus 'more expedient to leave to those with whom the responsibility of government might rest at the time, to adopt such measures as might appear to them best suited to the emergency.'[44] Consider Sir Robert Peel's statement on the Bank Bill on June 4, 1844:

> My Confidence is unshaken that we have taken all the Precautions which legislation can prudently take against the Recurrence of a pecuniary Crisis. It may occur in spite of our Precautions; and if it be necessary to assume a grave Responsibility, I dare say Men will be found willing to assume such a Responsibility.[45]

One man who took responsibility got into trouble. George Harrison, then president of the Federal Reserve Bank of New York in the late 1920s, opened the discount window wide at the time of the October 1929 stock market crash. He exceeded his instructions from the Board of Governors in Washington by buying $160 million in government bonds on the open market in October and another $210 million in November. The Board of Governors in Washington resented the New York bank because of the earlier high-handed dominance of the system by Benjamin Strong (who died in 1928), and had little compunction in reining in Harrison when he tried to emulate Strong's penchant for filling a power vacuum by strong leadership. Ambiguity as to whether there will be a lender of last resort, and who it will be, may be optimal in a close-knit society. The division in experience and outlook between Washington and New York handicapped more effective action in coping with the collapse of stock prices in 1929.

There was no hint of criticism or second-guessing when the Federal Reserve Board, under the new chairmanship of Alan Greenspan set about expansive open-market operations immediately after October 19, 1987, and poured in high-powered money 'right and left' to use Bagehot's expression. The Fed under Greenspan provided liquidity to cope with the Asian Financial Crisis in 1997, the debacle in Russian finances and the collapse of Long-Term Capital Management in the summer of 1998, in anticipation of the Y2K crisis in the last few months of 1999, and in response to the sharp decline in stock prices in 2000 and 2001.

To whom on what?

The rule laid down by Bagehot was that loans should be granted to all comers on the basis of sound collateral 'as largely as the public asks for them.'[46] But in his testimony before the 1875 inquiry, two years after the publication of *Lombard Street,* Bagehot resisted the suggestion that last-resort lending be turned over to a body of commissioners appointed by the government on the grounds that they might make loans to 'improper persons.' They would be subject to political pressure while the Bank of England is 'a body withdrawn from the political world and not subject to political pressures.'[47]

Bagehot's suggestion that central banks are immune from political pressure seems naive. The dilemma about collateral is that its soundness depends on when and whether the panic is stopped; the longer the panic continued, the sharper the decline in the prices of securities and bills of exchange and commodities and hence the less sound the collateral. In this case, it becomes necessary to look at the character of the borrower, something that J.P. Morgan was reported to consider exclusively. Here the dilemma relates to the wry comment that bankers lend money only to those that do not need it.

Central banks typically have rules.[48] When the rules cannot be easily broken—as in the Federal Reserve Act of 1913, which permitted only gold and negotiable bills of exchange but not government securities to be held as reserve against Federal Reserve notes and demand deposits—there is frequently trouble. There is also trouble when rules are too readily broken. The beauty of the Chancellor of the Exchequer's letter of indemnity was that it preserved the rule while violating it and did not create a precedent, at least not for a time. The Bank of France and the Reichsbank occasionally discounted only three-name paper. But discretion to reject paper because it was 'unsound' or the borrower because of his character gave the lender of last resort a life-or-death power that might not always be used with complete objectivity. The literature is filled with accusations of venality on the part of the directors of central banks. Protestant and Jewish directors of the Bank of France were alleged to have punished the Catholic (and worse-off) supporters of the Union Générale in 1882, while saving the insider Comptoir d'Escompte in 1888.[49] In the crisis of 1772, the Bank of England's issuance of new regulations about discounting and refusal to discount doubtful paper were interpreted as an attempt to break the Jewish houses in Amsterdam that had been most involved in the speculation. Then there was the Bank's decision to refuse the bills of Scottish banks, and finally to stop discounting altogether, which was probably 'a step taken quite deliberately to break up a group of Dutch speculators.'[50] Outsiders particularly suffered. The Bank of the United States was allowed to fail in New York in December 1930 by a syndicate of banks amid accusations that the Bank was being punished for its pushy ways.[51]

The rule of discounting for everyone with good paper evolved slowly in Great Britain. For a time 'the invariable practice' was respectable London names on paper with no more than two months to run; but this description of 1793 is accompanied by a statement that while a request from Manchester had been turned down (along with one from Chichester, where refusal helped to bring a bank down), £40,000 had been advanced to Liverpool banks. Only in July 1816 did the Bank, breaking a rigid precedent, agree to accept 'country securities of undoubted respectability if the firm cannot get enough London names.'[52]

The fact is that the Bank of England made advance on a wide range of different types of assets much beyond two-name paper. In 1816 the Bank broke its rule against lending on mortgages, undertaking a 'Transaction quite out of the ordinary course of Business' to relieve the distress of poor people in the Black Country. The Bank resolved to lend only in the old way 'on notes of respectable parties' but a few years later the Bank began a regular mortgage business on the ground that the volume of discounts and especially the income from discounts had collapsed—a private rather than a public purpose.[53] At one stage the Bank even made loans on the security of a mortgage on a plantation in the West Indies (ultimately the Bank foreclosed on this loan[54]) and on unimproved land in England. The land was unencumbered by mortgage but belonged to a duke, an indication that collateral and the character (or status) of the borrower were not unrelated. Loans were not made on land in Scotland or in Ireland.[55]

With the growth of railroads, Bank of England loans were made on the collateral of railroad debentures. In 1842, as the second railway mania got under way, the Bank voted to make an occasional loan to firms in difficulty and to well-tried firms for development.[56] The Bank of France began lending to a railroad syndicate in 1852; in fact, it was accused of supporting, if not starting, the feverish speculation in railroads.[57] Walter Bagehot thought the Bank of England mistaken for not lending on railroad debentures when it did so on consols and Indian securities; Bagehot stated that a railway was less liable to unforeseen accidents than the Empire of India.[58] But Indian securities were guaranteed by the Colonial Office and in effect were British government obligations.

Exchequer bills were issued on the collateral of goods, as were Admiralty bills in Hamburg. Clapham observed that many of the Bank's advances in 1825 were not actually on goods but rather on personal security;[59] the Bank loaned freely and was not 'over-nice.'[60] In a few weeks in 1847 the Bank advanced £2.25 million in both usual and unusual ways, including the securities of the Company of Copper Miners, through which it involuntarily acquired a copper works.[61]

The rule is that there is no rule. One does not lend to insolvent banks, except to avoid the mischief that would occur if the Lord Mayor of London were to go bankrupt (1793),[62] or to maintain for a time a payroll in Newcastle, a town used to banking disasters.[63] The Bank of France had never discounted as much as 4 million francs for anyone but Jacques Laffitte when Samuel Welles, an American banker, applied in 1837; he proved to be an exception.[64] (The Laffitte transaction had also been exceptional, with a political motivation.) The Conseil General could not abandon such an important bank, so it received a line of credit of 15 million francs.[65] In the crisis of 1830 the Bank of France discounted royal and municipal bonds, customs receipts, woodcutting receipts, obligations of the city of Paris, and canal bonds repayable by lottery.[66]

Some of the decisions that the lender of last resort must make are easy, such as whether to discount Treasury bills. Some are difficult, such as whether to take shaky collateral from shaky banks. The record is full of firms that were refused help, failed, and paid off 20 shillings to the pound, and of banks that were helped in one crisis but went down in the next. The 241-page appendix to Evans's book on the commercial crisis of 1857 was devoted to court records of bankruptcies in Britain between 1849 and 1858. The reading is doleful. G.T. Braine, who was refused accommodation by the Bank of England in 1848, paid 20 shillings to the pound and ended up with a surplus double that originally estimated. One also finds petitions in bankruptcy brought by the Bank, as against Cruikshank, Melville and Co., for the unpaid residue of a bill it drew on another bankrupt firm that had paid only 12s. 6d. to the pound.[67]

Even the judgment of history is not always helpful. The Bank of England first refused to help the three American 'W banks' (Wiggins, Wilsons and Wildes) in the fall of 1836 and then relented and advanced them credit in March 1837. Andréadès noted that the Bank took a bold step and had no occasion to regret its courage.[68] Clapham held on the contrary that the Bank lent most reluctantly and was not surprised when Wilsons and Wiggins failed at the end of May and Wildes thereafter and the consequence was 'a long, dreary tale of debt lasting 14 years.'[69] To Matthews, the Bank of England's aid to the three banks 'in the vain hope of avoiding their suspending was a matter of faulty judgment but the principle on which they operated was a sound one.'[70]

When and how much?

'Too little, and too late' is one of the saddest phrases in the lexicon not only of central banking but of all activity. But how much is enough? When is the right time?

Bagehot's rule is to lend freely at a penalty rate. 'Freely' means only to solvent borrowers and with good collateral, subject to the inevitable exceptions. It means rejecting the expedients that various central banks are tempted to indulge in crises. Early in 1772 the Bank of England tried to apply the brakes to overtrading by selective limitation of discounts and was criticized.[71] In 1797 the Bank began to prorate discounts, and Foxwell thought that might have been undertaken again in 1809.[72] Another technique when a central bank feels it is getting overcommitted is to tighten up on eligibility requirements for collateral, changing the maturity of eligible bills from 95 or 90 to 65 or 60 days, or adding to the number of names required. In May 1783 the Bank of England had discounted so heavily for its own clients that it departed from its regular practice and refused to make advances on subscriptions to government bonds issued that year. Clapham commented that fortunately no public or private catastrophe of the sort that starts a panic occurred that summer since the Bank had limited its capacity to meet one.[73] In this case the Bank was behaving like a private bank worried about its own safety rather than a public institution with the responsibility to provide for the safety and stability of the system.

The lender of last resort might supply funds to the system through open market purchases rather than through the discount mechanism. How much should the central bank expand the money supply? Were the $160 million in October 1929 and the additional $210 million through November 1929 adequate? In the view of the Federal Reserve Bank of New York they were not. The New York Fed was operating under a directive from the Board of Governors in Washington that permitted it to buy $25 million of government bonds a week. It violated this rule in October by buying $160 million, and on November 12 recommended to the Board that the limit of $25 million a week be removed and that the Open Market Investment Committee be authorized to buy $200 million of bonds for the system. After considerable negotiation, the Board reluctantly approved this request on November 27, and $155 million was purchased between November 27 and January 1, 1930. By this time, discounts were running off rapidly, interest rates had fallen sharply, and the need for a lender of last resort—to accommodate the liquidation of call loans in the market—was over.[74]

Some monetarists seem ambivalent on the role of the lender of last resort. Friedman and Schwartz quoted Bagehot approvingly on not starving a panic.[75] They asserted that the action taken by the Federal Reserve Bank of New York in buying $160 million in October 1929 was 'timely and effective' although they were gently skeptical about Harrison's claim that the open market purchases kept the stock exchange open.[76] Friedman was opposed to all discounting and believed the stock market crash was not a major factor in producing or deepening the depression.[77] An ultra-monetarist view maintains that the open market operations of the period constituted a renewal of the credit inflation of the 1920s.[78] But most monetarists believe that there is no need to have a lender of last resort so long as the money supply increases at a constant rate. In retrospect the open market operations were woefully inadequate in the weeks from mid-October to the end of November 1929. They enabled the New York banking system to take over the call loans of out-of-town banks but at the cost of reducing the amount of credit available for purchases of stocks, commodities, and real estate, which led to declines in their prices and unleashed the depression.[79]

The timing of the Federal Reserve Board under the chairmanship of Alan Greenspan in the Black Monday crash of October 1987 was impeccable, as also was the help for the U.S. capital market when the collapse of Long-Term Capital Management was avoided in September 1998.

Timing presents a special problem. As the boom mounts to a crescendo, it must be slowed without precipitating a panic. After a crash has occurred, it is important to wait long enough for the insolvent firms to fail, but not so long as to let the crisis spread to the solvent firms that need liquidity—'delaying the death of the strong swimmers,' as Clapham put it.[80] In a speech during the debate on the indemnity bill on December 4, 1857, Disraeli quoted the leader of an unnamed 'greatest discount house in Lombard Street' who said that 'had it not been for some private information which reached him, to the effect that in case of extreme pressure there would be an interference on the part of the Government, he should at that moment have given up the idea of struggling any further, and [that] it was only on that tacit understanding that he went on with his business.'[81] Questions could be raised about the equity of private information and of tacit understandings for insiders but not outsiders. Still, the remark underlines the importance of timing. Whether too soon and too much is worse than too little and too late is difficult to specify.

In 1857 the U.S. Treasury came to the rescue of the market too early and helped it inflate still further. In 1873 the response was too slow, no steps were taken during the first part of the year.[82] Sprague refers to 'the unfortunate delay of the Clearing House,' that is, the slowness of any authority to respond to the 1907 crisis, in which as in no other crisis since the Civil War, things were allowed to drag on too long.[83]

If the need for a lender of last resort is accepted after a speculative boom and it is believed that restrictive measures are not likely to slow the boom at the optimal rate without precipitating a collapse, the lender of last resort faces dilemmas of amount and timing. The dilemmas are more serious with open market operations than with a system of discounts. In the latter case, Bagehot specified the right amount: all the market will take—through solvent houses offering sound collateral—at a penalty rate. With open market operations the decision for the authorities is more difficult, but Bagehot was right not to starve the market. Given a seizure of credit in the system, more is safer than less since the excess can be mopped up later.

Timing is an art. That says nothing—and everything.

12
The International Lender of Last Resort

The primary argument for an international lender of last resort is the historical record of the transmission of deflationary pressure from one country to another. This transmission has often been associated with changes in exchange rates, both with devaluations when currencies have been pegged and with depreciations when they have not been pegged. The devaluation of the Finnish markka in 1992 transmitted deflationary pressure to Sweden, one of its major competitors in the production and sale of timber and other products. The depreciation of the Thai baht, the Malaysian ringgit, and the South Korean won in the second half of 1997 transmitted a massive deflationary impulse to the United States. The increase in the Japanese trade surplus in the 1990s had a deflationary impact on its major trading partners and especially the United States.

An international lender of last resort has a problem that has no domestic counterpart; as long as there are separate national currencies and national central banks, changes in exchange rates are inevitable. Some of these changes will be necessary, especially when a country has not been as successful as its major trading partners in achieving a low inflation rate; a reduction in the foreign exchange value of the country's currency may be a less costly way to return to equilibrium than unemployment associated with an overvalued currency. Some of these changes may be necessary because of a major structural shock, including the loss of an export market because of technological changes, the depletion of raw materials, and the productive gains in countries that are in earlier stages of industrialization. Some of the changes in exchange rates may not have been necessary, but instead were undertaken because a low value for the national currency was viewed as the preferred low-cost way to stimulate domestic employment and economic growth.

Changes in exchange rates can be an unnecessarily costly form of adjustment to a shock; the 'overshooting' of a country's currency as its market price increases relative to its long-run equilibrium value has almost always had a deflationary impact on the country's tradable goods sector. Conversely the 'undershooting' of a country's currency as its market price declines relative to its long-run equilibrium value can trigger a surge in the inflation rate. Moreover sharp real depreciations have often led to widespread failures of business firms and banks.

The massive episodes of currency undershooting have often been preceded by significant overshooting of the same currencies. The sudden reversal from overshooting to undershooting has almost always occurred as a result of a sudden reversal in the direction of cross-border movement of funds. Hence institutional innovations and policy innovations that reduce the scope of overshooting and undershooting enhance economic welfare.

The primary responsibility of a domestic lender of last resort is to reduce the likelihood that a shortage of domestic liquidity will cascade into a solvency problem and cause bankruptcies that would not have occurred in the absence of distress selling and precautionary selling. The domestic lender of last resort needs to walk a tightrope between avoiding saving financial institutions that are already bankrupt because of their risky investments or bad business decisions and saving their healthier competitors from insolvency that would occur as a result of the decline in the price levels and the tumble into deflation. The primary responsibility of an international lender of last resort is to provide liquidity to ameliorate the scope of the necessary changes in exchange rates and obviate those changes that are not required by the economic fundamentals.

International credits have been extended for at least four centuries, when governments have borrowed abroad, and when private bankers in one country have relied on their counterparts in other countries for assistance in meeting a sudden withdrawal of funds. In the 1920s the first concerted concern with a possible shortage of international liquidity—and more precisely of monetary gold—developed in response to the view that the surges in national price levels during and immediately after World War I would lead to a decline in gold production as well as to increases in both official and private demand for gold. Moreover it was feared that the establishment of new central banks in what had been the Austrian-Hungarian empire would lead to an increase in the demand for monetary gold. The thrust of several conferences sponsored by the League of Nations in the 1920s was the need for national central banks to hold a larger proportion of their international reserve assets in the form of liquid securities denominated in the British pound, the U.S. dollar, and other national currencies.

The International Monetary Fund was established in the 1940s to provide a formal arrangement for the extension of credit among national governments and to assist countries in coping with foreign exchange crises; the motivation was the belief that much of the destructive competitive behavior among countries in the interwar period that contributed to the advent of World War II had resulted from a shortage of international credits. Countries followed exchange rate policies and trade policies to stimulate domestic employment; the fallacy of composition was relevant and the policies that might have been successful for an individual country were costly for all countries as a group. When a country became a member of the IMF, it agreed to limit the range of movement in the foreign exchange value of its currency in the market around its parity; the country also agreed to seek the approval of the IMF before it changed the foreign exchange value of its parity by more than a modest amount. The IMF was endowed with a pool of gold and currencies from the capital subscriptions of its members. A member country could borrow from this pool to help finance a payments deficit.

A devaluation of a country's currency should almost always lead to an improvement in its international competitive position and a reduction in its trade deficit. The scope of the improvement is time-dependent and increases in the long run as firms within the country increase their export capacity and their ability to produce import-competing goods. So the country's currency could depreciate sharply in the short run before the supply and demand structures change and the country's trade deficit declines to a new and sustainable value. While these adjustments are occurring and before they have been completed, momentum-oriented traders in foreign currencies might induce an even sharper depreciation of the country's currency.

Undershooting and overshooting are inevitable developments in response to changes in the amount of cross-border capital flows. The scope of undershooting and overshooting often expands as traders in foreign exchange follow the canard that 'the trend is my friend.' In recent years the cliché of the 'vicious and virtuous cycle' was applied as the descriptive of this exchange market behavior. An earlier generation of economists used the term 'destabilizing speculation' for the same market developments.

At times these adjustments in currency values may occur in propitious circumstances, but at other times the circumstances are less than propitious. Thus in 1994 and 1995, Mexico needed a decline in the foreign exchange value of the peso because its current account deficit was much too large to be sustainable; the needed decline in the ratio of the current account deficit to its GDP was in the range of 3 to 4 percent of GDP. This necessary and inevitable decline would have dramatic impacts on Mexican saving, the fiscal position of the Mexican government, and Mexican GDP. When the shock occurred, there was a sharp outflow of capital from Mexico, and the change in the ratio of Mexico's current account balance to its GDP was briefly in the range of 10 to 12 percent. The shock to the Mexican economy was immense.

Similar sets of statements can be made about the depreciation of the foreign exchange value of the Argentinean peso in 2001. Or consider the throes of the South Korean economy after the won lost one-third of its value in the foreign exchange market in December 1997; prior to the crisis the country's current account deficit was 1 percent of its GDP. The scope of the overshooting of the Indonesian rupiah during the Asian crisis was extremely large.

While overshooting and undershooting are transitional phenomena associated with changes in the direction and scope of international capital flows, they have extremely powerful real effects on the domestic economies and some of these effects are permanent. One reason analysts have underestimated the extent of the changes in exchange rates associated with the move to new equilibrium values for individual currencies is that they have tended to ignore the permanent effects of overshooting and, especially, of undershooting.

An international lender of last resort would help countries moderate the deviations of market exchange rates from long-run equilibrium exchange rates. One inference from financial history is that in the absence of an international lender of last resort the economic depression that follows a financial crisis can be long and drawn out, as in 1873, 1890, and the early 1930s.

One problem in developing an international lender of last resort is formulating the legal framework and set of rules that would govern its activities. In the absence of a world currency, the international lender of last resort would necessarily lend the currency of one or several countries—most probably those with large holdings of international reserve assets or large payments surpluses—to the countries with large payments deficits. One inference from the historical record is that the lender of last resort would supply the currency of the country that is the leading financial center perhaps together with the currencies of a few other countries.

The debt-deflation cycle of the 1930s involved a feedback that encompassed business failures, bank failures, and declines in the price level. When businesses failed, their inventories were sold, which depressed the price level and reduced the net worth of other firms in the same industry. Business failures increased bank loan losses and the banks become less eager lenders; they refused to renew some maturing loans in the belief that the borrowers were on the proverbial slippery slope. The decline in the commodity price level meant that even though nominal interest rates were low, real interest rates were high and investment spending was depressed.

Japan was in the throes of a debt-deflation cycle at the end of the 1990s as its price level declined by 1 percent a year which led to an exceptionally high level of business failures. Hong Kong was in a debt-deflation cycle for six years following the Asian Financial Crisis and the handover of its sovereignty to China; the depreciation of the currencies of virtually all the other Asian countries meant that the international competitive position of firms producing in Hong Kong was declining.

The environment for the international lender of last resort differs from that of the domestic lender in two basic ways—one is that liquidity crises are often associated with changes in exchange rates and the other is that the rule of law is more fragile in the international context. The international lender of last resort also walks a tightrope, in this case between providing liquidity to countries so that unnecessary changes in exchange rates are avoided and minimizing the likelihood that its provision of liquidity would enable a country to postpone significantly the changes in the foreign exchange value of its currency that would be necessary for a return to the equilibrium value. In 1999 and 2000 Argentina would have borrowed and borrowed to avoid and delay the adjustments in its economy that were necessary to restore equilibrium. (After the devaluation, Argentina snubbed its creditors and wanted them to settle for twenty-five or thirty cents on the dollar.) Moreover, even when a change in the foreign exchange value of the country's currency is necessary, the extension of credit from the international lender of last resort may minimize the scope of undershooting of its currency in the move to a new equilibrium value. Finally, there are times when the determination of whether there is a need for a change in the foreign exchange value of a country's currency is a judgment call; the country's payments deficit might be reversed by developments in the business cycle or by changes in commodity prices—or there might be a miracle or just some good luck.

The analogy between the domestic lender of last resort and the international lender breaks—or at least bends sharply—on the fact that there is no good domestic counterpart to the changes in the foreign exchange values of national currencies. Normally, a domestic lender of last resort would not lend to an insolvent institution—except perhaps temporarily until losses or capital deficiency have been made good by a deposit guarantee agency or some other governmental group. Many international financial crises have involved changes in exchange rates associated with currencies that have become seriously overvalued. The problem is to determine when a country should change the foreign exchange value of its currency because of a fundamental disequilibrium—a term popularized by the IMF when the Bretton Woods system of adjustable parities was still viable. As long as countries retain the ability to change the foreign exchange value of their currencies, the international lender of last resort would have to determine when access to its funds would enable a country to delay a necessary change in the foreign exchange value of its currency and when such access would enable a country to avoid a change in the foreign exchange value that is not necessary.

The number and severity of financial crises in the last thirty-five years has been large. An effective international lender of last resort could have moderated the tumultuousness in financial markets. Consider some of the major currency crises of this period:

- Mexico, Brazil, and Argentina in 1982
- The British pound, the Italian lira, and other European currencies in 1992
- The Mexican peso in 1994
- The Thai baht, the Malaysian ringgit, and other Asian currencies in 1997
- The Russian ruble in 1998
- The Brazilian real in 1999
- The Argentinean peso in 2001

The United States cobbled together a financial assistance package for Mexico in 1995. Thailand, South Korea, Indonesia, and the Philippines received large credits from the IMF after their currencies had depreciated sharply. Russia received a large credit from the IMF in the spring of 1998, even though the devaluation of the ruble seemed inevitable; similarly

Argentina received a large credit from the fund in the early autumn of 2000 even though a major miracle would have been necessary if the parity of the peso with the U.S. dollar was to be maintained.

A historical view of international crises

Central bank history recognizes a distinction between internal and external drains. An external drain could generally be reversed by an increase in the interest rate; the quip was that an increase in the Bank of England's discount rate of 1 percent would 'draw gold from the moon,' although often there was a lag before the increase in interest rates would lead to the desired improvement in the country's holdings in gold. If investors viewed the increase in the discount rate as a sign of weakness and sold currency, the central bank might find it necessary to raise the interest rate further. At times the increase in interest rates would not be adequate to correct the imbalances—perhaps because the lags were long and the time limited—and it would be found necessary to obtain credits from some source other than the market to avoid a sharp depreciation. A central bank might borrow from other central banks. Domestic firms that owned foreign assets might sell them and remit the proceeds.

What is the appropriate public policy to reduce the likelihood of international financial crises and to ameliorate their impacts when they occur? In the financial crisis of 1846 to 1848, when bond prices all over Europe were plummeting, some by as much as 75 percent, and the Rothschild houses in Paris, Vienna, and Frankfurt were threatened with bankruptcy, Nathan Rothschild in London, with the help of Auguste Belmont, the Rothschild representative in New York, helped privately. Belmont shipped silver from New York to London that was then shared among the Rothschild brothers. Central banks helped by keeping interest rates low, but Nathan, as the effective lender of last resort, saved the day with New York assistance.[1] In the 1930s, Paul and Felix Warburg of Kuhn, Loeb in New York served in the same capacity for their brother, Max Warburg, in Hamburg, with credit of more than $9 million.[2]

Last resort lending centers on central banks as the providers of cash. In 1694 the Bank of England borrowed 2 million guilders from the States General in Holland to support the British Exchequer in remitting funds to the Continent to support British troops and allies during the Nine Years' War.[3]

In the years that followed (1695 to 1697) Amsterdam assisted the Bank of England by taking over its protested bills of exchange on the

Continent; the Dutch charged 10 percent for the service—a penalty rate in Bagehot terms, but it was, after all, business, not the provision of a public good.[4]

In the crisis of 1763 the Bank of England and London private bankers rescued their Dutch correspondents by granting, in distress, credits larger than those previously given in periods of prosperity. Five consignments of gold were shipped in August and two in September. In addition, the Bank of England and other banks delayed presenting bills for payment. Wilson comments that none of this was pure altruism. Instead, it represented a practical policy based on the knowledge that British prosperity was intimately associated with Dutch prosperity and that intensification of the Dutch crisis would cut off a source of capital for Great Britain.[5]

As the 1772 crisis reached a peak in January 1773, Anglo-Dutch trade was paralyzed. Amsterdam was helpless, and only the Bank of England, Wilson says, could rescue the city. On January 10, a Sunday, the Bank opened its windows and allowed specie to be drawn against presentation of notes and government stocks. Loads of bullion were sent on the first packet boat, and one Dutch banker was said to have drawn £500,000. At the same time, the Bank refused to discount doubtful paper, which had the effect of breaking many Jewish-owned banks in Amsterdam.[6] In the same crisis, Catherine the Great of Russia helped her best customers, the British merchants, the first of a number of occasions when czarist Russia assisted Western Europe in crisis.[7]

In the crisis of 1825 there was a rumor that the Bank of France was trying to add to the Bank of England's difficulties. Clapham insisted that instead France participated in an early example of international financial cooperation by shipping gold to London in exchange for silver.[8] That the price of gold in terms of silver was higher in London than in Paris (15.2 to 1 compared with 14.625 to 1) favored the exchange,[9] but the arrival via the Rothschild banks of £400,000 (mostly in sovereigns) from Paris on Monday, December 19, 1825, helped because the Bank of England coffers were virtually empty after the peak of the run on the previous Saturday.

Twice during the extended crisis of 1836 to 1839 the Bank of England sought help from the Bank of France and the city of Hamburg to maintain its liquidity. The first time the Bank of England drew bills on Paris for £400,000. In 1838 the Bank of England arranged for a line of credit and in 1839 drew on this line for £2 million, using Baring Brothers and ten Paris banks as intermediaries. A similar line of credit with Hamburg brought in £900,000 in gold, an arrangement possibly designed also to help Hamburg which needed silver.[10] In 1838 the Bank of England, not the most usual of gold dealers, sent 320,000 sovereigns to the United States in three ships and 360,000 sovereigns in two more. Clapham said the operation was without precedent, and damaging insofar as it encouraged American bankers to issue more securities in the British markets in 1838 and 1839, but he acknowledged that the Bank was wise to recognize the interlocking interests of Great Britain and the United States.[11]

The Bank of France borrowed 25 million francs from British capitalists in the second half of 1846, according to French sources;[12] a British source states that the sum was borrowed from the Bank of England in January 1847.[13] At that point, the emperor of Russia offered to buy 50 million francs of the French 3 percent *rente* to assist in financing the imports of wheat needed by France and Great Britain. Great Britain benefited since the French used half the money to repay the British advance.[14] Palmer, then governor of the Bank of England, testified before the Select Committee of Parliament that it was preferable to have an understanding with the principal banks in the United States, Hamburg, Amsterdam, and Paris than to ship gold.[15]

Central bank cooperation was not universally applauded. Viner wrote that the Bank of England in 1836 found itself obliged to appeal to France for help 'no doubt reluctantly' and added that the necessity was regarded in Great Britain as humiliating because it came at a time when relations between the two countries were not particularly cordial 'especially as it was reported that the followers of M. Thiers were boasting of the generosity of Frenchmen ... while recommending that under no circumstances should such liberality be repeated in future.'[16] Thomas Tooke thought the loan a 'discreditable expedient,' a 'circumstance of almost national humiliation.'[17] The Bank of France was criticized in Paris by some who thought it irresponsible, seeking to make a profit from the British arrangement rather than aiding those who implored its help on all sides at home.[18]

In the 1850s there was less international cooperation in crisis periods. Clapham wrote that the Bank of England contemplated joint action with the Bank of France in November 1857, but he did not indicate what the action was and said little beyond the statement that nothing came of it.[19] Perhaps the most interesting operation was the December *Silberzug* in Hamburg. Hamburg was on the end of the line of the rolling crisis that swept from New York (and Ohio) to Liverpool and then to the Continent, especially to Scandinavia. On December 4 the Hamburg Senate voted a 15 million mark banco fund composed of 5 million in Hamburg bonds and 10 million in silver that would be obtained by foreign borrowing. The next task was to borrow the money. Appeals for a loan were made to Rothschilds, Baring, and Hambros in London, to Fould in Paris, and to various political and financial bodies in Amsterdam, Copenhagen, Brussels, Berlin, Dresden, and Hanover. Each request was turned down. From Fould came this answer: 'Your message is not sufficiently clear.' From Berlin: 'Bruck and the Kaiser are not financially ambitious.' On December 8 when every bank in Hamburg except Heine's was threatened with bankruptcy, when captains of ships were unwilling to unload their cargos because they were concerned that they would not be paid, word came from Vienna that it would take the whole loan. A train bearing the silver (the *Silberzug)* arrived shortly.[20]

The silver was removed from the train, and loans in silver were made to Merck, Godeffroy, and Berenburg, Gossler and Co., among the leading bankers, plus five smaller ones. The panic ended on December 12 when it became known that there was enough silver. Some firms, like Donner & Co., which had initially been allotted 700,000 marks banco, turned out not to need any when confidence was restored. Böhme, who gave the most detailed account of the crisis, said that for years the episode kept coming up whenever Hamburgers and non-Hamburgers talked about currencies.[21] The political nature of the rescue operation was revealed in British diplomatic dispatches. From Hamburg the British consul noted that it was fortunate for Great Britain that Austria and not Prussia had brought the aid, since there would then be no pressure on Hamburg to join the Zollverein.[22] From Berlin on December 29 came a dispatch with a translation of Baron Manteuffel's statement to Hamburg that explained why Berlin had been unable to help. Lack of ambition gave way to a series of lame explanations that underlined that Berlin had 'missed an opportunity.'[23]

The distress in Scandinavia was relieved as the panic in Hamburg subsided. A positive item of international official aid, however, was a loan on December 18 by the Bank of England on promissory notes of the Norwegian government in support of overdue bills the bank held on Norwegian houses.[24]

At the outbreak of the Civil War in November 1860, panic in New York drew specie from Paris and London. French reluctance to raise the discount rate and the increasing departure of the French gold–silver ratio from the ratio in the market led France to exchange £2 million in silver for £2 million in gold with the Bank of England. The funds made available by this transaction failed to remedy the situation, so in 1861 the French bought gold in London at a price above the export point. The Bank of France then arranged through Rothschild and Baring to draw £2 million of bills on London.[25]

There was no international cooperation during the crisis of 1873 but there were two aspects that underline the sensitive political nature of central bank transactions. In the letter books for 1872–1873 the Bank of England refers to and denies a 'ridiculous rumor' that it had thought of applying for a loan to the Bank of France. And in the second week of November the governor of the Bank of Prussia—a predecessor of the Reichsbank, which was not established until 1875—wrote a letter to the Bank of England offering a loan in gold now or at any future time. (Clapham commented earlier that Germany was half drunk with victory and that Berlin had swelled up like Aesop's frog.) The Bank of England politely but curtly declined the offer: 'The Bank is not, nor has it been in want of such aid and need not avail itself of the arrangement you so kindly suggest.' Clapham adds that this suggestion from the nouveau riche would have seemed impertinent to the governor.[26]

In 1890 William Lidderdale, then the Governor of the Bank of England, prepared on two fronts for the crisis that would follow the revelation of Barings' position. In addition to the domestic guarantee, he arranged for the Russian government not to draw its £2.4 million deposit from Barings, and for loans of £3 million from the Bank of France and £1.5 million from the State Bank of Russia, both in gold. Lidderdale told the governor of the Bank of France that the ordinary operations of bank rate would have brought the gold in time and that there was nothing discreditable in using unusual measures to meet an unusually sudden storm. Nonetheless, Lidderdale and the City were uneasy about asking the French and the Russians for help. Clapham put it this way: 'Suppose for some political-financial reason they had been unwilling to oblige?'[27]

The sensitive character of such international assistance prior to World War I is revealed in the 1906–1907 incidents, when much discussion was devoted not to whether the Bank of France helped the Bank of England—which it clearly did—but whether the Bank of England had asked for such help or, if it did not, whether the steps taken by the Bank of France were largely in its own interest. In Sayers's account of the Bank from 1890 to 1914, in a chapter entitled 'Supposed Continental Support of the Bank,' the author concluded that the Bank of England did not ask for help. Sayers quotes *The Economist* in September 1906:

> Some talk of the Bank of France helping the Bank of England cope with the American demand for gold ... but it would not for a minute be supposed that the Bank would really put itself in so humiliating a position merely in order to permit American speculators getting gold here on easy terms.

Again in the fall of 1907, the Bank of France forwarded 80 million francs in U.S. gold eagles to London. The Bank of France report for 1907 refers to both incidents in its decisions. French journals cite the alleged reason: to relieve the Bank of England of the need to raise its discount rate, which implies that the Bank of England requested help. British sources emphasize that there was no announcement on the British side, as there was in 1890, and that the French did not want the Bank to increase its discount rate. Hartley Withers, financial editor of *The Times,* wrote later:

> The determination it [the Bank of England] showed finally compelled the Bank of France to take some share in the international burden, and to send three millions of its gold, not to America but to London, whence it knew it could rely on getting it back. It is commonly supposed the Bank of England asked it to carry out this operation, but this is quite untrue.[28]

Another view is that in dealing in sterling bills in London against gold in 1906, 1907, 1909, and 1910, the Bank of France was involved in open market operations which it did not undertake in Paris until 1938.[29]

London vs Paris as the world financial center

The general view among Anglo-Saxon students of economic history is that London was the world's financial center from the beginning of the nineteenth century until 1914, and that Paris, Berlin, Frankfurt, New York, and Milan were its satellites.

According to a German observer: 'England had a monopoly of capital exports to 1850. Then France moved in, largely for *gloire,* undertaking capital exports in the service of national policies, expansionary commercial interests, and the opening of new markets.'[30] In the 1850s Paris had a central role in international monetary relationships. Van Vleck wrote about the panic of 1857 that 'Just as France was the political nerve center of Europe during the first half of the nineteenth century, so during the years from 1850 to 1857, it was the center from which fluctuations in the economic cycle radiated.'[31]

The center for the economic cycle is not necessarily the pivot of the international financial system. Between 1820 and 1840 Paris assisted in clearing London's foreign payments in the Baltic, Russia, China, Latin America, and the United States and then between 1850 and 1870 became the 'first place in Europe for foreign exchange.'[32] If this view were correct, the situation was changed by the Franco-Prussian War. According to Bagehot:

> Since the Franco-German war, we may be said to keep the European reserves ... All great communities have at times to pay large sums in cash, and of that cash a great store must be kept somewhere. Formerly there were two such stores in Europe; one was the Bank of France, and the other the Bank of England. But since the suspension of specie payments by the Bank of France, its use as a reservoir of specie is at an end. No one can draw a cheque on it and be sure of getting gold or silver for that cheque. Accordingly the whole liability for such international payments in cash is thrown on the Bank of England ... all exchange operations are centering more and more in London. Formerly for many purposes, Paris was a European settling-house, but now it has ceased to be so ... Accordingly London has become the sole great settling-house in Europe, instead of being formerly one of two. And this preeminence London will probably maintain, for it is a natural preeminence ... The preeminence of Paris partly arose from a distribution of political power, which is already disturbed; but that of London depends on the regular course of commerce, which is singularly stable and hard to change.[33]

Sprague echoed this view from the United States in 1910, when he explained that the Bank of England raised its discount rate in 1907 to secure payment from other countries of money they owed the United States rather than to check the flow of gold to the United States. London was the central money market in the world and its interest rates were increased to avoid having to finance all the payments flowing to the United States.[34]

In contrast, Bonelli asserted that Paris was the center that regulated world liquidity when he discussed Italy's links to the 1907 crisis.[35] One of the most penetrating students of pre-World War I finance stated that

'Paris emerges in this study as the *strongest* [italics in original] financial center in the world before 1914, if the fact that its short-term rate was relatively the lowest is an indication of strength. This conclusion seems to contradict the generally held opinion that London was the world's money center.' Morgenstern attempted to reconcile these statements by distinguishing the abundance of funds in Paris and the 'machinery' in London for setting funds into motion.[36] The distinction seems forced. Each center had its own particular clients: Italy and Russia for Paris, the United States and the British colonies for London. Belgium, the Netherlands, and Germany were more closely linked to London than to Paris. Moreover London lent funds on a worldwide basis while Paris lent funds to a much smaller number of countries.

The lender of last resort after World War I

There was no international lender of last resort in the 1920–1921 crisis. Part of the slack was taken up by the depreciation of the various European currencies. In a crisis caused by balance-of-payments weakness and capital outflows, the depreciation of a country's currency led to increases in the domestic prices of tradable goods (i.e., the prices of goods and services that are exported or imported, and those capable of being exported and those that compete with imports). A sharp inflationary shock may produce another kind of crisis—out of money into goods—leading to hyperinflation, as happened in Eastern and Central Europe in 1923 in the newly independent countries that had been part of the Austrian-Hungarian Empire and were coping with new sets of boundaries and the lack of mechanisms for collection of taxes.[37] The scenario is similar to that of Paul Erdman's thriller *The Crash of '79,* in which the financial crisis is handled by printing massive amounts of currency and letting the U.S. dollar float, which led to a surge in the demand for goods.[38]

Most governments in Western Europe in the early 1920s sought to stabilize their currencies at their 1914 parities for gold because of tradition—restoring the status quo *ante bellum.* These countries often used stabilization loans, similar in some respects but not identical to loans from a lender of last resort, to dampen the depreciation of their currencies in the foreign exchange market. The French franc was under a speculative attack in 1924 for several reasons. Many foreigners had bought francs as the currency depreciated in 1919–1920 in anticipation of large revaluation gains from its subsequent appreciation toward its prewar parity—but they eventually gave up and sold.[39] Speculators in

Amsterdam, Vienna, and Berlin (perhaps stimulated by the German government) sold francs in anticipation that they would be able to purchase them in the future at much lower prices.[40] The story was that speculators who had profited from speculating in the German mark as it depreciated sharply in the hyperinflation of 1923–1924 then turned their attention to the French franc. Hundreds of thousands of Frenchmen with liquid securities denominated in the franc watched signals such as the legal ceiling on Bank of France advances to the French government approach.

On March 4, 1924, panic broke out. The franc, which had been 98 to the pound sterling on February 17 and 104 on February 28, went to 107 on March 4. The French government and the Bank of France met in emergency sessions. J.P. Morgan & Co. was willing to help if certain conditions were satisfied. The loan, a six-month revolving credit, should be for $100 million, not $50 million, which the bank, represented by Thomas W. Lamont, judged too small. The Bank of France resisted pledging its gold as collateral, and yielded only after a face-saving formula was found. In turn, the Bank regents, including Rothschild and de Wendel, exacted a conservative financial program from the government. The program was worked out on Sunday, March 9 and within three days the rout of the speculators began. The franc appreciated from a low of 123 francs to the pound to 78 by March 24. The Bank of France then intervened to limit further appreciation. The squeeze against the speculators was successful.[41] Lamont wrote that 'there has never been an operation that has given us more satisfaction.'[42]

Success was short lived. In 1926 there was another attack on the franc, and the currency depreciated to 240 francs to the British pound in July 1926. Subsequently the currency appreciated to 125 francs in response to conservative Poincaré reforms and a surge in interest rates that was designed to reassure the French holders of wealth and induce them to bring their funds back to Paris from London and New York.

Stabilization loans were arranged in the 1920s for Austria and Hungary under League of Nations auspices, and for a number of new central banks in Eastern Europe under various arrangements with London, Paris, and New York. The most widely known were the Dawes and Young loans undertaken to recycle German reparations. The Dawes loan stimulated U.S. purchases of foreign bonds. During the 1930s the suggestion was frequently put forward, with only partial irony, that what France needed was a stabilization loan in gold, since the French franc and the currencies of the other gold bloc countries had become overvalued as a consequence of successive devaluations of the British pound, the Japanese yen, and the U.S. dollar, and the imposition of exchange controls on foreign payments by Germany and Austria. The gold, it was said, should be mounted in a vehicle like a glass hearse and paraded through the streets of every town and village in France to convince the people that the authorities had an abundance of gold and thereby encourage them to dishoard from the *bas de laine* (wool sock) in which they kept their *louis d'or.*

The rolling deflation of 1931 underlines the need for an international lender of last resort in a way that differs in scale and therefore in kind from previous episodes. The issues involved include the need for loans of the appropriate magnitude, the political character of the transactions, and the need for some country or group of countries to accept responsibility for the stability of the system.[43] Those who wrote along similar lines included Jørgen Pedersen, R.G. Hawtrey, and other British economists whose advice to their government is set out in Susan Howson and Donald Winch's *The Economic Advisory Council, 1930–1939.*

Hawtrey presented a cogent analysis:

> The crisis of 1931 differed from earlier crises in its international character. Earlier crises were international in that the fall of prices and forced sales affected world markets. But only an unimportant part of debts were due to foreign creditors. In 1931 the outstanding characteristic of the panic was that foreign creditors of Germany and Eastern European debtors feared that the foreign exchange market would break down *even if the debtors remained solvent.* Against a panic-stricken withdrawal of foreign balances from London, it [raising Bank rate] was too tardy a remedy. Such a panic-stricken withdrawal *had never occurred before* ... the underlying cause of the trouble has been *monetary instability.* The industrial depression, the insolvencies, the bank failures, budget deficits and defaults, are all the natural outcome of a falling price level ... The need arises for an *international lender of last resort.* Perhaps some day the Bank for International Settlements ... But as things are, the function can only be undertaken by a foreign central bank or by a group of foreign central banks in co-operation.[44]

Hawtrey's theoretical insight into the wisdom of limits on these stabilization loans was penetrating:

> As a general rule, if credits are to be granted to a central bank in difficulties at all, they should be granted up to the full amount needed. There should be no limit. If the amount is inadequate and the exchange gives way after all, the sums lent are completely wasted ...

> It can be argued in favor of unlimited credits, that if they *had* been granted, there would have been no withdrawal of funds at all ... either no credits to the Bank of England or unlimited.
>
> But there is some risk. Unlimited credits would have enabled the country to remain on the gold standard, prolonging conditions that were rapidly becoming intolerable ... the lesson: if the country can maintain the monetary standard without undue strain, then grant unlimited credits; but if the effort of maintaining parity is excessive, no credits and allow the currency to depreciate.[45]

Howson and Winch set out a series of reports written by British economists to their government in the 1930s, including one from a Committee of Economists chaired by Keynes that included Henderson, Pigou, Robbins, and Sir Josiah Stamp as members, with Hemming and Kahn as secretaries. The reports advocated general cooperation among central banks, preferably through the Bank for International Settlements, both to fund short-term claims and to form a pool of currencies for loans that could be used to prevent currency debacles of the sort experienced in the early 1920s and to restore 'confidence in the financial stability of those many countries which are now the subject of distrust.'[46]

In July 1932, after Great Britain had gone off gold but before the World Economic Conference of 1933, the Cabinet Committee on Economic Information chaired by Stamp and including Citrine, Cole, Keynes, Sir Alfred Lewis, and Sir Frederick Leith-Ross as members, with Henderson and Hemming as secretaries, issued a report that discussed the 'international financial crisis.' The document quoted Bagehot, cited the crises of 1825 and 1847, and noted that Great Britain could no longer act as a lender of last resort, recommending that this function be performed by the Bank for International Settlements by the issue of 'paper gold,' to be called International Certificates.[47]

The first opportunity to halt the international disintermediation came in May 1931 with the collapse of the Credit Anstalt of Vienna, the leading Austrian bank. The central bank had maintained high interest rates to keep funds in Vienna which in turn contributed to the softness in the economy and large loan losses as asset prices declined. The publication of the Credit Anstalt's statement on May 11 revealed that it had lost 140 million schillings, about three-fourths of its capital. The Austrian government asked the League of Nations for financial assistance because the League had organized the stabilization loans in the 1920s and the League turned to the new Bank for International Settlements that had been established under the Young Plan of 1930 to assist in the transfer of German reparations. The Austrian government wanted to borrow 150 million schillings ($21 million). During the last two weeks of May the BIS arranged for a loan of 100 million schillings from eleven countries. By June 5 the funds from the loan were exhausted, and the Austrian National Bank requested another loan which was arranged by June 14, subject to the condition that the Austrian government get a two- to three-year loan of 150 million schillings. The French demanded that the Austrian government renounce its customs union agreement with Germany that had been announced two months earlier, but the Austrian government refused and fell. The Bank of England then offered a loan of 50 million schillings ($7 million) for a week. The Austrian government then stopped pegging its currency to gold, and the schilling depreciated.

The run shifted to Germany. The German banking position was weakened by excessive speculation, large loan write-offs, fraud, quarrels among the bankers, banks that had been buying their own shares and depleted liquid reserves—the full range of classic troubles.[48] The outsider was Jacob Goldschmidt of the Danatbank,[49] the product of the merger of the Darmstädter and the National banks. Other bankers, including Oskar Wasserman of the Deutsche Bank, detested Goldschmidt and his aggressive tactics. In 1927 the Berlin Handelsgesellschaft had stopped making loans to the Norddeutsche-Wolkämmerei (Nordwolle), an aggressive firm in the woolen industry. The Danatbank took on Nordwolle as a client. Nordwolle's failure, on June 17, 1931, brought down Danatbank; other banks were unwilling to support the bank because of their dislike of Goldschmidt. There were other complications, political and financial, but the internal financial turmoil led to massive withdrawals that were only briefly interrupted by the Hoover moratorium. On June 25 a loan for $100 million was arranged, including $25 million each from the Bank of England, the Bank of France, the Federal Reserve Bank of New York, and the Bank for International Settlements, for the period to July 16. Hans Luther, president of the Reichsbank, had wanted a larger loan and had asked that the exact amount of the loan be concealed, so the communiqué said only that discount facilities had been arranged in sufficient amount. When the amount of the loan became known and the Reichsbank's statement of June 23 showed that its reserve cover was at 40.4 percent, just above the minimum requirement of 40 percent, the motto became 'Devil take the hindmost.'[50]

New loans were discussed but were not forthcoming. The Germans wanted to borrow $1 billion. The French were willing to consider a loan of $500 million, but they wanted to impose political conditions. The U.S. government was worried about its prospective budget deficit of $1.6 billion and thought it highly unlikely that the U.S. Congress would approve lending more money to Germany. The U.S. government was willing to consider stabilization of existing loans to Germany, which the Reichsbank wanted as well as a further loan. In Great Britain the foreign secretary Arthur Henderson was attracted to the idea of a loan but Montagu Norman, governor of the Bank of England, held that the Bank had 'already lent quite as much as is entirely convenient.'[51] One argument against foreign loans was that the crisis was believed to have been caused by a flight of domestic capital rather than by withdrawals of funds by foreign investors. By July 20 the idea of a loan had been tacitly abandoned, 'brushed aside as impractical.'[52] Instead, the Germans relied on internal measures to halt the disintermediation at home and on a Standstill Agreement, imposed upon reluctant foreign bankers, to halt the external drain.

The speculative pressure then turned to Great Britain. The run began in mid-July 1931, stimulated partly by losses on the Continent, but also fed by the May and Macmillan reports of the large prospective domestic budget deficits and the unexpectedly high estimate of foreign funds in London that might be withdrawn. Since 1927 the Bank of France had converted British pounds to gold by a roundabout device; British pounds were sold in the spot foreign exchange market, and bought in the forward exchange market, then the Bank of France asked for gold on the dates when the forward exchange contracts matured.[53] The idea was to make it seem that the Bank of France was converting only its newly acquired British pound balances into gold, not its previously acquired balances. In the summer of 1931, the Bank of France cooperated fully and did not sell any of its British pound deposits and securities. At the end of July, the Federal Reserve Bank of New York and the Bank of France each loaned $125 million to the Bank of England. When these funds were depleted, the British government contemplated a one-year loan from the New York and Paris markets. The Bank of England reported that foreign bankers would not lend funds to Great Britain while it had such a large budget deficit. The British trade unions opposed a reduction in relief payments to the unemployed and withdrew support from the Labour government, which fell on August 24. Four days later, after the formation of a new 'national government' with MacDonald again prime minister and Snowden as the Chancellor of the Exchequer, $200 million was borrowed from a Morgan syndicate in New York and another

$200 million from a French syndicate in Paris. On one showing, the bankers held up the British government; their own explanation, echoing the Morgan statements to the French in the 1920s, was that they were not imposing political conditions but instead indicating the economic circumstances in which they felt they were justified in risking their own and their depositors' money.

On August 5, 1931, Keynes wrote to Prime Minister MacDonald, at the latter's request, to present a series of proposals for devaluation of the British pound and for the formation of a gold-based, fixed-exchange currency unit at least 25 percent below the current parity, which all empire countries, together with South America, Asia, Central Europe, Italy, and Spain—in fact, all countries—would be invited to join. The letter pointed out that if the British pound could not be successfully defended, it would be foolish to continue to borrow foreign currencies to support it.[54]

Loans of $400 million on top of $250 million were not enough, and the British stopped supporting the pound on September 21. The Bank of France did not show the restraint towards the United States that they had shown to the British, and together with other members of the gold bloc converted $750 million of U.S. dollar deposits into gold. The deflationary pressure exerted by this reduction in U.S. gold holdings, and by the depreciation of the British pound and of the currencies pegged to the pound weakened the U.S. banking system. The New York Fed did not ask for help or even for forbearance in conversion of U.S. dollar deposits into gold. The code of the central banker calls for a stiff upper lip, reminiscent of Walter Mitty refusing the blindfold before the firing squad. In 1929, when Harrison asked Norman whether the British pounds that the Federal Reserve Bank of New York had bought would be convertible into gold, he received the curt reply: 'Of course, the sterling is repayable in gold. This is the gold standard.'[55] In 1931 Harrison in turn offered to assist Moret in converting any or all of the Bank of France's dollars into gold.[56]

Five aspects of the 1931 story are especially striking: (1) the inability of Great Britain to act as a lender of last resort; (2) the unwillingness of the United States to act as a lender of last resort apart from the inadequate loan to Great Britain, the country of the 'special relationship;' (3) the desire of France to gain political objectives with respect to Austria and Germany; (4) the paranoia of Germany after 1923, preferring anything to a hint of inflation; and (5) the irresponsibility of the smaller countries.

This analysis has been questioned in a number of quarters. One analyst thought that something more far-reaching was required to restore the world economy after World War I, perhaps something on the order of the Marshall Plan after World War II.[57] Another considered that the German economy could not have been righted by a lender of last resort in 1931 since its authorities were determined to undo the Versailles treaty and especially its reparations clauses.[58]

Bretton Woods and the international monetary arrangements

There was an extended debate in the early 1940s about planning for multilateral economic institutions that would provide for greater economic stability than in the twenty years after World War I. An international credit institution would be established to help countries finance short-term balance of payments deficits (this became the International Monetary Fund). Another lending agency would be established to help countries finance their economic reconstruction after the war; this became the International Bank for Reconstruction and Development (IBRD or World Bank). An international trade organization would be established to resolve trade disputes and provide a forum for the reduction of trade barriers. The international trade organization never came into being, but its preamble, the General Agreement on Tariffs and Trade, provided the basis for an organization to deal with trade policy issues in a less ambitious way.

The debate about the international credit institution that became the International Monetary Fund (IMF) was primarily between the British and the Americans, who held different views about its structure and its financial resources. The British 'Keynes's plan' provided for an institution that would have its own money or unit of account. Member countries would be endowed with deposits in this institution which they could then transfer to other countries to finance their payments deficits. The American view, the 'White plan,' was that each member country would transfer gold and its own currency in the form of a noninterest bearing demand deposit to the institution to endow its capital. Each member country would have a quota based on the volume of its trade and its gold holdings. The size of each member country's quota would determine the amount of gold and its own currency that it would transfer to the institution. A member country would be able to 'buy' currency owned by the institution with its own currency; the amount of currencies that the member could buy would depend on the size of its quota.

The U.S. view prevailed; the Americans had all the money. The British got the Americans to agree to double the initial capital of the institution.

The fund's Articles of Agreement contained a set of rules for the management of the foreign exchange values of member country currencies. Each member country would be required to state a parity for its currency either in terms of gold or in terms of the U.S. dollar; would be required to limit the variation in the foreign exchange value of its currency to a narrow band around its parity; and would be required to obtain the approval of the IMF before changing the value of its parity by more than 10 percent relative to its initial parity.

Despite the motivation to establish a credit institution that would help avoid a repetition of the experiences of the 1930s, the structure of the fund meant it could not act as a lender of last resort because it did not have its own money. Instead the IMF could lend money to countries to help them finance their current account deficits within modest limits. Countries could retain exchange controls to limit capital flows that might complicate their ability to retain their parities. Loans from the IMF would have to be repaid. The lesson of 1931 concerning the need for a lender of last resort was not learned. At Bretton Woods, the IMF was created to finance current-account deficits, within moderate limits. Controls on capital flows would restrict speculative capital movements. The IMF provided loans in member currencies that would have to be repaid, rather than loans in a newly-created international money. There were narrow limits on the amount of loans to each country set by country quotas that were identical to their capital subscriptions to the IMF; the quota was divided into four tranches and no more than one tranche could be drawn on in a given twelve month period. Drawing on the first tranche was more or less automatic. Thereafter access to credit was a matter of grace on the part of the IMF rather than a matter of right as Keynes's plan had proposed.

During the period of economic recovery from World War II, the IMF and the World Bank were largely on the sidelines since most of the finance for economic reconstruction was provided under the Marshall Plan. The Bretton Woods system did not come into operation until 1958, after the devaluation of the French franc and the convertibility of the pound and the abandonment of restrictions on capital flows.

The inattention to financial flows soon had to be modified. It proved impossible to maintain convertibility on current accounts and controls over capital movements, since large capital transfers could take place through changes in the finance of exports and imports, the so-called 'leads and lags.' A country called upon to pay cash for imports instead of getting three months' credit, and forced to extend six months' credit for exports instead of three months, could quickly lose the value of six months of the average of exports and imports.

In 1960 the Articles of Agreement of the IMF were extended by the General Arrangements to Borrow (GAB), under which ten leading financial countries, the Group of Ten, pledged an additional $6 billion on top of $14.4 billion of the IMF's quotas (an increase from $7.8 billion when the IMF started in 1946), to be made available through the IMF in case of perverse capital flows that could not be handled by a country's own reserves and IMF quota. These amounts proved inadequate. Moreover, the IMF was found not to work in timely fashion. Decisions were taken by weighted voting by directors, many of whom represented more than one country. To frame a proposal, obtain instructions, and arrive at a decision to help a country in crisis could take three weeks.

There was an increase in cross-border capital flows in the 1950s and the 1960s. Economic distances were declining because of technological developments and the sharp decline in the costs of communication and storing information. Richard Cooper emphasized this development:

> A crude quantitative indicator of these developments is provided by contrasting the maximum daily speculation of under $100 million against the pound sterling, in the 'massive' run of August 1947, with the maximum daily speculation of over $1.5 billion in favor of the German mark in May 1969, and the movement of over $1 billion into Germany in less than an hour in May 1971. Moreover, as the barriers of ignorance fall further, there is no reason why $1.5 billion should not rise to $15 billion, or even $50 billion a day.[59]

The daily turnover in the foreign exchange market had reached $1 trillion by the late 1990s. The increase in the foreign exchange transactions in the currencies of the emerging market economies had been even more rapid.[60]

The increase in international capital flows challenged the ability of central banks to retain their parities. Some central banks experimented by selling their currencies in the forward foreign exchange market; these sales enabled them to maintain the parities without depleting their foreign exchange reserves—at least not until the dates that the forward exchange markets matured. And on those dates the central banks might 'roll over' or renew these contracts. A few observers believed that these forward exchange transactions would relieve central banks of the need to hold international reserve assets. The experience of the Bank of

England from 1964 to 1967 suggests the limits to this view; by late 1967 the amount of its commitments to deliver U.S. dollars in the spot foreign exchange market on the dates that the forward exchange contracts matured were several times larger than its holdings of international reserve assets, and market participants became increasingly reluctant to renew maturing forward exchange contracts. In 1964 the British had been able to postpone the devaluation of the British pound, but the devaluation became inescapable in 1967.

One of the major international financial innovations in the 1960s was the Basel Agreement that provided for the swap network. The United States had taken a leadership role in the development of the swap network—a series of bilateral credit lines between pairs of central banks in which each bank wrote up an amount of foreign currency as an asset and an equivalent amount of foreign exchange as a liability. Once the swap lines had been established, the foreign currency would be immediately available, although the money drawn under the swap lines would have to be repaid. The first swap was a $50 million arrangement between the Bank of France and the Federal Reserve Bank of New York in March 1962. In June the New York Fed entered into $50 million swap arrangements with the Dutch and Belgian central banks and a $250 million swap with the Bank of Canada. In July the New York Fed established a $250 million line with the Swiss National Bank. By October 1963 the swap network had been increased to $2 billion, by March 1968 to $4.5 billion, and by July 1973 to $18 billion.[61]

In 1961, when the British pound was under attack, representatives of the major central banks at a meeting of the Bank for International Settlements committed a total of $1 billion for credits. Charles Coombs, a senior vice president of the Federal Reserve Bank of New York, called this development a major breakthrough in international postwar finance.[62] The number was large enough to convince speculators that they could not break the parity of a currency. Most of the loan would be repaid with the funds obtained from the repatriation of flight capital.

The money available under the swap lines would be a country's first line of defense; the second line would be access to credits from the IMF. A number of countries used their swap lines: Canada used more than $1 billion in June 1962; Italy $1 billion in March 1963; and Great Britain $2 billion in the autumn of 1964. A $1.3 billion package was available for France in July 1968, which would have been extended to $2 billion in November for the defense of the devalued franc.[63] The French decision not to help the British in September 1965 has been characterized as a 'shocking repudiation of the central-banking free masonry.' The pressure to conform to the club, and the will to be different as a matter of foreign policy, were doubtless both intense. 'It cut no ice. The British got the support they wanted.'[64]

The approximate cause of the breakdown of the Bretton Woods arrangements was an effort by the U.S. and the German central banks to follow divergent monetary policies, even though their money markets were closely linked through the offshore deposit market. Any effort to follow divergent monetary policies would lead to massive capital flows. The Federal Reserve embarked on a policy of monetary expansion six to eight months before the presidential election, while Germany maintained high interest rates. Massive funds were shifted from the dollar area to the mark area.

The decline in interest rates on U.S. dollar securities led to the relaxation of lending standards, as in 1825, 1853, 1871, and 1885. Banks headquartered in New York, London, Tokyo, and other financial centers began to lend freely to Mexico, Brazil, Argentina, and other developing countries as well as to the Soviet Union and the countries in the Eastern bloc.

Further, the large flow of funds from New York to Germany and elsewhere made it impossible to sustain the system of pegged exchange rates. The United States made little or no effort to defend the new parity for the U.S. dollar that had been set in the Smithsonian Agreement. By February 1973 speculation that the mark would be revalued led to increasingly large flows of funds to Frankfurt; the Bundesbank stopped buying U.S. dollars, and the mark began to appreciate.

Most economists had thought that the adoption of floating exchange rates would kill the movement of interest-sensitive capital and that once currencies were floating central banks would be able to follow independent monetary policies without any untoward external effects. Economists differed about whether speculative capital movements would be stabilizing or, occasionally seriously destabilizing; the general view was that fear of exchange losses would deter capital flows. That view proved mistaken; many banks regarded currencies as a new asset class to be traded for a profit.

Under these new circumstances, the initial need for a lender of last resort proved to be domestic, though related to international finance—at least for a time. The changes in exchange rates encouraged speculators, including some who worked for banks. The Herstatt Bank of Cologne and the Franklin National Bank of New York lost money trading foreign exchange and each failed in June 1974. The closing of the Herstatt Bank in the middle of the trading day created a new problem because Herstatt had collected sums due to it on foreign exchange transactions but was closed before it had paid out the German mark counterpart that was due the other banks. For a time, the consortium that guaranteed its liabilities was interested only in domestic German obligations and was prepared to let the sums due to foreign banks go unrequited. Second thoughts prevailed, however; the total liabilities of the bank were covered, foreign as well as domestic, and there was no shockwave felt abroad. The Federal Deposit Insurance Corporation took over Franklin National deposits up to the limit of $40,000, and the Federal Reserve System, acting as lender of last resort, guaranteed the remaining liabilities.

The arrangements worked out at the Bank for International Settlements in the so-called Basel Protocol of March 1975 were supposed to settle the issue of national responsibility in the case of bank failure. A new problem developed in 1982 when the Luxembourg subsidiary of the Banco Ambrosiano of Milan defaulted on $400 million of liabilities to other European banks. The Bank of Italy refused to make good on these liabilities on the legal grounds that the Luxembourg unit of Ambrosiano was a subsidiary of the Milan bank which was incorporated under Luxembourg law and so its assets and liabilities were distinct from those of the bank's head office. This placed the Basel Protocol under a cloud.

The sharp increases in the price of oil in 1973 and again in 1979 led to a surge in the export earnings of the oil-producing countries and in their holdings of international reserve assets. Spending by the oil-producing countries also surged, including their purchases of real estate, office buildings, and shopping malls. Borrowing by oil importing countries increased. The increase in the price of oil accelerated oil exploration and production.

The combination of the increase in oil production in the North Sea and Mexico and elsewhere and the decline in demand due to the global recession in the early 1980s led to reductions in oil prices. By mid-1982 Mexico and many of the smaller oil-producing countries were in financial difficulties. Similarly the firms and financial institutions in Texas, Oklahoma, and Louisiana were encountering problems.

Credits under the swap agreements were limited to the major industrial countries and were not available to emerging markets in developing countries which depended on credits from the IMF when they incurred financial crises. But since many of these countries had a strong aversion to the conditions demanded by the IMF, they attempted to reschedule debt with the lending banks. It was a bit like Catch 22; often these banks insisted that the developing countries obtain a seal of approval from the IMF before they would refinance maturing loans. When financial conditions became acute, a 'bridge' loan might help the borrower during the period of negotiation.

The Federal Reserve Bank of New York extended a $1 billion bridge loan to Mexico in 1982, and the U.S. Treasury bought a billion dollars' worth of oil with current payments for future delivery to the U.S. Strategic Petroleum Reserve. These ad hoc loans enabled Mexico to muddle through and avoid default. The debtors liked this arrangement because otherwise they would have been cut off from international capital markets for a generation (if indications from history were any guide) and because they wanted more foreign capital to enhance their rates of economic growth. The creditors liked these arrangements because otherwise defaults by the borrowers would force them to write off the loans and recognize large loan losses. Whereas default in earlier periods was less of a concern to the credit system of developed countries, since it affected bonds held by individuals and not loans extended by banks, default on Third World debt in the 1980s might propagate runs on the major international banks.

Conditionality

The populist view is that the IMF has been excessively restrictive about the choice of monetary policies and fiscal policies by the emerging market countries. Most lenders, both domestic and international, stipulate conditions on their loans. Some French analysts were irked by the requirements laid down by J.P. Morgan & Co. in its 1924 stabilization loan,[65] although the standard response is that the lenders have an obligation to their depositors to ensure that their loans can be repaid. French conditions for loans to Austria and to Germany in 1931 were political. American and French loans to Great Britain later that summer were regarded by the Labour Party as a 'bankers' ramp' (in American, 'racket') as the lenders thought that the recommendations of the British May Committee to balance the budget and reduce unemployment benefits should be carried out.

Conditions have not been attached to the credits extended under swaps although there are 'understandings.' When the Bank for International Settlements makes a loan to Hungary under a swap, it knows that Hungary will obtain the funds to repay the loan from access to credit at the IMF. Conditions will be attached to that loan. When a G-7 member borrows from the IMF, as Great Britain did in 1976, conditions also apply.[66]

The Mexican crisis

The Mexican financial crisis of 1994 began with a peasant revolt in January and the assassination of the leading presidential candidate of the dominant political party. The flow of foreign investment slowed, and Mexico's ability to support the peso in the foreign exchange market rapidly became exhausted.[67] In April 1994, the United States and Canada came to the rescue, largely because of the 'special relationship' involved in the North American Free Trade Agreement Act of November 1993 between the three countries. A credit line of $6.7 billion was put together—the United States provided $6 billion, Canada $700 million. Mexican troubles continued. In December 1994 another crisis attack on the peso occurred, partly local capital flight, partly the withdrawal of funds by disenchanted American investors. In January 1995, the U.S. Treasury organized a $50 billion rescue fund including $20 billion from the U.S. Exchange Stabilization Fund, $18 billion from the IMF, $10 billion from European central banks organized by the BIS, and $2 billion from Canada.[68] The amount proved persuasive. The capital flows stopped and capital began to flow back to Mexico. Only $12.5 billion of the U.S. credit line was drawn, and in the fall of 1995 repayment started with the help of loans placed privately.

Several questions remain about the Mexican rescue operation in 1994–1995. One is whether the loans made in 1982 led the Mexicans to believe that they would be helped if they again encountered difficulties—the moral hazard question. Another is whether the large amounts of the credits created a precedent that would lead to future problems. Moreover, did the financial authorities forestall contagion and prevent the spreading of the crisis to Brazil and Argentina, as contagion spread from Austria in May 1931?

Bagehot enunciated the prescription that a lender of last resort should lend freely because low limits excite. Loans on a scale that seems beyond any possible need can be seen as lending freely.

The East Asian crisis

The financial crisis in East Asia that started in July 1997 involved euphoric lenders in developed countries, enamored of diversifying their portfolios, and the rapidly developing borrowing countries that wanted to increase their investments and their growth rates and had been pushed by the West to deregulate their financial markets. Other factors included crony capitalism in Indonesia, weak government in Thailand, enormous conglomerates (*chaebol*) in South Korea, bad bank loans everywhere. The catatonic state of economic policy in Japan robbed the area of what had been a strong source of demand, and the expansion of Japanese direct investment into lower wage areas and Japanese bank loans contributed to the increase in the current account deficits in most of these countries. European banks also made large bank loans in the region. The currencies of most of the countries had become overvalued in response to these capital inflows—and countries with large current account deficits and overvalued currencies are vulnerable to any shock that leads to a decline in the capital inflows.

The devaluation of the Thai baht in early July 1997 triggered the contagion effect, and the flow of foreign capital to other Asian countries slowed and then reversed. The President of Malaysia, Dr Mahathir, blamed foreign speculators, and specifically George Soros in the United States, who asserted that he had not sold the ringgit short while Malaysia was constructing two new buildings taller than those anywhere else in the world. Malaysia did not seek loans from the IMF but instead imposed controls on outflows of capital and interest of foreign investors. Thailand, Indonesia, and South Korea borrowed from the IMF. The amounts, on top of that for Mexico in 1994–1995, are set forth in Table 12.1 from the Bank for International Settlements.[69]

The report of the Bank for International Settlements noted that the $50 billion credit lines for Mexico had a 'psychological impact on the markets' and halted the erosion of domestic confidence.[70] These credit commitments also depleted the funds available for rescue operations in

Table 12.1 Official finance commitments (last-resort lending) ($U.S. billions)

Country	IMF	World Bank	Asian Development Bank	Bilateral Commitments	Total
Thailand	3.9	1.9	2.2	12.1	20.1
Indonesia	10.1	4.5	3.5	22.0[a]	30.0
South Korea	21.0	10.0	4.0	22.0	57.0
Total	35.0	16.4	*9.7*	56.1	117.1
Memo item					
Mexico	17.8	1.5	1.3[b]	21.0	51.6

[a]Including the use of a $5 billion Indonesian contingency reserve.
[b]InterAmerican Development Bank.

the future. At the end of 1998, the U.S. Congress agreed to the proposal of the Clinton Administration to increase IMF quotas and capital. The IMF was thus able to help Brazil when it needed assistance.

The IMF is not a central bank and it cannot create money; instead it can lend the money it has obtained from the capital subscriptions of its members and its own borrowings. The quota system of the IMF makes it different from a central bank, which can create domestic money.

A world central bank would be a more efficient lender of last resort than the IMF, but an improbable one. Outside the European Monetary Union, most large countries regard the issue and control of money as a mark of sovereignty; in the United States, these functions are enshrined in the Constitution.

The United States and the dollar

The United States took the lead in the 1940s, 1950s, and the 1960s in establishing a new set of international financial arrangements—the International Monetary Fund and the World Bank, the General Arrangements to Borrow, the Special Drawings Rights, the swap network, and the gold pool. Moreover the United States took the initiative at the end of the 1980s in assisting the developing countries to write down the value of their loans to major international banks so they might again be creditworthy. And the United States took a leadership role when individual countries like Mexico and Russia and South Korea had major international payments problems.

One of the major surprises at the beginning of the 1980s was the development of a persistent U.S. trade deficit. The U.S. had had trade surpluses for more than a hundred years. The persistent U.S. trade deficit that began about 1980 led to a dramatic change in the U.S. international financial position. In 1980, the United States was the world's largest creditor country; its net creditor position was larger than the combined positions of all other net creditor countries. By 2000 the United States had become the world's largest debtor, and its net debtor position was larger than the positions of all other net debtors as a group. The U.S. net debtor position has continued to increase.

There is an analogy between the persistent U.S. payments deficit in the 1950s and the 1960s and the persistent U.S. trade deficit in the 1980s and the 1990s and subsequently. The U.S. payments deficit developed because the demand for international reserve assets on the part of other countries was larger than the increases in the supply of new reserve assets from non-U.S. sources. The United States developed a persistent trade deficit because of the demand in other countries for U.S. dollar securities and U.S. real assets.

At the end of the 1960s and throughout the early 1970s, the willingness of foreign official institutions to continue to acquire reserve assets declined, which might reflect, if present indications are correct, the crises of the last two-thirds of the 1990s. The U.S. has also been the most successful economy during the 1990s, with some economic analysts suggesting that with low inflation, low unemployment, government budget surpluses in the making, and technical progress, it has entered a 'New Era' in which the business cycle has been dampened and financial crises, with fast Federal Reserve responses to trouble, tamed. Not all is completely solid, however. Prosperity has relied on increases in U.S. consumer spending and a decline in the household saving rate. Credit card debt has reached new heights. So have household bankruptcies. The increase in U.S. net international indebtedness may pose problems if foreign confidence in the value of the U.S. dollar declines. A strong, perhaps overstated warning by a British economist is entitled 'Seven Unsustainable Processes,' although the author is unwilling to discuss timing beyond saying that downturns are likely within the next five to fifteen years.[71] There is a possibility that the United States and its dollar may lose their positions in 'world economic and financial primacy.'[72]

Some political scientists place faith in what they call 'regimes,' habits of cooperation built up during periods of leadership (that they in turn call 'hegemony').[73] Such cooperation worked remarkably well in the 1980s, especially under the initiatives of Secretary of the Treasury James Baker, who abandoned the policy of benign neglect of the value of the dollar and worked out the Plaza Agreement of September 1985 and the Louvre Agreement of January 1987. Few observers place much reliance on the system of summit meetings among the G-7. These have strong overtones of ceremony and posturing. More suited to the working out of effective agreements is the G-5 among France, Germany, Japan, the United Kingdom and the United States.

Can the IMF and the World Bank offer an alternative to declining U.S. leadership? These institutions, established at Bretton Woods not to help the United States but to solve the problems of others, work slowly, a disability in a time of crisis that may require decisions in hours, not weeks. Moreover their funds may still prove to be too small to cope with markets today when those markets get the bit between their teeth and need the supplement of those of the G-7 central banks. This is particularly the case if the currency in difficulty is the dollar, rather than the yen, lira, franc, and so on, with smaller financial markets.

While the dollar has troubles, it continues to be used as a world unit of account, if decreasingly as a medium of exchange, for lack of an adequate substitute. Japan has troubles of its own in real estate loans at problem banks, and Germany has not yet completed integrating the GDR into its economy. Japan and Germany were good followers of the American lead, but held back from challenging it. Under President de Gaulle, France was continuously ready to challenge U.S. policies and the dominance of the dollar without, however, great success, and is now under President Jacques Chirac fully engaged with domestic and international difficulties. The European Union may grow in economic and financial strength and take over world economic primacy. At the moment, however, the world depends on U.S. leadership for lack of better; but the United States is holding back, preoccupied with its own political and economic difficulties, and reluctant to pay the cost of providing international public goods. Regimes work well in quiet times, but something more decisive in the way of leadership is called for in crisis, and the likelihood of escaping economic and financial crises in the years ahead seems small.

13
The Lessons of History and the Most Tumultuous Decades Ever

The monetary history of the last four hundred years has been replete with financial crises. The pattern was that investor optimism increased as economies expanded, the rate of growth of credit increased and economic growth accelerated, and an increasing number of individuals began to invest for short-term capital gains rather than for the returns associated with the productivity of the assets they were acquiring. The increase in the supply of credit and more buoyant economic outlook often led to economic booms as investment spending increased in response to the more optimistic outlook and the greater availability of credit, and as household spending increased as personal wealth surged. One of the earliest bubbles reviewed in this volume was the Dutch 'tulipmania' of the 1630s in which the buyers received credit from the sellers. Rational exuberance in the Netherlands morphed into irrational exuberance, the economy briefly boomed—and then the growth rate slowed as bulb prices tumbled. The South Sea Bubble in London and the Mississippi Bubble in Paris both occurred in 1720; each was associated with a new financial institution that arranged for sharp increases in the supplies of credit.

Some crises were triggered by the concern that particular borrowers had become over-extended. Occasionally several crises occurred within a relatively few years but the pattern was that these crises were infrequent, often no more than one a generation.

The U.S. stock price bubble in the last several years of the 1920s was a domestic event that responded to the remarkable developments in the U.S. economy, as automobile production surged and as much of the country became electrified; optimism about economic futures was pervasive. The increase in interest rates on U.S. dollar securities in 1928 in response to the increase in stock prices led to a reduction in U.S.

purchases of foreign bonds and complicated the ability of other countries to maintain their parities because access to dollar funds was more costly. The implosion of the stock prices in the last quarter of 1929 triggered a slowdown in global economic growth and a large number of countries suspended the convertibility of their currencies into gold in response to a decline in their export revenues and speculative pressure against their currencies. The hallmark of the 1930s was a sequence of currency crises, first the Austrian schilling, then the German mark, then the British pound, and then the U.S. dollar; finally the speculative pressure was deflected to the gold bloc currencies—the French franc, the Swiss franc, and the Dutch guilder. By the end of the 1930s, the alignment of currency values was similar to the alignment at the end of the 1920s, although the price of gold in terms of the U.S. dollar and most other currencies was 75 percent higher.

Some of these crises involved the failure of a large number of banks, some involved the lack of confidence in the ability of a country to maintain the parity for its currency and a few involved the implosion of a bubble in stock markets and in real estate markets. Virtually all of these bubbles were independent events; the coincidence of the bubbles in London and Paris in 1720 appeared largely to reflect the fact that financial innovation in Paris mimicked that in London.

The number of crises that were solely domestic events appears to have declined with the development of domestic lenders of last resort whose role was to provide cash to cope with a sharp decline in investor demand for speculative assets. The pattern in the sequence of currency crises in the 1930s was that investors would become concerned that a country would not be able to maintain the parity for its currency in terms of gold; the central bank would raise interest rates in the effort to convince the market about the strength of its commitment to its parity. The increase in interest rates would deflate the domestic economy; business bankruptcies and bank failures would increase. Then the central bank would abandon the effort to maintain its parity because the domestic costs were too high. Immediately the concern would shift to one or several other currencies that still retained their parities.

This sequence of devaluations led to the question as to whether an international lender of last resort would have enabled countries to maintain their parities and avoid the cycle of deflate-and-devalue. A domestic lender of last resort provides abundant credit to reduce the likelihood that a currency crisis will cascade into a liquidity crisis; the question in the international context is whether greater availability of credit from an international lender of last resort would have reduced the likelihood that countries would have needed to devalue because of a shortage of liquidity. Once one country had stopped pegging its currency to gold, the devaluations of the currencies of its major trading partners and competitors seemed inevitable. The similarity in the alignment of currency values at the end of the 1930s with the alignment ten years earlier suggests that the competitive advantage that each country gained from its devaluation was temporary, although the consequence of the effective increase in the prices of gold in terms of the U.S. dollar and other currencies was that the supply of international reserve assets surged.

The counter-factual question is whether a comparable increase in the supply of international reserve assets in the early 1920s, when the potential shortage of gold was first recognized, rather than toward the end of the 1930s, would have obviated some or many of the changes in the currency values in the interwar period. A larger volume of international reserve assets by itself would not have obviated the need for an international lender of last resort to provide credit to countries whose currencies were subject to a speculative attack. But a larger volume might have reduced the frequency of speculative attacks on currencies.

The inference from the changes in asset prices, the changes in currency values, and the number and severity of banking crises since the mid-1960s is that the lessons of history have been forgotten or slighted. These decades have been the most tumultuous in international monetary history in terms of the number, scope, and severity of financial crises. More national banking systems collapsed than at any previous comparable period; the loan losses of the banks in Japan, in Sweden and Norway and Finland, in Thailand and Malaysia and Indonesia, and in Mexico (twice) and in Brazil and Argentina ranged from 20 to 50 percent of their assets. In some countries the costs to the taxpayers of providing the money to fulfill the implicit and explicit deposit guarantees amounted to 15 to 20 percent of their GDPs. The loan losses in most of these countries were much greater than those in the United States in the Great Depression of the 1930s.

Occasionally the failure of a bank was a specific national event; Franklin National Bank of New York City and Herstatt AG of Cologne made large bets on the direction of changes in the prices of various currencies in the foreign exchange market that proved very costly to their capital and led to their demise. Crédit Lyonnais, the largest French bank, incurred loan losses that eventually reached more than 30 percent of its total assets and 3 percent of the country's GDP. But these bank failures were the exceptions; most of the bank failures in the 1980s and 1990s were systemic events that involved a large number of banks in a country, and in many episodes virtually all of a country's banks. Banks in many other countries also incurred large loan losses and would have failed if they had not been owned by their governments.

A few countries, including Japan and Norway, had banking crises without foreign exchange crises. Several, including South Africa and Brazil, had foreign exchange crises without banking crises; however the dominant pattern, demonstrated by Mexico, Argentina, Thailand, Malaysia, Russia, and many other countries, was one of banking and foreign exchange crises occurring at about the same time.

In the early 1980s many banks in Texas, Oklahoma, and Louisiana failed when the oil price declined sharply; during the same period many small banks in Iowa, Kansas, and other states in the agricultural Midwest became bankrupt because of the sharp decline in the value of real estate held as loan collateral. Several thousand U.S. thrift institutions lost more than their capital when short-term interest rates surged in the early 1980s. In the late 1990s, soon after the financial debacle in Russia, Long-Term Capital Management, then one of the largest U.S. hedge funds, collapsed and would have gone bankrupt without the injections of equity capital from its largest creditors mandated by the Federal Reserve.

Many developing countries, including Mexico, Brazil, and Argentina, defaulted on their external debts in the early 1980s. In the late 1980s both Argentina and Brazil experienced hyperinflation and their governments defaulted on their domestic debts; Argentina again defaulted in 2001.

There have been more foreign exchange crises than in any previous period of comparable length, beginning with the breakdown of the Bretton Woods system of adjustable parities for national currencies in the late 1960s and early 1970s. In August 1971 the United States abandoned efforts to maintain the parity for the U.S. dollar of $35 an ounce of gold that served as the centerpiece of the Bretton Woods. The new set of currency parities that were established in the Smithsonian Agreement of January 1972 was maintained for about a year and then in February 1973 the German mark and the Japanese yen and the currencies of most other industrial countries began to float.

The range of movement in the foreign exchange values of many national currencies relative to the currencies of their major trading partners was much larger than in any previous period. Initially these large movements in exchange rates were attributed to the market participants' lack of familiarity with freely floating exchange rates. The foreign exchange values of the Mexican peso, the Brazilian cruzeiro, the Argentinean peso, and the currencies of many other developing countries plummeted in the early 1980s. The Finnish markka, Swedish krona, British pound, Italian lira, and other European currencies lost 30 percent of their values relative to the German mark in the autumn of 1992 when the European Exchange Rate Mechanism broke up.

Moreover the scope of 'overshooting' and 'undershooting' of currency values relative to the values inferred from the differences in national inflation rates was much larger than in any previous period. The sharp depreciation of the U.S. dollar in the late 1970s was much greater than the decline that would have been forecast on the excess of the U.S. inflation rate over the inflation rates in Germany and in Japan. Then in the early 1980s the U.S. dollar appreciated by 60 percent even though U.S. inflation remained higher than the inflation rate in Germany. In the late 1990s the U.S. and European inflation rates were similar but the newly-established euro—the successor currency to the German mark, French franc, Italian lira, and the currencies of the other countries that joined the European Monetary Union—depreciated by 30 percent following its establishment at the beginning of 1999, and then appreciated by a large amount between 2002 and 2004. The scope of overshooting and undershooting of the currencies of the developing/emerging market countries was larger than for the industrial countries. The Mexican peso lost nearly half of its foreign exchange value during that country's presidential transition at the end of 1994 and the beginning of 1995. The foreign exchange values of the Thai baht, the Malaysian ringgit, the Indonesian rupiah, and the South Korean won declined by 50 to 70 percent in the last six months of 1997. The Russian ruble depreciated sharply in August 1998, and the Brazilian real was devalued extensively in January 1999. The Argentinean peso lost more than two-thirds of its value in January 2001.

There were more asset price bubbles between 1980 and 2000 than in any earlier period. Japan experienced the 'mother of all asset price bubbles' in the second half of the 1980s. Real estate prices increased by a factor of nine, stock prices increased by a factor of six, and Japanese financial wealth surged. The Japanese economy boomed. Finland, Norway, and Sweden also experienced bubbles in their real estate markets and their stock markets at this same time. There were bubbles in the real estate and stock markets in Thailand, Malaysia, Indonesia, and several nearby countries in Southeast Asia in the first half of the 1990s. U.S.

stock market wealth doubled in the late 1990s and the values of the firms in the dot.com and information technology industries increased by a factor of four.

The failures of banks, the overshooting and the undershooting of exchange rates around their long-run equilibrium values, and the bubbles in real estate and stock markets were systematically related and resulted from various shocks that led to large changes in the scope and direction of cross-border money flows. The failure of the banks—which primarily occurred in three waves—resulted from the sharp depreciations of their national currencies or from the sharp declines in the values of real estate and of stocks during the crash phase of the financial cycle. These crashes were preceded by manias that led to large cross-border flows of money to individual countries whose economies were then performing well; the foreign exchange value of their currencies increased and the prices of real estate and of stocks increased significantly.

Several of these shocks were true surprises but several were 'predictable'; a 'predictable shock' seems like an oxymoron since by definition a shock is not predictable. However the increasing reliance on cash from new foreign investments to pay the interest on the outstanding foreign indebtedness that developed in the mania phase of the expansions in Mexico in the 1970s and again in the 1990s and in Thailand, Malaysia, and Indonesia in the 1990s could not be sustained for an indefinite period. At some stage it was inevitable that the lenders would reduce the rate of growth of their loans to these increasingly indebted borrowers, although the details and the timing of these moves could not have been predicted. The likelihood that these countries could adjust to the decline in the inflow of foreign funds without a sharp depreciation of their currencies was low. Similarly at some stage it was inevitable that Japanese real estate prices would stop increasing; when that happened, many of the investors that recently had purchased real estate with large amounts of borrowed money would be likely to be in a cash bind because the interest payments on their loans would be larger than their rental income.

The causes of the financial tumult

The financial tumult since the early 1970s resulted from the impacts of monetary shocks and credit market shocks on the direction and scope of the flows of funds across national borders. Several of the shocks were monetary and involved unanticipated changes in the rates of money supply growth and the accompanying changes in anticipated inflation rates and in interest rates. Some of these shocks involved the relaxation or elimination of financial regulations that facilitated changes in the allocation of bank loans and the amount of credit available to specific groups of borrowers; borrowers that formerly had been penalized by regulations suddenly became attractive to the lenders. In several cases a credit shock and a monetary shock occurred at about the same time and had complementary impacts on the flow of funds across national borders.

An increase in the flow of funds to a country induces increases in the prices of both its currency in the foreign exchange market and the securities and other assets available in the domestic market; the increases in these prices during the mania phase of the expansions caused market prices to increase above their long-run equilibrium values. Some of the shocks triggered a pattern of money flows from lenders to borrowers that could not be sustained indefinitely. A decline in the flow of money from abroad almost always led to a depreciation of the country's currency in the foreign exchange market; in some cases this decline triggered crashes in asset prices of 50 or 60 percent or more.

The first major shock in this extended period was the increase in the annual U.S. inflation rate to the range of 5 and 6 percent in the second half of the 1960s; in the previous twenty years the annual U.S. inflation rate was almost always below 3 percent and usually below the inflation rates in Germany and its neighboring countries in Western Europe. The annual U.S. payments deficit surged because a decline in the foreign exchange value of the U.S. dollar seemed increasingly likely; either the U.S. dollar would be devalued or the German mark and the Japanese yen and other currencies would be revalued. Investors and firms moved funds from the United States to avoid losses from these anticipated changes in parities or to profit from them. Because the United States was reluctant to devalue the U.S. dollar and Germany and France and Japan were reluctant to revalue their currencies, the payments imbalance increased, with the result that the foreign exchange reserves of Germany and Japan and of other countries with payments surpluses increased at a more rapid rate. Then in 1971, when the U.S. economy slowed and the inflation rate declined the Federal Reserve adopted a more expansive monetary policy, and the decline in interest rates on U.S. dollar securities led to an even larger flow of short-term funds from New York to foreign financial centers.

The global inflation in the early 1970s was an unprecedented peace-time event that followed from the combination of the growth of the

U.S. money supply, which followed from the easing of monetary policy, and the growth in the money supplies in Germany and other countries in Western Europe and in Japan in response to their increasingly large payments surpluses.

The more rapid increase in the U.S. inflation rate than in those of Germany, the Netherlands, and Switzerland at the end of the 1960s meant that a realignment of adjustable parities for national currencies was inevitable. Because the U.S. inflation rate exceeded the inflation rate in Germany by more than 2 percent a year, the system of adjustable parities was not viable and hence the abandonment of parities for the German mark and other European currencies was inevitable.

The rapid increases in money supply growth in the United States and other industrial countries in the early 1970s contributed to a global economic boom, surges in demand for primary products, and sharp increases in the prices of oil and other commodities. The rates of growth of GDP in the countries that produced these commodities increased. The Saudi Arabian embargo of oil shipments to the United States and the Netherlands following the Yom Kippur War of October 1973 triggered a surge in the demand for petroleum and the oil price increased sharply; the decline in oil supplies following the Iraqi invasion of Iran in 1980 had a much larger impact on global inflation.

Investors responded to the increases in the anticipated global inflation rate by increasing their purchases of gold and other precious metals, collectibles, real estate, and other 'hard assets.'

As the world inflation rate increased in the early 1970s, there was a credit market shock that led to a surge in bank loans to Mexico, Brazil, Argentina, and other developing countries; these loans increased at the rate of 30 percent a year during the decade. Banks headquartered in many European countries and in Japan used U.S. dollars obtained in the offshore deposit markets in London, Zurich, and Luxembourg to make loans to governments and government-owned firms in Latin America and 'poach' on what had been the traditional turf of U.S. banks. The U.S. banks responded by competing aggressively to avoid an erosion of their share of this loan market. They also wanted to circumvent the regulations that limited the growth of their domestic loans and assets. The external indebtedness of this group of borrowers increased at the rate of 20 percent a year.

The next major shock was the change in the operating procedures of the Federal Reserve in October 1979 (the so-called 'Volcker shock') that almost immediately shattered the anticipations of accelerating inflation;

the market price of gold peaked ten weeks after this policy had been adopted. Previously the Federal Reserve had stabilized interest rates and market forces had determined the rate of growth of credit; under the new policy the Fed sought to limit the rate of growth of credit.

The sharp decline in the rate of growth of bank loans led to a surge in interest rates on U.S. dollar securities. Investment spending fell, a world recession followed, and the prices of petroleum and other commodities dropped sharply.

Mexico and other developing countries were squeezed by the scissors-like increase in the interest rates on their foreign loans and the decline in both the volumes and the prices for their exports. The surge in interest rates on U.S. dollar securities and the subsequent decline in the price of petroleum led to massive failures of U.S. banks in Texas and the other oil-producing areas. Similarly many banks in the grain-producing Midwestern states failed as the prices of farmland fell. Interest rates paid by U.S. thrift institutions on their short-term deposits increased rapidly and in many cases began to exceed the interest rates that the thrifts were earning on their long-term mortgage loans, thus depleting their capital.

The combination of the much higher interest rates on U.S. dollar securities and the sharp reduction in the anticipated U.S. inflation rate led to an increase in investor demand for U.S. dollar securities and the U.S. dollar began to appreciate at a rapid rate.

The liberalization of regulations applied to banks in Japan in the first half of the 1980s was a major credit market shock. Previously Japanese banks were subject to extensive regulations that limited both the interest rates they could pay on their deposit liabilities and the rates they could charge on their loans; moreover administrative guidance required that these banks extend loans to industrial firms in those industries that the government bureaucrats believed were strategically important. One motive for financial deregulation was that the industrial demand for bank loans had declined so that allocation of credit among borrowers on a preferential basis was no longer necessary, and another was that the U.S. authorities demanded that U.S. banks and other U.S. financial firms have access to the banking and capital markets in Tokyo on terms comparable to those available to Japanese banks in the United States.

Financial deregulation enabled the banks headquartered in Tokyo and in Osaka both to increase their real estate loans in Japan and to increase the numbers of their foreign branches and subsidiaries. The flow of savings from Japan to the United States and various European countries surged; the cliché in both New York and Tokyo was 'Where will the U.S.

Treasury get the money to finance its fiscal deficit if the Japanese stop buying U.S. government securities?' These newly-established foreign branches of Japanese banks rapidly increased their loans in their host countries, using the funds obtained in the offshore deposit market; these newly-established branches wanted to increase their market share and so they charged lower interest rates than their home country competitors. Moreover Japanese investors began to purchase real estate—office buildings, apartment buildings, golf courses, and ski resorts—in the major U.S. cities and in the major financial centers in other industrial countries; most of these purchases were funded with money borrowed from the foreign branches of Japanese banks.

The depreciation of the U.S. dollar in the foreign exchange market that began in the spring of 1985 induced the central banks in Japan and various countries in Western Europe to buy U.S. dollars in the foreign exchange market to limit the appreciation of their currencies and the result was that the rates of money supply growth in these countries quickened.

The decision of the newly-appointed Chair of the Board of the Bank of Japan at the beginning of 1990 to restrict the rate of growth of bank loans for real estate imploded the asset price bubble in Japan; real estate prices and stock prices declined by 30 percent in 1990 and by 25 percent in 1991. The rate of growth of the Japanese economy slowed dramatically. The Japanese yen appreciated significantly in the foreign exchange market as the country's exports surged relative to its imports. Japanese firms responded to the adverse impact of the increase in the foreign exchange value of the yen on their profitability by increasing their investments in productive facilities in China and Thailand and the other countries in Southeast Asia that would be used primarily as sources of supply for markets in Japan, the United States, and other industrial countries; many of these investments involved assembly-type activities of high value-added components that were imported from Japan. Japanese banks followed Japanese firms and rapidly increased their loans in these countries.

The development of the Brady Bonds in 1989 and 1990 enabled Mexico and other developing countries to convert bank loans that had been in default into long-term bonds that were partially guaranteed by the U.S. government; this innovation effectively ended the period of financial isolation ('the lost decade') for these borrowers.

Mexico then began to prepare for its membership of the North American Free Trade Agreement; a contractive monetary policy was adopted to reduce the inflation rate, hundreds of government-owned firms were privatized, and government regulations on international trade and business practices were liberalized. Foreign direct investment in Mexico surged as U.S., European, and Japanese firms rapidly increased their manufacturing facilities in Mexico. United States money market funds were attracted to the high interest rates on peso securities; U.S. pension funds and mutual funds increased their purchases of stocks of a new asset class—'emerging market securities.'

Then at the beginning of 1994 there were several political incidents that led to a decline in the flow of funds to Mexico. There was an Indian uprising in its southernmost province and two months later the leading presidential candidate of the dominant political party was assassinated. The decline in the flow of foreign funds to Mexico meant that the country was no longer able to finance its current account deficit which had increased to 6 percent of its GDP.

The flow of foreign funds to Thailand slowed significantly in late 1996 because the nonbank finance companies that were owned by the Thai banks were incurring large losses on their consumer loans; these finance companies had been established to circumvent the regulations on bank loans. In effect the losses that the finance companies incurred were the losses of the banks once-removed. The Bank of Thailand was unable to maintain the foreign exchange value of the Thai baht once its international reserve assets had been nearly depleted at the beginning of July 1997. The depreciation of the baht triggered the contagion effect that rippled through the Asian countries and led to a sudden decline of their imports relative to their exports of $150 billion.

Several of these shocks were true surprises: the political events in Mexico in the first few months of 1994 could not have been foreseen. Still the rate of increase in stock prices and real estate prices in Japan at the end of the 1980s was too high to be sustained and so were the levels of these prices; once these prices stopped increasing, a crash was inevitable. Similarly the Mexican current account deficit in 1994 was too large to be sustained and some trigger eventually would have led to a decline in these loans if the political shocks had not occurred. Similarly the current account deficits of Thailand and Malaysia in 1996 were too large to be sustained. Something would have triggered a decline in capital inflows and a depreciation of their currencies, although the nature of the catalyst for the decline in inflows could not have been foreseen. The implosion of the bubbles in real estate prices and stock prices in Japan and the subsequent bubbles in Thailand and Malaysia was inevitable; bubbles always implode. Similarly it was inevitable that there would have been a reversal in the foreign exchange value of the U.S. dollar from its extreme overvaluation in the mid-1980s.

The impacts of the monetary shocks and credit market shocks

The striking feature of the period since the early 1970s is the variability of cross-border flows of money as measured by the changes in the ratio of trade balances of individual countries to their GDPs, which have been much larger than in any previous period. When the Mexican economy was booming and foreign funds were flowing into the country, its trade deficit reached 7 percent of its GDP. When Mexican and foreign funds were withdrawn as the country experienced a financial crisis, its trade surplus reached 4 percent of its GDP. This change was massive and sudden, and had powerful impacts on the foreign exchange value of the peso and on the prices of peso securities and real assets in Mexico as well as on the inflation rate and the solvency of Mexican firms, households, and banks.

These sharp changes in the ratios of the trade balances to GDP in many countries resulted from sharp changes in the volume and direction of cross-border flows of funds. The Minsky story of the cyclical variability in the supply of credit can be extended to the cyclical variability in the pattern of cross-border flows of money. An increase in the flow of funds to a country led to an increase in the foreign exchange value of its currency and to increases in the prices of securities and other assets traded in that country. The increase in the flow of cross-border funds to a country was often associated with increases in the rates of growth of domestic credit and the result was an economic boom.

Some of the credit market and monetary shocks led to increases in the flow of money to a country and increases in the prices of commodities, currencies, stocks, and real estate available in that country. As long as the prices of currencies and stocks were increasing, the rates of return to the owners of these securities and currencies were high and likely to be increasing; optimism about the economic future increased. Then another shock would trigger a reversal in the cross-border flows of funds; and the result was a financial crash that featured sharp declines in the prices of currencies, securities, and other assets.

These manic-type shocks resulted from extensive changes in the preferences of investors for securities and other assets denominated in different currencies. Investors became concerned that the U.S. inflation rate would increase in the 1970s; they sold U.S. dollar securities to get the funds to buy securities denominated in the German mark, the Swiss franc, and the British pound, and the U.S. dollar depreciated much more quickly than would have been inferred from the excess of the U.S. inflation rate over the inflation rates in the country's major trading partners. During the same period the price of gold increased 'because gold was a good inflation hedge,' although the annual percentage increases in the price of gold in the second half of the 1980s were much greater than the annual percentage increases in the U.S. price level. Early in 1980 investors became convinced that the U.S. inflation rate would decline; they sold securities denominated in the German mark and other foreign currencies to get the funds to buy U.S. dollar securities and the U.S. dollar appreciated at a rapid rate.

One possible explanation for the greater variability of cross-border capital flows in the last thirty years is that shocks, and especially those that involved a change in the stance of monetary policy, have been larger than in earlier periods—periods when currencies were pegged or when there was a commitment to parities for national currencies. One of the major arguments in the case for floating exchange rates is that when currencies are no longer pegged, central banks have greater independence to change their monetary policies to achieve their domestic economic objectives. When a currency was not pegged to gold or to some other currency, central banks could vary their own interest rates and the rates of growth of their money supply. In effect the commitment to a parity for a national currency constrained changes in the central bank's monetary policy and especially the adoption of a more expansive monetary policy; this commitment to a parity for the currency meant that the national inflation rate could not differ significantly from the inflation rates in the country's major trading partners. In the absence of a commitment to a parity, the policies adopted by central banks would lead to changes in the current and anticipated inflation rates which in turn would lead to changes in cross-border flows of funds. Hence the explanation for the much larger swings in the cross-border flow of funds is that changes in monetary policies and anticipated inflation rates have been larger.

The much greater variability in the cross-border flow of funds in part reflected that the monetary shocks were much greater than when currencies had been pegged; these shocks led to changes in investor estimates of the inflation rates in a particular country and hence of the anticipated spot exchange rates at some distant future date. The expansive U.S. monetary policies of the late 1960s and the early 1970s led investors to revise their estimates of the U.S. inflation rate upward and to revise downward their estimates of the anticipated value for the U.S. dollar in the foreign exchange market; investors sold U.S. dollar securities to get the funds to buy foreign securities, and their purchases of the foreign currencies led to the sharp decline in the foreign exchange value of the U.S. dollar. In effect, the purchases of the German marks, Swiss francs, and other foreign currencies by these investors contributed to the decline in the foreign exchange value of the U.S. dollar that they anticipated.

If as a group these investors were to increase the proportion of nondollar securities in their portfolios, then the United States would have to have a larger current account surplus, which would require that the U.S. dollar depreciate more rapidly than would be inferred from the difference in national inflation rates. The U.S. dollar would increasingly undershoot the values inferred from the differences in national inflation rates as long as investors sought to increase the rate at which they acquired nondollar securities.

Similarly the adoption of a much more contractive U.S. monetary policy in the autumn of 1979 soon led investors to reduce their estimates of the U.S. inflation rate and hence to revise upward their estimates of the foreign exchange value of the U.S. dollar. Their purchases of U.S. dollars in the foreign exchange market led to the appreciation of the U.S. dollar; if as a group investors were to increase the proportion of U.S. dollar securities in their portfolios, the United States would need to develop a current account deficit and a trade deficit. The increase in the foreign exchange value of the U.S. dollar relative to the value that would be inferred from the difference in national inflation rates was inevitable as long as the investors wanted to acquire U.S. dollar securities at a faster rate.

Overshooting and undershooting were inevitable whenever investors wished to increase or reduce their holdings of securities denominated in a particular currency. The earlier clichés applied to large and rapid deviations between the market exchange rates and the exchange rates that were consistent with the differences in national inflation rates—the 'vicious and virtuous cycle' and 'destabilizing speculation'—reflected the impacts of sudden changes in the pattern of cross-border flows of funds. Changes in anticipated inflation rates—more precisely changes in the differential in national inflation rates—would lead to overshooting and undershooting because of the impact of the changes in these differentials on the anticipated spot exchange rates. In contrast the monetary shock that impacted Japan in the second half of the 1980s as the Bank of Japan intervened in the foreign exchange market to limit the appreciation of the yen did not appear to have a major impact on its anticipated foreign exchange value and hence on the scope of currency overshooting.

Because the bubble in Japanese stocks and real estate affected both Japanese purchases of foreign securities and foreign purchases of Japanese securities, the changes in the demand for yen securities led to changes in the foreign exchange value of the yen. Similarly credit market shocks had no direct impacts on the anticipated inflation rates and hence no direct impacts on the anticipated foreign exchange values of individual currencies in the long run. The credit market shocks in the last thirty years have had major impacts on the foreign exchange value of the Mexican peso, Thai baht, and the U.S. dollar because they led to changes in the amounts of the securities denominated in these currencies that investors wished to hold.

A second, complementary, explanation for the greater variability in the ratios of trade balances to GDPs is that when currencies are not pegged, a shock of a given magnitude in the form of an increase in demand for securities denominated in a currency has a larger immediate impact on the country's GDP induced by the increase in the prices of securities and real estate traded in the country. When a currency was pegged, the immediate impact on a country of an increase in the inflow of saving was that the central bank's holdings of international reserve assets increased and its monetary liabilities increased correspondingly. The price of securities available in the country also increased in response to the increase in the purchases by the foreign investors. The sellers of securities to these foreign savers would use the funds to buy other securities from other domestic residents, and the prices of securities would increase.

When a currency was not pegged, a comparable increase in the foreign demand for securities denominated in this currency initiated the adjustment process to ensure that the country's trade balance changed by the amount that corresponded to the increase in the flow of savings from abroad. The invisible hand operated to ensure that the immediate impact of the increase in the flow of savings from other countries was that domestic investment spending increased as the cost of capital declined and household consumption spending increased in response to the increase in household wealth. Most of the increase in the aggregate spending would be that of households, since in most countries consumption spending is three or four times larger than investment spending. The flip-side of the increase in consumption spending was that household saving declined. (In contrast, there was no comparable change in the savings-investment relationship when the currency was pegged, since the counterpart of the increase in the flow of saving from abroad could be a change in the central bank's holdings of international reserve assets.) The inevitable outcome of the adjustment process was that domestic saving declined relative to domestic investment in the country that received an increase in the cross-border flow of saving.

The invisible hand that induced the changes in the relationship between saving and investment in both the countries that experienced an inflow of saving from abroad and the countries that were the source of these savings operated through changes in relative prices and changes in relative incomes. The relative price change reflected the fact that the currency of the country that received an increase in the inflow of foreign saving appreciated in the foreign exchange market (which is the floating exchange rate counterpart of the increase in the central banks' holdings of foreign exchange when the currency was pegged). By itself the appreciation of the country's currency did not have a direct impact on household saving, although to the extent that the increase in the demand for imports led to a decline in spending on domestic goods domestic GDP would decline.

The invisible hand led to an increase in the rate of growth of GDP in the country that experienced an increase in the inflow of saving. This resulted from the increase in consumption spending induced by the increase in household wealth as the prices of securities and other assets rose. As the wealth of some investors increased, they reduced their saving from current income because their 'wealth targets' had been achieved by the increases in the prices of their securities and other assets.

Thus the reason for the increase in the variability in the ratios of the changes in the trade balances to GDP is that the initial increase in the flow of saving to a country triggered changes in the adjustment process that led to increases in the rates of return on securities and other assets available in the country. The increase in wealth contributed to the economic boom. In effect there was a feedback mechanism from the initial increase in the flow of saving to the increase in the rates of return that induced further inflow of foreign funds. The economic boom was prolonged and pervasive; many of the participants may have failed to recognize that the cross-border pattern of flows of cash could not be sustained.

Thus the stylized fact is that an increase in the flow of saving to a country leads to an increase in the price of that country's currency in the foreign exchange market and an increase in the prices of securities available in that country. Hence the rates of return to owners of these securities may prove to be higher than anticipated and the increases in the prices of these securities operate like a feedback effect and attract more funds from other countries. Moreover the prices of securities in the countries that are experiencing an increase in the flow of saving to other countries will be declining, and some of the owners may foresee further declines and so continue to move funds to avoid further losses.

One of the patterns in the data is that the flow of savings to a country was associated with an economic boom; this was evident in Mexico and other developing countries in the 1970s, in Mexico, Thailand, and other Asian countries in the first half of the 1990s, and in the United States in the second half of the 1990s. The appreciation of the currencies of this group of countries reduced the inflationary pressures associated with a robust economic expansion and the increase in export prices relative to import prices led to an increase in the rate of economic growth. The inflow was also associated with a nonsustainable pattern of cash flows because some of the borrowers in the country were obtaining the cash to pay the interest to their creditors from their creditors. The continuation of the economic boom may explain why the lenders—at least a large number of them—failed to recognize that eventually there would be an adjustment.

The variability in the flows of national savings across countries conforms with the Minsky model that changes in the supply of credit are procyclical. Increases in the inflow of foreign saving to countries were often associated with increases in the rates of growth of domestic credit.

Could an international lender of last resort have made a significant difference?

The financial tumultuousness of the years since the mid-1960s is a result of the large variability of cross-border flows of funds. The increase in the flow of funds to a country led to an increase in the foreign exchange value of its currency and to the increase in prices of securities and other assets in the country. The asset price bubbles in Finland, Norway, and Sweden in the second half of the 1980s resulted from the increase in the inflow of cross-border funds; similarly the asset price bubbles in Thailand, Malaysia, and the other Asian countries in the early 1990s followed from the increase in the flow of savings from Japan and elsewhere.

The foreign exchange crises in a large number of countries resulted from the reversal in the cross-border flow of funds. In many of these cases the rate of increase in the flow of funds was not sustainable; a slackening of the rate of inflow would have led to the depreciation of the currency of the country that had been experiencing the inflow, and a modest initial depreciation of its currency would have triggered a massive depreciation.

The roles of the lender of last resort in the domestic context have counterparts at the international level. The domestic lender of last resort might on occasion note that there was irrational exuberance in the stock market or the real estate market or some other markets. The counterpart is that an international lender of last resort might note that the increase in the external indebtedness of one or several countries was too rapid to be sustainable and that the adjustment to a sustainable rate could be costly and perhaps messy. Investors and other market participants would be left to draw their own conclusions about the implications of the statement.

Domestic lenders of last resort provide liquidity to reduce the likelihood that increases in investor demand for less risky securities would escalate into a solvency crisis as the prices of the riskier assets declined sharply. Domestic lenders of last resort have been established to enhance the stability of the financial system although not necessarily of individual financial banks. The counterpart rationale for an international lender of last resort is to reduce the sharp depreciation of a national currency after the end of a mania that led unsustainably large flows of funds to a country. During the manic phase, the country's currency would appreciate in response to the increase in the inflow of funds. When the inflows of capital decline, the country's currency is likely to depreciate. Undershooting would be inevitable because exporters could not immediately respond to the change in relative prices and their improvement in their international competitive positions induced by the depreciation of the currency; lags would be inevitable before they could increase their production of exportable goods and identify and connect with the foreign customers. In some countries the temporary severe depreciation of the currency during the period when the currency undershoots would imperil the solvency of domestic firms that had debts denominated in foreign currencies because of the sharp increases in the domestic currency equivalent of their debt servicing payments to their foreign creditors. The bankruptcy of these firms could imperil the solvency of domestic banks and other financial institutions.

The U.S. Treasury took the initiative in acting as a lender of last resort to Mexico at the time of that country's financial crisis at the end of 1994; the credit to Mexico involved funds from the U.S. government as well as from the International Monetary Fund. The announcement of the availability of these funds limited the further depreciation of the peso. If a comparable initiative had been taken one or several weeks earlier, the undershooting of the peso would have been smaller, and the adverse impacts of the depreciation of the peso on the Mexican economy would have been less severe.

One role of the international lender of last resort would be to suggest that the volume of international capital flows to a country was too large to be sustainable and that the eventual adjustment to the reduction in the capital inflows would lead to a depreciation of the currency. When the depreciation occurred, the international lenders could provide credits to reduce the scope of undershooting. The ready availability of credits would limit the contagion effect.

The International Monetary Fund was established in the 1940s to act as an international lender of last resort. The motive for establishing the IMF was that much of the financial instability in the 1920s and especially in the 1930s could have been avoided or mitigated if there had been an international lender of last resort. The fund staff visits each of the member countries twice a year to discuss the country's economic policies. The fund has rarely sounded the alarm that a member country was embarked on a non-sustainable pattern of international borrowing—that its current account deficit was too large to be sustainable, and that the transition to a sustainable value for its current account would be likely to be costly in terms of its economic stability—and that there was more likely to be a 'hard landing' than a 'soft landing'. Nor has the IMF been able to provide the credits at the time of the crash to avoid extensive and debilitating undershooting.

Whether the shortfall in the performance of the IMF relative to the ambitions that led to its establishment has resulted from the failures of analysis or policy or member country truculence is a topic for another book.

Appendix

A Stylized Outline of Financial Crises, 1618 to 1998

Year	1618–1623	1636–1637	1690–1696
Countries (city)	Holy Roman Empire	Dutch Republic	England
Related to	Thirty Years' War	Boom in war against Spain	Glorious Revolution 1688; war with France 1689–1697
Preceding speculation in	Subsidiary coin, exchanging bad for good	Shares of Dutch East India Company, real estate, exotic tulip bulbs, common tulip bulbs, canals	East India Company, treasure, new companies, lotteries
Monetary expansion from	Debasement of coins by weight, fineness, denomination	None (?), down payments in kind	Coin debasement, Bank of England established 1694
Speculative peak	Feb. 1622	Feb. 1637	1695
Crisis (crash, panic)	Feb. 1622	Feb. 1637	1696
Lender of last resort	None	None	None

Year	1720		1763	1772	
Countries (city)	England	France	Amsterdam	Britain	Amsterdam
Related to	Treaty of Utrecht, 1713	Death of Louis XIV, 1715	End of Seven Years' War	Seven Years' War (10 years after)	
Preceding speculation in	South Sea Company stock; government debt	Mississippi Company, Banque Générate, Banque Royale	Commodities, esp. sugar (?)	Housing, turnpikes, canals	East India Co.
Monetary expansion from	Sword Blade Bank	John Law banks	*Wisselruitij* (chain of accommodation bills)	Ayr Bank; country banks	*Wisselruitij;* Bank of Amsterdam
Speculative peak	Apr. 1720	Dec. 1719	Jan. 1763		June 1772
Crisis (crash, panic)	Sept. 1720	May 1720	Sept. 1763		Jan. 1773
Lender of last resort	Bank of England (??)	None	Bank of England	Bank of England	City of Amsterdam

Year	1792	1793	1797	1799	1810	1815–1816
Countries (city)	United States	England	England	Hamburg	England	England
Related to	Constitution adopted, 1789	Reign of Terror (France)	Collapse of *assignats;* French landing, Fishguard	Break in Continental blockade	Wellington's peninsula campaign	End of Napoleonic War
Preceding speculation in	Recovery of U.S. bonds	Canal mania	Securities, canals	Commodities	Exports to Brazil (and Scandinavia)	Export commodities, Continent and United States
Monetary expansion from	Treasury accepted public securities at par for stock of Bank of the U.S.	Capital flows from France	Country banks	*Wechselreiterei*	Country banks	Banks
Speculative peak	Jan. 1792	Nov. 1792	1796	1799	1809	1815
Crisis (crash, panic)	Mar. 1792	Feb. 1793	Feb.–June 1797	Aug.–Nov. 1799	1810, Jan. 1811	1816
Lender of last resort	U.S. Treasury open market purchases, deferred customs receipts	Exchequer bills	Exchequer bills, abandon gold	Admiralty bills	Exchequer bills	?

Year	1819		1825	1828	1836	1837	1838
Countries (city)	England	United States	England	France	England	United States	France July 1830 Monarchy
Related to	Waterloo (five years after)		Success of Baring loan; decline in interest rates	Decline in interest rates	Textile boom	Jackson presidency	
Preceding speculation in	Commodities, securities	Manufacturing behind embargo	Latin American bonds, mines, cotton	Canals, cotton, building sites	Cotton, railroads	Cotton, land	Cotton, building sites
Monetary expansion from	Banks generally	Bank of the U.S.	Bonds sold in installments, country banks	Paris banks	Joint-stock banks	Wildcat banks; retention of silver	Regional banks
Speculative peak	Dec. 1818	Aug. 1818	Early 1825		Apr. 1836	Nov. 1836	
Crisis (crash, panic)	None	Nov. 1818 to June 1819	Dec. 1825	Dec. 1827	Dec. 1836	Sept. 1837	June 1837
Lender of last resort	None needed	Treasury specie deposits	Bank of England	Paris, Basel banks, Bank of France banks		Bank of France and Bank of Hamburg helped Bank of England	

Year	1847	1848		1857	
Countries(city)	England	Continent	United States	England	Continent
Related to	1846 potato blight, wheat failure			End of Crimean War	
Preceding speculation in	Railways, wheat	Railways, wheat, building (Cologne)	Railroads, public lands	Railroads, wheat	Railroads, heavy industry
Monetary expansion from	Installment sale of railway securities	Regional banks	Gold discoveries, clearinghouse	Bank mergers, clearinghouse	Crédit Mobilier, new German banks
Speculative peak	Jan. 1847	Mar.–Apr. 1848	End of 1856	Mar. 1857	
Crisis (crash, panic)	Oct. 1847	Mar. 1848	Aug. 1857	Oct. 1857	Nov. 1857
Lender of last resort	Suspension of Bank Act of 1844	Bank of England loan to Bank of France; Russian purchase of French *rentes*	Capital inflow from England	Suspension of Bank Act of 1844	Silberzug (Hamburg)

Year	1864	1866	1873		1882
Countries (city)	France	England/Italy	Germany/Austria	United States	France
Related to	End of Civil War	General limited liability	Franco-Prussian indemnity	Fraud exposed in 1872 campaign	Expansion into southeastern Europe
Preceding speculation in	Cotton	Shipping companies generally	Building sites, railroads, securities, commodities	Railroads, homesteading, Chicago bldg.	Stocks of new banks, Lyons
Monetary expansion from	Crédit Mobilier	Joint-stock discount houses	New industrial banks, broker banks, construction banks	Short-term credit, inflow of European capital	Securities bought on margin
Speculative peak	1863	July 1865	Fall 1872	Mar. 1873	Dec. 1881
Crisis (crash, panic)	Jan. 1864	May 1866	May 1873	Sept. 1873	Jan. 1882
Lender of last resort	Maturities of bills extended	Suspension of Bank Act; Italy abandoned fixed parity	None	None	Limited help from Paris banks

Year	1890	1893		1907		1920–1921
Countries (city)	England	United States	Australia	United States	France/Italy	Britain, United States
Related to	Argentine clearing of southern lands; Brazil, coffee; Chile, nitrates; South Africa, gold	Sherman Silver Act, 1890	Growth of cities	Russo-Japanese war (?), San Francisco earthquake (??)		End of postwar boom
Preceding speculation in	Argentine securities, private companies going public	Silver, gold	Land, gold mines	Coffee, Union Pacific	Industrial borrowing from banks	Securities, ships, commodities, inventories
Monetary expansion from	Goschen conversion	Contraction	Capital inflow	Trust companies	Società Bancaria Italiana	Banks
Speculative peak	Aug. 1890	Dec. 1892	1891	Early 1907 Mar. 1906		Summer 1920
Crisis (crash, panic)	Nov. 1890	May 1893	Spring 1893	Oct. 1907 Aug. 1907		Spring 1921
Lender of last resort	Baring liabilities guaranteed; Bank of France, Russian gold loans to Britain	Repeal of Sherman Silver Act of Aug. 1893	None	$100 million inflow from Britain	Bank of Italy	None

Year	1929	1931–1933	1950s, 1960s	1974–1975
Countries (city)	United States	Europe	Worldwide	United States, Worldwide
Related to	End of extended postwar boom	Cut-off of U.S. foreign lending	Convertibility without macroeconomic coordination	Collapse of Bretton Woods: OPEC 1973 price rise
Preceding speculation in	Land to 1925, stocks 1928–1929	Not applicable	Foreign exchange	Stocks, REITs, office buildings, tankers, Boeing 747s
Monetary expansion from	Stocks bought on margin	U.S. lending	Not applicable	Eurodollar market flooding in 1970–1971
Speculative peak	Sept. 1929	1929	Speculation in currencies of	1973
Crisis (crash, panic)	Oct. 1929	Austria, May 1931; Germany, June 1931; Britain, Sept. 1931; Japan, Dec. 1931; United States, Mar. 1933	France, 1958; Canada, 1962; Italy, 1963; Britain, 1964; France, 1968; United States, 1973, etc.	1974–1975
Lender of last resort	FRBNY open-market operations (inadequate)	Feeble efforts in United States, France	BIS swap network	BIS swap network

Year	1979–1982	1982–1987
Countries (city)	United States, World	United States
Related to	Third World syndicated bank loans, OPEC 1979 price rise in oil, real estate in southwest United States, U.S. farmland, dollar	Stock market, luxury housing, office buildings, dollar
Monetary expansion from		Capital inflow
Speculative peak	1979	Dollar, 1985; stocks, 1987; real estate, 1987
Crisis (crash, panic)	Dollar, 1979; farmland, 1979; oil, 1980; Third World debt, 1982	Stocks, Oct. 19, 1987
Lender of last resort	IMF; FRBNY, U.S. govt. for Mexican debt, Farm Loan Bank Board	FRBNY open-market operations banks, FDIC, FSLIC dollar, swaps

Year	1990	1994–1995	1997–1998
Countries (city)	Japan	Mexico	Thailand, Indonesia, Malaysia, Korea, Russia, Brazil
Related to	Nikkei shares index; real estate	Deregulation; capital inflow and outflow; domestic boom	Deregulation, capital inflow and outflow; borrowing abroad
Monetary expansion from	Interest-rate reduction 1986	Capital inflow, bank lending, domestic new banks 1991, nationalized banks privatized 1991	Bank lending; construction boom; crony capitalism
Speculative peak	First half 1989	1994–1995	1997–1998
Crisis (crash, panic)	Jan. 1990	1994–1995	1997–1998
Lender of last resort	Ministry of Finance and Bank of Japan slow to react	U.S. Stabilization Fund; IMF; IADB	IMF; World Bank; ADB; bilateral country loans

Notes

1. Financial Crisis: A Hardy Perennial

1. Ezra Vogel, *Japan as Number One: Lessons for America* (Boston: Harvard University Press, 1979).
2. C.P. Kindleberger, *The World in Depression, 1929–1939,* 2nd ed. (Berkeley: University of California Press, 1986).
3. See Robert D. Flood and Peter W. Garber, *Speculative Bubbles, Speculative Attacks and Policy Switching* (Cambridge, Mass.: MIT Press, 1994), who believe in 'fundamentals' as determining economic behavior, unless governments change the rules. One particular change in the last quarter of the twentieth century was deregulation of financial markets.
4. Edward Shaw, *Financial Deepening in Economic Development* (New York: Oxford University Press, 1973); and Roland I. McKinnon, *Money and Capitalism in Economic Development* (Washington, DC: Brookings Institution, 1973). A detailed study of regulation in developing countries is 'A Survey of Financial Liberalization' by John Williamson and Molly Mohar, *Essays in International Finance,* no. 221 (Princeton, NJ: International Finance Section, November 1998).
5. *Recent Innovations in International Banking* (Basel: Bank for International Settlements, 1986).
6. See Kindleberger, 'Panic of 1873', in *Historical Economics* (New York: Harvester Wheatsheaf, 1990), pp. 310–25; idem, 'International Propagation of Financial Crises'; Henrietta M. Larson, *Jay Cooke, Private Banker* (Cambridge, Mass.: Harvard University Press, 1936); and Matthew Simon, *Cyclical Fluctuations in the International Capital Movements of the United States, 1865–1897* (New York: Arno, 1979).

2. Anatomy of a Typical Crisis

1. Joseph A. Schumpeter, *Business Cycles: a Theoretical, Historical and Statistical Analysis of the Capitalist Process* (New York: McGraw-Hill, 1939), vol. 1, chap. 4, esp. pp. 161ff.
2. Hyman P. Minsky, *John Maynard Keynes* (New York: Columbia University Press, 1975); and idem, 'The Financial Instability Hypothesis: Capitalistic Processes and the Behavior of the Economy', in C.P. Kindleberger and J.-P. Laffargue, eds, *Financial Crises: Theory, History and Policy* (Cambridge: Cambridge University Press, 1982), pp. 13–29. For a view of the work of Hyman Minsky in historical context, see Perry Mending, 'The Vision of Hyman P. Minsky', in *Journal of Economic Behavior and Organization,* vol. 39 (1999), pp. 125–58.

3. See R.C.O. Matthews, 'Public Policy, and Monetary Expenditure', in Thomas Wilson and Andrew S. Skinner, eds, *The Market and the State: Essays in Honour of Adam Smith* (Oxford: Oxford University Press, Clarendon Press, 1976), p. 336.
4. See James B. Stewart, *Den of Thieves* (New York: Touchstone Books [Simon & Schuster], 1991, 1992), p. 97: 'What really fueled the takeover boom [in the 1980s] was the sight of other people making money, big money, by buying and selling companies.'
5. See C.P. Kindleberger, *The World in Depression, 1929–1939,* 2nd ed. (Berkeley: University of California Press, 1986), pp. 1–3.
6. Robert D. Flood and Peter W. Garber, *Speculative Bubbles, Speculative Attacks and Policy Switching* (Cambridge, Mass.: MIT Press, 1964), pp. 73–4, 85, 96, 98, etc.
7. Alvin Hansen, *Business Cycles and National Income* (New York: W.W. Norton, 1957), p. 226.
8. Newspaper accounts state that George Soros's Quantum Fund made a profit of $1 billion going short of the British pound and the Italian lira in 1992–93 and lost $600 million shorting the yen in the spring of 1994.

3. Speculative Manias

1. John F. Muth, 'Rational Expectations and the Theory of Price Movements', *Econometrica,* vol. 29 (July 1961), pp. 313–35.
2. Harry G. Johnson, 'Destabilizing Speculation: a General Equilibrium Approach', *Journal of Political Economy,* vol. 84 (February 1976), p. 101.
3. Milton Friedman, 'The Case for Flexible Exchange Rates', in *Essays in Positive Economics* (Chicago: University of Chicago Press, 1953). On one occasion, Friedman moved to a different position: 'Destabilization speculation is a theoretical possibility, but I know of no empirical evidence that it has occurred even as a special case, let alone as a general rule.' Milton Friedman, 'Discussion' of C.P. Kindleberger, 'The Case for Fixed Exchange Rates, 1969', in Federal Reserve Bank of Boston, *The International Adjustment Mechanism* (Boston: Federal Bank of Boston, 1979), pp. 114–15.
4. See Fernand Braudel, *The Structures of Everyday Life,* vol. 1 of *Civilization and Capitalism: the Limits of the Possible,* trans. Siân Reynolds (New York: Harper and Row, 1981), pp. 220, 221, 281, 315, 318, 335, etc.
5. H.M. Hyndman, *Commercial Crises of the Nineteenth Century* (1892; 2nd ed. [1932], reprinted, New York: Augustus M. Kelley, 1967), p. 96.
6. Walter Bagehot, *Lombard Street: a Description of the Money Market* (1873; reprint ed., London: John Murray, 1917), p. 18.
7. Sir John Clapham, *The Bank of England: a History* (Cambridge: Cambridge University Press, 1945), vol. 2, p. 326.
8. Adam Smith, *An Inquiry into the Nature and Causes of the Wealth of Nations* (1776; reprint ed., New York: Modern Library, 1937), pp. 703–4.
9. Alfred Marshall, *Money, Credit and Commerce* (1923; reprint ed., New York: Augustus M. Kelley, 1965), p. 305.

10. More and more economic theorists are moving away from unswerving reliance on the assumption that market participants are uniformly intelligent, informed, and independent in thought, introducing such concepts as asymmetric information (different knowledge available to different participants), cognitive dissonance (unconscious suppression of information that fails to fit a priori views), herd behavior, procrastination that results in failure to act in timely fashion, and so on. Those interested should consult the work especially of George Akerlof and Richard Thaler. For relevant studies, see Frederic S. Miskin, 'Asymmetric Information and Financial Crises: a Historical Perspective', in R. Glenn Hubbard, ed., *Financial Markets and Financial Crises* (Chicago: University of Chicago Press, 1991), pp. 69–108; and Thomas Lux, 'Herd Behavior, Bubbles and Crashes', *Economic Journal,* vol. 105 (July 1995), pp. 881–96.
11. Gustav LeBon, *The Crowd: a Study of the Popular Mind* (London: T. Fischer, Unwin, 1922).
12. Charles Mackay, *Memoirs of Extraordinary Delusions and the Madness of Crowds* (1852; reprint ed., Boston: L.C. Page Co., 1932).
13. John Carswell, *The South Sea Bubble* (London: Cresset Press, 1960), p. 161.
14. David Cass and Karl Shell, 'Do Sunspots Matter?' *Journal of Political Economy,* vol. 91, no. 2 (April 1983), pp. 193–227. This concept of a completely extraneous event was included in the first edition more or less randomly. Since 1983, however, 'sunspots' has become a word of art to cover general uncertainty as opposed to the 'fundamentals' that feature in rational expectations.
15. Irving Fisher, *The Purchasing Power of Money: its Determination and Relation to Credit, Interest and Crises,* 2nd ed. (New York: Macmillan, 1911), esp. chap. 1, dealing with crises; Knut Wicksell, *Interest and Prices* (London: Macmillan, 1936) (first published 1898).
16. Henrietta M. Larson, *Jay Cooke, Private Banker* (Cambridge, Mass.: Harvard University Press, 1934).
17. John Berry McFerrin, *Caldwell and Company: a Southern Financial Empire* (Chapel Hill: University of North Carolina Press, 1939; reprint, Nashville: Vanderbilt Press, 1969).
18. Peter Temin, *Did Monetary Forces Cause the Great Depression?* (New York: W.W. Norton, 1976), pp. 90–3.
19. Joan Edelman Spero, *The Failure of the Franklin National Bank: Challenge to the International Banking System* (New York: Columbia University Press, 1980).
20. Bagehot, *Lombard Street,* pp. 131–2.
21. George W. Van Vleck, *The Panic of 1857: an Analytical Study* (New York: Columbia University Press, 1953), p. 31.
22. R.C.O. Matthews, *A Study in Trade-Cycle History: Economic Fluctuations in Great Britain, 1832–1842* (Cambridge: Cambridge University Press, 1954), pp. 49, 110–11; and M.C. Reed, *Investment in Railways in Britain: a Study in the Development of the Capital Market* (London: Oxford University Press, 1976).

The ladies and clergymen—in American parlance, 'widows and orphans'—may more properly belong to a third stage when the securities have become seasoned in the market. The French call such investments suitable for 'the father of a family'. Charles Wilson, in *Anglo-Dutch Commerce and Finance in the Eighteenth Century* (Cambridge: Cambridge University Press, 1941), produces a number of variations on investor groups: in the Netherlands 'spinsters, widows, retired naval and army officers, magistrates, retired merchants, parsons and orphanages' (p. 118); 'hundreds of other merchants ... as well as thousands of civil servants, magistrates, widows and orphans and charitable institutions' (p. 135); 'widows, parsons, orphanages, magistrates and civil servants' (p. 162); 'country gentry, wealthy burghers and officials of Amsterdam, widows and wealthy spinsters' (p. 181); 'spinsters, theologians, admirals, civil servants, merchants, professional speculators, and the inevitable widows and orphans' (p. 202).

In the quotation from Bagehot that constitutes one of the epigraphs of this book, owners of the blind capital who lacked the wisdom to invest it properly were characterized in the excised portion as 'quiet ladies, rural clergymen and country misers' and again as 'rectors, authors, grandmothers'. See Bagehot, 'Essays on Edward Gibbon', quoted in Theodore E. Burton, *Financial Crises and Periods of Industrial and Commercial Depression* (New York: Appleton, 1902), pp. 321–2.

In his essay on Lord Brougham (1857), Bagehot quotes his subject on the crisis of 1814:

> 'The frenzy, I can call it nothing less ... descended to persons in the humblest circumstances, and the farthest removed by their pursuits, from commercial cares ... Not only clerks and labourers, but menial servants, engaged the little sums which they had been laying up for a provision against old age and sickness...
>
> The great speculators broke; the middling ones lingered out a precarious existence, deprived of all means of continuing their dealings either at home or abroad; the poor dupes of the delusion had lost their little hoards and went on the parish.'
>
> (Norman St John-Stevas, ed., *Bagehot's Historical Essays* (New York: New York University Press, 1966), pp. 118–19)

Another British expression for the naive and innocent who were drawn into the last phases of a bubble is 'greengrocers and servant girls'. The American 1929 categories were 'bootblacks and waiters', whereas a more modern characterization is 'house painters and office girls' (John Brooks, *The Go-Go Years* (New York: Weybright and Talley, 1973, p. 305)). Classes of current well-to-do amateurish and sometimes badly advised investors in the United States include successful doctors and dentists and professional athletes.

23. Max Wirth, *Geschichte der Handelskrisen,* 4th ed. (1890; reprint ed., New York: Burt Franklin, 1968), p. 480.
24. Ilse Mintz, *Deterioration in the Quality of Bonds Issued in the United States, 1920–1930* (New York: National Bureau of Economic Research, 1951).
25. Benjamin Stein, 'The Day Los Angeles's Bubble Burst', *New York Times,* December 8, 1984.
26. 'For Investors, Condo Craze Ends: Once Hot Market Makes Do Without Speculators', *Boston Globe,* February 14, 1988.
27. Homer Hoyt, *One Hundred Years of Land Values in Chicago* (Chicago: University of Chicago Press, 1933), p. 136.
28. Johnson, 'Destabilizing Speculation', p. 101.
29. Larry T. Wimmer, 'The Gold Crisis of 1869: Stabilizing or Destabilizing Speculation under Floating Exchange Rates', *Explorations in Economic History,* 12 (1975), pp. 105–22.
30. Christina Stead, *House of All Nations* (New York: Knopf, 1938).
31. Carswell, *South Sea Bubble,* pp. 131, 199.
32. Ibid., p. 120.
33. Clapham, *Bank of England,* vol. 2, p. 20. Hyndman, a socialist, sarcastically ascribes this example to the 1820s: 'The most ridiculous blunders were made by the class which was supposed to be carrying on business for the general benefit. Warming-pans were shipped to cities within the tropics, and Sheffield carefully provided skaters with the means of enjoying their favorite pastime where ice had never been seen. The best glass and porcelain were thoughtfully provided for naked savages, who had hitherto found horns and cocoa-nut shells quite hollow enough to hold all the drink they wanted.' (See H.M. Hyndman, *Commercial Crises of the Nineteenth Century* (1892; 2nd ed., 1932, reprinted, New York: Augustus M. Kelley, 1967), p. 39.) Clapham is right and Hyndman wrong. The source for both is J.R. McCullough, *Principles of Political Economy,* 2nd ed. (Edinburgh, 1830), which refers to 1810 not 1825.

    The announcement of the formation of the South Sea Company in May 1711 produced expectations of a strong demand for British goods in Latin America that would provide 'a triumphant solution to the [British] financial problem and need for expansion for the support of our way of life'. Booming markets were anticipated in 'Colchester bays [a type of cloth], silk handkerchiefs, worsted hose, sealing wax, spices, clocks and watches, Cheshire cheese, pickles, scales and weights for gold and silver' (see John Carswell. *The South Sea Bubble* (London: Cresset Press, 1960), p. 55.).
34. William Smart, *Economic Annals of the Nineteenth Century* (1911; reprint ed., New York: Augustus M. Kelly, 1964), vol. 2, p. 292.
35. Matthews, *Trade-Cycle History,* p. 25.
36. D. Morier Evans, *The History of the Commercial Crisis, 1857–1858, and the Stock Exchange Panic of 1859* (1859; reprint ed., New York: Augustus M. Kelley, 1969), p. 102.
37. Max Wirth, 'The Crisis of 1890', *Journal of Political Economy,* vol. 1 (March 1893), p. 230.

38. P.L. Cottrell, *Industrial Finance, 1830–1914: the Finance and Organization of English Manufacturing Industry* (London: Methuen, 1980), p. 169. Cottrell notes that the Guinness flotation was for £6 million, was handled by Baring, and was oversubscribed many times.
39. A.C. Pigou, *Aspects of British Economic History, 1918–25* (London: Macmillan, 1948).
40. J.S. Mill, *Principles of Political Economy, with some of their Applications to Social Philosophy* (1848; 7th ed., reprint ed., London: Longmans, Green, 1929), p. 709.
41. Maurice Lévy-Leboyer, *Les banques européennes et l'industrialisation internationale dans la première moitié du XIXe siècle* (Paris: Presses universitaires de France, 1964), p. 715.
42. Charles Wilson, *Anglo-Dutch Commerce and Finance in the Eighteenth Century* (Cambridge: Cambridge University Press, 1941), p. 25. For a series from the early seventeenth century, see J.G. Van Dillen, 'The Bank of Amsterdam', in *History of the Principal Public Banks* (The Hague: Martinus Nijhoff, 1934), p. 95.
43. For 1822 and 1824, see Smart, *Economic Annals,* vol. 2, pp. 82, 215. For 1888, see W. Jett Lauck, *The Causes of the Panic of 1893* (Boston: Houghton Mifflin, 1907), p. 39.
44. A. Andréadès, *History of the Bank of England* (London: P.S. King, 1909), pp. 404–5, see also p. 249.
45. O.M.W. Sprague, *History of Crises under the National Banking System* (1910; reprint ed., New York: Augustus M. Kelly, 1968), pp. 35–6.
46. Great Britain, *Parliamentary Papers* (*Monetary Policy, Commercial Distress*), 'Report of the Select Committee on the Operation of the Bank Acts and the Causes of the Recent Commercial Distress, 1857–59' (Shannon: Irish University Press, 1969), vol. 4; Consular report from Hamburg, no. 7, January 27, 1858, p. 438.
47. This statement appears in italics in Donald H. Dunn's fictionalized book, *Ponzi, the Boston Swindler* (New York: McGraw-Hill, 1975), p. 98.
48. *The Collected Works of Walter Bagehot,* ed. Norman St John Stevas (London: *The Economist,* 1978), vol. 11, p. 339.
49. Wirth, *Handelskrisen,* p. 109.
50. Wirth, 'Crisis of 1890', pp. 222–4; Alfred Pose, *La monnaie er ses institutions* (Paris; Presses universitaires de France, 1942), vol. 1, p. 215. Lauck puts the cost of the rescue operation at 25 million francs from the leading banks and 100 million francs from the Bank of France; see *Causes of the Panic of 1893,* p. 57.
51. Ronald I. McKinnon, *Money and Capital in Economic Development* (Washington, DC: Brookings Institution, 1973).
52. Carlos F. Diaz-Alejandro, 'Goodbye Financial Repression, Hello Financial Crash', *Journal of Development Studies,* vol. 18, no. 1 (Sept–Oct 1985), pp. 1–24.
53. Ronald I. McKinnon and Donald J. Mathieson, 'How to Manage a Repressed Economy', *Essays in International Finance,* no. 145 (Princeton, NJ: International Finance Section, Princeton University, 1981).

54. Wirth, *Handelskrisen,* p. 519. An apparent parallel can be found in a major exhibition in Melbourne, Australia, to celebrate the hundredth anniversary of European settlement, which boosted the city's economy briefly. See Geoffrey Searle, *The Rush to be Rich: a History of the Colony of Victoria* (Melbourne: Melbourne University Press, 1971), pp. 285–7.
55. J.W. Beyen, *Money in a Maelstrom* (New York: Macmillan, 1959), p. 45.
56. The expression is that of Gerald Malynes in 1686, quoted in Violet Barbour, *Capitalism in Amsterdam in the 17th Century* (Ann Arbor: University of Michigan Press, 1963), p. 74.
57. William R. Scott, *The Constitution and Finance of English, Scottish and Irish Joint-Stock Companies to 1720,* 3 vols (London, 1922), as summarized by J.A. Schumpeter, *Business Cycles* (New York: McGraw-Hill, 1939), vol. 1, p. 250.
58. Carswell, *South Sea Bubble,* p. 139.
59. Hans Rosenberg, *Die Weltwirtschaftskrise von 1857–59* (Stuttgart-Berlin: W. Kohlhammer, 1934), p. 114.
60. David Divine, *Indictment of Incompetence: Mutiny at Invergordon* (London: Macdonald, 1970).
61. C.P. Kindleberger, 'The Economic Crisis of 1619 to 1623', *Journal of Economic History,* vol. 51, no. 1 (March 1991), pp. 149–75.
62. Wirth, *Handelskrisen,* p. 92.
63. Ibid., p. 458.
64. Bertrand Gille, *La Banque et le crédit en France de 1815 à 1848* (Paris: Presses universitaires de France, 1959), p. 175.
65. Lévy-Leboyer, *Banques européennes,* p. 673.
66. Gille, *Banque et crédit,* p. 304.
67. Honoré de Balzac, *César Birotteau* (Paris: Livre de Poche, 1972), esp. pp. 13–14.
68. Leland H. Jenks, *The Migration of British Capital to 1875* (New York: Knopf, 1927), p. 34.
69. Rosenberg, *Weltwirtschaftskrise,* pp. 50, 100–1. See also Stewart L. Weisman, *Need and Greed: the Story of the Largest Ponzi Scheme in American History* (Syracuse: University of Syracuse Press, 1999).
70. Carswell, *South Sea Bubble,* p. 171.
71. Ibid., pp. 140, 155.
72. Ibid., p. 159.
73. Guy Chaussinand-Nogaret, *Les financiers de Languedoc au XVIIIe siècle* (Paris: S.E.V.P.E.N., 1970), p. 146. This author observed that the financiers were much more realistic than John Law, stimulating the speculation *(agiotage)* but keeping themselves aloof from the fever and ruining the system by converting their notes when they judged the moment to be the most favorable. Ibid., p. 129.
74. Clapham, *Bank of England,* vol. 2, p. 239.
75. T.S. Ashton, *Economic Fluctuations in England, 1700–1800* (Oxford: Oxford University Press, Clarendon Press, 1959), p. 151.
76. Ibid., p. 127.

77. See the review of Johannes van der Voort, *De Westindische Plantage van 1720 tot 1795* (Eindhoven: De Witte, 1973), in *Journal of Economic History*, vol. 36 (June 1976), p. 519.
78. Wilson, *Anglo-Dutch Commerce*, pp. 169–87; Ashton, *Economic Fluctuations*, pp. 127–9; Clapham, *Bank of England*, vol. 1, 242–9; Martin G. Buist, *At Spes non Fracta, Hope & Co., 1770–1815: Merchant Bankers and Diplomats at Work* (The Hague: Martinus Nijhoff, 1974), pp. 21ff.
79. Arthur D. Gayer, W.W. Rostow and Anna J. Schwartz, *The Growth and Fluctuation of the British Economy, 1790–1850* (Oxford: Oxford University Press, Clarendon Press, 1953), vol. 1, p. 92.
80. Ruth Benedict, *Patterns of Culture* (Boston: Houghton Mifflin, 1934).
81. See Herman van der Wee, *The Growth of the Amsterdam Market and the European Economy* (The Hague: Martinus Nijhoff, 1963), vol. 2, p. 202; J.A. Van Houtte, 'Anvers', in Amitore Fanfani, ed., *Città Mercanti Dottrine nell' Economia Europea* (Milan: A. Guiffre, 1964), p. 311; Simon Schama, *The Embarrassment of Riches: an Interpretation of Dutch Culture of the Golden Age* (Berkeley: University of California Press, 1988), pp. 347–50; Ernest Baasch, *Holländische Wirtschaftsgeschichte* (Jena: Gustav Fischer, 1927), p. 240, quoting Büsch.
82. Schama, *The Embarrassment of Riches*, pp. 503, 505.
83. Clement Juglar, *Des crises commerciales et leur retour périodiques en France, en Angleterre et aux Etats-Unis*, 2nd ed. (1889; reprint ed., New York: Augustus M. Kelley, 1967).
84. Theodore E. Burton, *Financial Crises and Periods of Industrial and Commercial Depression* (New York: D. Appleton, 1902), pp. 39–41.
85. The real prices of Australian land rose from 100 in 1870 to 450 in 1895, fell to about 360 before 1900, and then took off again to 600 by 1905. See Kevin H. O'Rourke and Jeffrey G. Williamson, *Globalization and History* (Cambridge, Mass.: MIT Press, 1999), Figure 3.1.
86. Francis W. Hirst, *The Six Panics and Other Essays* (London: Methuen, 1913), p. 2.
87. Michel Chevalier, *Lettres sur l'Amérique du Nord*, 3rd ed. (Brussels: Société belge du librairie, 1838), vol. 1, pp. 261–2.
88. Ibid., vol. 2, pp. 151 ff.
89. Andréadès, *Bank of England*, p. 404.
90. Louis Wolowski, testimony before Ministére des Finances et al., *Enquête sur les principes et les faits généraux qui régissent la circulation monétaire et fiduciaire* (Paris: Imprimerie imperiale, 1867), vol. 2, p. 398.
91. Wilson, *Anglo-Dutch Commerce*, p. 77, quoting Isaac de Pinto, *Jeu d'Actions* (eighteenth century).
92. Fritz Stern, *Gold and Iron: Bismarck, Bleichröder, and the Building of the German Empire* (London: Allen & Unwin, 1977), p. 500, quoting Constantin Franz in 1872.
93. Oskar Morgenstern, *International Financial Transactions and Business Cycles* (Princeton, NJ: Princeton University Press, 1959), p. 550.
94. Robert Bigo, *Les banques françaises au cours du XIXe siècle* (Paris: Sirey, 1947), p. 262.

95. Stead, *House of All Nations,* p. 233.
96. Ibid., p. 244.

4. Fueling the Flames: The Expansion of Credit

1. At least as far as I can tell from limited sources. Typically at the height of the bubble, sellers had no bulbs, and some (many?) buyers made down-payments, if at all, in kind, that is, in personal possessions or commodities, presumably because they lacked cash. The difference between the value of the down-payment and the negotiated price was personal credit. See N.W. Posthumus, 'The Tulip Mania in Holland in the Years 1636 and 1637', *Journal of Economic and Business History,* vol. 1 (1928–29), reprinted in W.C. Scoville and J.C. LaForce, eds, *The Economic Development of Western Europe,* vol. 2, *The Sixteenth and Seventeenth Centuries* (Lexington, Mass.: D.C. Heath, 1969), P. 142; Simon Schama, *The Embarrassment of Riches: an Interpretation of the Dutch Culture in the Golden Age* (Berkeley: University of California Press, 1987), p. 358; Robert P. Flood and Peter M. Garber, *Speculative Bubbles, Speculative Attacks and Policy Switching* (Cambridge, Mass.: MIT Press, 1994), p. 60.
2. Peter Temin, *The Jacksonian Economy* (New York: W.W. Norton, 1969), pp. 79–82.
3. Jean Bouvier, *Le Krach de l'Union Générale, 1878–1885* (Paris: Presses universitaires de France, 1960), pp. 129–34.
4. 'Kuwait's Great $70 Bn Paper Chase', *Financial Times,* September 25, 1982; 'Kuwait Aide Says Speculators Own "Price of Follies"', *International Herald Tribune,* October 29, 1982; 'Kuwaities Try a New Exchange', *New York Times,* December 16, 1984, sec. D.
5. Milton Friedman, *The Optimum Quantity of Money and Other Essays* (Chicago: Aldine, 1969), pp. 1–50.
6. Jacob Viner, *Studies in the Theory of International Trade* (New York: Harper, 1937), pp. 232–3.
7. J.G. Van Dillen, 'The Bank of Amsterdam', in *History of the Principal Public Banks* (The Hague: Martinus Nijhoff, 1934), pp. 79–123.
8. Eli F. Heckscher and J.G. Van Dillen, eds, 'The Bank of Sweden in its Connection with the Bank of Amsterdam', in ibid., p. 169.
9. Walter Bagehot, 'The General Aspect of the Banking Question', no. 1, a letter to the editor of *The Economist,* February 7, 1857, in *The Collected Works of Walter Bagehot,* ed. Norman St John Stevas (London: *The Economist,* 1978), vol. 9, p. 319.
10. Great Britian, Committee on the Working of the Monetary System, *Report* (Radcliffe Report), Cmnd 827 (London: H.M. Stationery Office, August 1959), pp. 133–4, 391–2.
11. Ibid., pp. 134, 394.
12. James S. Gibbons, *The Banks of New York, their Dealers, the Clearing House and the Panic of 1857* (New York: D. Appleton, 1859), pp. 376–7.
13. J.S. Mill, in *Westminster Review,* vol. 41 (1844), pp. 590–1, quoted in Jacob Viner, *Studies in International Trade,* p. 246.

14. See Benjamin M. Friedman, 'Portfolio Choice and the Debt-to-Income Relationship', *American Economic Review,* vol. 75, no. 2 (May 1985), pp. 338–43; and idem, 'The Roles of Money and Credit in Macro-economic Analysis', in James Tobin, ed., *Macroeconomics, Prices, and Quantities: Essays in Memory of Arthur Okun* (Washington, DC: Brookings Institution, 1983), pp. 161–89.
15. Samuel L. Clements (Mark Twain) and Charles Dudley Warner, *The Gilded Age: a Tale of Today* (New York: Harper & Brothers, 1873; reprint ed., author's national ed., 10 vols, 1915), vol. 1, p. 263.
16. For an extended discussion see C.P. Kindleberger, 'The Quality of Debt', in D.B. Papadimitriou, ed., *Profits, Deficits and Instability* (Basingstoke: Macmillan, 1992). reprinted in idem, *The World Economy and National Finance in Historical Perspective* (Ann Arbor: University of Michigan Press, 1995), pp. 117–30.
17. See Hyman P. Minsky, 'The Financial-instability Hypothesis: Capitalist Processes and the Behavior of the Economy', in C.P. Kindleberger and J.P. Laffargue, eds, *Financial Crisis: Theory, History and Policy* (Cambridge: Cambridge University Press, 1982), pp. 13–39.
18. See the comments on the Minsky paper by J.S. Flemming, Raymond W. Goldsmith, and Jacques Melitz, in ibid., pp. 39–47.
19. 'Revco Drugstore Chain in Bankruptcy Filing', *New York Times,* July 29, 1988, sec. D.
20. Henry Kaufman, *Interest Rates, the Markets and the New Financial World* (New York: Times Books, 1986).
21. Alfred Marshall noted that paper money was used in China 2,000 years before his writing, and that the apt term *flying money* was given there to bills of exchange 1,000 years ago. See Appendix E, 'Notes on the Development of Banking, with Special Reference to English Experience', in *Money, Credit and Commerce* (1923; reprint, New York: Augustus M. Kelley, 1965), p. 305n.

    In Europe the bill of exchange was developed by Italian merchants to balance accounts at fairs. Net debtors at the end of trading paid in bills drawn on a fair in a different location or on the next fair at the same place. This 'private money' was needed because there was not enough coin (money of the prince) to square accounts. See Marie-Therèse Boyer-Xambeu, Ghislain Deleplace, and Lucien Gillard, *Private Money and Public Currencies: the 16th-century Challenge,* translated from the French (Armonk, NY: M.W. Sharpe, 1984).
22. T.S. Ashton, 'The Bill of Exchange and Private Banks in Lancashire, 1790–1830', in T.S. Ashton and R.S. Sayers, eds, *Papers in English Monetary History* (Oxford: Oxford University Press, Clarendon Press, 1953), pp. 37–8.
23. Francis C. Knowles, *The Monetary Crisis Considered* (1827), referring to the House of Lords Committee on Scottish and Irish Currency of 1826; quoted in J.R.T. Hughes, *Fluctuations in Trade, Industry and Finance: a Study of British Economic Development, 1850–1860* (Oxford: Oxford University Press, Clarendon Press, 1960), p. 267.

24. Ibid., p. 258.
25. Kurt Samuelsson, 'International Payments and Credit Movements by Swedish Merchant Houses, 1730–1815', *Scandinavian Economic History Review,* vol. 3 (1955), p. 188.
26. For an early example of such attitudes, see the hypothetical discussion of the board of directors at a New York bank in the 1850s by James S. Gibbons, *The Banks of New York, their Dealers, the Clearing House, and the Panic of 1857* (New York: D. Appleton, 1859), p. 50. A director is pleading the loan application of a Mr. Black, 'rich beyond a contingency', who wants to build a new house on Fifth Avenue for $60,000 and to spend $40,000 to furnish it, and proposes expanding his firm's discount line at the bank by the whole amount. Another director objects:

    > Mr. President, my notion is, that we have no right to discount any thing at the Board but a *bona fide* commercial note that will be paid when due. And on top of that the indorser must be able to take it up himself, if the drawer should fail or die. Don't you see that we are discounting this paper to pay for Mr. Black's house and furniture, just for his single enjoyment? This isn't commercial paper, sir! It's accommodation paper in the true sense.

    Gibbon's book, with chapters on the various tasks in a bank, is a mid-nineteenth-century precursor to Martin Mayer's *The Bankers* (New York: Ballantine Books, 1974).
27. R.G. Hawtrey, *The Art of Central Banking* (London: Longmans, Green, 1932), pp. 128–9.
28. See Herman E. Krooss, ed., *Documentary History of Banking and Currency in the United States* (New York: Chelsea House, 1969), vol. 1, p. 31.
29. Viner, *Studies in International Trade,* pp. 245ff., esp. pp. 249–50.
30. Adam Smith, *An Inquiry into the Nature and Causes of the Wealth of Nations* (1776; reprint ed., New York: Modern Library, 1937), pp. 293–7.
31. R.G. Hawtrey, *Currency and Credit,* 3rd ed. (New York: Longmans, Green 1930), p. 224.
32. Arthur D. Gayer, W.W. Rostow, and Anna Jacobson Schwartz, *The Growth and Fluctuation of the British Economy, 1790–1850* (Oxford: Oxford University Press, Clarendon Press, 1953), vol. 1, p. 105.
33. Great Britain, *Parliamentary Papers* (*Monetary Policy, Commercial Distress*), 'Report of the Select Committee on the Operation of the Bank Acts and the Causes of the Recent Commercial Distress, 1857–59' (Shannon: Irish University Press, 1969), vol. 4, p. 113, question 1661, and p. 115, question 1679.
34. Albert E. Fr. Schäffle, 'Die Handleskrise von 1857 in Hamburg, mit besonderer Rucksicht auf das Bankwesen', in Schäffle, *Gesammelte Aufsätze* (Tübingen: H. Haupp'schen, 1885), vol. 2, p. 31.
35. Wirth, *Handelskrisen,* p. 91.
36. See C.P. Kindleberger, *The World in Depression, 1929–1939,* 2nd ed. (Berkeley: University of California Press, 1986), p. 133 and note.
37. Bouvier, *Le Krach,* pp. 130–1.

38. After the bank's dissolution, the French prosecutor of Bontoux wrote that there had been grave irregularities in the issuance of the shares and in the increases in capital. Subscriptions to the capital had been made by the bank both in its own name and in the names of fictitious client subscribers. A rival bank, the Banque de Lyon et de la Loire, formed in April 1881 with a capital of 25 million francs (raised to 50 million in November) and with one-quarter of its capital theoretically paid in, was similarly a bubble. Of 50,000 shares originally issued, more than half had not paid amounts due, and the bank had less than half of the 6.5 million francs of capital claimed at the outset.

    The Union Générale also bought its own securities in the open market and, as we shall see, loaned money to others to buy them. (Bouvier, *Le krach,* pp. 123, 164–5, 167.)
39. Ibid., p. 131.
40. Ibid. For prices, see tables 7 and 8, pp. 136 and 144; for the shortfall, see p. 144.
41. Ibid., tables 7 and 8, pp. 136, 144, 145.
42. John Carswell, *The South Sea Bubble* (London: Cresset Press, 1960), p. 171.
43. Bouvier, *Le krach,* pp. 112, 113.
44. Federal Reserve System, *Banking and Monetary Statistics* (Washington, DC: Board of Governors of the Federal Reserve System, 1943), p. 494.
45. Alexander Dana Noyes, *The Market Place: Reminiscences of a Financial Editor* (Boston: Little, Brown, 1937), p. 353.
46. Peter H. Lindert, *Key Currencies and Gold, 1900–1913,* Princeton Studies in International Finance, no. 24 (August 1969).
47. Jeffrey G. Williamson, *American Growth and the Balance of Payments, 1830–1913: a Study of the Long Swing* (Chapel Hill: University of North Carolina Press, 1964).
48. Alvin H. Hansen, *Business Cycles and National Income* (New York: W.W. Norton, 1957), chaps. 13, 15.
49. A.C. Pigou, *Industrial Fluctuations* (London: Macmillan, 1927), pt. 1, chap. 7, and p. 274.
50. Milton Friedman and Anna J. Schwartz, *A Monetary History of the United States, 1867–1960* (Princeton, NJ: Princeton University Press, 1963). Chapter 10 of the book is published separately as *The Great Contraction, 1929–1933* (Princeton, NJ: Princeton University Press, 1965).
51. This assertion was made by Thomas A. Mayer in a seminar on money and the Great Depression, University of California, Berkeley, May 11, 1977.
52. Peter Temin, *Did Monetary Forces Cause the Great Depression?* (New York: W.W. Norton, 1976), passim.
53. Ben S. Bernanke, 'Nonmonetary Effects of the Financial Crisis in the Propagation of the Great Depression', *American Economic Review,* vol. 73, no. 3 (June 1983), pp. 237–76.
54. Frederic S. Miskin, 'Illiquidity, Consumer Durable Expenditure, and Monetary Policy', *American Economic Review,* vol. 66 (September 1976), pp. 642–54.

55. See Minsky's review of Temin, in *Challenge,* vol. 19, no. 1 (September/October 1976), pp. 44–6; and see Milton Friedman, 'The Monetary Theory and Policy of Henry Simons', in Friedman, *Optimum Quantity of Money,* pp. 81–93.
56. Henry Simons, *Economic Policy for a Free Society* (Chicago: University of Chicago Press, 1948).
57. Friedman, 'Henry Simons', p. 83.
58. See Friedrich A. Hayek, 'Choice in Currency: a Way to Stop Inflation', Occasional Paper no. 48 (London: Institute of Economic Affairs, 1982); Roland Vaubel, 'Free Currency Competition', *Weltwirtschaftliches Archiv,* vol. 113 (1977), pp. 435–59; Richard H. Timberlake, 'Legislative Construction of the Monetary Control Act of 1980', *American Economic Review,* vol. 75, no. 2 (May 1985), pp. 97–102; Leland B. Yeager, 'Deregulation and Monetary Reform', *American Economic Review,* vol. 75, no. 2 (May 1985), pp. 103–7: Lawrence H. White, *Free Banking in Britain: Theory, Experience and Debate* (New York: Cambridge University Press, 1984); George Selgin, *The Theory of Free Banking* (Totowa, NJ: Rowan and Littlefield, 1989). For a defense of central banking, see Charles Goodhart, *The Evolution of Central Banks* (Cambridge: Cambridge University Press, 1989).
59. 'The Post-1990 Surge in World Currency Reserves', *Conjuncture,* 26th year, no. 9 (October 1996), pp. 2–12.
60. Pascal Blanqué, 'U.S. Credit Bubble.com', *Conjuncture,* 29th year, no. 4 (April 1999), pp. 12–21.
61. Graciela L. Kaminsky and Carmen W. Reinhart, 'The Twin Crises: the Causes of Banking and Balance-of-Payments Problems', *American Economic Review* (June 1999), pp. 433–500.
62. Gayer, Rostow, and Schwartz, *Growth and Fluctuation,* vol. 1, p. 300.
63. Hughes, *Fluctuations,* p. 12.
64. Ibid., p. 261.
65. Elmer Wood, *English Theories of Central Banking Control, 1819–1858, with Some Account of Contemporary Procedures* (Cambridge, Mass.: Harvard University Press, 1939), p. 147.
66. Andréadès, *History of the Bank of England* (London: P.S. King, 1909), pp. 356–7.
67. Wirth, *Handelskrisen,* p. 463.
68. Ibid., pp. 515–16.
69. E. Victor Morgan, *The Theory and Practice of Central Banking, 1797–1913* (Cambridge: Cambridge University Press, 1943), pp. 184–5.
70. O.M.W. Sprague, *History of Crises under the National Banking System* (1910; reprint ed., New York: Augustus M. Kelley, 1968), p. 241.
71. Gibbons, *Banks of New York,* p. 375.

5. The Critical Stage

1. *The Collected Works of Walter Bagehot,* ed. Norman St John Stevas (London: *The Economist,* 1978), vol. 9, p. 273.

2. Milton Friedman, 'In Defense of Destabilizing Speculation', in *The Optimum Quantity of Money and Other Essays* (Chicago: Aldine, 1969), p. 288.
3. Harry G. Johnson, 'The Case for Flexible Exchange Rates, 1969', in Federal Reserve Bank of St Louis, *Review,* vol. 51 (June 1969), p. 17.
4. John Carswell, *The South Sea Bubble* (London: Cresset Press, 1960), p. 139.
5. W.R. Brock, *Lord Liverpool and Liberal Toryism, 1820–1827* (Cambridge: Cambridge University Press, 1941), p. 209.
6. R.C.O. Matthews, *A Study of Trade-cycle History: Economic Fluctuations in Great Britain, 1832–1842* (Cambridge: Cambridge University Press, 1954), p. 162.
7. Maurice Lévy-Leboyer, *Les banques européennes et l'industrialisation internationale dans la première moitié du XIX*[e] *siècle* (Paris: Presses universitaires de France, 1964), pp. 618–20.
8. Ibid., p. 713.
9. Wladimir d'Ormesson, *La grande crise mondiale de 1857: L'histoire recommence, les causes, les remèdes* (Paris-Suresnes: Maurice d'Hartoy, 1933), pp. 110ff.
10. Hans Rosenberg, *Die Weltwirtschaftskrise von 1857–59* (Stuttgart: Verlag von W. Kohlhammer, 1934), p. 210.
11. Max Wirth, *Geschichte der Handelskrisen,* 4th ed. (1890; reprint ed., New York: Burt Franklin, 1968), p. 463.
12. Fritz Stern, *Gold and Iron: Bismarck, Bleichröder, and the Building of the German Empire* (London: Allen & Unwin, 1977), p. 242.
13. *The Economist,* April 21, 1888, p. 500. This citation and the following one were brought to the author's attention by Richard C. Marston.
14. Ibid., May 5, 1888, pp. 570–1.
15. M.J. Gordon, 'Toward a Theory of Financial Distress', *Journal of Finance,* vol. 26 (May 1971), p. 348.
16. Carswell, *South Sea Bubble,* p. 170.
17. Sir John Clapham, *The Bank of England: a History* (Cambridge: Cambridge University Press, 1945), vol. 2, p. 257.
18. Edouard Rosenbaum and A.J. Sherman, *M.M. Warburg & Co., 1758–1938: Merchant Bankers of Hamburg* (New York: Holmes & Meier, 1979), p. 129.
19. D.P. O'Brien, ed., *The Correspondence of Lord Overstone* (Cambridge: Cambridge University Press, 1971), vol. 1, p. 368.
20. Michel Chevalier, *Lettres sur l'Amérique du Nord,* 3rd ed. (Brussels: Société belge du librairie, 1838), vol. 1, p. 37.
21. Jean Bouvier, *Le krach de l'Union Générale* (Paris: Presses universitaires de France, 1960), pp. 129, 133, 137.
22. Wirth, *Handelskrisen*, p. 508.
23. D. Morier Evans, *The History of the Commercial Crisis, 1857–1858, and the Stock Exchange Panic of 1859* (1859; reprint ed., New York: Augustus M. Kelley, 1969), p. 203.
24. Testimony of Louis Adolphe Thiers, Ministère des Finances et al., *Enquête sur les principes et les faits généraux qui régissent la circulation monétaire et fiduciaire* (Paris: Imprimerie imperiale, 1867), vol. 3, p. 436.

25. Stephen A. Schuker, *The End of French Predominance in Europe, the Financial Crisis of 1924 and the Adoption of the Dawes Plan* (Chapel Hill: University of North Carolina Press, 1976), pp. 87, 104.
26. Arthur D. Gayer, W.W. Rostow, and Anna J. Schwartz, *The Growth and Fluctuation of the British Economy, 1790–1850* (Oxford: Oxford University Press, Clarendon Press, 1953), vol. 1, p. 190.
27. Ibid., p. 312.
28. Bouvier, *Le krach,* pp. 29, 130.
29. James G. Gibbons, *The Banks of New York, their Dealers, the Clearing House, and the Panic of 1857* (New York: D. Appleton, 1859), p. 94.
30. See Clément Juglar, *Des crises commerciales et leur retour périodique en France, en Angleterre et aux Etats-Unis,* 2nd ed. (1889; reprint ed., New York: Augustus M. Kelley, 1967), p. 427.
31. W.T.C. King, *History of the London Discount Market* (London: George Routledge & Sons, 1936), p. 232.
32. O.M.W. Sprague, *History of Crises under the National Banking System* (1910; reprint ed., New York: Augustus M. Kelley, 1968), p. 127.
33. Ibid., p. 33.
34. Ibid., p. 36.
35. Bouvier, *Le krach,* p. 133.
36. Christina Stead may be referring to this episode in *The House of All Nations* (New York: Simon & Schuster, 1938), when she has one of her characters, Stewart, say: '"My first job. By jove we had fun. At one time they had a short position in Union Pacific which exceeded the floating supply. Were they ruined? Not that time. They came to terms with them . . . they had to, otherwise a world panic would have resulted".'
37. Sprague, *History of Crises,* pp. 237–53.
38. See C.P. Kindleberger, 'Asset Inflation and Monetary Policy', *Banco Nazionale del Lavoro Quarterly Review,* no. 192 (March 1995), pp. 17–35.
39. Carswell, *South Sea Bubble,* pp. 136–7, 158.
40. Evans, *Commercial Crisis,* p. 13.
41. Gayer, Rostow, and Schwartz, *Growth and Fluctuation,* p. 307.
42. W. Jett Lauck, *The Causes of the Panic of 1893* (Boston: Houghton Mifflin, 1907), pp. 59–60.
43. Oskar Morgenstern, *International Financial Transactions and Business Cycles* (Princeton, NJ: Princeton University Press, 1959), p. 523.
44. Part of the reason Germany sold Russian bonds was political, as was the basis for German buying of Italian bonds. The French bought Russian bonds and sold Italian bonds. But Germany did float a Mexican loan of £10.5 million in 1888, so one cannot make the case that the domestic boom in Germany required capital that in nonpolitical circumstances would have gone abroad. See Fritz Stern, *Gold and Iron: Bismarck, Bleichröder, and the Building of the German Empire* (London: Allen & Unwin, 1977), pp. 427, 433, 442. Professor Stern has indicated that there is nothing in the Bleichröder correspondence that bears on German selling of Argentine securities.
45. Johan Åkerman, *Structure et cycles économiques* (Paris: Presses universitaires de France, 1955–57), vol. 2, p. 292.

46. E. Ray McCartney, *Crisis of 1873* (Minneapolis: Burgess Publishing Co., 1935), pp. 58, 71.
47. Wirth, *Handelskrisen,* p. 110.
48. George W. Van Vleck, *The Panic of 1857: an Analytical Study* (New York: Columbia University Press, 1943), p. 68.
49. H.S. Foxwell, introduction to Andréadès, *History of the Bank of England,* p. xvii.
50. E. Victor Morgan, *The Theory and Practice of Central Banking, 1797–1913* (Cambridge: Cambridge University Press, 1943), p. 109.
51. Elmer Wood, *English Theories of Central Banking Control, 1819–1858* (Cambridge, Mass.: Harvard University Press, 1939), p. 183.
52. R.G. Hawtrey, *Currency and Credit,* 3rd ed. (New York: Longmans, Green, 1927), p. 28.
53. Clapham, *Bank of England,* vol. 2, p. 153.
54. Leone Levi, *History of British Commerce* (London: John Murray, 1872), p. 233.
55. Joan Edelman Spero, *The Failure of the Franklin National Bank: Challenge to the International Banking System* (New York: Columbia University Press, 1980), pp. 66, 71, 85, 91.
56. Milton Friedman and Anna J. Schwartz, *A Monetary History of the United States, 1867–1960* (Princeton: Princeton University Press, 1963), p. 339.
57. Lauck, *Causes of the Panic of 1893,* chap. 7.
58. Sprague, *History of Crises,* p. 253.
59. Thomas Joplin, *Case for Parliamentary Inquiry into the Circumstances of the Panic, in a Letter to Thomas Gisbourne, Esq. M.P.* (London: F. Ridgeway & Sons, n.d. [after 1832]), pp. 14–15.
60. Robert Baxter, *The Panic of 1866, with its Lessons on the Currency Act* (1866; reprint ed., New York: Burt Franklin, 1969), pp. 4, 26.
61. Clapham, *Bank of England,* vol. 2, p. 101.
62. Ibid., p. 100.
63. Rosenberg, *Weltwirtschaftskrise,* p. 118.
64. Van Vleck, *Panic of 1857,* p. 74.
65. Rosenberg, *Weltwirtschaftskrise,* p. 121.
66. Sprague, *History of Crises,* p. 113.
67. Alvin H. Hansen, *Cycles of Prosperity and Depression in the United States, Great Britain and Germany: a Study of Monthly Data, 1902–1908* (Madison: University of Wisconsin, 1921), p. 13.
68. H.S. Foxwell, 'The American Crisis of 1907', in *Papers in Current Finance* (London: Macmillan, 1919), pp. 202–3.

6. Euphoria and Economic Booms

1. Peter M. Garber, 'Tulipmania', in Robert P. Flood and Peter M. Garber, *Speculative Bubbles, Speculative Attacks, and Policy Switching* (Cambridge, Mass.: MIT Press, 1994), p. 72.
2. N.W. Posthumus, 'The Tulip Mania in Holland in the Years 1636 and 1637', *Journal of Business and Economic History,* vol. 1 (1928–29), reprinted

in W.C. Scoville and J.C. LaForce, eds, *The Economic Development of Western Europe,* vol. 2, *The Sixteenth and Seventeenth Centuries* (Lexington, Mass.: D.C. Heath, 1969), p. 169.

3. Simon Schama, *The Embarrassment of Riches: an Interpretation of Dutch Culture in the Golden Age* (New York: Knopf, 1987), p. 358. Schama's source is Krelage, *Bluemenspekulation.*
4. Jonathan I. Israel, *The Dutch Republic: its Rise, Greatness and Fall, 1477–1806* (Oxford: Clarendon Press, 1995), p. 533. Jan de Vries and Ad van der Woude state that in the summer of 1636, speculation in commodity derivatives spread far beyond the circle of tulip fanciers, its flame being fanned by severe outbreaks of bubonic plague that released inhibitions (*The First Modern Economy: Success, Failure and Perseverance of the Dutch Economy, 1500–1815* (Cambridge: Cambridge University Press, 1997), pp. 150–1).
5. Jan de Vries, *Barges and Capitalism: Transportation in the Dutch Economy* (Wageningen: A.G. Bidragen, 1978), pp. 52ff.
6. Israel, *The Dutch Republic,* p. 533.
7. Garber, 'Tulipmania', pp. 71–2.
8. Israel, *The Dutch Republic,* chap. 33.
9. Ibid., p. 869.
10. Homer Hoyt, *One Hundred Years of Land Values in Chicago: the Relationship of the Growth of Chicago to the Rise in Land Values, 1830–1933* (Chicago: University of Chicago Press, 1933).
11. Quoted in Hoyt, *Land Values,* p. 165. This suggests that the 'greater fool theory'—a speculator buying an asset he believes is overpriced because he thinks he can sell it to a greater fool, widely quoted today—goes back at least a century.
12. Fritz Stern, *Gold and Iron: Bismarck, Bleichröder, and the Building of the German Empire* (London: Allen & Unwin, 1977), p. 161.
13. Hoyt, *Land Values,* p. 102. One stimulus to the boom was the huge fire of October 6, 1871, which destroyed somewhat more than one-fourth of the 60,000 houses in the city.
14. Hoyt, *Land Values,* p. 401.
15. 'How to Ruin a Safe Bet: Did Rockefeller Center Financiers Reach Too Far?', *New York Times,* October 5, 1995, pp. D1, D11.
16. Keizai Koho Center, *Japan 1994: an International Comparison* (Tokyo, 1993), Chart 11–3, 'Increase in Land Prices in Japan', p. 83.
17. Koichi Hamada, 'Bubbles, Busts and Bailouts', in Mitsuaki Okabe, ed., *The Structure of the Japanese Economy* (London: Macmillan, 1995), pp. 263–86.
18. Masahiko Takeda and Philip Turner, 'The Liberalization of Japanese Financial Markets: Some Major Themes', *BIS Economic Papers,* no. 34 (November 1992), graph 8, p. 53.
19. Takeda and Turner, 'Liberalization of Japanese Financial Markets', pp. 99–121.
20. Ibid., Table A-l, pp. 120–1.
21. Ibid., pp. 58–65. Hamada calls the revelations 'scandals' (p. 9).

22. Herman Kahn, *The Emerging Japanese Superstate: Challenge and Response* (Englewood Cliffs, NJ: Prentice-Hall, 1970).
23. 'Erosion in Japan's Foundation: Real Estate Crash Threatens the Entire Economy', New *York Times,* October 4, 1995.
24. David Asher and Andrew Smithers, 'Japan's Key Challenges for the 21st Century', SAIS (School for Advanced International Studies) Policy Forum Studies, April 1998.
25. Keizai Koho Center, *Japan 1994,* Charts 5–0, p. 52, and 4–19, p. 44.
26. See C.E.B. Borio, N. Kennedy, and S.D. Prowse, 'Exploring Aggregate Price Formation across Countries: Measurement, Determinants and Monetary-Policy Implications', *BIS Economic Papers,* no. 40 (Spring 1994), p. 46: 'It has been widely accepted that the primary goal of monetary policy should be price stability.'
27. See Armen A. Alchian and Benjamin Klein, 'On a Correct Measure of Inflation', *Journal of Money, Credit and Banking,* vol. 5, no. 1 (February 1973), pp. 172–91.

7. International Contagion

1. Herbert Hoover, *The Memoirs of Herbert Hoover* (New York: Macmillan, 1952), vol. 3, pp. 61–2.
2. Milton Friedman and Anna J. Schwartz, *A Monetary History of the United States, 1867–1960* (Princeton: Princeton University Press, 1963), pp. 359–60.
3. Quoted in Leone Levi, *History of British Commerce* (London: John Murray, 1872), p. 234.
4. S. Saunders, quoted in D. Morier Evans, *The History of the Commercial Crisis, 1857–1858, and the Stock Exchange Panic of 1859* (1859; reprint ed., New York: Augustus M. Kelley, 1969), p. 13.
5. R.C.O. Matthews, *A Study in Trade-Cycle History: Economic Fluctuations in Great Britain, 1832–1842* (Cambridge: Cambridge University Press, 1954), p. 69.
6. Friedman and Schwartz, *Monetary History,* p. 360.
7. Jørgen Pedersen, 'Some Notes on the Economic Policy of the United States during the Period 1919–1932', in Hugo Hegelund, ed., *Money Growth and Methodology: Papers in Honor of Johan Åkerman* (Lund: Lund Social Science Studies, 1961), reprinted in J. Pedersen, *Essays in Monetary Theory and Related Subjects* (Copenhagen: Samfundsvienskabeligt Forlag, 1975), p. 189.
8. R.T. Naylor, *The History of Canadian Business, 1867–1914,* vol. 1, *The Banks and Finance Capital* (Toronto: James Lorimer & Co., 1975), p. 130.
9. Clément Juglar, *Des crises commerciales et leur retour périodique en France, en Angleterre et aux Etats-Unis,* 2nd ed. (1889; reprint ed., New York: Augustus M. Kelley, 1967), pp. xiv, 17, 47, 149, and passim.
10. Wesley C. Mitchell, introduction to Willard L. Thorp, *Business Annals* (New York: National Bureau of Economic Research, 1926), pp. 88–97.

11. Oskar Morgenstern, *International Financial Transactions and Business Cycles* (Princeton, NJ: Princeton University Press, 1959), chap. 1. esp. sec. 6; on international stock exchange panics from 1893 to 1931, see table 139, pp. 546–7, and chart 72, p. 548.
12. C.P. Kindleberger, 'The International (and Interregional) Aspects of Financial Crises', in Martin Feldstein, ed., *The Risk of Economic Crisis* (Chicago: University of Chicago Press, 1991), pp. 128–32.
13. Friedman and Schwartz, *Monetary History,* p. 308.
14. See C.E.V. Borio, N. Kennedy, and S.D. Prowse, 'Exploring Aggregate Price Fluctuations across Countries: Measurement, Determinants, and Monetary Policy Implications', *BIS Economic Papers,* no. 40 (April 1994), Graph A.1, p. 74.
15. C.P. Kindleberger, 'The Economic Crisis of 1619 to 1623', *Journal of Economic History,* vol. 51, no. 1 (March 1991), esp. pp. 159–61.
16. Johan Åkerman, *Structure et cycles économiques* (Paris: Presses universitaires de France, 1957), vol. 2. pp. 247, 255.
17. John Carswell, *The South Sea Bubble* (London: Cresset Press, 1960), pp. 84, 94,100, 101.
18. Ibid., pp. 151, 160–1, 166. There may be some doubt about this. P.G.M. Dickson maintains that the Canton of Berne still held £287,000 of South Sea annuities in 1750 (*The Financial Revolution in England: a Study in the Development of Public Credit, 1688–1756* (New York: St Martin's Press, 1967), p. 90).
19. Charles Wilson, *Anglo-Dutch Commerce and Finance in the Eighteenth Century* (Cambridge: Cambridge University Press, 1941), pp. 103, 124.
20. Carswell, *South Sea Bubble,* p. 167.
21. Ibid., pp. 178, 199. In *The Great Mirror of Folly* [*Het Groote Tafereel der Dwaasheid*], *an Economic Bibliographical Study* (Boston: Baker Library, Harvard Graduate School of Business Administration, 1949), Arthur H. Cole observes that Holland had a full-scale bubble between April and October 1720, stimulated by the excitements of Paris and London. Forty new companies were floated in thirty mostly smaller towns, in the amount of 350 million guilders. Shares of the Dutch East India Company tripled in this period, and those of the West India Company went from 40 to 600 before the bubble burst (pp. 5, 6).
22. T.S. Ashton, *Economic Fluctuations in England, 1700–1800* (Oxford: Oxford University Press, Clarendon Press, 1959), p. 120.
23. George Chalmers, *The Comparative Strength of Great Britain* (London, 1782), p. 141, quoted in Ashton, *Economic Fluctuations,* p. 151.
24. E.E. de Jong-Keesing, *De Economische Crisis van 1763 te Amsterdam* (Amsterdam, 1939), pp. 216–17.
25. Wilson, *Anglo-Dutch Commerce,* p. 168.
26. De Jong-Keesing, *Economische Crisis van 1763,* p. 217.
27. Ernst Baasch, *Hollandische Wirtschaftsgeschichte* (Jena: Gustav Fischer, 1927).
28. Max Wirth, *Geschichte der Handelskrisen,* 4th ed. (1890; reprint ed., New York: Burt Franklin, 1968), p. 87.

29. Stephan Skalweit, *Die Berliner Wirtschaftskrise von 1763 und ihre Hintergründe* (Stuttgart/Berlin: Verlag W. Kohlhammer, 1937), p. 50.
30. Wilson, *Anglo-Dutch Commerce,* p. 168; Alice Clare Carter, *Getting, Spending and Investing in Early Modern Times: Essays on Dutch, English and Huguenot Economic History* (Assen: Van Gorcum, 1975), p. 63.
31. William Smart, *Economic Annals of the Nineteenth Century,* vol. 1 (1911; reprint ed., New York: Augustus M. Kelley, 1964), pp. 529–30.
32. Arthur D. Gayer, W.W. Rostow, and Anna J. Schwartz, *The Growth and Fluctuation of the British Economy, 1790–1850* (Oxford: Oxford University Press, Clarendon Press, 1953), vol. 1, p. 159.
33. Smart, *Economic Annals,* vol. 1, chap. 31.
34. Murray N. Rothbard, *The Panic of 1819: Reactions and Policies* (New York: Columbia University Press, 1962), p. 11.
35. Bray Hammond, *Banks and Politics in America from the Revolution to the Civil War* (Princeton, NJ: Princeton University Press, 1957), chap. 10, esp. pp. 253–62.
36. Maurice Lévy-Leboyer, *Les banques européennes et l'industrialisation international dans la première moitié du XIXe siècle* (Paris: Presses universitaires de France, 1964), pp. 464–79.
37. Åkerman, *Structure et cycles économiques,* p. 294.
38. Maurice Lévy-Leboyer, 'Central Banking and Foreign Trade: the Anglo-American Cycle in the 1830s', in C.P. Kindleberger and J.-P. Laffargue, eds, *Financial Crises: Theory, History and Policy* (Cambridge: Cambridge University Press, 1982), pp. 66–110.
39. R.G. Hawtrey, *Currency and Credit,* 3rd ed. (New York: Longmans, Green, 1927), p. 177.
40. Lévy-Leboyer, *Banques européennes,* pp. 570–83.
41. Juglar, *Crises Commerciales,* p. 414.
42. D. Morier Evans, *The Commercial Crisis, 1847–48* (1849; reprint ed., New York: Augustus M. Kelley, 1969).
43. Richard Tilly, *Financial Institutions and Industrialization in the Rhineland, 1815–1870* (Madison: University of Wisconsin Press, 1970), p. 112.
44. Alfred Krüger, *Das Kölner Bankiergewerbe vom Ende des 18. Jahrhunderts bis 1875* (Essen: G.D. Baedeker Verlag, 1925), pp. 12–13, 35, 49, 55–6, 202–3. Reference courtesy of Professor Richard Tilly.
45. This is discussed in a Swedish study of the crisis of 1857: P.E. Bergfalk, *Bidrag till de under de sista hundrade aren inträffade handelskrisershistoria* (Uppsala: Edquist, 1859), referred to in Theodore E. Burton, *Financial Crises and Periods of Industrial and Commercial Depression* (New York: Appleton, 1902), pp. 128–9.
46. Sir John Clapham, *The Bank of England: a History* (Cambridge: Cambridge University Press, 1945), vol. 2, p. 226.
47. Hans Rosenberg, *Die Weltwirtschaftskrise von 1857–1859* (Stuttgart: Verlag von W. Kohlhammer, 1934), p. 136.
48. Åkerman, *Structure et cycles économiques,* p. 323.
49. Clapham, *Bank of England,* vol. 2, p. 268. R.G. Hawtrey makes the point that the crisis was not isolated but a sequel to the Continental crisis of 1864. See *Currency and Credit,* p. 177.

50. Shepard B. Clough, *The Economic History of Modern Italy* (New York: Columbia University Press, 1964), p. 53.
51. David S. Landes, *Bankers and Pashas: International Finance and Economic Imperialism in Egypt* (Cambridge, Mass.: Harvard University Press, 1958), p. 287.
52. Wirth, *Handelskrisen,* pp. 462–3.
53. Larry T. Wimmer, 'The Gold Crisis of 1869: a Problem in Domestic Economic Policy and International Trade Theory' (PhD diss., University of Chicago, 1968); U.S. Congress, House, *Gold Panic Investigation,* 41st Cong., 2nd sess., H. Rept. 31, March 1, 1870.
54. Wirth, *Handelskrisen,* p. 464.
55. U.S. Congress, House, *Gold Panic Investigation,* p. 132.
56. C.P. Kindleberger, 'The Panic of 1873', paper presented to the NYU-Salomon Brothers Symposium on Financial Panics, reprinted in *Historical Economics: Art or Science?* (New York: Harvester/Wheatsheaf, 1990), pp. 310–25.
57. Henrietta M. Larson, *Jay Cooke, Private Banker* (Cambridge, Mass.: Harvard University Press, 1936).
58. Homer Hoyt, *One Hundred Years of Land Values in Chicago: the Relationship of the Growth of Chicago to the Rise in Land Values, 1830–1933* (Chicago: University of Chicago Press, 1933), pp. 101–2, 117.
59. R. Ray McCartney, *Crisis of 1873* (Minneapolis: Burgess, 1935), p. 85.
60. Morgenstern, *International Financial Transactions,* p. 546.
61. Fritz Stern, *Gold and Iron: Bismarck, Bleichröder, and the Building of the German Empire* (London: Allen & Unwin, 1977), p. 189.
62. Morgenstern, *International Financial Transactions,* p. 548.
63. L.S. Pressnell, 'The Sterling System and Financial Crises before 1914', in C.P. Kindleberger and J.-P. Laffargue, eds, *Financial Crises,* pp. 148–64.
64. O.M.W. Sprague, *History of Crises under the National Banking System* (1910; reprint ed., New York: Augustus M. Kelley, 1968), p. 132.
65. C.P. Kindleberger, 'International Propagation of Financial Crises: the Experience of 1888–93', in idem, *Keynesianism vs. Monetarism and Other Essays in Financial History* (London: Allen & Unwin, 1985), pp. 226–39.
66. Franco Bonelli, 'The 1907 Financial Crisis in Italy: a Peculiar Case of the Lender of Last Resort in Action', in C.P. Kindleberger and J.-P. Laffargue, eds, *Financial Crises,* pp. 51–65.
67. Franco Bonelli, *La crisi del 1907: una tappa dello sviluppo industrial in Italia* (Turin: Fondazione Luigi Einaudi, 1971), pp. 31–2.
68. Ibid., p. 34.
69. Ibid., pp. 42–3.
70. Frank Vanderlip, 'The Panic as a World Phenomenon', *Annals of the American Academy of Political and Social Science,* vol. 31 (January–June 1908), p. 303.
71. Andrew McIntyre, 'Political Institutions and the Economic Crisis in Thailand and Indonesia', *Asian Economic Bulletin,* vol. 15, no. 3 (December 1998), pp. 363–72. McIntyre believed that the extreme, if disparate, character of government policy in the two countries made the crisis worse in each.

72. Rusian L. Margulin, 'Russian Financial Crisis of 1988', written for a class in financial history at the Stern School of New York University taught by Professor Richard E. Sylla, who kindly made the paper available. The paper is especially useful in providing a detailed chronology of events from 1967, almost day by day from May 1998 to mid-September, and the use of a number of Russian items in the bibliography from websites.
73. 'Turmoil in Brazil: Markets Rally but More Convulsions Are Possible', *New York Times,* January 16, 1999, pp. Al, B4.

9. Frauds, Swindles, and the Credit Cycle

1. See Norman C. Miller, *The Great Salad Oil Swindle* (New York: Coward, McCann, 1965).
2. Hyman P. Minsky, 'Financial Resources in a Fragile Financial Environment', *Challenge,* vol. 18 (July/August 1975), p. 65.
3. Martin F. Hellwig, 'A Model of Borrowing and Lending with Bankruptcy', Princeton University Econometric Research Program, Research Memorandum no. 177 (April 1975), p. 1.
4. Daniel Defoe, *The Anatomy of Change-Alley* (London: E. Smith, 1719), p. 8. See also the title of Jean Carper's book on fraud, *Not with a Gun* (New York: Grossman, 1973).
5. Jacob van Klavaren, 'Die historische Erscheinungen der Korruption', *Viertelsjahrschrift für Sozial- und Wirtschaftsgeschichte,* vol. 44 (December 1957), pp. 289–324; vol. 45 (December 1958), pp. 433–69, 469–504; vol. 46 (June 1959), pp. 204–31. See also idem, 'Fiskalismus—Mercantilismus—Korruption: Drei Aspecte der Finanz- und Wirtschaftspolitik während der Ancien Regime', ibid., vol. 47 (September 1960), pp. 333–53.
6. E. Ray McCartney, *The Crisis of 1873* (Minneapolis: Burgess, 1935), p. 15.
7. John Carswell, *The South Sea Bubble* (London: Cresset, 1960), p. 13.
8. Maximillian E. Novak, *Economics and the Fiction of Daniel Defoe* (Berkeley: University of California Press, 1962), p. 103.
9. Bray Hammond, *Banks and Politics in America from the Revolution to the Civil War* (Princeton, NJ: Princeton University Press, 1957), p. 268.
10. Carswell, *South Sea Bubble,* pp. 222–4.
11. William G. Shepheard, Wall Street editor of *Business Week,* in preface to Donald H. Dunn, *Ponzi, the Boston Swindler* (New York: McGraw-Hill, 1975), p. x.
12. Milton Friedman, 'In Defense of Destabilizing Speculation', in *The Optimum Quantity of Money and Other Essays* (Chicago: Aldine, 1969), p. 290.
13. Quoted in Max Winkler, *Foreign Bonds, an Autopsy: a Study of Defaults and Repudiations of Government Obligations* (Philadelphia: Roland Swain, 1933), p. 103.
14. E. Victor Morgan, *The Theory and Practice of Central Banking, 1797–1913* (Cambridge: Cambridge University Press, 1943), p. 177.
15. Honoré de Balzac, *Melmoth réconcilié* (Geneva: Editions de Verbe, 1946), pp. 45–50.

16. Dunn, *Ponzi,* p. 188.
17. Introduction by Robert Tracey to Anthony Trollope, *The Way We Live Now* (1874–75; reprint ed., New York: Bobbs-Merrill, 1974), p. xxv.
18. Sir John Clapham, *The Bank of England: a History* (Cambridge: Cambridge University Press, 1945), vol. 1, p. 229.
19. Charles Wilson, *Anglo-Dutch Commerce and Finance in the Eighteenth Century* (Cambridge: Cambridge University Press, 1941), p. 170.
20. George W. Van Vleck, *The Panic of 1857: an Analytical Study* (New York: Columbia University Press, 1943), p. 65.
21. Earl J. Hamilton, 'The Political Economy of France at the Time of John Law', *History of Political Economy,* vol. 1 (Spring 1969), p. 146.
22. Jacob van Klavaren, 'Rue de Quincampoix und Exchange Alley: Die Spekulationsjähre 1719 und 1720 in Frankreich und England', *Viertelsjahrschrift für Sozial- und Wirtschaftsgeschichte,* vol. 48 (October 1961), pp. 329ff.
23. Dunn, *Ponzi,* p. 247.
24. Max Wirth, *Geschichte der Handelskrisen,* 4th ed. (1890; reprint ed., New York: Burt Franklin, 1968), p. 510.
25. William Robert Scott, *The Constitution and Finance of English, Scottish and Irish Joint-Stock Companies to 1720* (Cambridge: Cambridge University Press, 1911), vol. 3, pp. 449ff.; and D. Morier Evans, *The Commercial Crisis, 1847–48,* 2nd ed., rev. (1849; reprint ed., New York: Augustus M. Kelley, 1969), pp. 33–4. A separate list for the South Sea Bubble, prepared by a contemporary and less detailed, is set out in Wirth, *Handelskrisen,* pp. 67–79.
26. A. Andréadès, *History of the Bank of England* (London: P.S. King, 1909), p. 133.
27. Carswell, *South Sea Bubble,* p. 142.
28. Scott, *Joint-Stock Companies,* p. 450.
29. Hans Rosenberg, *Die Weltwirtschaftskrise von 1857–59* (Stuttgart: W. Kohlhammer, 1934), p. 103.
30. Wirth, *Handelskrisen,* p. 480.
31. Anthony Trollope, *The Three Clerks* (New York: Harper & Brothers, 1860), p. 346.
32. Carswell, *South Sea Bubble,* p. 177.
33. Fritz Stern, *Gold and Iron: Bismarck, Bleichröder, and the Building of the German Empire* (London: Allen & Unwin, 1977), p. 358.
34. Ibid., pp. 396–7.
35. U.S. Senate, Committee on Finance, 72nd Cong., 1st sess., *Hearings on Sales of Foreign Bonds of Securities,* held December 18, 1931, to February 10, 1932 (Washington, DC: U.S. Government Printing Office, 1932).
36. OMW. Sprague, *History of Crises under the National Banking System* (1910; reprint ed., New York: Augustus M. Kelley, 1968), p. 341.
37. Quoted in Wirth, *Handelskrisen,* p. 80.
38. Honoré de Balzac, *La maison Nucingen,* in *Oeuvres complètes* (Paris: Calmann Lévy, 1892), p. 68.
39. Carswell, *South Sea Bubble,* pp. 176, 181.

40. Wirth, *Handelskrisen,* p. 491.
41. Emile Zola, *L'Argent* (Paris: Livre de Poche, n.d.), p. 125.
42. Wirth, *Handelskrisen,* p. 491.
43. Zola, *L'Argent,* p. 161.
44. Jean Bouvier, *Le krash de l'Union Générale* (Paris: Presses universitaires de France, 1960), p. 36.
45. *The Economist,* October 21, 1848, pp. 1186–8, quoted in Arthur D. Gayer, W.W. Rostow, and Anna J. Schwartz, *The Growth and Fluctuation of the British Economy, 1790–1850* (Oxford: Oxford University Press, Clarendon Press, 1953), p. 316.
46. Rosenberg, *Weltwirtschaftskrise,* p. 101.
47. Stern, *Gold and Iron,* chap. 10 ('Greed and Intrigue') and p. 364.
48. Novak, *Economics of Defoe,* pp. 14–15 and 160 n. 35.
49. Ibid., p. 16, note 50.
50. Maurice Lévy-Leboyer, *Les banques européennes et l'industrialisation internationale dans la première moitié du XIXe siècle* (Paris: Presses universitaires de France, 1964), pp. 632–3.
51. Ibid., p. 503, note 90.
52. Bouvier, *Le krach,* p. 124.
53. Ibid., p. 161, note 50.
54. Stern, *Gold and Iron,* chap. 11.
55. Theodore Dreiser's *Trilogy of Desire* consists of three novels: *The Financier* (1912), *The Titan* (1914), and *The Stoic* (1947). See *The Titan* (New York: World, 1972), pp. 371–2.
56. Ibid., pp. 515–40.
57. Henry Grote Lewin, *The Railway Mania and its Aftermath, 1845–1852* (1936; reprint ed., rev., New York: Augustus M. Kelley, 1968), pp. 262, 357–64.
58. See Paul W. Gates, *Illinois Central Railroad and its Colonization Work* (1934; reprint ed., Cambridge, Mass.: Harvard University Press, 1968), pp. 66, 75–6; John L. Weller, *The New Haven Railroad: the Rise and Fall* (New York: Hastings House, 1969), p. 37n; Van Vleck, *Panic of 1857,* p. 58.
59. See Willard L. Thorp, *Business Annals* (New York: National Bureau of Economic Research, 1926), p. 126.
60. Watson Washburn and Edmund S. Delong, *High and Low Financiers: Some Notorious Swindlers and their Abuses of our Modern Stock Selling System* (Indianapolis: Bobbs-Merrill, 1932), p. 13.
61. Ibid., pp. 85, 101, 144, 309.
62. Barrie A. Wigmore, *The Crash and its Aftermath: a History of Security Markets in the United States, 1929–1933* (Westport, Conn.: Greenwood, 1985), pp. 344–8.
63. Ibid., pp. 358–60.
64. James S. Gibbons, *The Banks of New York, their Dealers, the Clearing House, and the Panic of 1857* (New York: D. Appleton, 1859), p. 104.
65. Ibid., p. 277.
66. John Kenneth Galbraith, *The Great Crash, 1929,* 3rd ed. (Boston: Houghton Mifflin, 1972), pp. 133–5.

67. David F. Good, *The Economic Rise of the Hapsburg Empire, 1750–1914* (Berkeley: University of California Press, 1984), p. 165.
68. D. Morier Evans, *Facts, Failures and Frauds* (1839; reprint ed., New York: Augustus M. Kelley, 1968), p. 235.
69. See Robert Shaplen, *Kreuger: Genius and Swindler* (New York: Knopf, 1960).
70. Carswell, *South Sea Bubble,* pp. 225, 265–6.
71. Bouvier, *Le krach,* pp. 211, 219.
72. Herbert I. Bloom, *The Economic Activities of the Jews of Amsterdam in the Seventeenth and Nineteenth Centuries* (Williamsport, Pa.: Bayard Press, 1937), p. 199.
73. Carswell, *South Sea Bubble,* p. 210.
74. Dreiser, *The Titan,* p. 237.
75. Christina Stead, *House of All Nations* (New York: Simon & Schuster, 1938), p. 643.

10. Policy Responses: Letting It Burn Out, and Other Devices

1. Thomas Joplin, *Case for Parliamentary Inquiry into the Circumstances of the Panic, in a Letter to Thomas Gisborne, Esq., M.P.* (London: James Ridgeway & Sons, n.d. [after 1832]), p. 10 (apropos the panic of 1825).
2. Sir John Clapham, *The Bank of England: a History* (Cambridge: Cambridge University Press, 1945), vol. 2, p. 236 (apropos the panic of 1847).
3. E. Victor Morgan, *The Theory and Practice of Central Banking, 1797–1913* (Cambridge: Cambridge University Press, 1943), p. 133.
4. The episode is noted in A. Andréadès, *History of the Bank of England* (London: P.S. King, 1909), p. 334. For an extended discussion, see Rudiger Dornbusch and Jacob Frenkel, 'The Gold Standard and the Bank of England in the Crisis of 1847', in Michael Bordo and Anna J. Schwartz, eds, *A Retrospective on the Classical Gold Standard, 1821–1931* (Chicago: University of Chicago Press, 1984), pp. 233–64.
5. Ministère des Finances et al., *Enquête sur les principes et les faits géneraux qui régissent la circulation monétaire et fiduciare* (Paris: Imprimerie impériale, 1867), vol. 1, p. 456.
6. 'The Revulsion of 1857—its Causes and Results', *New York Herald,* n.d., quoted in D. Morier Evans, *The History of the Commercial Crisis, 1857–1858, and the Stock Exchange Panic of 1859* (1859; reprint ed., New York: Augustus M. Kelley, 1969), p. 121.
7. Herbert Hoover, *The Memoirs of Herbert Hoover* (New York: Macmillan & Co., 1952), vol. 3, p. 30.
8. Murray N. Rothbard, *America's Great Depression,* 3rd ed. (Kansas City: Sheed & Ward, 1975), p. 187.
9. Paul Johnson, *Modern Times: the World from the Twenties to the Eighties* (New York: Harper & Row, 1983), p. 244.
10. Ernst Baasch, *Holländische Wirtschaftsgeschichte* (Jena: Gustav Fischer, 1927), p. 238.
11. Joplin, *Parliamentary Inquiry,* pp. 14–15.

12. Great Britain, *Parliamentary Papers, Monetary Policy, Commercial Distress* (1857; Shannon: Irish University Press, 1969), vol. 1, pp. 427, 431.
13. D. Morier Evans, *The Commercial Crisis, 1847–1848,* 2nd ed. (1849; reprint ed., New York: Augustus M. Kelley, 1969), p. 89n.
14. Evans, *Commercial Crisis,* p. 181.
15. Parliamentary Papers, *Commercial Distress,* p. xii.
16. Ibid., vol. 4, appendix 20; *Foreign Communications Relative to the Commercial Crisis of 1857,* Hamburg consular circular no. 76, November 23, 1857, pp. 435, 440, 441.
17. Henrietta M. Larson, *Jay Cooke, Private Banker* (Cambridge, Mass.: Harvard University Press, 1936), p. 80.
18. W.C.T. King, *History of the London Discount Market* (London: George Routledge & Sons, 1936), p. 243.
19. Theodore Dreiser, *The Financier* (1912), in *Trilogy of Desire* (New York: World Publishing, 1972), p. 491.
20. W. Jett Lauck, *The Causes of the Panic of 1893* (Boston: Houghton, Mifflin, 1907), p. 102.
21. *The Commercial and Financial Chronicle,* May 16, 1884, p. 589, quoted in O.M.W. Sprague, *History of Crises under the National Banking System* (1910; reprint ed., New York: Augustus M. Kelley, 1968), p. 112.
22. W.R. Brock, *Lord Liverpool and Liberal Toryism, 1820–1827* (Cambridge: Cambridge University Press, 1941), pp. 209–10 (cited by Clapham, *Bank of England,* vol. 2, p. 108).
23. Clapham, *Bank of England,* vol. 2, p. 332.
24. Stephan Skalweit, *Die Berliner Wirtschaftskrise von 1763 und ihre Hintergründe* (Stuttgart: Verlag W. Kohlhammer, 1937), pp. 49–73.
25. Arthur D. Gayer, W.W. Rostow, and Anna J. Schwartz, *The Growth and Fluctuation of the British Economy, 1790–1850* (Oxford: Oxford University Press, Clarendon Press, 1953), vol. 1, p. 272.
26. Larry T. Wimmer, 'The Gold Crisis of 1869: a Problem in Domestic Economic Policy and International Trade Theory' (PhD diss., University of Chicago, 1968), p. 79.
27. Andréadès, *Bank of England,* p. 137, citing Henry D. McLeod, *Theory and Practice of Banking,* 3rd ed. (London: Longman Green, Reader & Dyer, 1879), p. 428.
28. John Carswell, *The South Sea Bubble* (London: Cresset Press, 1960), p. 184.
29. Andréadès, *Bank of England,* p. 151.
30. Alexander Dana Noyes, *The Market Place: Reminiscences of a Financial Editor* (Boston: Little, Brown, 1938), p. 333.
31. Sprague, *History of Crises,* p. 259.
32. Ibid.
33. Ibid., p. 181.
34. Max Wirth, *Geschichte der Handelskrisen,* 4th ed. (1890; reprint ed., New York: Burt Franklin, 1968), p. 521.
35. Maurice Lévy-Leboyer, *Les banques européennes et l'industrialisation internationale dans la première moitié du XIXe siècle* (Paris: Presses universitaires de France, 1964), p. 480, text and note 5.

36. George W. Van Vleck, *The Panic of 1857: an Analytical Study* (New York: Columbia University Press, 1943), p. 80.
37. Sprague, *History of Crises,* pp. 120, 182–3.
38. Ibid., pp. 75, 291–2.
39. Jacob H. Schiff, 'Relation of a Central Bank to the Elasticity of the Currency', *Annals of the American Academy of Political and Social Science,* vol. 31 (January–June 1908), p. 375. For a more contemporary account, see Jean Strouse 'The Brilliant Bailout', *New Yorker* (November 23, 1998), pp. 62–77.
40. Myron T. Herrick, 'The Panic of 1907 and Some of its Lessons', *Annals of the American Academy of Political and Social Science,* vol. 31 (January–June 1908), p. 309.
41. John Kenneth Galbraith, *The Great Crash, 1929,* 3rd ed. (Boston: Houghton Mifflin, 1972), pp. 107–8.
42. For a discussion of the rescue committee *(Aufhilfsfonds)* in Vienna, see Eduard März, *Österreich Industrie- und Bankpolitik* in *der Zeit Franz Josephs I: Am Beispiel der k.k. priv. Österreichischen Credit-Anstalt für Handel und Gewerbe* (Vienna: Europa Verlag, 1968), pp. 177–82. März notes (p. 179) that the best account of the crisis is that of Josef Neuwirth, *Bank und Valuta in Österreich,* vol. 2, *Die Spekulationskrisis van 1873* (no publishing data given).
43. Lévy-Leboyer, *Banques européennes,* pp. 470–1.
44. Bertrand Gille, *La banque en France au XIXe siècle* (Paris: Droz, 1970), p. 93.
45. Parliamentary Papers, *Commercial Distress,* vol. 4, appendix, consular dispatch from Hamburg, no. 75, p. 434.
46. Ibid., p. 435.
47. Hans Rosenberg, *Die Weltwirtschaftskrise von 1857–1859* (Stuttgart/Berlin: Verlag von W. Kohlhammer, 1934), p. 129.
48. Parliamentary Paper, *Commercial Distress,* vol. 4, appendix, consular dispatches from Hamburg, nos. 77, 80, 81, 82, 84, 86, pp. 435–7.
49. Albert E. Fr. Schäffle, 'Die Handelskrise von 1857 in Hamburg, mit besonderer Rücksicht auf das Bankwesen', in *Gesammelte Aufsätze* (Tübingen: H. Raupp'schen, 1885), vol. 2, pp. 44, 45, 52, 53.
50. Clapham, *Bank of England,* vol. 2, p. 156.
51. Ibid., p. 331. For more detailed accounts of the Baring crisis and rescue, see L.S. Pressnell, 'Gold Reserves, Banking Reserves and the Baring Crisis of 1890', in C.R. Whittlesey and J.S.G. Wilson, eds, *Essays in Money and Banking in Honour of R.S. Sayers* (Oxford: Clarendon Press, 1968), pp. 67–228; and idem, 'The Sterling System and Financial Crises before 1914', in C.P. Kindleberger and J.-P. Laffargue, eds, *Financial Crises: Theory, History and Policy* (Cambridge: Cambridge University Press, 1982), pp. 148–64.
52. Diary of John Biddulph Martin, in George Chandler, *Four Centuries of Banking* (London: B.J. Batsford, 1964), vol. 1, p. 330.
53. Ellis T. Powell, *The Evolution of the Money Market (1384–1915): an Historical and Analytical Study of the Rise and Development of Finance as*

a Central Coordinated Force (1915: reprint ed., New York: Augustus M. Kelley, 1966), p. 528.

54. Ibid., p. 525.
55. 'New York Fed Assists Hedge Fund Bailout', *New York Times,* September 24, 1998, pp. Al, C11.
56. There are some purists or masochists who think that bank runs are an optimal response of depositors, and good for the system, with panic as a form of monitoring. 'If depositors believe that there are some underperforming banks, but cannot decide which ones may become insolvent, they may force out all the undesirable ones by a systemwide panic.' This is from Charles W. Calomoris and Gary Gorton, 'The Origins of Banking Panics: Models, Facts and Bank Regulation', in R. Glenn Hubbard, ed., *Financial Markets and Financial Crises* (Chicago: University of Chicago Press, 1991), pp. 120–1.
57. Hoover, *Memoirs,* vol. 3, pp. 211–12.
58. 'Bank Board Doubles Texas Cost Estimate', *New York Times,* July 8, 1988, sec. D.
59. 'Treasury Says Savings Aid Should Not Tax the Taxpayer', *New York Times,* August 3, 1988, sec. D.
60. Wirth, *Handelskrisen,* p. 100.
61. Andréadès, *Bank of England,* pp. 187–9; Clapham, *Bank of England,* vol. 1, pp. 263–5.
62. Gayer, Rostow, and Schwartz, *Growth and Fluctuation,* vol. 1, p. 34.
63. William Smart, *Economic Annals of the Nineteenth Century* (1911; reprint ed., New York: Augustus M. Kelley, 1964), vol. 1, pp. 267–8.
64. Ibid., p. 271.
65. Ian Giddy, 'Regulation of Off-Balance Sheet Banking', in *The Search for Financial Stability: the Past Fifty Years* (San Francisco: Federal Reserve Bank of San Francisco, 1985), pp. 165–77.
66. Edward J. Kane, 'Competitive Financial Reregulation: an International Perspective', in R. Portes and A. Swoboda, eds, *Threats to International Financial Stability* (Cambridge: Cambridge University Press, 1987), pp. 111–45.
67. Stanley Zucker, *Ludwig Bamberger: German Liberal Politician and Social Critic, 1823–1899* (Pittsburgh: University of Pittsburgh Press, 1975), p. 78.
68. Wirth, *Handelskrisen,* pp. 110–11.

11. The Domestic Lender of Last Resort

1. François Nicholas Mollien, *Mémoires d'un Ministre du Trésor Public, 1780–1815* (Paris: Fournier, 1845), vol. 2, pp. 298ff.
2. Ministère des Finances et al., *Enquête sur les principes et les faits généraux qui régissent la circulation monétaire et fiduciaire* (Paris: Imprimerie impériale, 1867), vol. 2, pp. 31–2.

3. Murray N. Rothbard, *America's Great Depression,* 3rd ed. (Kansas City: Sheed & Ward, 1975), p. 167.
4. Herbert Spencer, from 'State Tampering with Money and Banks', in *Essays: Scientific, Political and Speculative* (London: Williams & Norgate, 1891), vol. 3, p. 354, quoted by Charles Lipson, *Standing Guard: Protecting Foreign Capital in the Nineteenth and Twentieth Centuries* (Berkeley: University of California Press, 1985), p. 45.
5. T.S. Ashton, *Economic Fluctuations in England, 1700–1800* (Oxford: Oxford University Press, Clarendon Press, 1959), p. 112.
6. Ibid., p. 111.
7. E. Victor Morgan, *The Theory and Practice of Central Banking, 1797–1913* (Cambridge: Cambridge University Press, 1943), p. 240.
8. Maurice Lévy-Leboyer, *Les banques européennes et l'industrialisation internationale dans la première moitié du XIXe siècle* (Paris: Presses universitaires de France, 1964), p. 490.
9. See F.A. Hayek's introduction to Henry Thornton, *An Enquiry into the Nature and Effect of the Paper Credit of Great Britain* (1802; London: Allen & Unwin, 1939; reprint, London: Frank Cass, 1962), p. 38.
10. Thornton, *Paper Credit,* pp. 187–8.
11. *The Collected Works of Walter Bagehot,* ed. Norman St John Stevas (London: *The Economist,* 1978), vol. 11, p. 149.
12. Ibid., vol. 9, p. 267.
13. Thomas Joplin, *Case for Parliamentary Inquiry into the Circumstances of the Panic, in a letter to Thomas Gisborne, Esq., M. P.* (London: James Ridgeway & Sons, n.d. [after 1832]), p. 29.
14. Jacob Viner, *Studies in the Theory of International Trade* (New York: Harper & Bros., 1937), p. 233.
15. D.P. O'Brien, 'Overstone's Thought', in D.P. O'Brien, ed., *The Correspondence of Lord Overstone* (Cambridge: Cambridge University Press, 1971), vol. 1, p. 95. (A bodkin is a dagger, stiletto, ornamental hairpin, or a blunt needle with a large eye.)
16. Milton Friedman and Anna J. Schwartz, *A Monetary History of the United States, 1867–1960* (Princeton, NJ: Princeton University Press, 1963), pp. 418–19. The metaphor of an avalanche is also used by Alfred Marshall in stating that prompt action by the Bank of England in regard to the rate of discount often checks unreasonable expansions of credit, 'which might otherwise grow, *after the manner of a fall of snow on a steep mountain side'* and become an avalanche (Marshall's emphasis). See Marshall, *Money, Credit, and Commerce* (1923; reprint ed., New York: Augustus M. Kelly, 1965), pp. 258–9.
17. Walter Bagehot, *Lombard Street: a Description of the Money Market* (1873; reprint ed., London: John Murray, 1917), p. 160.
18. Elmer Wood, *English Theories of Central Banking Control, 1819–1858* (Cambridge, Mass.: Harvard University Press, 1939), p. 147.
19. J.H. Clapham, *The Bank of England: a History* (Cambridge: Cambridge University Press, 1945), vol. 2, p. 289.
20. Bagehot, *Lombard Street,* pp. 161–2.

21. Clapham, *Bank of England,* vol. 2, p. 108.
22. Marshall, *Money, Credit, and Commerce,* p. 307. In their concluding chapter on the Dutch Republic, Jan de Vries and Ad van der Woude note that in 1780 the Dutch international banking sector lacked but one critical feature: effective credit-creating institutions to maintain liquidity in time of crisis *(The First Modern Economy* (Cambridge: Cambridge University Press, 1997), p. 683).
23. Bertrand Gille, *La banque en France au XIXe siècle: Recherches historiques* (Geneva: Librairie Droz, 1970), p. 32.
24. Bertrand Gille, *La Banque et le crédit en France de 1815 à 1848* (Paris, Presses universitaires de France, 1959), p. 367.
25. Michel Chevalier, *Lettres sur l'Amérique du Nord,* 3rd ed. (Paris: Charles Gosselin, 1838), p. 37, note 1.
26. Ministère des Finances et al., *Enquête,* vol. 3, pp. 411–12.
27. Ibid., vol. 2, pp. 129–30.
28. Jean Bouvier, *Un siècle de banque française* (Paris: Hachette Littérature, 1973), pp. 83–4.
29. See Rondo Cameron, *France and the Economic Development of Europe, 1800–1914* (Princeton, NJ: Princeton University Press, 1961), pp. 191ff.
30. Maurice Lévy-Leboyer, *Histoire économique et sociale de la France depuis 1848* (Paris: Les Cours de Droit, Institut d'Etudes Politiques, 1951–52), p. 121.
31. Cameron, *France and Europe,* p. 117.
32. Alfred Pose, *La monnaie et ses insitutions* (Paris: Presses universitaires de France, 1942), p. 215.
33. Jean Bouvier, *Le krach de l'Union Générate, 1878–1885* (Paris: Presses universitaires de France, 1960), pp. 150, 152–53.
34. Esther Rogoff Taus, *Central Banking Functions of the United States Treasury, 1789–1941* (New York: Columbia University Press, 1943), pp. 22, 23, 29.
35. Ibid., pp. 39–131.
36. C.A.E. Goodhart, *The New York Money Market and the Finance of Trade, 1900–1913* (Cambridge, Mass.: Harvard University Press, 1969), p. 120.
37. George W. Van Vleck, *The Panic of 1857: an Analytical Study* (New York: Columbia University Press, 1943), p. 106.
38. O.M.W. Sprague, *History of Crises under the National Banking System* (1910; reprint ed., New York: Augustus M. Kelley, 1968).
39. Myron T. Herrick, 'The Panic of 1907 and Some of its Lesson', *Annals of the American Academy of Political and Social Science,* vol. 31 (January–June 1908), p. 324.
40. Ridgely's essay in *Annals* was more narrowly entitled 'An Elastic Credit Currency as a Preventive for Panics', but the papers of the others, except for Seligman, were unqualified in their advocacy of central bank currency elasticity.
41. Note Bagehot's characterization of the character of the then members of the court of the Bank of England: 'A board of plain, sensible prosperous English merchants; and they have both done and left undone what such a board might be expected to do and not to do. Nobody could expect

great attainments in economical science from such a board; laborious study is for the most part foreign to the habits of English merchants' (Walter Bagehot, *Lombard Street: a Description of the Money Market* (1873; reprint ed., London: John Murray, 1917), p. 166). Later he is more critical: 'Unluckily ... directors of the Bank of England were neither acquainted with the right principles, nor were they protected by a judicious routine. They could not be expected themselves to discover such principles. The abstract thinking of the world is never to be expected from people in high places ... No doubt when men's own fortunes are at stake, the insight of the trader does somehow anticipate the conclusions of the closet' (p. 169).

42. Wood, *English Central Banking Control,* pp. 169–70.
43. Franco Bonelli, *La crisi del 1907: una tappa dello sviluppo industriale in Italia* (Turin: Fondazione Luigi Einaudi, 1971), passim and esp. p. 165.
44. Leone Levi, *History of British Commerce, 1763–1870,* 2nd ed. (London: John Murray, 1872), pp. 311–12.
45. Great Britain, *Parliamentary Papers, Monetary Policy, Commercial Distress* (1857; Shannon: Irish University Press, 1969), vol. 3, p. xxix.
46. *Collected Works of Walter Bagehot,* vol. 9, p. 147.
47. Ibid., vol. 11, pp. 149–50.
48. See C.P. Kindleberger, 'Rules vs. Men: Lessons from a Century of Monetary Policy', in Christoph Buchheim, Michael Hutter, and Harold James, eds, *Zerrissene Zwischenkriegsheit: Wirtschaftshistorische Beitrage: Knut Borchardt zum 65. Geburstag,* reprinted in C.P. Kindleberger, *The World Economy and National Finance in Historical Perspective* (Ann Arbor: University of Michigan Press, 1995), pp. 181–200.
49. Bouvier, *Le krach,* chap. 5.
50. Charles Wilson, *Anglo-Dutch Commerce and Finance in the Eighteenth Century* (Cambridge: Cambridge University Press, 1941), pp. 176–7.
51. Friedman and Schwartz, *Monetary History,* p. 309 and esp. pp. 309–10n; Peter Temin, *Did Monetary Forces Cause the Great Depression?* (New York: W.W. Norton, 1976).
52. Clapham, *Bank of England,* vol. 1, p. 261; vol. 2, p. 58.
53. Ibid., vol. 2, pp. 59–60.
54. Ibid., vol. 1, p. 249.
55. Ibid., vol. 2, pp. 82–4.
56. Ibid., p. 145.
57. Alain Plessis, *La Politique de la Banque de France de 1851 à 1870* (Geneva: Droz, 1985), pp. 89, 99, 107. The Banque also loaned on Paris bonds, but not on those of Marseilles or Bordeaux; ibid., pp. 105–6.
58. Bagehot, *Lombard Street,* p. 195.
59. Clapham, *Bank of England,* vol. 2, p. 59.
60. W.C.T. King, *History of the London Discount Market* (London: George Routledge & Sons, 1936), p. 36.
61. Clapham, *Bank of England,* vol. 2, pp. 206–7.
62. Ibid., vol. l, p. 261.

63. D. Morier Evans, *The History of the Commercial Crisis, 1857–1858, and the Stock Exchange Panic of 1859* (1859; reprint ed., New York: Augustus M. Kelley, 1969), p. 80.
64. Lévy-Leboyer, *Banques européennes,* p. 559.
65. Ibid., p. 647.
66. Ibid., p. 492.
67. Evans, *Commercial Crisis,* pp. i–ii, vi–xviii.
68. A. Andréadès, *History of the Bank of England* (London: P.S. King, 1909), p. 266.
69. Clapham, *Bank of England,* vol. 2, p. 157. He refers to it later as 'the long drawn out W bank affair' (ibid., p. 337).
70. R.C.O. Matthews, *A Study in Trade-Cycle History: Economic Fluctuations in Great Britain, 1832–1842* (Cambridge: Cambridge University Press, 1954), p. 173.
71. Clapham, *Bank of England,* vol. 1, p. 245.
72. H.S. Foxwell, preface to Andréadès, *Bank of England,* p. xvii.
73. Clapham, *Bank of England,* vol. 1, p. 256.
74. See Friedman and Schwartz, *Monetary History,* pp. 339, 363–7.
75. Ibid., p. 395.
76. Ibid., p. 339.
77. See Milton Friedman, 'Rediscounting', in *A Program for Monetary Stability* (New York: Fordham University Press, 1960) pp. 35–6.
78. Paul Johnson, *Modern Times: the World from the Twenties to the Eighties* (New York: Harper & Row, 1983), p. 244.
79. Friedman and Schwartz, *Monetary History,* pp. 334–5.
80. Clapham, *Bank of England,* vol. 2, p. 102.
81. Evans, *Commercial Crisis,* p. 207.
82. Taus, *Central Banking,* pp. 55, 70.
83. Sprague, *History of Crises,* p. 256.

12. The International Lender of Last Resort

1. Niall Ferguson, *The House of Rothschild: Money's Prophets, 1798–1847* (New York: Viking, 1998), chap. 16, Table 16a on p. 461, shows the course of bond prices in Vienna, Paris, Rome, and London. Ferguson states that 'the London house was not the lender of last resort at all'; but Alphonse, Nathan's grandson, was sent to New York to turn Belmont away from preoccupation with the Mexican indemnity and focus on Europe (pp. 466–70).
2. Ron Chernow, *The Warburgs: the Twentieth-Century Odyssey of a Remarkable Jewish Family* (New York: Random House, 1993), p. 328.
3. R.D. Richards, 'The First Fifty Years of the Bank of England, 1694–1744', in *History of the Principal Public Banks,* compiled by J.G. Van Dillen (The Hague: Martinus Nijhoff, 1934), p. 234.
4. Violet Barbour, *Capitalism and Amsterdam in the 17th Century* (1950; reprint ed., Ann Arbor: University of Michigan Press, 1966), p. 125.

5. Charles Wilson, *Anglo-Dutch Commerce and Finance in the Eighteenth Century* (Cambridge: Cambridge University Press, 1941), pp. 168–9.
6. Ibid., p. 176.
7. Sir John Clapham, *The Bank of England: a History* (Cambridge: Cambridge University Press, 1945), vol. 1, p. 249.
8. Alain Plessis, *La Politique de la Banque de France de 1850 à 1870* (Geneva: Droz, 1985), chap. 4, esp. pp. 241–5.
9. Knut Wicksell, *Lectures on Political Economy* (New York: Macmillan, 1935), vol. 2, pp. 37–8.
10. Jacob Viner, *Studies in the Theory of International Trade* (New York: Harper & Bros., 1937), p. 273; Clapham, *Bank of England,* vol. 2, p. 169.
11. Clapham, *Bank of England,* vol. 2, pp. 164–5.
12. Clément Juglar, *Des crises commerciales et leur retour périodiques en France, en Angleterre et aux Etats-Unis,* 2nd ed. (1889; reprint ed., New York: Augustus M. Kelley, 1967), p. 417.
13. E. Victor Morgan, *The Theory and Practice of Central Banking, 1797–1913* (Cambridge: Cambridge University Press, 1943), p. 148.
14. Arthur D. Gayer, W.W. Rostow, and Anna J. Schwartz, *The Growth and Fluctuation of the British Economy, 1790–1850* (Oxford: Oxford University Press, Clarendon Press, 1953), vol. 1, p. 333.
15. British Parliamentary Papers, *Causes of Commercial Distress: Monetary Policy* (Shannon: Irish University Press, 1969), vol. 1, p. 153, question 2018.
16. Viner, *Studies in International Trade,* p. 273.
17. Clapham, *Bank of England,* vol. 2, p. 170.
18. Bertrand Gille, *La Banque et le crédit en France de 1818 à 1848* (Paris: Presses universitaires de France, 1959), p. 377.
19. Clapham, *Bank of England,* vol. 2, p. 229.
20. Helmut Böhme, *Frankfurt und Hamburg: Des Deutsches Reiches Silber und Goldloch und die Allerenglishte Stadt des Kontinents* (Frankfurt-am-Main: Europaïsche Verlagsanstalt, 1968), pp. 255–68.
21. Ibid., pp. 267–74.
22. Parliamentary Papers, *Commercial Distress,* vol. 4, appendix 20, consular dispatch no. 7, January 27, 1858, p. 441.
23. Ibid., dispatch no. 393 from Berlin, December 29, 1857, pp. 450–1.
24. Clapham, *Bank of England,* vol. 2, p. 234.
25. Morgan, *Theory and Practice of Central Banking,* p. 176.
26. Clapham, *Bank of England,* vol. 2, pp. 291–4.
27. Ibid., pp. 329–30, 344.
28. Quoted in R.S. Sayers, *Bank of England Operations 1890–1914* (London: P.S. King, 1936), p. 111 from Hartley Withers, *The Meaning of Money.*
29. J.-L. Billoret, 'Systéme bancaire et dynamique économique dans un pays a monnaie stable: France, 1896–1914', thesis, Faculty of Law and Economic Science, Nancy, 1969, quoted in Jean Bouvier, *Un siècle de banque française* (Paris: Hachette Littérature, 1973), p. 240.
30. Hans Rosenberg, *Die Weltwirtschaftskrise von 1857–1859* (Stuttgart: Verlag von W. Kohlhammer, 1934), p. 38.
31. George W. Van Vleck, *The Panic of 1857: an Analytical Study* (New York: Columbia University Press, 1943), p. 42.

32. Billoret, 'Systeme bancaire', as quoted in Bouvier, *Un siècle de banque française,* p. 238.
33. Walter Bagehot, *Lombard Street: a Description of the Money Market* (1873; reprint ed., London: John Murray, 1917), pp. 32–4.
34. O.M.W. Sprague, *History of Crises under the National Banking System* (1910; reprint ed., New York: Augustus M. Kelley, 1968), pp. 248–85.
35. Franco Bonelli, *La crisi del 1907: una tappa dello sviluppo industriale in Italia* (Turin: Fondazione Luigi Einaudi, 1971), p. 42.
36. Oskar Morgenstern, *International Financial Transactions and Business Cycles* (Princeton, NJ: Princeton University Press, 1959), pp. 128–37.
37. See League of Nations, *The Course and Control of Inflation after World War I* (Princeton, NJ: League of Nations, 1945).
38. Paul E. Erdman, *The Crash of '79* (New York: Simon & Schuster, 1976).
39. Stephen A. Schuker, *The End of French Predominance in Europe, the Financial Crisis of 1924 and the Adoption of the Dawes Plan* (Chapel Hill: University of North Carolina Press, 1976), p. 67.
40. J.N. Jeanneney, 'De la Spéculation financière comme arme diplomatique: A propos de la première bataille de franc (November 1923–Mars 1924)', *Relations internationales,* no. 13 (Spring 1978), pp. 9–15, is persuaded that the German government organized the bear raid on the franc. Schuker is skeptical: (*The End of French Predominance in Europe*), p. 56. Jean-Claude Debeir, 'La crise du franc de 1924: Une exemple de la spéculation "internationale"'. *Relations Internationales,* no. 13 (Spring 1978), p. 35, lays considerable blame for financing the attacks on American banks but states that the French did most of the speculation.
41. Schuker, *The End of French Predominance,* chap. 4.
42. Ibid., p. 111.
43. C.P. Kindleberger. *The World in Depression, 1929–1939,* 2nd ed. (Berkeley: University of California Press, 1986), esp. chaps 7, 14.
44. R.G. Hawtrey, *The Art of Central Banking* (London: Longmans, Green, 1932), pp. 220–4; all italics are in the original. Hawtrey is prescient to a degree. Since the International Monetary Fund takes time to make credit decisions as a lender of last resort, and the Bank for International Settlements can act quickly, the latter has operated in a number of recent financial crises by providing 'bridge loans', that is, short-term finance (though limited in amounts) to countries with immediate needs. These loans would then be repaid with funds from credits from the International Monetary Fund. See Harold James, *International Monetary Cooperation since Bretton Woods* (Washington, DC: International Monetary Fund, 1995; New York and Oxford: Oxford University Press, 1996), pp. 361–2, 389, 557, 562, 592.
45. Hawtrey, *The Art of Central Banking,* pp. 229–32; italics are in the original.
46. Susan Howson and Donald Winch, *The Economic Advisory Council, 1930–1939: a Study in Economic Advice during Depression and Recovery* (Cambridge: Cambridge University Press, 1977), pp. 188–9. The personnel of the various committees are given in ibid., appendix 1, pp. 354–70.
47. Ibid., pp. 272–81.

48. This discussion is largely based on Karl Erich Born, *Die deustsche Bankenkrise, 1931: Finanzen und Politik* (Munich: R. Piper & Co. Verlag, 1967).
49. Ibid., p. 86.
50. Ibid., p. 83.
51. Norman to Harrison, cable, July 3, 1931, in Federal Reserve Bank of New York files.
52. Stephen V.O. Clarke, *Central Bank Cooperation, 1924–31* (New York: Federal Reserve Bank of New York, 1967), p. 44. This was after discussion by both sides, with the British and Americans saying no (Kindleberger, *World in Depression,* p. 153). The Germans for their part were debating a plan of Wilhelm Lautenbach of the Economics Ministry, which called for suspending service on foreign debt and expanding spending (ibid., p. 171, n. 5). The Lautenbach plan came up again after the British pound went off gold in September 1931. See Knut Borchardt and Hans Otto Scholtz, eds, *Wirtschaftspolitik in der Krise* (Baden-Baden: Nomos, 1931 [1991]). This is a transcript of the riveting debate in the Reichsbank among German officials and economists.
53. Clarke, *Central Bank Cooperation,* pp. 121, 148.
54. Howson and Winch, *Economic Advisory Council,* pp. 88–9.
55. Ibid., p. 162.
56. Kindleberger, *World in Depression,* pp. 168, 184.
57. D.E. Moggridge, 'Policy in the Crises of 1920 and 1929', in C.P. Kindleberger and J.-P. Laffargue, eds, *Financial Crises: Theory, History and Policy* (Cambridge: Cambridge University Press, 1982), pp. 171–87.
58. Stephen A. Schuker, *American 'Reparations' to Germany, 1919–33: Implications for the Third-World Debt Crisis,* Princeton Studies in International Finance no. 61 (Princeton, NJ: International Finance Section, Princeton University Press, 1988).
59. Richard N. Cooper, 'Economic Interdependence and Foreign Policy in the Seventies', *World Politics,* vol. 24 (January 1972), p. 167.
60. See bank for International Settlements, *Annual Report* no. 63 to March 31, 1993, p. 196; and no. 64 to March 31, 1994. World turnover rose from $10 billion to $20 billion a day in 1973, to $80 billion in 1983, before soaring to over $1 trillion a day in 1995: *The Economist,* vol. 337, no. 7936 (October 14, 1995), p. 10. For emerging markets and the European Monetary Union, see Bank for International Settlements, 68th *Annual Report* to March 31, 1998, p. 11, and chart p. 115.
61. Charles A. Coombs, *The Arena of International Finance* (New York: Wiley), pp. 77, 79, 81, 83, 195, 202, 292.
62. Coombs, *Arena,* p. 37.
63. Ibid., pp. 81, 85, 111, 121, 127, 134, 181, 185.
64. Susan Strange, 'International Monetary Relations', in Andrew Schonfield, ed., *International Economic Relations of the Western World, 1959–71* (Oxford: Oxford University Press, for the Royal Institute of International Affairs, 1976), vol. 2, p. 136.
65. See Debeir, 'La crise du franc du 1924'.

66. Kathleen Burk and Alec Cairncross, *'Goodbye Great Britain': the 1976 IMF Crisis* (New Haven, Conn.: Yale University Press, 1992).
67. For background, see the paper on Mexico, by Ernesto Zedillo in Donald R. Lessard and John Williamson, eds, *Capital Flight and Third World Debt* (Washington, DC: Institute for International Economics, 1987), pp. 174–85. The crisis itself is discussed at length in the *New York Times* issues from 21 to December 29, 1994.
68. 'President Clinton Sidesteps Congress Using Emergency Authority', *New York Times,* February 1, 1995, p. Al.
69. Bank for International Settlements, *Annual Report,* no. 68, p. 134.
70. Ibid.
71. Wynne Godley, 'Seven Unsustainable Processes', a special report of the Levy Institute, Annandale-on-Hudson, New York, 1999.
72. C.P. Kindleberger, *World Economic Primacy, 1500–1990* (New York: Oxford University Press, 1996), chaps 10, 12.
73. Robert O. Keohane, *After Hegemony: Cooperation and Discord in the World Political Economy* (Princeton, NJ: Princeton University Press, 1984).

Index